3D Studio for Beginner

Jim Lammers

Michael Todd Peterson

New Riders Publishing, Indianapolis, IN

3D Studio for Beginners

By Jim Lammers and Michael Todd Peterson

Published by:
New Riders Publishing
201 West 103rd Street
Indianapolis, IN 46290 USA

Printed in the United States of America 1 2 3 4 5 6 7 8 9 0

CIP data available upon request

Warning and Disclaimer

This book is designed to provide information about the 3D Studio program. Every effort has been made to make this book as complete and as accurate as possible, but no warranty or fitness is implied.

The information is provided on an "as is" basis. The authors and New Riders Publishing shall have neither liability nor responsibility to any person or entity with respect to any loss or damages arising from the information contained in this book or from the use of the discs or programs that may accompany it.

Publisher	*Don Fowley*
Associate Publisher	*Tim Huddleston*
Product Development Manager	*Rob Tidrow*
Marketing Manager	*Ray Robinson*
Managing Editor	*Tad Ringo*

Product Director
Steven Elliott

Senior Acquisitions Editor
Jim LeValley

Software Specialist
Steve Weiss

Production Editor
Laura Frey

Copy Editors
Fran Blauw
Gail Burlakoff
Cliff Shubs

Technical Editor
Alan Sommer

Marketing Copywriter
Tamara Apple

Acquisitions Coordinator
Tracey Turgeson

Publisher's Assistant
Karen Opal

Cover Designer
Karen Ruggle

Book Designer
Kim Scott

Cover Art Illustrator
Roger Morgan

Manufacturing Coordinator
Paul Gilchrist

Production Manager
Kelly Dobbs

Production Team Supervisor
Laurie Casey

Graphics Coordinator
Dennis Clay Hager

Graphic Image Specialists
Clint Lahnen
Dennis Sheehan

Production Analysts
Angela D. Bannan
Bobbi Satterfield
Mary Beth Wakefield

Production Team
Dan Caparo
Nathan Clement
Kim Cofer
Kevin Foltz
Erika Millen
Beth Rago
Gina Rexrode
Erich J. Richter
Christine Tyner
Karen Walsh

Indexer
Bront Davis

About the Authors

Jim Lammers is a professional animator specializing in broadcast and industrial video in the Kansas City area. When not animating, he writes articles for computer graphics-oriented magazines including *3D Artist* and *Planet Studio*. He also operates a computer bulletin board service (BBS) specializing in 3D Studio called the Rendering Plant BBS. He can be reached via CompuServe (73261,66) and Internet (trinity@sky.net).

Michael Todd Peterson is currently a lecturer at the University of Tennessee School of Architecture, where he teaches an introductory computer course and sponsors independent study on advanced visualization with 3D Studio. He also owns a consulting firm, MTP Graphics, that specializes in AutoCAD and 3D Studio. He has used AutoCAD for 8 years and 3D Studio for 3 years. He graduated from the University of Tennessee College of Architecture in 1992 and is currently pursuing a Master's degree in Computer Science.

Trademark Acknowledgments

All terms mentioned in this book that are known to be trademarks or service marks have been appropriately capitalized. New Riders Publishing cannot attest to the accuracy of this information. Use of a term in this book should not be regarded as affecting the validity of any trademark or service mark. 3D Studio is a registered trademark of Autodesk, Inc.

Acknowledgments

Jim Lammers wants to thank his wife, Gail, for her undying support as this book took shape. He also thanks Laura Frey and the staff at New Riders Publishing who have been extremely patient as this book progressed. Mr. Lammers would also like to thank the talented artists who contributed to the CD-ROM that accompanies this book: Herb Shemwell, Eric Peterson, Mark Pennel, Gary Baker, and Jeff Beith.

Michael Todd Peterson would like to thank his friends and all the helpful people at NRP who graciously gave him the opportunity to work on this book.

New Riders Publishing would like to acknowledge Eric Peterson for his contribution to the cover art.

Contents at a Glance

Table of Contents

Introduction

Three-dimensional graphics, once the domain of universities and research centers, are now an applied art. Or is that applied science? The mixture of math, computer assistance, and aesthetics in 3D computer graphics makes its practitioners some of the most diversely skilled professionals around. You can see the results of their work everywhere—in the courtroom, in movies, in games, in schools. You can visualize objects still in the design phase, fly through keyholes, and visit places only imagined. All of it looks as realistic as the animator's skill allows.

The graduation of 3D animation from high-budget movies to more commonplace video productions and courtrooms follows the evolution of low-priced animation software and the computational power of the desktop personal computers that it runs on. At the forefront of 3D animation software is Autodesk's 3D Studio, a professional animation system designed for both versatility and speed. Its versatility enables it to tackle jobs of all sizes and requirements. Its speed enables an animator to get his or her work done on schedule. Even a user with a single, lower-end PC can create fairly elaborate animations that the computer is able to render out in a reasonable amount of time.

With each new release, 3D Studio expands the boundaries of animators who use it. As the power and capabilities of this PC-based professional animation software grow, the complexity that faces the first-time user can be discouraging. At the same time, you see animations produced by 3D Studio that motivate and inspire. If you've attempted to scale the 3D Studio mountain and found it too steep, *3D Studio for Beginners* will give you the foothold to ascend confidently. Intermediate users will be able fill in some of the details missed in their initial explorations with the software.

Who Should Use This Book

This book assumes, out of necessity, that the reader brings certain skills to the table at the outset. For 3D Studio to run reliably and quickly, you must set up and manage your system effectively. However, the skills of using your computer's operating system and getting the various hardware of your system to coexist peacefully is not covered here. Hopefully, you've kept your system simple and made this task easier.

In addition to hardware and software skills, good animators must have good aesthetic sense before they begin learning the mechanics of their tools. The end result of their work is nearly always judged on how it looks, and it is quite easy to end up with ugly results. There is no "Lookin' Good" button.

Both beginners and advanced users of 3D Studio can benefit from some study of the basics of good design. Because the nature of 3D Studio is to use virtual cameras, objects, and lights, books that cover the art of photography can provide a lot of compositional guidance and ideas.

This book is ideal for the beginner who has already spent time combining computers with imaging or drawing. Computer software such as CorelDRAW! and Photoshop contain features and proceedures that are similar to parts of 3D Studio. With some patience the less experienced user should be able to follow the book's tutorials. Much of the way computers deal with 2D images and 3D scenes becomes more apparent as a user works with them over time.

Getting the Most Out of This Book

The CD-ROM included with this book contains helpful files for using the tutorials. In some cases, the final project file that results from a tutorial is available on the CD in the event that you lose track of where a tutorial is headed. The tutorials do not assume that you have any files loaded from the CD, so that you can work through the book even if you do not have a CD-ROM reader. The tutorials do build on each other, often using the results of a preceding tutorial to start a new tutorial. Because of this, the best approach is to work through the book from the beginning.

How This Book Is Organized

3D Studio for Beginners is arranged into progressive sections. Each new chapter assumes you are fluent with the commands and procedures already discussed, so starting at the front of this book and working to the back is the most effective way to learn. The appendix is separate, and is intended as a powerful reference that you will continue to use after you have completed and mastered the material in this book.

The Chapters

Chapter 1, "Three-Dimensional Computer Graphics," provides important background information about 3D graphics in general, and details about how 3D Studio works internally. Understanding these concepts enables you to know why images and animations sometimes come out differently than expected, or why a desired effect is not directly possible. Also, some of the terminology used in this book is explained.

Chapter 2, "Meet 3D Studio," takes the user through the entire 3D animation process with 3D Studio on a simple project. Standard use of all the 3D Studio modules is described in detailed, but simple, tutorials.

Chapter 3, "Introduction to 3D Modeling," provides a more in-depth look at the process of modeling (creating objects in 3D space). Tutorials take the user into the primary features of the model-making modules of 3D Studio.

Chapter 4, "Lights, Camera, Set Design," introduces materials, lights, and cameras. The process of creating a well-lit scene is presented along with the primary features of 3D Studio's materials-making module.

Chapter 5, "Directing the Show: Action!" discusses the fourth dimension, time, in relation to the objects in the scenes that have been created. The animation module's primary features are covered in tutorials, and the concepts of 3D Studio's approach to animation are described.

Chapter 6, "3D Studio on a Higher Plane," is designed to get the now intermediate user thinking about controlling 3D Studio more definitively. The chapter includes various topics that relate to efficiency and quality during the creation or rendition of scenes.

Chapter 7, "Advanced Modeling Techniques," deals with creating more complex objects in 3D Studio. The methods for building difficult types of objects are described as the tutorials delve into the details of 3D Studio's model-making modules.

Chapter 8, "Advanced Lighting/Materials Techniques," covers lighting and materials more fully and completely. Tutorials describe the process of inventing virtually any surface material style within 3D Studio.

Chapter 9, "Advanced Animation Techniques," explains how to create complex animations. The advanced use of 3D Studio's animation module is described through tutorial example. Character animation is a major topic of the chapter.

Chapter 10, "Advanced Keyframing Techniques," covers the process of placing, controlling, and manipulating keys using KeyInfo and TrackInfo. Advanced topics such as morphing are briefly discussed.

Chapter 11, "Video Post," covers the Video post module. The process of combining rendered images in this module is described, from overlaying simple 2D effects, to building complex multilayered animations.

Chapter 12, "Output Issues," gives guidelines for the various forms of outputting the animations and scenes made in 3D Studio. This practical look at the issues of print, video, and film output explains the best approach and helps the artist avoid common problems.

The appendix that follows Chapter 12 contains the commands on the Menu Bar and their descriptions.

Sidebar Icons

There are special sidebar sections throughout this book, designed to point out important information or warn of potentially dangerous situations.

Caution

Warns of possibly unwanted results of using a given 3D Studio feature (see fig. I.1).

CAUTION

Figure I.1
The Caution symbol used throughout this book.

Usage Tip

The Usage Tip gives additional information about a 3D Studio command or feature (see fig. I.2).

USAGE
TIP

Figure I.2
The Usage Tip icon.

Design Tip

The Design Tip gives additional ideas for creative usage of a 3D Studio feature (see fig. I.3).

DESIGN
TIP

Figure I.3
The Design Tip icon.

Note

A Note lists an alternate reference in the book or gives an explanation about how 3D Studio reacts (see fig. I.4).

NOTE

Figure I.4
The Note icon.

Hardware Issues

3D Studio is software designed for IBM-PCs and compatibles. 3D Studio is totally dependent on a properly set up PC with adequate computing power to run properly. Few applications push the limit of a computer's speed as 3D Studio does, and so its important to distinguish between the minimum computer requirements, and the minimum requirements for a serviceable animation workstation. After all, a bicycle is as capable as an automobile for traveling across the continent, but practical people tend to favor traveling in an automobile.

"Official" 3D Studio Hardware Requirements

The bare minimum required to allow 3D Studio to run is a PC with a 386 processor, a math coprocessor, 8 megabytes (MB) of RAM, a mouse, and about 20 MB of hard disk space. If you have a 486SX type computer, it has no math coprocessor, and must be upgraded with an "overdrive" processor upgrade. The 486DX systems and Pentium systems already have an integral math coprocessor.

Real 3D Studio Hardware Requirements

Computer graphics software is notoriously hungry for system resources. 3D Studio is no exception; it is perhaps the most demanding application available for PCs. After you have designed an animation, the system will compute each frame of the animation unattended. This process can take days. More importantly, when designing an animation, getting a feel for the final output requires computing a single frame, or a low-quality version of part of the animation. A more powerful system will speed up the process of reacting to new results, and increase your productivity dramatically. A more practical minimum system than the "official minimum system" would a 486DX2-66 system with 16 MB of RAM. A 17-inch, high resolution monitor also is important to ease eyestrain and allow you to view the tightly spaced gridlines of 3D objects (called "meshes" or "wireframes") with finer detail.

3D Studio uses temporary space on the hard drive while operating, both as a substitute for RAM when all the RAM is used up, and for temporary storage of the images that will later be combined to create an animation file (called a Flic). You should have at least 100 MB of hard drive space available for this purpose. 3D Studio behaves erratically when it runs out of hard drive space while computing an animation, and there is no way to know exactly how much hard drive space will be required to complete computation of an animation. It is very disappointing to find your computer "locked up" after two days of computing a final animation!

When your system begins to use the hard drive as a substitute for RAM, your animation computations will slow down, sometimes to a crawl. This book will show you ways to optimize your animation designs for better efficiency without loss of quality, but at a certain point it becomes necessary to add RAM. Most professional animators who use 3D Studio consider 32 MB to be a practical configuration, and some add as much as 128 MB.

The Hardware Key

3D Studio is copy protected by a hardware key, a small plug that the software seeks when it is running. You must plug the hardware key, or "dongle," into the parallel port connector on the back of your PC. It usually is installed into the back of the computer and then the printer cable is attached to the device. In some cases, the program will not see the dongle, and 3D Studio will terminate with the message "SentinelPro must be plugged into parallel port." If this occurs, one possible fix is to start 3D Studio with the printer turned on. Another potential problem is that on newer computers, the parallel ports are sometimes an advanced type called "bidirectional." Unfortunately, in this case you must get a basic plug-in parallel port expansion board for your PC and set it up as the first parallel port (LPT1).

When to Upgrade Your Hardware

Clearly, you can't always start out with a top-of-the-line system. But as you progress, if you find your system painfully slow, some guidelines for improvement are suggested as follows.

If your CPU is less than a 486DX, you should get a complete new system first. Some items can be transferred from your old system, such as RAM, hard drive, mouse, and monitor. You can always benefit from a faster CPU with 3D Studio.

Upgrade to at least 16 MB as a second priority. 3DS will tell you how much swap space it is using at any moment by pressing the ? key. If your hard drive light flashes constantly while an animation is computed (or rendered), follow the listed steps for reducing your animation's RAM requirements. If this is not enough to minimize swapping activity, it's time to add RAM. Most PCs will accept RAM in certain increments only (that is, the next step from 16 MB is 32 MB), so you should check your PC's manual before making a memory purchase.

Finally, if your monitor is blurry or low-resolution, your eyes will thank you to upgrade to a large (17-inch or more), high resolution monitor. Your video adapter works in concert with the monitor and may limit resolution or display in an interlaced mode (where the alternating horizontal lines of the screen flicker annoyingly). Due to this problem, the computer sometimes must be upgraded at the same time as the monitor. If you plan to spend dozens of hours at your workstation building your 3D Studio skills, your physical health demands a better monitor!

Older Versions of 3DS

Some users might be learning 3D Studio on older versions of 3D Studio than Release 4. In some cases, the differences are minimal, but each major release of the software contains substantial changes. The basic operation of 3D Studio remains the same, but this book makes use of some functions that only more current versions of the software contain.

Release 2: Differences from This Book

Release 2 of 3D Studio differs significantly from Release 4, so much so that this book would be difficult to use with the software. This book does not attempt to describe alternate procedures for those using R2 of 3D Studio. *AutoCAD 3D Design and Presentation* from New Riders Publishing has several chapters that focus on the Release 2 version of 3D Studio.

Release 3: Differences from This Book

Release 3 is only different from Release 4 in a few ways. You will encounter few difficulties using R3 with this book. Inverse Kinematics, Quick Preview, and the Keyframer Script Utility are the major missing 3D Studio utilities in Release 3. All are accessed in R4 as plug-in utilities, and are thus easy to master separately from the core of 3D Studio.

Getting Ready to Run

The next section deals with installing and setting up 3D Studio. You might already have 3D Studio running, but it is worthwhile to confirm that you have chosen video modes appropriately, as described following. Although a default video installation will usually run, it will use the lowest quality video mode that is common to all video display hardware. Also, you might want to reset your swap drive based on issues that are discussed in the next section. Installing 3D Studio is a three-step process: installing the software, installing the hardware key, and configuring the display.

Installing the Software

Simply put the disk labeled "disk 1" into your floppy disk drive and type **install** at the prompt. Before the installation process begins, you are asked to select a drive to use as a temporary swap file area. Ideally, this would be a 40 to 100 MB section of the hard drive (a partition) that has no other files on it. The necessity for this is due to a phenomenon called *fragmenting* that occurs when files are written and erased over time from a disk. Eventually, the open space on the drive is in physically separate areas of the magnetic disk, and performance begins to drag as each file read must be picked up from multiple places around the drive. If a drive has no files on it, the space is guaranteed to be contiguous, and your swapping activity will occur at optimal speed.

CAUTION

Make sure that when you specify this drive it is not a drive that uses disk-compression software. If you have Disk Doubler, Stacker, DoubleSpace, or similar software active, you need to adjust your hard drive configuration so that at least one drive letter is non-compressed, and use that as your swap area.

Installing the Hardware Key

Make sure the hardware key is installed in your parallel port connector on the back of your PC. The installation program will run regardless of the key, but 3DS will only run for a few seconds before exiting with an error if the lock is not found.

Configuring 3DS for Your Graphics Card

One area in which the PC market has progressed to many variations is the video adapter card. Each card is capable of several resolutions (the number of pixels displayed horizontally and vertically) at several color quantities. Typical resolutions are 640×480, 800×600, and 1024×768. Typical color quanities are 16, 256, 32,000, and 16 million.

Additionally, a graphics card can display images in either interlaced or non-interlaced mode. Interlaced mode used with 3D Studio usually is perceived as "flickery" and can be truly headache-inducing over long periods.

Critical to your best use of 3D Studio is to configure the program for the video card your computer uses for graphics displays. Don't overlook this important detail!

To configure 3D Studio for your video card at any time, instead of typing the usual "3DS" at the prompt, type **3DS VIBCFG**. The program will display a special menu for configuring and testing your video setup. You will need to know what kind of video card is in your system (model and make). Remember that it is okay to experiment with these settings—they can easily be reset or adjusted further—until you find the most pleasant interface for your work.

For guidance, the best settings for the modules listed in the configuration screen are as shown in table I.1.

Table I.1
Optimal Settings for 3D Studio Modules

Module	Setting
Main Editor screens	Use the highest resolution possible. Use the "test" offered as you choose a driver to confirm the clarity of the settings. You might notice blurriness or interlace flicker, especially in the text at the center of the text screen. You might want to downgrade to a lower display resolution if this is the case. A monitor is sometimes unable to handle certain modes, even though your video card can output them. If a tested mode doesn't appear or strobes during the test, this is the case. Always use a 256-color display for the editor screens because this is the display mode that 3D Studio expects for highest redraw speed and appropriate colors for certain operations.
Materials Editor screen	This screen should have as much color depth as possible. If you have an older graphics adapter, you might be limited to 256 colors. Most newer graphics adapters, however, include at least a 32,000-color mode (often called "high-color"), and many include a 16 million color mode

Module	Setting
	(often called "true color"). Besides offering more accurate feedback on color adjustment, a lot of time will be saved with the high/true color modes because 256-color displays are palletted. Palletted displays require 3D Studio to count each unique color of an image and calculate the best 256 colors to display to give the user a reasonable approximation of what the image "really" looks like. This will be evident as 3D Studio displays first a rough version of the image, pauses, and then displays a more correctly colored version.
Rendering output screen	The rendering display should also have the highest color depth possible, for the same reasons given for the Materials editor. Even if you are intending to create disk-based animations that only have 256 colors, it's advisable to use a true/high color mode as you refine your scenes and create test renders to judge the improvements made, because the visual effect caused by palletting can't be predicted. The resolution chosen is usually entirely dependent on the final scene resolution. 3D Studio renders a scene at a smaller resolution than the resolution the screen is set to, and the image appears in the upper left corner. However, when you try to render larger than the screen resolution, 3D Studio truncates the size without asking you. Also, doubling the resolution usually quadruples the render time (640×480 takes 12 minutes to render if 320×240 took 3 minutes) so don't choose a large resolution unless you need it. Typically this screen is set to 640×480 or 800×600 at most.

This chapter serves as an introduction to 3D computer animation and computer based graphics. Some of the terms and explanations might be familiar to you if you've worked with CAD, painting, or drawing programs on a PC before. Although this chapter does not incorporate tutorials, some of the most vital information to understanding how 3D Studio works is contained within it. Also, this chapter lets you know what not to expect 3D Studio to do, to avoid confusion as you progress as an animator. In addition, much of the terminology that you will use to describe your work methods and problems to other animators is explained within.

This chapter will discuss the following:

- Common jobs of all 3D animation programs

- How packages like 3D Studio let you work in three dimensions

- The building blocks of 3D Studio

- The aspects of real-world optics that 3D Studio can and cannot emulate

Three-Dimensional Computer Graphics

As computer-created imagery becomes more and more a part of entertainment and other fields, the acronym CGI has become prevalent. CGI stands for computer generated imagery, and describes virtually any visual information that comes from a computer. Most of the time we think of some sort of shaded 3D graphics because video games and movies include these kinds of computer graphics, and draw attention to the fact that a computer is generating the image.

Unlike other forms of imaging, three-dimensional computer graphics accomplish their work by creating a virtual 3D environment. The 3D-design approach should be familar to you because you live in a three-dimensional world. The drawback is that in three-dimensional graphics, it's not enough just to design an object's 2D profile. Instead, most objects must be created in three dimensions—a task that is often tedious and time-consuming. In 3D graphics, the object-creation process is more like sculpting than drawing because true 3D images require the artist to add depth, as well as the two-dimensional qualities of height and width. The 3D-design process is made even more difficult by the fact that our interface to the object creation process is a flat, two-dimensional video screen. Once all the parts of the subject have been created in 3D Studio, however, you can view the object from every angle and even fly through it.

The Geometric Fundamentals

Now that you are dealing with three dimensions, you must go back to geometry class for a way to describe the elements of your work. Cartesian coordinates refer to using an imaginary grid to fix a point in space, and this is the system that 3D Studio uses. A letter is assigned to each of the three dimensions (X, Y, Z), so that a position exactly based on three numbers describes your position in each of the three dimensions.

In 3D Studio, the X position refers to the position of an object across the width of the front-view screen. The Y position refers to the position of an object across the height of the front view. The Z position refers to the depth of an object in the scene viewed from the front. To say that an object is at position 1, 3, 9 describes its position as 1 to the right, 3 up, and 9 in. If a line is drawn between two of these points in 3D space, it exists as an infinitely thin connecting line between two infinitely thin, exact points in space. This type of geometry is referred to as vector-based.

In the typical three-dimensional design workspace, objects exist as geometry, with lines that are anchored at x, y, and z coordinates. In 3D Studio the animator builds a scene from geometric objects made up of triangular faces. Viewed from edge-on, each triangle is a flat planar object that is infinitely thin. The triangles are *vector* objects like those in other drawing software such as AutoCAD and CorelDRAW!, so a corner of a triangle can be viewed at any zoom level without appearing blocky.

This vectorized part of 3D Studio, however, usually is seen and used only by the animator. The vectors (triangles and wireframes) are used only to create the skeleton that underlies the finished 3D objects, which you then can render. 3D Studio's rendered output is always a bitmap, or raster image. A *bitmap* or *raster image* is a flat 2D image made up of a grid of pixels. It can be grayscale or color, but because it has a finite number of pixels, at some zoom level, the individual pixels become apparent to the eye. 3D Studio's rendered bitmaps can be loaded into paint software such as Photoshop and Fractal Design Painter for further editing.

3D versus 2D

Many draw and paint packages offer effects and special modes that simulate 3D. Sometimes these are as simple as drop shadows. *Drop shadows* are a copy of an image element colored black, blurred, and offset underneath the original to fool the eye into seeing the element as though it were floating above the shadow. Some programs can apply lines to simulate a perspective extrusion of a logo or other element. In all these cases, all the object's elements remain flat; you can't rotate the object and view its sides. The drop shadows or lines drawn to add perspective are just adding an illusion of depth; no depth really exists. With a true 3D program, however, the perspective is dynamic and real. The camera can be moved about to adjust the perspective, or view the sides and back of the created scene.

Perhaps the happiest attribute of using a 3D program comes after the objects are created and rendered. Often when a 3D-style image is required for an illustration, the technique is imitated painstakingly with an airbrush or other media. The final image created this way is fixed when complete. If the client then wants the viewpoint a little to the left or an object needs to appear like chrome instead of wood, the 2D artist has to start over or tell the client to live with the imperfect version. In a 3D program, these edits would take but a few minutes, and the computer could recalculate the image unattended. Further, simple animation such as camera fly-around can be added in seconds, and again the computer will create the images unattended.

How 3D Computer Graphics Work

Most commercial 3D computer graphics systems work similarly to 3D Studio—geometric elements are defined to exist in 3D space, the material properties of these geometric elements are defined in some way, and then the scene is rendered by scanning it from the perspective of a 2D image plane, one pixel at a time. The following sections take you through an introductory step-by-step process of turing a 2D outline into a 3D image. See Chapter 2, "Meet 3D Studio," for greater detail on this process.

The 2D Outline

First, there's the creation of the 2D outline, or frame. 2D shapes are usually used as a starting point in creating new objects. Different views of the subject can be drawn and scanned into the computer, to be used for tracing. Sometimes plastic sheets with these images penned or Xeroxed on are taped to the screen as a guide while creating the initial reference 2D shapes. Once these shapes are drawn, the 3D aspects of modeling the object begin in earnest.

Extruding the Frame

Next, the frame is extruded, or lofted, to give it depth and make it a real 3D object. The shape can be spun, scaled, or deformed in a variety of ways as it is extruded. Alternatively, the object can be constructed in three dimensional space directly, by adding and subtracting basic geometric objects from other objects. The final objects are bent, twisted, and scaled and finally placed in position when complete. The computer can be used to copy a single designed object many times, to complete subjects such as fences or the wheels of a train. The computer is also capable of creating objects by a formula, with the animator giving the program only a few controlling variables. These programs are often used to create random but predictable objects such as trees and shrubs.

Wrapping the Frame

Next, the object's exterior appearance is decided. Besides just simple colors, objects can be covered papier-mache style with 2D images in a variety of ways. In addition to color adjustment, other surface variables are adjusted to control such things as glossiness, transparency, and reflectivity. Because the computer controls these attributes, the animator can create materials from combinations of variables that would not normally be seen in the physical world.

Lighting and Cameras

Then lighting and cameras are brought in, so that you can perfect your view.

The lights and camera are positioned in the scene just like their real-life counterparts. Each light can illuminate the surroundings at nearly any color or power. These computer-simulated lights are highly adjustable. They can shine on only specified objects, cast sharp or blurred shadows, diminish quickly or shine on forever. Computer simulated lights can even have negative value, and reduce the light from other sources in their vicinity. The computer camera is placed in the composition to provide a point of view for the scene.

Rendering the 3D Object

Finally, the computer is asked to take all these steps into account, and create a rendering of the 3D object.

Each pixel traces a line from the viewer's eye, through the pixel, and into the scene. It is up to the renderer how this *eye ray* will react to the objects it intersects in 3D space. Some rendering programs allow the ray to bounce from a reflective object to other objects in the scene. Some 3D rendering programs (called ray tracing renderers) allow transparent objects to bend the eye ray as it passes through, based on transparency properties. In any case, the internal calculations involve intersecting a line (the eye ray) with an object that can be defined by a geometric equation. When an intersection test succeeds, the rendering program alters the color of the pixel based on all material properties assigned to it. The calculations for this color altering are complex and diverse and are often named after their inventors, such as Phong or Gouraud. The mathematical calculations of geometry tests and shading are performed hundreds of thousands of times, even to generate relatively simple scenes. Even for a computer, this many calculations takes time to compute.

The earliest approach to the process of handling the enormous number of calculations for rendering was brute force; the fastest supercomputers were programmed and left running for hours or days. Quickly, new methods began to evolve to speed up the process by requiring fewer calculations. Rather than testing the eye ray against every single object, for example, one speed improvement adds invisible *bounding objects* to groups of closely spaced objects. The bounding object is a simple shape, such as a box, that envelops several smaller and more complex objects, but is not rendered. This bounding object becomes the object against which the ray will test for all the objects within it. Over time more speed enhancing techniques were added, and are now commonly used in most rendering systems. 3D Studio's creators have put high priority on improving rendering speed without sacrificing image quality.

The Animation Process

The animation process is made up of the following major tasks: modeling, material assignment, setting lights and cameras, and applying changes over time. In some cases, objects from sources such as the World Creating Toolkit CD-ROM that comes with 3D Studio can be used, and the animator can go directly to assigning materials. Materials creation often involves using a program other than 3D Studio to paint the images that will be applied as materials. After the materials, lights, and camera are adjusted to yield acceptable still renders, animation can be added. Because animation is a series of related still images, or frames, the animations are created by assigning positions for the moving objects at different frame numbers. 3D Studio then handles the gradual repositioning of the objects at the frame numbers between the ones where positions were assigned. Other types of animation such as scaling an object, or lights changing color, are handled in a similar way. See Chapter 9, "Advanced Animation Techniques," for an in-depth discussion of animation.

Modeling

In its initial state, 3D Studio is a completely void virtual universe. To create a virtual world, you need to fill it with objects. *Modeling*, or designing, 3D structures for computer graphics is accomplished through a variety of approaches. 3D Studio can create basic geometric objects on command, such as spheres, cones, and cubes. These objects are easily manipulated—bent, squashed, and cut up—to create the final product. More complex objects are created by drawing a set of 2D cross-sections of an object, which 3D Studio connects to form a 3D object.

Some modeling subjects are so complex and organic as to almost rule out traditional modeling, such as a bust of Beethoven or the Statue of Liberty. These types of objects are usually modeled by using a 3D *digitizer*—a device that can capture points in 3D space for programs such as 3D Studio (see fig. 1.1). A pointing device is held against a scale model of the subject, and the stylus's position is recorded by 3D Studio as a vertex. Digitizing an object can be time-consuming because each point on the object must be entered individually. To automate the process, laser-based 3D scanners can automatically capture an entire object in seconds. These scanners, however, cost tens of thousands of dollars (see fig. 1.2) and can sometimes choke 3D Studio with the complexity of the scans they produce.

One other approach to modeling is not to model yourself, but to use pre-modeled objects. Most common objects probably have been modeled by one of the companies that sells 3D geometry sets. The bust of Beethoven and Statue of Liberty are available, as well as most cars, anatomical structures, animals, planes, and so forth. Other objects are available by modem; many BBSs (bulletin board systems) carry 3D mesh objects created by other animators that are freely available.

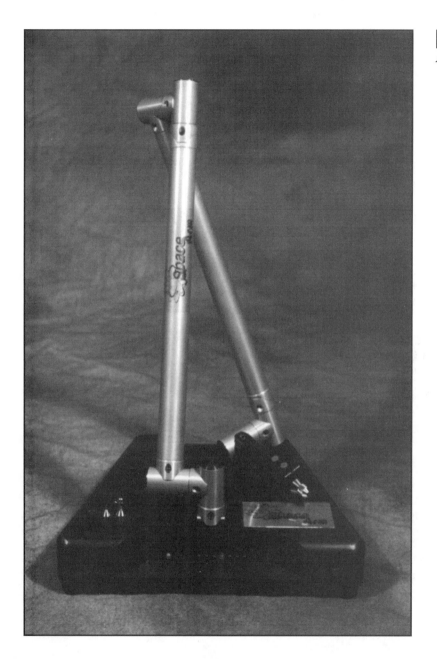

Figure 1.1

A stylus digitizer.

Materials

In any 3D scene, each object has some characteristic appearance. Whether it's glass, chrome, wood, or something totally new, the surfaces for each face are defined by the animator. These surfaces are called *materials* in 3D Studio. Many material styles are included with 3D Studio, and some animators use these built-in materials heavily.

In addition to the materials included with 3D Studio, many more are available quickly by simply swapping the applied 2D material (called a texture map) with another. Included on the CD-ROM that ships with 3D Studio, for example, are hundreds of different images of subjects such as wood, marble, and scratched metal. Many of these are designed to be tilable, so that the image can repeat on a large 3D surface without obvious rectangular borders appearing at each instance of the image. Many CD-ROMs filled with tilable images of every conceivable material are for sale on the open market, and are valuable to animators using any 3D software.

Lighting

Various types of light can be used to create a mood within a scene and focus the attention of the viewer. Each light's range of illumination can be set to imply the power of the light and the scale of the scene. Additionally, shadows can be selectively cast by certain lights to add to the realism and depth of the rendered images. A special kind of light called ambient light is set to provide a minimum amount of light on all objects in a scene.

The lighting in a scene heavily influences the way the materials look. At least one light is placed somewhere in every scene to illuminate the objects. The lights can be any color, illuminate only certain objects, or even project an image or a movie.

Camera

Part of this stage of animation is setting up the camera. Like real cameras, the cameras' position and field of view in 3D Studio can be adjusted to exaggerate or diminish the apparent scale of the objects in your images. An extremely wide field of view can simulate a fisheye lens. Like a photographer, you can use the placement of the camera to play a major part in the composition of your animation.

The camera can move about in an animation, but the direction it points when created is treated as its starting point, so it should be placed appropriately. More than one camera can be created, and sometimes various animated camera views are edited together to create a more dynamic animation that cuts from one view to another as it progresses.

Animating

After creating your models, fixing your lights, and placing your cameras, your scene's time-based characteristics come to the fore. Animation includes more than the movement of objects. Other time-variable actions include objects that change color over time, or whose textures move about; objects that reshape themselves over time, such as a character's smile turning into a frown; lights that change color and move; and the camera that moves or changes angle of view.

Animation consists of a series of related still images that give the impression of continuous movement when played back sequentially. The human eye fills in the movements between each image, if the images occur fast enough. Animations created in 3D Studio are usually played back on video, film, or computer, which usually displays 12 to 30 images per second. With this in mind, the animator can pick a certain point in time for an action to complete, and easily calculate the exact frame that correlates to that point in time. For example, if the playback rate is known to be 30 frames per second, then the point that is six seconds in to the animation should occur at frame 180 (6×30=180).

Animation originally was performed by hand-creating each separate image. Animators would draw and color hundreds of images for a few seconds of animation. Much of the terminology and concepts of traditional animation have been recycled for the process of 3D computer animation. Each individual image of an animation is called a frame, as in the frames of film all early animation used. Extreme points of motion are called keyframes by traditional animators, because they are the important points of motion to capture correctly. The in-between frames that occur between each pair of keyframes are called tweens, as a shortened form of the word. Animation studios used their master animators to draw the keyframes, and the frames that displayed the gradual changes between each keyframe were filled in by the apprentice animators. With 3D Studio, the computer will handle the tedious tweens between the keyframes that you will create.

Hardware limitations make testing your 3D Studio animation changes difficult. Clearly, you can't perform an overnight render after each small edit to an animation to see if your changes have achieved a particular desired effect. For this reason, animation can be one of the more difficult tasks of 3D Studio. 3D Studio does, however, provide a variety of aids to evaluate changes to animations while refining a scene. By using these aids appropriately, animation development becomes much more straight-forward.

Like modeling organic mesh objects, trying to animate organic movement such as walking a dog, can be very challenging. To speed this process, a technique known as motion capture is often used to record movements. Motion capture sensors are available for translating real-world move-ments into 3D Studio animation. Typically, twelve or more sensors are attached to each major skeletal joint of a human actor, and then the actor performs the motions the 3D animated character is to perform. The tiny nuances of human motion can be recorded and applied to objects in 3D Studio.

Like meshes, some types of animation can be purchased. This pre-packaged animation is often called *clip motion* after the clip art used by brochure designers. Common clip motion exists for realistic character motion, such as walking or running. The motion files are usually recorded from an actor with a motion capture system.

Three Dimensions, Three Hats: Sculptor, Set Designer, and Director

Animators must adopt many different mindsets to get their job done. These mindsets parallel their professional counterparts in the real world: sculptor, set designer, and director. Each of these skills is an art unto itself, and the animator who approaches her creation with the dedication of a top sculptor, set designer, and director gets more effective results.

Sculptor

Making a model is usually a fairly straightforward procedure. Complex shapes, however, often require the modeler to adjust isolated parts of a model to complete the object. At this stage, the process is much like sculpting. Parts of the model are pushed, pulled, and bent to achieve the desired look. Models can be added to and subtracted from other models to create new shapes, or even twisted and pulled like taffy with plug-in modules purchased separately.

NOTE

Third-party utility programs for 3D Studio are called Plug-Ins or IPAS routines. Besides twisting and stretching, these add-on programs allow you to add ripples to a surface, fill an area with falling snowflake particles, or even add a glowing aura to a specific object in a rendered image. Most of these utilities are commercial products from a variety of software developers not affiliated with the creators of 3D Studio. However, there are many excellent plug-ins for 3D Studio that are freely available, some of which are included with the CD-ROM that is part of this book.

If you're an experienced CAD user, the transition to modeling in 3D Studio should be fairly easy. Because the rendered output of 3D Studio does not require a high degree of precision, the model-creating parts of 3D Studio are less exacting than a CAD program. If you want the precision, on the other hand, 3D Studio can import from most 3D CAD programs directly through the DXF format, and AutoCAD release 13 can output 3DS files directly.

USAGE TIP

If you use a 2D package that will save DXF-format files, you might be able to import them into 3D Studio and use them as the basis for your new 3D models

During the process of creating the props, characters, and sets that will be used in the 3D animated production, the sculptor must remember how objects will ultimately be colored, and from what angles they will be viewed. If the animation is technical, the goal is usually accuracy, but if the animation is for artistic purposes, the sculptor must consider what each object is supposed to represent in the story.

Set Designer

When lighting and materials are applied, the animator as set designer emphasizes lighting as much as materials. Each object's surface characteristics are chosen and applied. New textures are created and perfected in the Materials Editor. In some cases, the animator actually photographs needed textures and scans them into the computer.

Lighting is often the most difficult aspect of set design in 3D animation. Lights often don't behave as expected—they are the least reality-based characters in 3D Studio's virtual world. Also, because 3D Studio doesn't calculate the secondary light created when light reflects from an object to other nearby objects, it's tempting to over-compensate with more and brighter lights. It should not be surprising, then, that an animation is most commonly ruined by over-lighting, which washes out an image's color and contrast.

Using the set designer's mentality, these problems are solved one at a time by the animator. Attention is focused on the subject of the animation by illuminating it the most and directing the camera to it. The drama of the scene is composed by the shadows cast around the subject, and overall light in the peripheral areas. Colored lights provide additional mood, just as in the complex colored lighting you might have observed at plays and musical productions. The camera can add fog to dim out objects beyond a certain distance. As a computer animator, you can take advantage of additional light features such as excluding certain objects from illumination by the light, or making the light subtractive.

Camera placement also belongs in the set design area if you are creating a still image. The lighting and camera positions usually work in concert to give the mood and composition of the computer artist's vision.

Director

A completely different set of skills is required to use time as a value for changing your characters. As a director, the animator must consider all the changes that occur during the length of the animation. Just as a director blocks out the actors' movements on stage during the first rehearsal, the animator will set the positions of the objects first. After the object motions are in synch with the script, the camera movements are blocked out. In some cases, you can simply link the camera's target to the moving objects.

Objects that animate or change shape over time, such as a character's walk or facial expression, are animated next. Lights that move or change color also are animated at this time. Finally, other animated effects, such as materials that change over time, and animated nuances, such as slight deformations on a bouncing object, are added.

The best results are often the product of carefully scripted animation. For simple scenes, the animator might be able to mentally pace out the animation's progress and apply it to the 3D scene being edited. Most professional animators use a previsualization tool called storyboarding, where certain important frames are sketched out, with arrows drawn in each picture to indicate motion. Notations about sound, light, and other important changes are written beside each drawn out frame. When customers are involved, storyboards provide an excellent way to confirm that you are creating the animation that the customer expects.

During the creation phase, the animation-in-progress has to be viewed to confirm each change. Different techniques are used to minimize the time it takes to get the necessary feedback as you go along.

CGI-to-English, English-to-CGI Dictionary

Understanding the terms used in this book is critical to following the tutorials. A glossary of important terms follows.

Materials | The properties of an object's appearance. Includes color, shininess, transparency, textures, bumpiness, reflections, and any other surface characteristics. Water, gold, wood, marble, and red plastic are examples of materials one might use in 3D Studio.

24-bit color | (TrueColor, 16-million-color mode) 24-bit color is determined by the brightness scale. The brightness scale of the range of each primary color was divided until the difference between two adjacent shades in the range was not noticeable. This turned out to be 256 total brightness levels each for red, green, and blue. Because there are 3 primary colors and each has an 8-bit range, this color quality is said to be 24-bit color. The 16 million colors come from multiplying the 256 shades of red with 256 shades of green and the 256 shades of blue to arrive at all the possible colors that could be displayed on a 24 bit color system. The result is roughly 16 million colors. (See fig. 1.3.)

Additive color | In additive color, the primary colors are not the red, yellow, and blue, as in the color wheel you learned in art class, instead they are red, green, and blue. By altering the intensities of these three colors, any other shade can be produced. Televisions and computer monitors use additive color: they start with a dark screen and then illuminate the primary colors to achieve all the colors in an image.

Subtractive color | In subtractive color, the primary colors are red, yellow, and blue. A white light, for example, shines on the painting's canvas, and the pigments there subtract from the canvas light reflected to create the colors we see when we look at the painting.

Figure 1.3

Color gradation becomes less stratified with more bits.

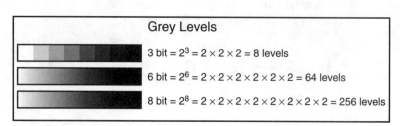

Grey Levels

3 bit = 2^3 = 2 × 2 × 2 = 8 levels

6 bit = 2^6 = 2 × 2 × 2 × 2 × 2 × 2 = 64 levels

8 bit = 2^8 = 2 × 2 × 2 × 2 × 2 × 2 × 2 × 2 = 256 levels

1

Character Animation	Animation that includes anthropomorphic characters, or assignment of anthropomorphic motion to inanimate objects. Usually more difficult than mechanical animation in that the characters have emotions and move with the subtlety of a human.
Industrial Animation	Animation of a non-broadcast nature, usually designed for a company to show only to it's employees or another company. Often technical in nature, the budget and standards required of industrial animation are usually lower than broadcast animation.
Forensic Animation	Animation designed for the courtroom. Usually used to support the testimony of an expert witness. Often, forensic animations recreate an accident or a crime.
Primitive	A single building-block element of 3D geometry. The only true primitive in 3D Studio is the flat triangular face. Using collections of triangles, 3D Studio can make other primitives, such as cones, spheres, boxes, and cylinders.
Pixel	*Pixel* is a contraction of "picture element." Computer images consist of a grid of rectangular color swatches. A single rectangle is a pixel. In computer images, the detail level apparent in an image depends on the fineness of the grid of pixels. As demonstrated in figure 1.4, at some zoom level of a computer image the pixels become evident.

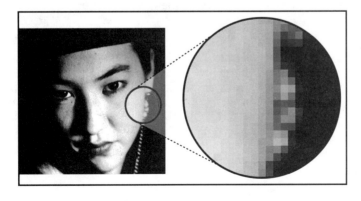

Figure 1.4

All digital images are made up of rectangular pixels of solid color.

Render

Rendering is the computer's unattended processing of all the data created by the animator to create an image. Animators create many test renders as they tune up their creations, and eventually create a final render. The final render usually is set to the highest output quality (where test renders sometimes sacrifice quality for speed), and often require many hours to generate a short animation.

Resolution

The size of a bitmap image, usually given as the number of pixels across, and then the number of pixels high.

Video

Televisions and computers display video images quite differently. When referring to the video signal sent to a television set or output by a VCR, the signal should be termed a television signal (or more accurately, an NTSC video signal). When referring to video from a computer, the signal is usually described as a VGA or SVGA signal. Displaying a computer image on a television monitor requires a special computer card to do the complex conversion of the two disparate signals.

Texture Map

Besides the usual glass and red plastic, it is also possible to take a 2D image and wrap it around a mesh object. Any image used as surface coloring in a 3D scene is called a texture map. Texture maps render quickly and are easily prepared in a paint program from scanned images. 3D Studio's CD-ROM offers hundreds of excellent texture maps. Many are tilable—they can be repeated across an object without apparent edges where the copies meet.

Mesh (wireframe, dataset)

Describes any 3D object. These words are often used interchangeably, but at least for 3D Studio users, mesh is the most common. Wireframe files can exist in many different formats, so be sure that if you are getting a mesh for 3D Studio, that it is in 3DS, PRJ, ASC, or DXF format. Other mesh file formats must be converted to one of these formats with a third party product such as Syndesis' Interchange.

Antialias

A method of avoiding the jaggedy look of 3D rendered scenes by appropriately blending the colors
of the objects hit in proportion to how much of the
pixel each color covers (see fig. 1.5).

Vector

A vector is a line between two points. In math, it
usually is considered to have a direction implied
also, where one end of the line is treated as a
pointer. In computer graphics, the term vector-
based is used to refer to the fact that a program
records and uses exact points for the curves and
polygons it displays, and can allow the user to zoom
infinitely on a feature without any loss of detail or
quality. CorelDRAW! and Adobe Illustrator can be
described as vector-based illustration programs.

Raster

A raster image is made up of a finite number of rows
and columns of pixels. Raster images can be black
and white, greyscale, or color, but at some zoomed in
level, the pixels that make up the image are evident.
A fax is a black and white raster image, and the
limited number of pixels is often evident where a
curved line is approximated on the fax by a collection of square pixels.

Bitmap

A bitmap is a raster image. Technically, a bitmap
refers to raster images that contain pixels that are
either solid black or solid white. The term is often
used incorrectly to describe any raster image.

Vertex

A point in three dimensional space. A vertex has no
dimension, and consists only of a specified location.
A vertex may be designated in 3D Studio by a dot or
a tiny plus sign (see Display/Geometry/Vertices).

Face

A face is a single triangle, described by any three
vertices in 3D Studio. All 3D Studio objects are
made up of faces. Each face can have a different
material. Faces can penetrate each other or be
stretched in any extreme direction. Faces that share
two common vertices can have smoothing assigned
to them so that they will render without an obvious
seam between them.

Element

An element is any group of faces that share common
vertices. Sometimes objects will appear to share
vertices but are still separate elements, such as a
3D model of a tire and its rim.

| Object | An object is a named entity in 3D studio. An object can be made of many elements, each consisting of many faces, but the conglomerate unit will have a single name and will always move, rotate, and scale as a whole. |
| Broadcast animation | Animation designed for display to the public. This term is also used to describe the highest quality animation work for television and film. |

Figure 1.5

Aliasing artifacts are most evident in jagged boundaries of rendered objects.

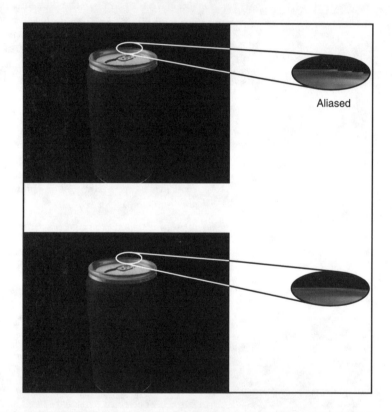

NOTE

Experienced desktop publishers are prone to give resolutions in "DPI" or dots per inch. In video, film, or computer-file animation, this is a misleading way to measure image size, in that there is no "inch;" the display screen will be whatever size it is, and the animation will play back within the screen's borders. For clarity, always measure your bitmap images for 3D Studio in terms of pixels.

Triangles, Lights, and Cameras: The Building Blocks of 3D Studio

Although some rendering programs allow geometric primitives such as spheres and cylinders to be used in designing, in 3D Studio only triangles are allowed. The reason for this is speed—when a sphere is calculated with its true geometric formula, the calculations are always much slower than rendering a spherical object made of hundreds of triangular patches.

Triangles

The user might expect this approach to create a faceted-looking object instead of a sphere. 3D Studio, however, uses a method of smoothing along the surface of each triangle so that seams don't appear between edges. The drawback to this form of rendering is that even though the all-triangle sphere looks correct in the middle, the edges appear faceted and give away the triangular origin of the sphere. The reason for this is that 3D Studio can only smooth triangles if there is a triangle to smooth; if a pixel does not intersect at least one triangle of the sphere, it will continue past the sphere. Figure 1.6 illustrates a wireframe of a high- and low-density sphere, and figures 1.7 and 1.8 illustrate the various renderings of these wireframes.

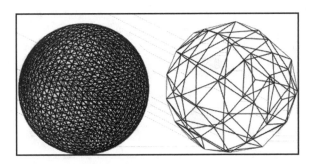

Figure 1.6

Wireframe of a high-density and low-density sphere, both made up entirely of triangles.

Some objects appear to be made of anything but triangles at first glance. The reason for this is that 3D Studio does not always show the user every edge of every triangle. The working area would get quite cluttered with every triangle visible (see fig. 1.9), so appropriate edges are hidden by 3D Studio during object creation. You can view all the triangles at any time by using the command Display/Geometry/All lines in the 3D Editor. Figure 1.10 shows the rendered versions of objects with different edges visible. Notice that they all render the same.

Figure 1.7

Flat-shaded rendered high-density and low-density spheres.

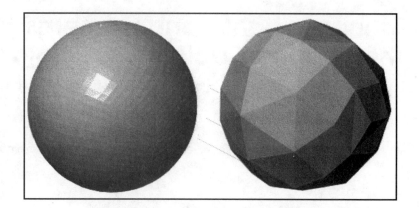

Figure 1.8

Smooth-shaded rendered high-density and low-density spheres - only the silhouettes reveal which is which at this point.

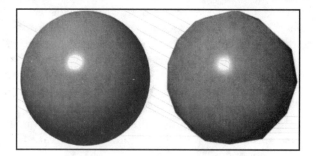

Figure 1.9

Wireframes of three copies of the same object, each with different edges visible. Note that the leftmost mesh displays every edge, and the triangular makeup of the object is apparent.

Figure 1.10

Rendered version of figure 1.9—all objects render identically.

1

Lights

Besides triangles, the other two entities of 3D Studio are lights and cameras. Three types of lights are listed in the menu: ambient, omni, and spot. The ambient setting is really not a light type, it is an adjustment to determine the brightness and color of the light that falls on all objects no matter where they are in a scene. This variable is most often adjusted to compensate for the fact that objects in 3D Studio don't bounce light no matter what material is applied to them.

Omni lights can be any color and intensity, and illuminate in a spherical pattern. Because they cast no shadows, their light is not blocked by any object and they will illuminate any face in the scene that is turned toward them. Omni lights are used to cast a broad, directional light over an area when shadow-casting is not required.

Spot lights radiate light out in a conical fashion from a central point. If their shadow casting attribute is turned on, they will cast shadows and be blocked by objects that cast the shadow. Because of their conic shape, they cannot open to beyond a 179 degree spread. Spot lights are used to cast primary lighting in a scene and cast the shadows that add drama and fix an object's position in space for the viewer.

Cameras

Cameras are not required to render a scene. The renderer can render from any of the viewports that are flat (also called orthographic) just as easily. The camera is used to create a view of the scene that includes perspective.

The camera will show as a pyramid-like shape when created (if the Show Cone button in the light adjustment dialog is set to YES). Think of this camera pyramid as a framer: the eye of the viewer is at the apex, and the frame that crops what the eye sees is the square base (see fig. 1.11). When 3D Studio renders from a camera view it is filling in this square frame with the rendered image (figure 1.12). In perspective, the ray of light that represents each pixel is shot from the eye through the pixel being rendered into the scene. The rays radiate from the centerpoint of the camera that is the viewer's eye. When rendering from an orthographic view (see fig. 1.13), the rays are all parallel, which yields a flat looking image (see fig. 1.14). This is because perspective comes from the single point view (the eye point of the camera) and in the parallel rays of the orthographic projection the viewing eye is essentially being moved to a parallel point for each pixel rendered.

Figure 1.11

A camera looks into the scene from a single point, and therefore always will exhibit perspective.

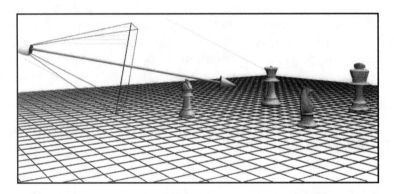

Figure 1.12

The rendered image that fills up the camera view frame.

Figure 1.13

An orthographic view that moves the viewer's eye to parallel points to view the scene from a given angle.

Figure 1.14

Parallel rays cause the projection to appear flat and without perspective.

3DS versus Reality

Although 3D Studio seems to have the parameters necessary to emulate most of the properties of the real world, it is still quite limited in many respects. Often, trying to accomplish a style of image with 3D Studio exactly as you would in the real world is not the best or most effective way. In some cases, the reality approach won't work at all.

Like in real movie sets, the important thing is the final images recorded. Houses and other structures found at movie sets will have no back side if the script doesn't require the viewer to see the back. Shadows of trees that ripple across an actress may simply be a light with a tree-shadow gel in front of it. Don't get bogged down trying to create an entire universe if all you need is a cityscape in the background of your animation.

The lights that 3D Studio use are especially unlike real-world lights. A default-setting light in 3D Studio has no falloff; it shines with equal intensities at all distances from the source similar to the way we perceive sunlight. Adding six bright omni lights to a scene will illuminate it as if there were six suns in the sky! Every object will be so illuminated that all the shadow and depth of the scene will be lost, and the scene will appear flat and washed-out.

What 3DS Cannot Do

Sometimes new 3D Studio users are befuddled by the lack of a particular effect in a scene. In some cases, they have overlooked a switch, but in many cases they are looking for an effect that 3D Studio simply cannot accomplish. As powerful as 3D Studio is, there are some real-life phenomena that it does not attempt to emulate.

Radiosity

Radiosity is the effect that almost every surface has of radiating—or reflecting—the light that strikes it. The moon's surface would not be described as shiny, yet the sunlight it reflects at night is strong enough to see by. Similarly, you may notice that if a person is wearing a bright green shirt, the underside of that person's chin has a greenish cast also. This diffuse complex radiation of light plays a large part in the way real scenes appear, but the effect requires enormous rendering power. Usually this effect is simulated with the deft use of local dim lights.

Refraction

Refraction occurs in light rays that pass through any two transparent objects with different densities. This effect is commonly and accurately modeled by some rendering programs with a process called *ray tracing*. However, 3D Studio does not account for refraction effects, because it uses a faster rendering method that does not allow the rays to bend as ray tracing does. For this reason, you can usually tell when a glass object has been rendered by 3D Studio because the surfaces seen through the glass are not distorted by refraction.

There is a technique, however, for simulating refraction in 3D Studio described in *3D Studio Special Effects* (New Riders Publishing). Also, it is possible to use a third-party ray tracing program with 3D Studio scene files. Ray tracers are nearly always slower than 3D Studio's renderer, by a factor of 3–30 times for complex scenes.

Depth of Field

Depth of field is a term that describes the in-focus area of a camera. When a real camera is focused on an object, objects that are nearer to or farther from the camera than the focused object will appear blurred. The blur effect is stronger as the objects get farther from the focused on area. More sophisticated cameras can open up the aperture of the camera to cause a very shallow depth of field. In 3D Studio, the camera has a depth of field similar to a pinhole aperture camera, where everything in the image is sharply in focus.

Depth of field effects are simulated by using a third-party utility that works within 3D Studio to blur the rendered image in the desired areas.

Complex Reflection

3D Studio is incapable of bouncing a ray from the viewer off of an object that is supposed to be reflective. This doesn't stop 3D Studio from simulating the effect of an object reflecting it's surroundings. 3D Studio works around the problem by creating a texture map to apply to the object. In essence, the camera is placed at the center of the reflective object, a render is completed of the scene from this view, and the resultant image is wrapped around the reflective object. This process can be run at every frame of an animation if the animator sets a particular switch. 3D Studio also can accomplish flat reflection maps creating a similar reflection texture, this time with the camera temporarily repositioned to render from the angle of reflection from the shiny object.

How effective are these workarounds to true reflection? In the case of flat reflection maps, the effect is perfect. In the case of the textured reflection map, the effect is usually fairly good. In the context of a moving animation, the texture mapped reflection system seems just as effective as the time-consuming reflected-ray approach that 3D Studio does not support. Sometimes, however, it is apparent that a curvy reflective object in a scene is not properly reflecting the world around it, usually in large scale paper prints.

Shaped Lights

3D Studio's omni light sources are spherical in nature. The spotlights can emit a round or square beam of light, but it will always be a focused beam. When an illuminated object such as a neon sign or glowing sword is moving about a scene, the effect of the light it emits has to be simulated with a collection of omni and spot lights that are attached to the moving source of illumination. Also, the spotlights can act as a slide projector by selecting an image in the Spotlight Adjust dialog box. Specially created images applied to spotlights can help simulate the effect of non-circular sources of light.

Volume-Related Effects

All 3D Studio objects are made up of infinitely thin triangles. The objects should be thought of as hollow shells with a veneer surface; there is nothing inside an object. Because of this, effects that relate more to volume than to flat surfaces must be simulated in some way. Flying through a cloud or a pool of fire is not directly possible. Usually full screen smoke and cloud effects are accomplished with multiple planes of semi-transparent images that move about in front of the camera. Fire and wispy smoke are more difficult to simulate due to their complex motion. These are handled by third-party plug-in utilities for 3D Studio that fill a simple cube object with animated particles.

Caustics

This effect is best illustrated by the wavy shadows and light seen at the bottom of a swimming pool when the sun is overhead. Light that falls on transparent curvy objects is bent into and out of focus. This bright and dark shadow must fall onto a surface to be observed (like the pool floor). This effect is a by-product of refraction, which, as mentioned previously, is not supported in 3D Studio. The effect is usually simulated with a spot light that acts as a slide or movie projector. Specially created images or sequences of images are shined on the appropriate area by the spotlight.

Colored Shadows

Only one type of light can create shadows that take the shadow-casting object's transparency into account: the ray traced-shadow spotlight. Although it can take transparency into account, it does so only in terms of total opacity, so the shadow varies as a greyscale. A red translucent object will thus only create a medium dark grey shadow. There is a technique for working around this limitation. It is described thoroughly in *3D Studio Special Effects* from New Riders Publishing.

Summary

The fundamentals of computer graphics provide an understanding of the progress that enabled 3D Studio to evolve. Comprehending 3D Studio's internal processing of the data you create for it will help you anticipate problems and work within its limitations for the highest quality output. The terminology and concepts of computer imaging and graphics are the foundation for the work you will create, but it will become more clear as you work with 3D Studio. This chapter could be returned to after more exploration with 3D Studio, and many of the concepts and terms will be more apparent. As you begin to create with 3D Studio, and wear the different hats of sculptor, set designer, and director, remember to include the artistic vision and meaning that each imparts in their craft.

Now that you've explored the theory of 3D Studio, the next chapter takes you into its usage. Each of the procedures discussed in this chapter are applied in typical fashion to the creation of a simple animation in the next chapter.

Chapter Snapshot

Now that you have been acquainted with the terms and functions of 3D Studio, it is time to put these to use. This chapter will introduce the fundamental concepts and usage of 3D Studio including the following:

- The different types of structures of 3D Studio

- The different types of rendering

- An introduction to the commands and icons of 3D Studio

- An exploration of 3D Studio's five main modules

2

Meet 3D Studio

3D Studio combines five main modules with several specialized plug-in programs. You use the first two modules—the 2D Shaper and the 3D Lofter—together as a modeling system to create the 3D geometry that will make up all the objects that you eventually will render and use in your animations. At its simplest, the 2D Shaper defines the outline through which the 3D Lofter extrudes an object, like the circular opening of a toothpaste tube causes the contents to extrude in a cylindrical fashion (see figures 2.1 and 2.2).

The 3D Editor is where the 3D stage is set: modifying the existing models, adding predefined objects (such as spheres and cylinders), placing the lights and cameras, choosing the initial positions of all the objects, and selecting and placing all the materials. You will use the Materials Editor module to create and edit surface attributes. Finally, animation is handled in the Keyframer module.

Figure 2.1

Figure 2.1

A circle can be extruded to create a cylinder.

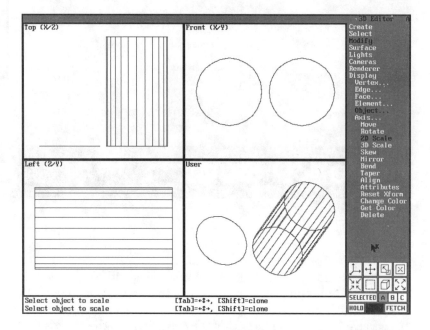

Figure 2.2

Text is extruded to create a three-dimensional object.

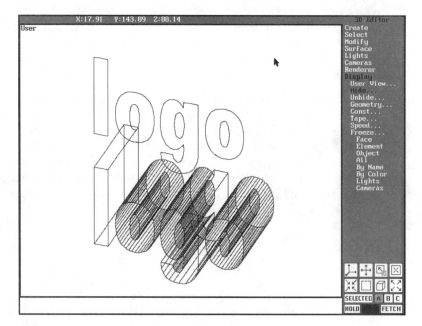

Objects, Faces, Vertices, Edges, and Elements

As was discussed in Chapter 1, "Three-Dimensional Computer Graphics," every item that you render in 3D Studio consists of triangles. Individual triangles, a triangle's parts, and groups of triangles have different names in 3D Studio. Similarly, the program's commands are grouped to act on parts of a triangle (vertices), a whole triangle (face), and groups of triangles (element, object).

Faces and Vertices

In 3D Studio, the sole building block of any 3D object is the triangular face. Each face is made up of one face and three vertices. The *vertices* are the end points of the triangle on which each face is hung. Faces can share vertices. A flat square, for example, might be composed of four vertices and two faces. Vertices can exist without any faces attached, but rendering this will show empty space—the vertices are simply isolated points in 3D space. A face cannot, however, be created without existing vertices. When you delete a face in the 3D Editor, 3D Studio will ask if you want to delete the isolated vertices—the vertices that now are left disconnected from all faces.

Faces that share edges can have the seam between them smoothed, but the silhouette will reveal a corner where they join. This is due to the fact that during rendering if a given pixel does not intersect a triangle, 3D Studio cannot guess where a bent triangle might have been intersected instead. Also, even though 3D Studio can smooth the seams between triangles, if the angles to be smoothed are too extreme, the smoothing can take on a streaked appearance and will look unnatural. Therefore, objects with rounded edges tend to take a large number of faces and vertices to keep the edges from appearing faceted, and to keep the smoothing natural.

Each face can have a unique material assigned to it. Often, a single object can have sections that require different colors. A rocket booster object, for example, might be striped along its body, and have different colored fins. In 3D Studio, each of the needed materials would be assigned to only the faces that make up those subsections (body, fins) of the rocket booster.

Face Editing

You can manipulate 3D objects in almost any way you want within 3D Studio. You can, for example, detach (disconnect) faces from one object and attach them to another object. You can detach a selection of faces as a group and use that group to create an entirely new object, and so on.

Because detailed objects are typically made up of thousands of faces, you will rarely build an object one face at a time. Professional animators, however, frequently edit their objects by selecting groups of faces to delete or by selecting groups of vertices to "pull out." Models are usually touched up and perfected in the 3D Editor this way.

Edges

The *edges* of a face can be displayed or hidden. Most objects have many hidden edges. You can force the hidden edges of an object to be revealed by selecting the Display/Edges/All lines command in the 3D Editor (see figure 2.3). Typically, edges are visible only where an object bends sharply or reaches its outer limits. This helps the animator to see what's going on and also speeds screen redraws. Edges are only a visual cue for the animator and are usually seen only during the creation stage within 3D Studio.

It is sometimes desirable, however, to actually render wireframe objects, where the displayed edges are rendered instead of the object's faces. This is often useful for more easily modeling subjects that are gridlike, such as birdcages and wire fences.

Objects and Elements

A group of faces and vertices make up an *object*, which always is assigned a unique name in the 3D Editor. A collection of three vertices can define a face. A collection of one or more *contiguous* (where faces share one or two common vertices) faces defines an element. A collection of one or more elements defines an object. A complex object can be made up of one or more *elements*, which usually are the separate parts of the object. If you have a complex model of a car, for example, the car is a single object, and each wheel is an element (see figure 2.4).

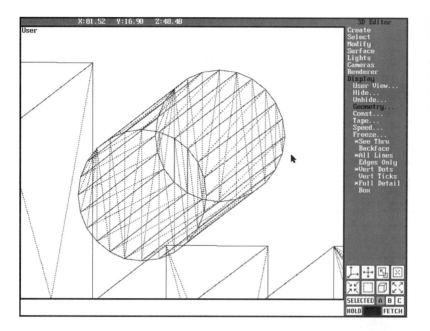

Figure 2.3

With all lines displayed, the triangular nature of all 3D Studio objects is revealed.

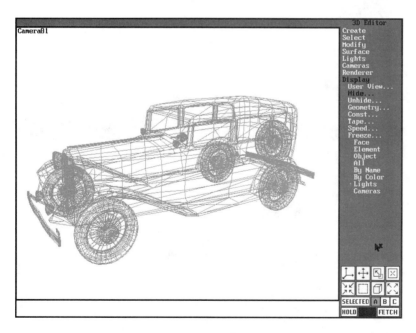

Figure 2.4

The entire car is the object in this figure, and each wheel is an element.

Before You Get Started

Before you dive into 3D Studio, there are a few basic buttons and commands you need to know about. These are the key buttons and commands that you will use repeatedly as you work with 3D Studio.

Hot Keys

As you click on the options that appear at the top of the 3D Studio screen, pull-down menus appear. On each menu, many of the commands list a key combination beside the name of the command. These keyboard shortcuts, called *hot keys*, can help you move very quickly within 3D Studio. The most important hot keys to learn now are the F1 through F5 keys, which let you quickly choose among the five main modules, as follows. Figure 2.5 shows the Materials Editor, the module that appears when you press F5.

F1   The 2D Shaper

F2   The 3D Lofter

F3   The 3D Editor

F4   The Keyframer

F5   The Materials Editor

Figure 2.5

The Materials Editor.

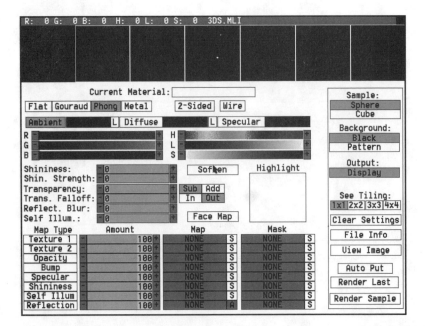

Although there are links between the modules, in many ways they are independent, simultaneously running programs. You can toggle from one to the other at any time with the F1 through F5 keys, and you should explore this now to get familiar with the standard layout of each module.

USAGE TIP

2

> While you're flipping through the modules, take a minute to make sure that the Materials Editor has the correct color depth and resolution, as you configured in the Introduction of this book. If you want to change the screen display settings, restart 3D Studio with the command **3DS YIBCFG** and follow the setup described in this book's Introduction.

Viewport Control Icons

In the lower right corner of the 2D Shaper, 3D Lofter, 3D Editor, and Keyframer modules, there is a panel that contains several icons that act as pushbuttons. You can use these icons to adjust your view in the many windows (called *viewports*) when you are working in a scene. Only one viewport is active, or *current*, at a time; when a viewport is active, it has an outline around it.

The following icons are common to all four modules.

Table 2.1

The Universal Icon Pushbuttons

Icon		*Purpose*
Pan	⊕	To pan the view, click the area in the viewport that you want to pick up, move the pointer to where you want the picked up area to be dropped, and click again.
Zoom In	⤢	Left-click this icon to magnify the center of the selected viewport (roughly a 2× zoom). Right-click this icon to zoom in all the viewports.
Zoom Out	⤡	This icon has the inverse effect of the Zoom In icon. Left-click this icon to zoom out the selected viewport (roughly a 2× zoom). Right-click this icon to zoom out all the viewports.

continues

Table 2.1, Continued
The Universal Icon Pushbuttons

Icon		Purpose
Zoom Extents		Left-click this icon to adjust the zoom and pan so that all the objects neatly fit within the current viewport. Right-click this icon to achieve the same effect in all the non-camera viewports.
Zoom Region		Use this icon to select a portion of a viewport's display to fill the viewport. Click in the active viewport in one corner to drop the zoom window, then move the mouse diagonally and click again to specify the zoom.
Full-Screen Toggle		This icon makes the selected viewport temporarily fill the full screen. Clicking the icon again restores the original multi-viewport view.

Four of the icon buttons adjust the zoom level of a viewport. The Zoom In and Zoom Out buttons work from the center of the active viewport and expand or reduce the scene. The Zoom Extents button alters both zoom and pan to fill a viewport with every displayed object, light, and camera. The Zoom Region button brings a selected area of a viewport to the full viewport. Zooming is critical to make minute adjustments at close magnification and check the overall scene at a zoomed-out magnification. The Zoom Out button can be right clicked several times after a right-clicked Zoom Extents to get an entire scene into a small area in the center of each viewport, which is useful when placing cameras and lights that need to cover the entire scene.

Panning about the scene is useful for bringing to center a part of the view that is close to, but off the screen. Use the Pan, Zoom In, and Zoom Extents buttons to alternate editing sections of your scene close-up and zooming back out to the full scene.

Menu Bar

The menu bar is broken down into five categories: Info commands, File commands, View commands, Program commands, and Network commands. These commands are used to manipulate your way through a drawing or animation. A complete listing and description of these commands is found in Appendix A, "Menu Bar Commands."

Exploring the Five Main Modules

To get an understanding of how each module relates to the others and creates a rendered animation, this first series of tutorials takes you through all the steps of creating a simple, but complete, animation in 3D Studio. You'll learn the basic use of the five modules while creating the most popular of computer-rendered subjects, the flying logo.

Using the 2D Shaper

2

The 2D Shaper is very similar to vector-based drawing programs such as CorelDRAW! and Adobe Illustrator. You use the 2D Shaper to set up the flat, two-dimensional shapes from which you will create 3D objects.

For the shapes to be used as an outline for extrusion, they must follow certain rules. They have to be *closed* shapes; that is, they must be connected in a loop so that there are no end points. They cannot intersect themselves in any way, like a figure-8. You can have nested shapes so that one item is a hole within the other, such as the letter O, but you cannot have two shapes that intersect each other. All these restrictions make sense when you imagine how a circle might be lofted into a cylinder, or two nested circles might be lofted into a tube. Figure 2.6 shows examples of acceptable and unacceptable shapes.

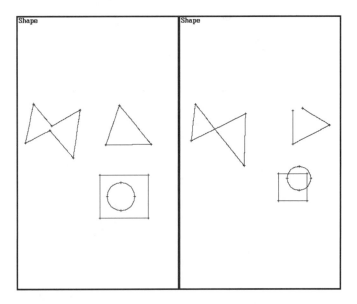

Figure 2.6

Acceptable and unacceptable shapes in the 2D Shaper.

The drawing tools for creating squares, circles, text, and lines are listed on the right menu, under Create. After you create your basic shapes and lines, the vertices and segments can be adjusted, deleted, welded, and scaled.

The 2D Shaper lets you create text from font files. There are many fonts that come with 3D Studio, and you can also use any PFB format PostScript font file to create text directly in the 2D Shaper.

Creating Text in the 2D Shaper

Return to the 2D Shaper by pushing F1	2D Shaper appears
Choose Create/Text/Font from the right side menu	The Font File dialog box offers a selection of fonts (see figure 2.7)
Select the 3D Studio font file NORMANBL.FNT and click on OK	The font name is accepted. This font will be used for any new text created until you select a different font file
Choose Create/Text/Enter	The Enter Text dialog box appears (see figure 2.8)

Figure 2.7

Selecting a font from the Font File dialog box.

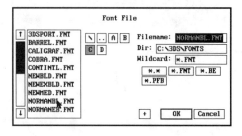

Figure 2.8

The Enter Text dialog box.

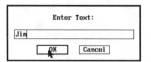

Type in **logo**	3D Studio accepts the text. Like the font, this text will be used for any new text created until different text is set here
Click OK	
Choose Create/Text/Place	Moving the mouse cursor through the active viewport shows crosshairs across the viewport

Click the mouse in the upper left corner of the viewport	A frame is drawn when the mouse cursor is moved away from the selected point (see figure 2.9)
Size the frame to be a square that mostly fills the viewport. Click the left mouse button	The text appears in the viewport (see figure 2.10)

The text might be the appropriate scale for the font. It might appear elongated or squashed, but sometimes this is desired. Usually, though, a font is designed to look correct at a certain height and width ratio. 3D Studio uses the font's internal proper ratio if you hold Ctrl while sizing the text frame. With this in mind, back up a step and use Ctrl to maintain the proper ratio while you re-create the text.

Click on the UNDO icon in the icon panel, located in the lower left corner of the viewport	The text just entered disappears
While holding down Ctrl, click in one corner of the viewport	A frame is drawn when the mouse cursor is moved away from the selected point. This time, the frame keeps a constant aspect ratio
Size the frame and click the left mouse button	The text appears in proper scale (see figure 2.11). You are now ready to import your two-dimensional text into the 3D Lofter, where you will give it depth

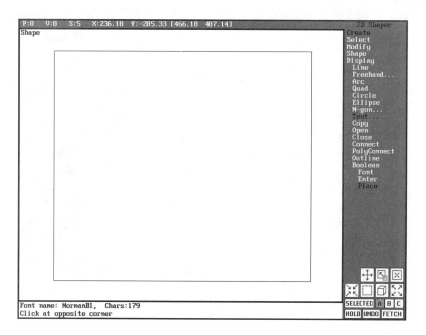

Figure 2.9

Drawing a bounding rectangle to place the text object in.

continues

continued

Figure 2.10

The placed text.

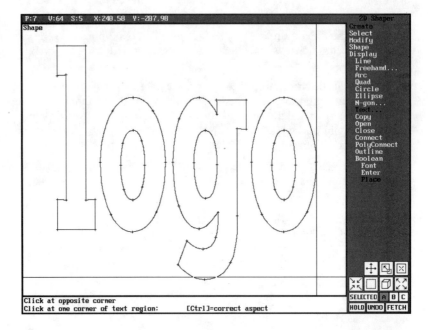

Figure 2.11

Properly sized text, scaled to the font's internal correct width and height.

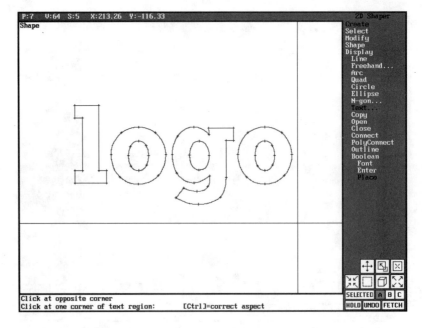

Because many different shapes can coexist in the 2D Shaper at one time, you have to tell 3D Studio which shapes to bring into the 3D Lofter. Any group of closed and non-intersecting shapes can be moved to the 3D Lofter, but at least one shape should be assigned. An *assigned* shape is a shape that is marked for movement to the 3D Lofter, as the following exercise shows. For example, with the text just entered, you could assign just a single letter or the whole word for lofting. Similarly, just the central circle of an O shape might be used in the 3D Lofter.

> **NOTE**
>
> An Assign command is used to select shapes for the 3D Lofter. Don't confuse this with the Select command, which is used to pick groups of shapes to modify. Assigned shapes are yellow; selected shapes are red. If a shape is both selected and assigned, it is dark orange.

Assigning a Shape for the 3D Lofter

Select Shape/All	All the text in the 2D Shaper switches to yellow, with the vertices remaining white

Shape/Assign can be used to pick shapes one at a time. Assigning an assigned shape makes it unassigned. Before moving on to the 3D Lofter, the assigned shape should always be computer-checked to make sure that the 3D Lofter will accept it.

Choose Shape/Check	A message appears stating Shape OK, Vertices: 35, where 35 is the number of vertices that make up the assigned shape (see figure 2.12)
Click Continue	The dialog box disappears

Occasionally, an error message is returned, but the FNT fonts that come with 3D Studio nearly always work. When there is an error, 3D Studio flags problem areas with little red boxes. Zooming in closely to these areas usually reveals the problem with the assigned shape or shapes.

At this point, the text is brought into the 3D Lofter.

Press the F2 key	Switches to the 3D Lofter, which is empty at this point

Although the shapes in the 2D Shaper have been assigned, they still must be brought into the 3D Lofter, as the next exercise explains.

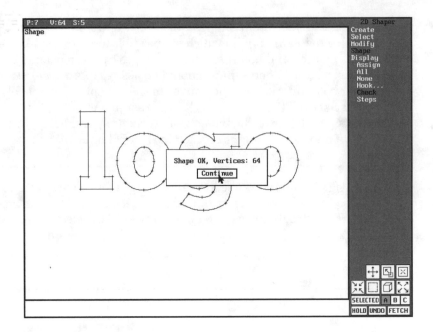

Figure 2.12

Shape OK dialog box returns from a successful shape check.

Using the 3D Lofter

The 3D Lofter creates 3D objects for your scenes by combining a shape with a path. The shape defines the perimeter of the 3D object to be lofted, and the path defines the direction in which the shape will be lofted. The path can be edited in 3D space within the 3D Lofter. For example, an oval-track shape can be created in the 2D Shaper, imported into the 3D Lofter, and then edited in 3D space to prevent the bugle tubing from running through itself. A circle lofted on this path creates a paper-clip effect instead of a bugle. However, the 3D Lofter enables a shape to be modified in many ways as it moves along the path, including scaling. Appropriately scaling a circle to larger and smaller sizes at different parts of the bugle-shaped path would create a good 3D bugle object.

NOTE

Extrusion is used here to describe simple lofting such as a circle to a cylinder or a triangle to a prism. Lofting describes the creation of any object with 3D Studio's 3D Lofter.

The most common usage of the 3D Lofter is simple extrusion. The default path built into the 3D Lofter is a simple, straight path. There are tick marks along the path to indicate intermediate steps. 3D Studio allows a user-definable number of steps to be used for both the path and shape each time you loft an object.

Because all the triangles that make up a 3D object are flat, you must decide how complex to make an object. Complexity slows rendering speed, but results in a better-looking finished object as the object gets closer to the viewer. Therefore, you have to decide during the lofting stage how complex (how many triangles) the object will be, based on how close the camera will get to the object during the animation.

In the following exercise, you will use the 3D Lofter to add depth to the text you created earlier.

Lofting the Text

Multiple shapes can be lofted at the same time, as long as they don't overlap. If one shape encloses another, the inner shape will loft as a hole in the outer shape. Lofting the text created in the last exercise will illustrate this.

Choose Shapes/Get/2D Shaper	The text shape currently assigned in the 2D Shaper from the last exercise appears in the 2D Shaper viewport (see figure 2.13). It is visible in 3D Space in the other viewports

Now you must adjust the detail level of the text. Because there are no curved lines in the objects you will create, you must set the number of line segments, or *steps*, between each vertex that will approximate the curves. This will create a polygonal effect.

Step settings are used to segment the 2D Shaper's spline curves for the flat faces used by the 3D Editor. You can change this setting either in the 2D Shaper or the 3D Lofter; both reflect any changes made. If steps are set to 0, a circle will appear as a square because there are only four vertices with a single line segment between each to approximate the curve. Increasing shape steps will yeild an 8-sided, then a 16-sided, then a 32-sided, and so on approximation of a circle. Although the higher steps yield smoother curves, the resulting objects take longer to render. Therefore you have to adjust this setting for your smoothness and rendering speed needs.

Choose Shape/Steps	The Set Steps dialog box appears (see figure 2.14)
Adjust the slider to 1 and click on OK	The shape is redrawn and looks angular in its previously curvy areas (see figure 2.15)
Choose Shape/Steps again	The Set Steps dialog box reappears
Adjust the slider to 10 and click on OK	The text is now very smooth in the curvy areas (see figure 2.16)

continues

continued

Figure 2.13

The assigned shape is imported into the 3D Lofter.

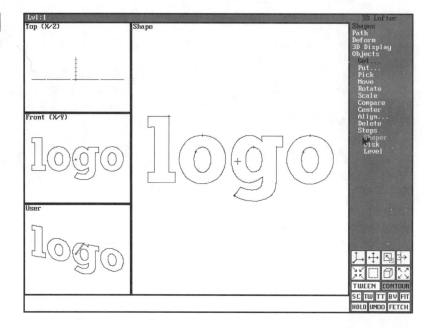

Figure 2.14

Adjusting the number of segments to approximate a curve with the Set Steps Dialog.

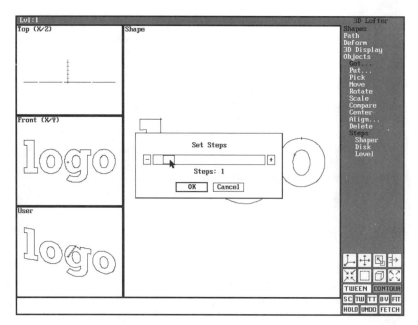

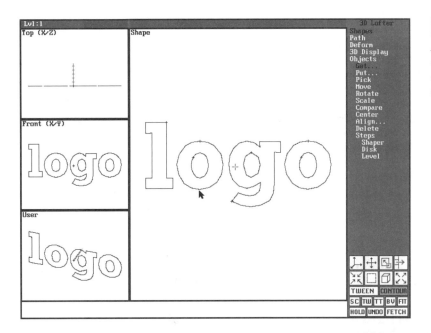

Figure 2.15

A low number of steps yields coarse approximations of curves.

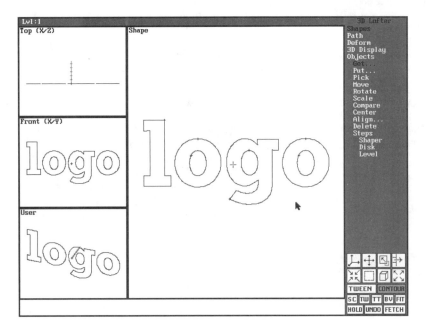

Figure 2.16

With 10 segments approximating the curves between each point, the shape looks quite smooth in the curved areas.

continues

continued

You need to set this detail level each time because setting more steps in the 2D Shaper creates more faces in the 3D Editor. Those extra faces use precious RAM, slow rendering speed, and slow redraw speed when you're working with the object in the 3D Editor and Keyframer. The key consideration is how close the object will be viewed. You want to avoid the faceted-edge look with a minimum number of vertices. At some magnification, faceting will be obvious, regardless of the number of steps, and at a distance, even an octagon appears circular. Thus, you must make a decision on this important factor every time you loft a curvy object. For this example, five steps should be sufficient.

Choose Shape/Steps	The Set Steps dialog box appears
Set the number of steps to 5 and click on OK	The dialog disappears and the shape is redrawn
Choose Objects/Preview	The Preview Controls dialog box appears
The Contour button should be selected by default. Select High Detail for both Shape and Path, then click on Preview (see figure 2.17)	The preview is displayed in the viewports. The text shape is drawn at each step of the path in all viewports (see fig. 2.18)

This preview should give some idea of how the object will look. However, re-lofting an object that didn't quite come out right is easy, so don't agonize over the lofting phase. The best approach is to simply create the 3D object and view it, then re-loft with adjustments if necessary.

Select Objects/Make	The Object Lofting Controls dialog box appears (see figure 2.19)
The name field is highlighted at the top of the dialog. Type **Logo** for the name	The name of the object about to be created is set to Logo
Accept the default perimeters and click on Create	An Object Creation Progress dialog box appears temporarily, then disappears. The 3D Lofter screens are displayed just as before. Where is the three-dimensional object you just created? It was placed directly into the 3D Editor module. Switch to that module now by pressing the F3 key (see figure 2.20)

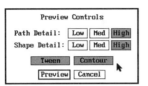

Figure 2.17

The Preview Controls dialog box.

Figure 2.18

A preview of how the object will be lofted.

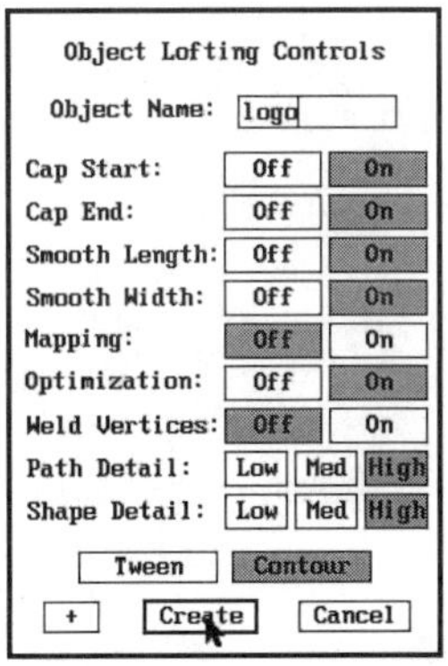

2

Figure 2.19

The Object Lofting Controls dialog box—this is the last step to creating a 3D object from the 3D Lofter.

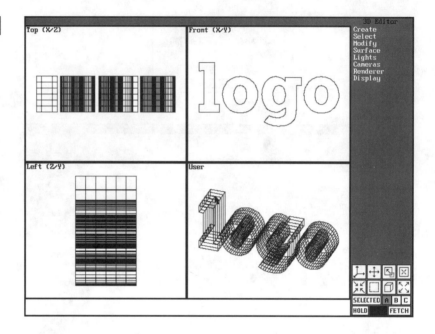

Figure 2.20

The just-created object generated by the 3D Lofter with its current settings.

Using the 3D Editor

The 3D Editor is probably where you will spend the most time in 3D Studio. All material assignments, object placement, lights, cameras, and general scene design are handled here. Much of the 3D Lofter's output objects are further altered, copied, and positioned in the 3D Editor.

If you are creating a single, still image and not an animation, most of the editing of the scene is handled in the 3D Editor. In the case of an animation, the 3D Editor is used to set up the scene completely for the initial position of the animation before moving on to the Keyframer.

In the 3D Editor, you are working in true three-dimensional space. You will notice the labels top, left, and front in the upper left corner of each viewport. You can switch the active viewport (with the white outline around it) among the six standard views by pressing the following keys:

F   Front

K   Back

L   Left

R   Right

T   Top

B   Bottom

A seventh mode is possible that allows all the viewing angles between the six listed previously. The U key puts a viewport into User View mode. The User View initially displays an adjustable XYZ axis icon. You move the mouse to alter the axis rotation in the view, and then click the mouse to view the scene from the chosen User View.

Some viewports might initially be listed as No View Defined in the upper left corner, but these can be quickly switched to any of the views previously listed by activating the view and pressing the proper key for one of the six viewpoints.

In the context of the previous exercise, the 3D Editor is useful for checking lofted objects; you can adjust them in the 3D Editor or go back to the 3D Lofter and re-loft if necessary. Because you just lofted the text in the last exercise, it should be visible in the viewports.

An obvious flaw in your lofted text is that there are multiple shape instances along the sides of the object. That is, when you view the image from the side, you can see that multiple path steps have created unneeded faces. Because every face uses memory and slows rendering, you should minimize them where possible. If a logo object such as this is later going to be bent in the 3D Editor, it may be desirable to have the interim steps along the logo's sides to allow segments for such bending. In your case, however, all the extra faces along the sides of the logo are wasted.

You should now correct the wasted faces problem by taking a step back; return to the 3D Lofter and adjust the parameters.

Checking Lofted Objects in the 3D Editor

Press F2 to jump to the 3D Lofter	The 3D Lofter screen appears, just as you left it
Choose Path/Steps	The Set Path Steps dialog box appears
Set the slider to 0 and click on OK (see figure 2.21)	The screen redraws, and the straight path now has no tick marks between the endpoints (see figure 2.22)
Select Objects/Make	The Object Lofting dialog box appears, with the same setting as the last use

continues

continued

Click on Create

You are asked about renaming this created object or deleting the one presently in the 3D Editor (see figure 2.23)

Click Delete Old

An Object Creation Progress dialog box appears temporarily, then disappears. The 3D Lofter screens are displayed just as before

You might have noticed a faster creation time this time, due to fewer faces being created. Now check the object in the 3D Editor.

Press F3 for the 3D Editor

The 3D Editor appears (see figure 2.24)

Figure 2.21

Adjusting the path steps to 0.

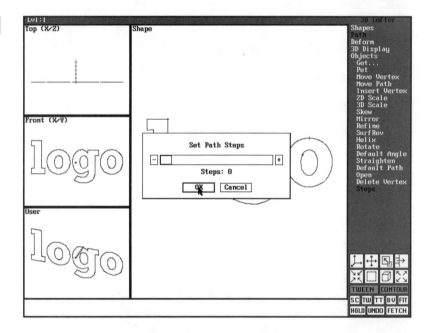

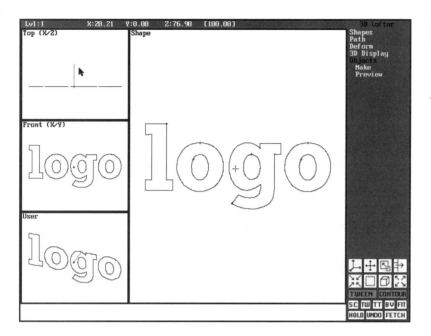

Figure 2.22

The new path has no ticks between its start and end points.

2

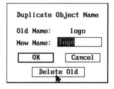

Figure 2.23

The Duplicate Object Name dialog box appears when the object you are attempting to create is named exactly the same as an object already in the 3D Editor.

Figure 2.24

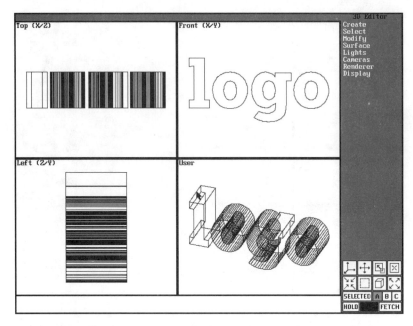

Figure 2.24

The new object, with far fewer faces, describing exactly the same shape.

The object created is clearly correct in the left viewport. As a wireframe, it might not be as beautiful, but it will render faster and look the same. 3D Studio novices commonly ignore the path steps and create thousands of unneeded faces. Rendering speed and RAM usage complaints are sometimes completely the result of this oversight.

Adjusting Objects in the 3D Editor

An object can be lofted correctly but still not be quite right. It's often much faster to adjust the object in the 3D Editor, where other parts of the scene are visible for comparison. In this example, the extrusion of the text is too long. In the following exercise, you will quickly scale the text to the desired depth, leaving the height and width unmodified.

Scaling the Text in the 3D Editor

Choose Modify/Object/2D Scale	Selection highlighted on right side menu
Click in the top viewport to activate it	Top viewport has white line around it

The mouse pointer is now a uniform scale icon that looks like four arrows. Hit Tab repeatedly and it cycles through horizontal scaling, vertical scaling, and uniform scaling. When the icon is set for vertical scaling (and looks like an up/down arrow), click on the logo object.

A rectangle appears (called the bounding box) that encompasses the periphery of the selected object (see figure 2.25). When the mouse is slid left or right, the box vertically enlarges or contracts.

Size the box so that the logo is ⅓ as thick as it is high and click the mouse

The logo is redrawn with new dimensions (see fig. 2.26)

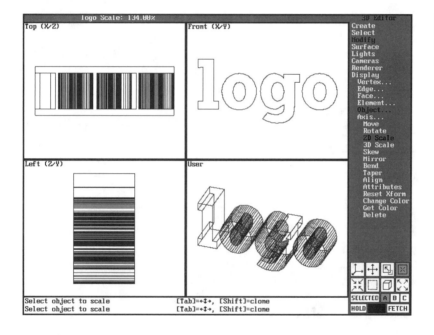

Figure 2.25

Scaling the object in depth only.

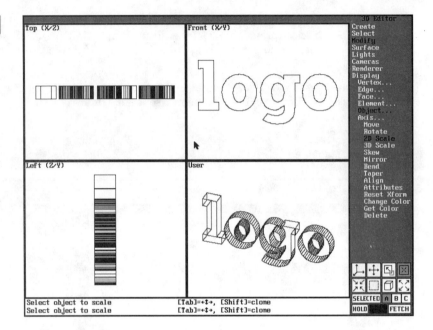

Figure 2.26

The scaled logo is redrawn after the mouse is clicked.

NOTE

You must select objects at corners or along edges, not in the airspace within an object.

Notice that with 2D scaling, the object is only affected in the plane in which you modified it (the top plane in this case). In the other views, it is clear that the object is less deep, but it is the same size as before when viewed from the front.

Adding Light in the 3D Editor

The 3D world is barren and black when you begin. After you create your objects, you need to illuminate them with lights if you plan to take a picture of the scene.

3D Studio offers three kinds of lights: ambient, omni, and spot. For the purpose of this introduction, you'll only use omni lights to illuminate your logo. *Omni* lights are not obstructed by anything; they shine right through walls to illuminate objects on the other side. They don't cast shadows. They can be any color and brightness level.

Adding Lighting to the Logo

First, you need some space around the logo so that the lights can be placed a distance away.

Right-click the Zoom Extents button	All four viewports re-zoom to perfectly contain a view of the logo
Right-click the Zoom Out button twice	All four viewports zoom out each time the button is depressed (see figure 2.27)
Choose Lights/Omni/Create	Create is highlighted in the menu
In the top viewport, click where the light is to be created. Put the light behind and to the left of the logo (see figure 2.28)	The Light Definition dialog box appears with light settings (see figure 2.29) and a light name field
Click in the name field and type **backlight**	The name changes from Light01 to backlight

You don't want a strong bright light at this point; you are creating a back light for effect.

Adjust the L slider down to 80 (L stands for luminance, or brightness.)	The color sample box darkens and the RGB sliders move together to lower values (refer to figure 2.29)
Click on Create	The box disappears, and a yellow asterisk-like object appears in 3D space in all four viewports. This symbol represents the light

Notice that when the object was placed in 3D space from the top viewport, the program assumes the construction plane. That is, the light appears at a default height in the front and side viewports. Generally, after a light is created, its position is adjusted in the other viewports.

Right-click on the Zoom Extents icon	The light is visible in all viewports
Choose Lights/Omni/Move	Move is highlighted in yellow
Click on the left viewport to activate it	The left viewport becomes active and has a white line around it
Click on the light in the left viewport	The light symbol is moved up by the mouse cursor and can be moved within the viewport
Move the light up so it is above and behind the logo, some distance back	The light is dropped in the new place
Click the mouse when the light is in position	

Figure 2.27

Zooming out from the centered object.

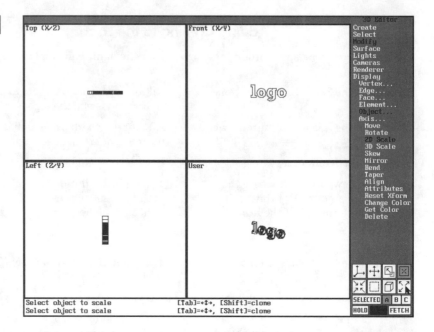

Figure 2.28

Placing a new light.

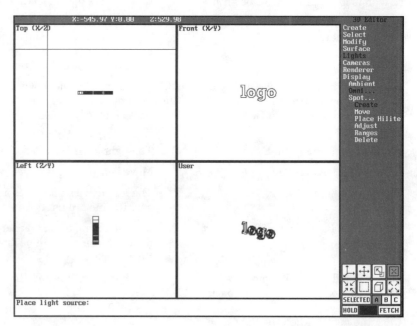

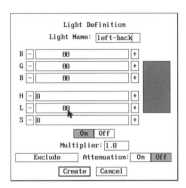

Figure 2.29

Adjusting the new light's parameters in the Light Definition dialog box.

2

You can create new objects, lights, and cameras in the 3D Editor by moving existing objects, lights, and cameras while pressing Shift. Shift is used as the clone key, as shown in the prompt during the moving operation. In the following exercise, you will use this method to create more lights.

Adding More Lights to the Logo

Lights/Omni/Move should still be active	Check the right menu; Move should be highlighted
Click on the top viewport to activate it	The top viewport becomes active
While holding Shift, click on the light in the top viewport	The original light remains, but a light icon is grabbed by the mouse cursor (see fig. 2.30)
Move the cursor to the right rear of the logo and click the mouse	The Light Definition dialog box appears asking for the name of the new light
Type in **rerear**	The name appears in the name field of the dialog box
Click on Create	The Light Definition dialog box disappears and the viewports show 2 lights behind and above the logo (see figure 2.31)
While pressing Shift, click on one of the two lights in the top viewport again	A new light is being moved by the cursor
Place this light in front of the logo and in the center in the top viewport and click the mouse	The Light Definition dialog box to name the light appears again

continues

continued

Type **front**	The name appears in the name field
Click on Create	The name front is accepted for the new light
Move this new center light in the front viewport by activating the front viewport and clicking on the new light icon in the center	The light is picked up and is controlled by the mouse movement

Place the light below the logo in the center (see figure 2.32).

(see figure 2.32)

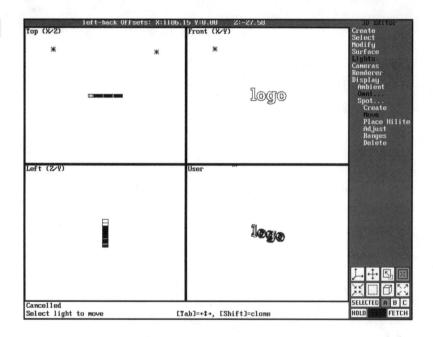

Figure 2.30

Copying a light with the Move command while Shift is held.

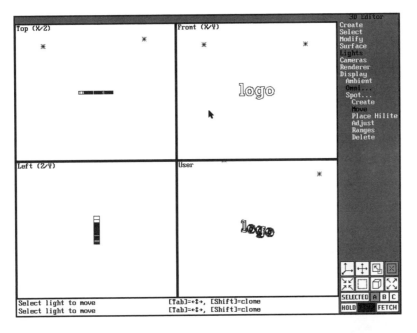

Figure 2.31

The new light appears.

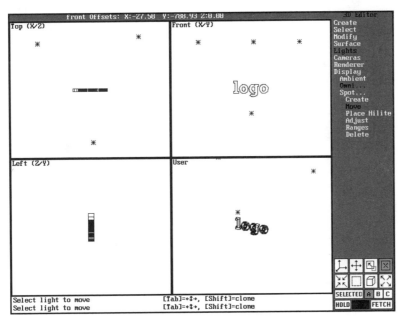

Figure 2.32

Moving the third light source.

Now you have basic three-point lighting around the logo. Currently, all lights have the same brightness level. In this case, however, the front light should be brighter than the two back lights because you want to emphasize the front side in this exercisre. The following exercise shows you how to adjust it.

Adjusting Your Lights

Choose Lights/Omni/Adjust	The menu item is highlighted
Click on the front light in one of the viewports	The Light Definition dialog box appears, similar to the Omni Light Adjust dialog that appeared when Lights/Omni/Create was used earlier
Adjust the L slider to 140 to brighten this light	The RGB sliders move up, and the color patch brightens (see figure 2.33)
Click on OK	The dialog box disappears

Adjusting the brightness of the third light source.

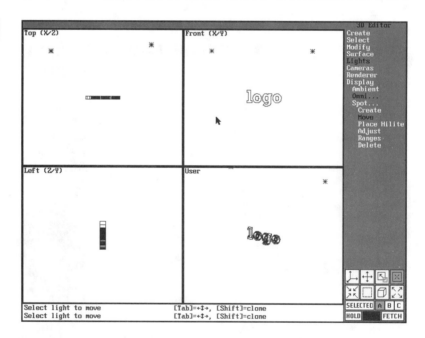

Setting Up Cameras in the 3D Editor

You now have the logo geometry and a lighting scheme. The next step is to create a camera. A *camera* views the scene in perspective from any position you place it. The camera cannot be set to focus at certain distances—every part of the scene will render in perfect focus—but you can adjust the field of view to zoom your camera in and out of your scene.

The following exercise shows you how to add a camera to your logo scene.

Creating a Camera

Choose Cameras/Create

The menu item is highlighted

Activate the top viewport by clicking on it

The viewport becomes active

Click the mouse in the position where the viewer is located. In this case, the viewer should be in front of the logo, to the left

When moved from the spot clicked upon, the mouse leaves a line. The line is the indicator of which way the camera is looking (see figure 2.34)

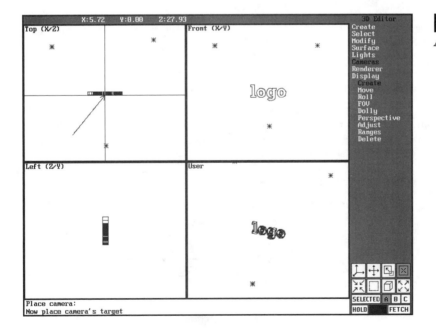

Figure 2.34

Adding a camera.

continues

continued

Click on the center of the logo	The Camera Definition dialog box appears with the camera adjustment settings (see figure 2.35)

The 48mm default camera simulates the perspective of the human eye. Lower millimeter settings yield a more powerful flared perspective, and higher millimeter settings give a less noticeable flattened perspective in the camera view.

Now, click on Create to accept the default settings	The camera symbol appears
Type **viewer**	The camera's name changes from camera01 to viewer
Click the show cone ON button	The ON button is highlighted in red

A blue line appears with a rectangular cone in all four viewports (see figure 2.36). The cone indicates the width of the field of view from the camera's position at the point. Like the light creation, the camera and camera target are at a default height when first created in the top viewport. Usually the camera position needs adjustment. To see what the camera sees and confirm correct placement, switch one of the viewports to a camera view.

Activate the lower right viewport by clicking in it	The viewport becomes active
Type **C** on the keyboard	The viewport switches to camera view (see figure 2.37)
Choose Camera/Move	The menu item is highlighted

Click on the camera or camera target in the left viewport.

The camera or camera target that you clicked on moves with the mouse, and the camera viewport displays the scene objects as a cube shape (Box mode) as they reflect what the camera is seeing from its current adjustment. Next, you can move the camera view so that it is slightly below the logo (see figure 2.38).

The Camera Definition dialog box.

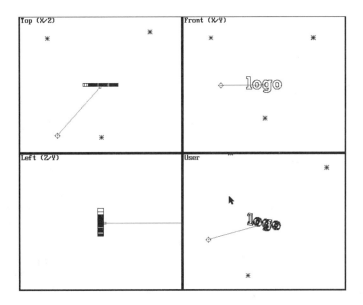

Figure 2.36

The camera symbol appears in all four viewports, indicating the camera's viewport.

2

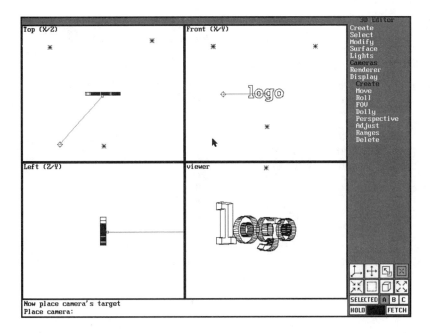

Figure 2.37

The lower right viewport now displays the camera view.

continues

continued

Figure 2.38

Interactively aligning the camera.

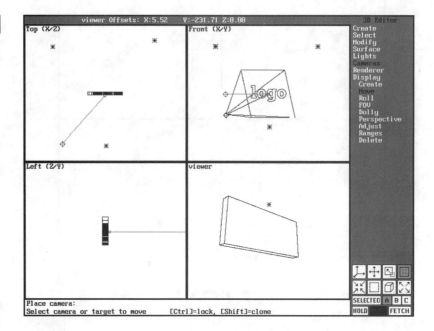

More than one camera can be placed in the scene. If only one camera is present, the viewport immediately switches to that camera view. If there are two or more, the Select Camera dialog box will ask you to select which camera view to display.

Saving your work frequently is a good idea in any computer program. In 3D Studio, it is even more advantageous, because sometimes a series of edits does not work out as you'd hoped, leaving you with an unusable scene. Saving the file before beginning each new major series of edits gives you multiple backups if needed.

Save the project by choosing File/Save Project	The Select a project file to save dialog appears
Click in the filename area, and type **logo01**	The typed in text appears in the filename area
Click on the OK button in the dialog	The dialog disappears and the file is saved
Click in the viewport to place the camera	The camera icon is redrawn in the selected point. The camera viewport displays the logo in correct position (see figure 2.39)

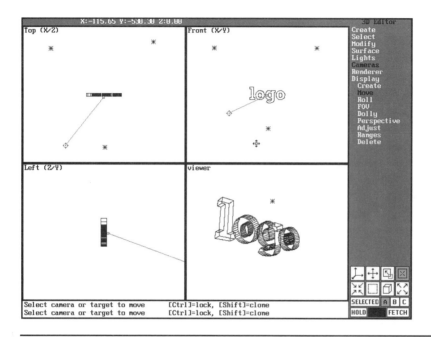

Figure 2.39

The viewport with the now-aligned camera.

2

USAGE TIP

For quick temporary saves, use the HOLD and FETCH buttons at the lower right of the screen, in the icon panel. Usually these are used for short term backup when testing a major change. Clicking HOLD stores your project in a temporary file on the disk. Clicking FETCH loads the file saved by HOLD, replacing all the data in 3D Studio. After exiting 3D Studio, the data saved by a HOLD operation is lost, so important backup files should be saved by using File/Save or File/Save Project.

Always create the camera in the top viewport to be sure that it is aligned to the horizon and doesn't roll inappropriately. The camera has an inherent sense of up, and aligns itself so that it is level with the horizon of the scene. When the camera is pivoted over a point that is perfectly down, it will roll quickly to try to align itself to the horizon. If the cyber-camera is unclear on where the scene's horizon is, it might roll at the wrong point.

Creating Materials in the 3D Editor

When an object is created, its surface has the properties of a material called Default (similar to matte white). When rendered, the object appears

USAGE TIP

as if it has been painted with flat white paint. Many other materials are available, and you can create virtually any material within 3D Studio with its Materials Editor. In the following exercise, you'll select a material that came predefined with the program in the default collection of 3D Studio materials.

Adding a Surface to the Logo

Choose Surface/Material/Choose

The Material Selector dialog box appears that lists a variety of surface names (see figure 2.40)

Use the slider bar and arrows to bring the RED PLASTIC material into view. Click on RED PLASTIC and click on OK to accept this as the current material (you can double-click on a selection to choose the material and accept it). The dialog box disappears.

Choose Surface/Material/Assign/Object

The menu item is highlighted

Click on the logo to assign the material

A confirmation dialog box appears (see figure 2.41)

Click on OK to confirm your choice

Figure 2.40

Choosing a material from the Material Selector dialog box.

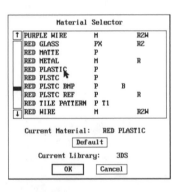

Figure 2.41

A dialog box confirms your assignment of a material to an object.

Rendering in the 3D Editor

Now the scene is complete. A red plastic logo is illuminated with three lights and is viewed from a camera. Now you can render the scene, as shown in the following exercise, to check that materials and lighting are appropriate.

Rendering the Logo

Choose Renderer/Render view	The menu item is highlighted
Activate the camera viewport	The viewport's outline appears
Click in the viewport to be rendered, in this case the camera viewport for the camera is called viewer	The Render Still Image dialog box appears with a variety of renderer settings (see figure 2.42)
Click the Render button to begin a single frame render to your display screen	A large display screen appears with a gauge at the top to indicate progress

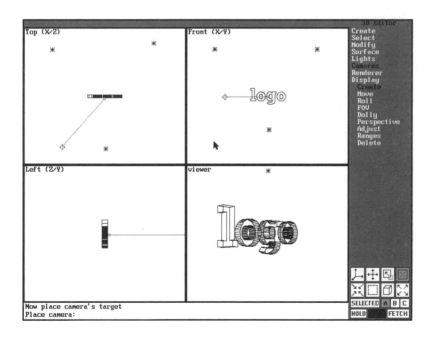

Figure 2.42

The Render Still Image dialog, with its default settings.

You can press the spacebar to switch between this screen and the rendering in progress.

If your system cannot display more than 256 colors (or was set up during the 3DS VIBCFG process to render only to a 256-color mode), then the rendering will appear crude and paint-by-number as it is rendered. When rendering to a 256-color display is complete, 3D Studio redisplays the image after a delay with a more optimal 256-color palette selection.

If the lighting or camera angle is not perfect in the rendering, each can be adjusted with the same procedures as before (Lights/Omni/Adjust and Cameras/Move), and the scene re-rendered to judge the effects.

If the materials are not exactly right, they must be adjusted in the Materials Editor. Suppose, for example, that you decide that the red plastic in the rendered final image is close, but you want a more red-orange plastic appearance on the logo. Press F5, and you are switched to the Materials Editor, where you can make the change.

Using the Materials Editor

All the materials used in 3D Studio are built in the Materials Editor (see fig. 2.43). The interface is rather formidable looking, but each part of it has its place in creating complex, lifelike surface attributes. Examples from the collection of materials that comes with 3D Studio can be loaded and examined for ideas and inspiration.

There are seven square areas at the top that indicate the current selected material (with a white outline) and also render an example of that material. The name of the active material is displayed in the bar below the seven squares. The material is applied to a sample object, a cube or a sphere, and the switch for this can be found on the right side of the screen. After tweaking any parameter, the sample render can be updated by pressing the spacebar (the Render Sample button does this also).

Sample windows   Color status

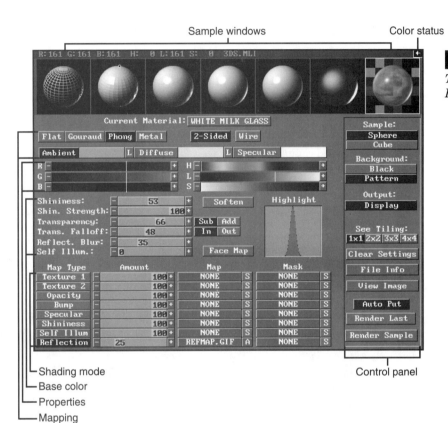

Figure 2.43

The Materials Editor.

Shading mode
Base color
Properties
Mapping

Control panel

The Shading Mode Controls

Below the current material indicator are four shading mode buttons and two special attribute buttons. Their usage is described in table 2.1.

Table 2.1
The Shading Mode Controls

Shading Button	Purpose
Flat shading	Flat shaded mode renders without taking any smoothing information into account. All the faces of a flat shaded object appear flat and faceted. Flat shaded objects will display highlights across entire faces because of their lack of smoothing. Flat shading is not commonly used, but renders the fastest of the four modes.

continues

Table 2.1, Continued
The Shading Mode Controls

Shading Button	Purpose
Gouraud Shading	Gouraud shading uses a simple form of smoothing to simulate roundness with the flat faces used by 3D Studio. Highlights are created by averaging the overall angle of nearby faces to approximate a given face's implied roundness. Shiny Gouraud objects have highlights that appear much like flat shaded objects with a blurred outward appearance. Gouraud shading renders slower than Flat shading, but faster than Phong shading.
Phong shading	Common mode. Allows every variation of texture and can produce colored specular highlights. Phong is especially effective at simulating glossy plastic.
Metal shading	Used almost exclusively to simulate metallic surfaces such as chrome, brass, copper, and gold. Metals reflect light in a unique way that is difficult to simulate with Phong shading.
Special Attributes	
2-Sided and Wire	Special attributes that can be applied to the shading modes.
Wire attribute	Used to render an object in a manner similar to the way it appears in the 3D Editor, as a wireframe mesh. It is a rarely used effect, but can be useful for grid-style objects such as bird cages.

The Color Controls

Below the Shading Mode buttons are the Material Color controls. When Flat, Gouraud, or Phong shading are active, there are three colors to modify: Ambient, Diffuse, and Specular (see table 2.2). Metal shading only displays Ambient and Diffuse colors.

Table 2.2

The Materials Color Controls

Material Color Button	Purpose
Ambient	The color the object has in areas not directly lit. If the ambient color is set too bright, objects with that material might look *flat*—some of the depth is lost. Usually, the ambient is kept very dark.
Diffuse	The main color of the object. In the real world, an object reveals its true diffuse color in full sunlight (and in the dark, all objects appear black). Diffuse color is the most commonly altered part of solid-colored materials.
Specular	The color of the highlight on shiny objects. If an object has the shininess set to zero, it cannot have a specular highlight. Usually, the specular color is set to white, or a near-white that is tinted the color of the diffuse color swatch.

Materials that are assigned to objects in a scene are saved with the scene and kept with it. They can be brought into the Materials Editor for modification at any time.

The current scene has a red plastic material applied to the logo. In the following exercise, you will edit the red plastic to make it appear orange, while keeping the plastic look.

Editing the Logo's Materials

This exercise picks up where the previous exercise ended. Make sure you are in the Materials Editor by pressing F5.

Move the mouse to the Material menu at the top of the screen. Click on the Get from Scene option (pressing **F** accomplishes the same thing)	A list of all active materials is displayed. In this case, the list only includes the red plastic material (see figure 2.44)
Click on the RED PLASTIC listing to highlight it and click on OK	The material is put into the active sample window, and all the sliders and variables are positioned to reflect the settings associated with the loaded material

continues

continued

Figure 2.44

The Get Material From Scene dialog box — only materials that have been used in objects in the 3D Editor will show up on this list.

Observe the settings for red plastic. Note that the diffuse color shares the intense red characteristic of the material as viewed in the previous rendered camera view of your logo. Editing the diffuse color is all that is required to create an orange plastic from the red plastic.

Activate the Diffuse color button by clicking on it

The Diffuse button switches on, turning red (see figure 2.45)

Figure 2.45

Selecting the Diffuse color for editing.

Diffuse color button

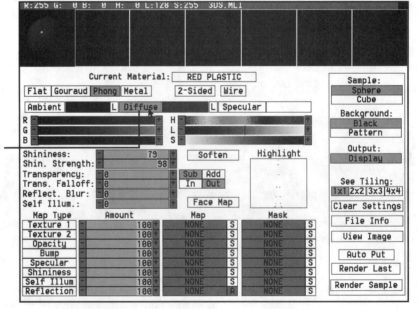

2

Two ways to adjust color are presented beneath the color swatches. Any color can be produced by either method. In this case, all you need is a different hue, so the HLS (Hue, Luminance, and Saturation) sliders are used rather than the RGB sliders (Red, Green, and Blue).

Slide the position indicator in the H slider bar area to the right by clicking and dragging it. Release the mouse button when the color appears to be correct	The diffuse color swatch changes color as the slider is adjusted (see figure 2.46)
Press the spacebar to re-render the sphere with the new diffuse color	An orange plastic sphere is rendered in the sample window

The material has been adjusted to the desired color, but needs to be assigned to the logo. The new material could just be PUT back to the scene. PUT is the complement of GET, used earlier, and accessed in the top menu. In this case, the material cannot really be described as red plastic anymore. To keep things straight (especially as your projects get more complex), it is a good idea to change the material name and then assign it to the logo.

Click in the Current Material button bar	A dialog appears to enable you to edit the name
Change the material name to Orange Plastic and click on OK	The dialog disappears and the new name is reflected in the Current Material button

This material needs to be the current, active material to be assigned in the 3D Editor.

Under the Material menu in the menu bar at the top of the screen, click on the Put to Current option	A dialog box appears to make sure this is what you want to do (see figure 2.47)

Figure 2.46

Moving the hue of the diffuse color toward orange.

Figure 2.47

Making the new material current.

Click on OK	The dialog box disappears

Now, ORANGE PLASTIC is the current material to be assigned in the 3D Editor. Go back to the 3D Editor by pressing F3. The 3D Editor appears with the logo mesh, lights, and camera created and edited in earlier exercises.

Choose Surface/Material/Assign/Object	The menu item is highlighted
Click on the logo mesh	A dialog box appears, confirming that you want to assign ORANGE PLASTIC to the selected object. The fact that it lists the modified name ORANGE PLASTIC assures that the operations in the Materials Editor worked
Click on OK	The dialog box disappears

You can re-render at this point using the Renderer/Render View option. You should see an orange logo with plenty of white highlights making it appear plastic-like.

Now that you have an initial scene that looks right, it's time to animate the logo. Press F5 to switch to the Keyframer.

Using the Keyframer

Animation is created in the Keyframer (see fig. 2.48). Virtually everything that changes over the course of the animation is set up in this module.

Animating scenes in 3D Studio is perhaps the most difficult part of 3D Studio because it is difficult to get instantaneous feedback on changes as they are made. In one sense, animation creation can never be instantaneous because the animation itself plays back over a period of time, and you can only review the adjustments made by viewing a segment of time. In 3D Studio it often takes more time because you must create renderings to accurately check your final work.

An important tool for checking your work quickly is the frame slider bar at the bottom of the screen. If you click and drag the frame slider left and right, the viewports will play the animation in box mode for the frames indicated on the slider. Traditional cel animators often check their work in progress by putting a corner of a pencil sketch between each finger of one hand and viewing the animation as the images are fanned across the field of view. Isolated sections of movement can be similarly previewed with the slider bar technique.

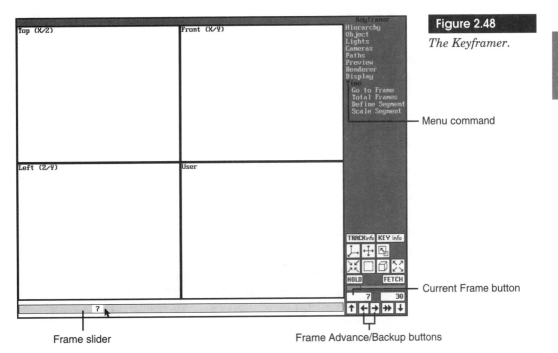

Figure 2.48

The Keyframer.

— Menu command

— Current Frame button

— Frame Advance/Backup buttons

Frame slider

Understanding Keyframes

Cel animation, where each frame is hand-drawn and colored (such as Warner Brothers cartoons or Disney animated features), has a rich, long history. Many of the problems associated with animation were tackled decades ago by cel animation pioneers. Don't overlook books on animation oriented to cel animation technique. They can still be quite useful to the 3D computer animator.

The term keyframe comes from traditional cel animation. In professional animation studios, drawings are made by artists with two different job titles: master animators and assistant animators. There are fewer master animators, and they are more highly skilled and better paid than the assistant animators. To maximize the usage of the studio's talent pool, the task of drawing the characters in the extreme positions of the motions in a particular scene falls to the master animator. The assistant animators then create the drawings between each extreme motion point to complete a fluidly animated scene. The cel animators call the extreme position drawings *keyframes* and the in-between drawings *tweens*.

In 3D Studio, the keyframes are created by the operator, and the tweens are handled by 3D Studio for you. Much of the tedious, time-consuming nature of traditional animation is alleviated by the ease of interactive animation design in 3D Studio's Keyframer module.

The Keyframer, at first glance, looks very similar to the 3D Editor. The main differences between the Keyframer and the 3D Editor are the new collection of menu options on the right, the frame slider at the bottom of the screen, and the frame indicators in the lower right corner of the screen.

The numbers in the lower right corner list the current frame and the total number of frames. Clicking on either brings up a dialog box where you can change the current frame or total frames. The active segment bar just above the values adjusts the current range of frames active for editing. This is used to isolate a section of the animation temporarily for certain procedures.

The critical thing to remember about the Keyframer is that any changes made are assigned a point in time: the current frame. The animator must always check the current frame indicator before making any changes to be sure that the current time point in the animation is the time where the new changes should occur. Changes to the animation in frame 0, the initial frame, will be reflected in the 3D Editor. If, for example, the animator adjusts the camera position at frame 15, assuming that the current frame is 0, he or she will later be startled to see that the camera jerks radically from frame 0 to frame 15, from the original position to the edited position.

The default settings in the Keyframer give a 30-frame animation with the current frame set at 0. All the modifications previously made to the scene in the 3D Editor are, of course, carried over to the Keyframer. All of the initial positions, light colors and intensities, and camera and camera target positions are set as keyframes at frame 0. If you return to the 3D Editor and alter the scene, the changes will be reflected in the keyframe at frame 0.

Returning to the logo scene created in the previous exercises, now use the Keyframer module to add motion and light changes.

Keyframing the Logo

Click on the down arrow icon located in the icon panel at the lower right corner of the screen	The current frame indicator switches to 30; all of the geometry in the viewports is now black
Make sure one of the viewports is a camera view. If necessary, choose one of the four viewports, activate it, and type **C** to switch to the camera view (see figure 2.49)	One of the four viewports displays the view from the camera's perspective
Choose Cameras/Move from the command column	The menu item is highlighted
In the top viewport, adjust the camera and camera target so the logo is viewed from the opposite side	The camera viewport reflects the adjustment (see figure 2.50)
Click and hold in the frame slider at the bottom of the screen. With the mouse button held, slide the mouse left and right	The animation of the camera movement is previewed in the viewports

The camera and camera target now have two keyframes each: a starting point and an ending point. Because the start position occurs at frame 0 and the end point occurs at frame 30, gradual movement of the camera and camera target between the two points is produced by 3D Studio. Adjust the object, using the following steps:

First, make sure that the current frame is frame 30. Every time an adjustment is made in the Keyframer, the current frame must be confirmed.

If the current frame is not frame 30, either click on the down arrow icon or slide the frame slider to the right	The current frame indicator displays 30
Choose Object/Squash	The menu item is highlighted
Activate the left viewport by clicking in the window	The viewport becomes active

Click on the logo and, without moving the mouse, click again.

If you accidentally move the mouse after the first click, right-clicking the mouse will escape the adjustment	The logo becomes white but otherwise appears the same

You have just set a keyframe at frame 30. The object has not changed, but because you want the object to return to its original shape after a keyframe in the middle of the animation (frame 15), you set the ending keyframe while the object remains unmodified in the frames between 0 and 30.

continues

continued

Figure 2.49

Adding the camera viewport.

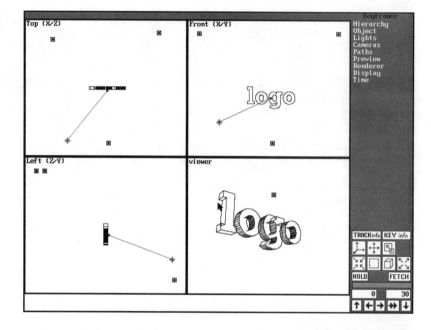

Figure 2.50

Moving the camera at frame 30.

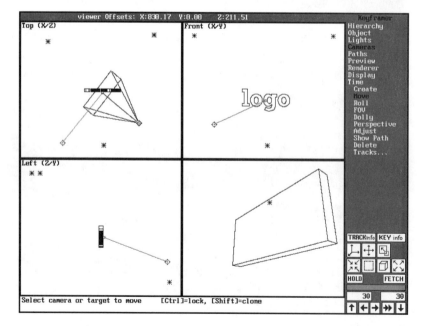

Click on the current frame indicator, below the icon panel

The Go To Frame dialog box asks for the new current frame

Type **15** and click on OK (see fig. 2.51)

The dialog box disappears

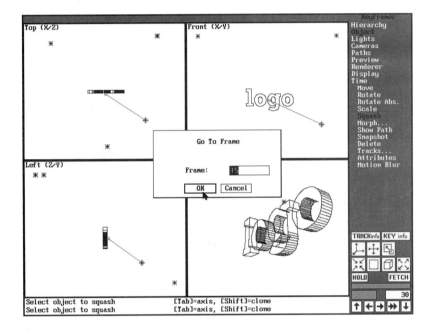

Figure 2.51

Moving to frame 15.

All the objects in the scene are black again, and the current frame is listed as frame 15.

Activate the front viewport by clicking in it

The front viewport becomes active

Object/Squash should still be active on the right menu. Click on the logo and slide the mouse left and right

A dotted rectangular outline that bounds the logo changes shape from tall and thin to short and wide (see figure 2.52)

Adjust the logo to be moderately tall and thin and click the mouse again (see figure 2.53)

The newly shaped logo appears in white

Figure 2.52

Squashing the logo at frame 15.

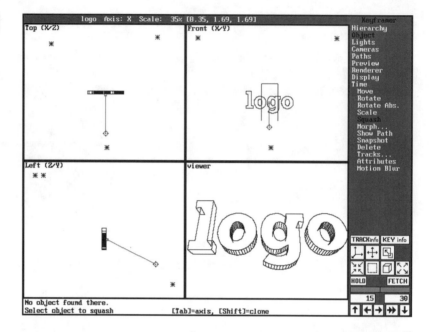

Figure 2.53

The logo object as it will appear at frame 15, modified by the squash procedure.

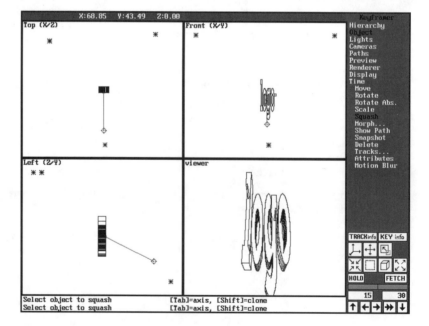

The logo now has three keyframes, occurring at frames 0, 15, and 30. You can now preview the animation you just created.

Click and drag the mouse left and right in the slider bar at the bottom of the screen, as before. A box the size of the logo changes shape from its original shape to tall and thin, then returns to its original shape. As this happens, the camera flies across the logo.

You can preview the animation with all its lines by clicking the right arrow icon. The playing animation will loop from frame 30 to frame 0 and repeat continuously. Because of the time required for 3D Studio to draw the complete mesh as each frame passes, playback might be considerably slower than final output. Right-click the mouse to stop the playback. To view a more full-speed animation, you must create a *Flic*—an animation playback file that contains a stack of images. Because at this point you have a pretty clear idea of how the action will happen, and from your renders in the 3D Editor you have a pretty clear idea of how a rendered still will look, you can go on to a fully rendered animation.

Before creating the final render, in the next exercise you will generate a preview. Previews are monochrome, flat shaded versions of the animation that 3D Studio can create very quickly. Although color is not included, previews offer an excellent idea of the pacing and direction of an animation.

Creating a Preview

Choose Preview/Make and click in the camera viewport	The Make Preview Dialog appears
Click on the Preview button	A gauge appears to indicate progress as the preview file is created. When the preview file is created, the gauge disappears, and the preview displays, looping continuously
Stop the preview playback by right-clicking the mouse, or pressing Escape	The preview stops playing and 3D Studio's interface reappears

To view this preview again without regenerating, choose Preview/ Play.

USAGE TIP

Rendering the Animated Logo

Choose Renderer/Render view in the right menu	The menu item is highlighted
Click in the camera viewport to activate it, then again to choose the viewport as the rendered viewport	The Render Animation dialog box appears with all the rendering settings

You need to create a Flic. You can make it at a smaller resolution to speed the render time: standard VGA 320×200. Note that all Flics created by 3D Studio are movies with 256 total colors available for the entire animation. Because each frame is originally rendered in Truecolor, and then color reduced to conform to the 256 best-choice colors of all of the frames, you might notice that the final animation's colors are color-banded (the paint-by-number look) and jittery. This will be especially severe in long animations of very colorful scenes.

Click the Configure... button in the Render Animation dialog box	The Device Configuration dialog appears
Click on the 320×200 button to set that resolution	The Width: and Height: data boxes reflect the new resolution
Click on the Flic button to choose Flics as the file format to output	The button turns red
Click on the Medium button	The Medium button turns red (see figure 2.54)
Click on OK	The dialog box disappears, revealing the previous Render Animation dialog box
At the bottom of the Render Animation dialog box, activate the Disk button.	Creates an animation that is saved to your hard drive. The Disk button turns red
Click on the All button in the Frame area. This ensures that all the frames are included in the animation	The All button turns red (see figure 2.55)
Click on the Render button	A prompt for the file name appears

Note where the file is being created (drive and subdirectory), choose a file name, and click on OK.

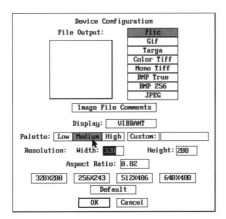

Figure 2.54

The Device Configuration dialog box.

2

Figure 2.55

The Render Animation dialog, ready to render a complete animation.

The dialog box disappears and a Rendering in Progress dialog box appears. The gauge repeatedly grows from left to right. The frame counter at the bottom of the dialog box shows which of the 30 frames is being rendered. You can switch between viewing the current frame and this dialog box using the spacebar, but if you press Escape, the animation rendering will abort. The best choice is to take a five minute break. When all the frames are rendered, the computer will review all the frames, which are temporarily stored on the hard drive. It then chooses an optimal palette (displaying counting colors), and applies that palette of 256 colors to the animation (displaying converting colors). The Keyframer module redisplays when rendering is complete.

Now you are ready to view your rendered animation.

Viewing a Rendered Animation

Choose Display/View/Flic

The Select Flic file to load dialog box prompts for the FLI or FLC file to play back (see figure 2.56)

Use the file name you entered previously and click on OK.

The animation plays back in a loop until you press Esc or the right mouse button. The left and right arrow keys slow down and speed up the animation.

Choose File/Save Project from the top menu

A dialog box for the file name appears, labeled "Select a mesh file to save"

Choose a name for this project and click on OK

The dialog box disappears

Figure 2.56

The Select Flic file to load dialog box.

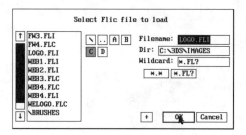

Your work in all five modules is saved in their current state under this file name. If you choose File/Save instead, the 2D Shaper, 3D Editor, and Materials Editor are not included. This book uses the logo tutorial animation file again later.

Having followed all the exercises to this point, you have modeled an object, added lights, materials, and a camera, and keyframed in the standard manner of all 3D Studio animators. More exercises will follow to get into the details of each module, but there is no reason not to repeatedly create other logo animations with variations on the procedures in the tutorial. Experimentation is the key to becoming a 3D Studio master!

Introducing IK, Text Editor, and Fast Preview

There are other modules in 3D Studio besides the five main modules covered so far. 3D Studio's designers allow external programs called IPAS routers or plug-ins to be created and activated within 3D Studio, and these programs have access to all of the data 3D Studio contains. The fact that plug-ins from third-party developers (IPAS routines) can completely take over the 3D Studio interface makes them seem like separate, unique modules that are part of 3D Studio. Most plug-in routines must be purchased separately from 3D Studio, but several important plug-ins are included with Release 4 of 3D Studio. In fact, these plug-ins are the primary change between Releases 3 and 4. The plug-in modules added with Release 4 consist of Inverse Kinematics (IK), keyscripter, fast preview, and match perspective.

Inverse Kinematics (IK)

Inverse kinematics is an enhancement to the Keyframer. It is used in cases where there are sliding or rotating joints in an object, especially character animation. After taking certain steps to prepare a mesh in the Keyframer, the IK module is activated and the object to be manipulated is selected. Within IK, joints are defined as rotating (like a ball and socket joint) or telescoping, and limits are set (such as knee joint, constrained to a limited rotational range). At this point, IK allows a special type of animation that is end-effector oriented. That is, instead of the usual keyframer technique of bending an arm, then a forearm, then a wrist, and then a finger to make a mannequin mesh point at a given object, IK enables you to simply point the mesh object's finger, and all the other parts react appropriately. IK allows two methods: interactive and follow object. For IK to be possible, separate objects must be linked to create joints that can rotate and slide. Linking is discussed more thoroughly in Chapter 9, "Advanced Animation Techniques."

In *interactive* mode, a keyframer-like screen is brought up and the usual technique of selecting a frame and then adjusting the mesh is used (see fig. 2.57). In the *automated* mode, a *follow object* is animated normally in the Keyframer. The IK module can then point the end effector (such as a pointing hand) at the follow object.

Figure 2.57

The interactive segment of the IK module.

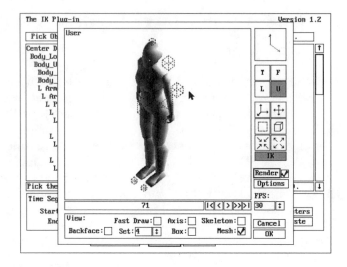

The Keyscripter

The keyscripter (see figure 2.58) enables a user to write programs to control animation. The program language is a form of computer programming language that is a unique hybrid of BASIC and C. A keyscript can alter and create keys based on existing objects, animation, or from scratch. As keyscripts proliferate, many of the tedious tasks of keyframing can be handled quickly by the appropriate script. Some facility with programming keyscripts will empower an animator to adjust a keyscript when it's close but not quite right for the task needed. This book discusses using keyscripts, but the details of programming are beyond it.

Fast Preview

Fast preview generates a smooth-shaded, colorized animation very quickly (see figure 2.59). It is invoked from the Keyframer in any viewport, and Flics are then generated in any desired resolution. Textures are not used—the color of the objects is set by the material's diffuse color setting only. In the past, animation previews were usually handled by using the Preview/Generate menu option, but this new previewer creates far superior animation files more quickly.

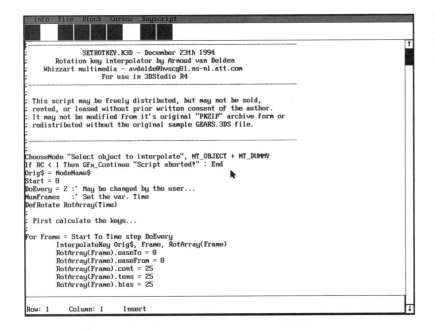

Figure 2.58

*The keyscripter
editing interface.*

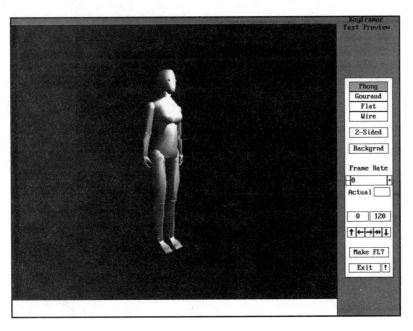

Figure 2.59

*The Fast Preview
interface.*

Camera Control and Match Perspective

This feature, illustrated in figure 2.60, can be thought of as the fast preview for the 3D Editor. Any of the 3D Editor's viewports are switchable to this smooth-shaded, diffuse-colored viewer. While in this mode, the camera and camera target position can be moved, and most camera settings can be adjusted. The term *match perspective* comes from the fact that a photograph can be placed into the background of this viewer, and camera perspective (the millimeter setting from an earlier exercise) can be adjusted to match the photograph. This enables 3D-rendered objects to be more accurately merged with photographs.

Figure 2.60

The Camera Control and Match Perspective interface.

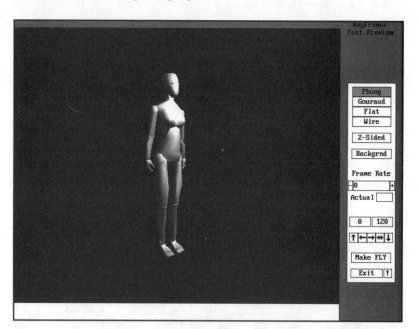

Summary

This chapter has touched on the basic steps of creating animation with 3D Studio. You have modeled, applied lighting, added a camera, applied materials, and then animated the scene. These steps are the building blocks of virtually all animation you will create with 3D Studio. Now that you have touched on each of the major parts of 3D Studio, the following chapters will explore in detail the major steps of creating animation, beginning with modeling in Chapter 3.

Chapter Snapshot

This chapter discusses the usage of the 2D Shaper and 3D Lofter modules to create new 3D objects. In addition, an external plug-in module is used as a modeling aid.

In this chapter, you will learn the following:

- Creating objects with the 2D Shaper and 3D Lofter

- Interactively viewing shaded objects with the VIEW.PXP plug-in

- Combining shapes in the 2D Shaper

- Importing 2D objects from the 2D Shaper to the 3D Editor

- Creating custom paths in the 2D Shaper

- Using Snap and Grid to create precise shapes

3

Introduction to 3D Modeling

The word *modeling*, which comes up often in 3D work, describes any process that creates three-dimensional information used to define an entity. The term usually refers to the interactive process in which you use a computer's mouse, keyboard, and screen to create 3D entities. Often this is done in a manner similar to that of a drafter who uses a CAD program to create 2D shapes. Much of the modeling process is more freeform than the drafting process, however, and is done in 3D space. Pieces of an object can be bent, twisted, or pulled out to complete a model. Often, simple 3D shapes, such as cones and spheres, are combined in various ways to build a 3D object directly (see fig. 3.1).

Modeling with a computer is similar in many ways to real-world modeling. The modeler is trying to re-create an object from the real world. Sometimes precision is critical, but sometimes the artist is free to add his or her own variations to the model. In some cases the object being modeled doesn't exist! Professional modelers, for example, often create clay mock-ups of car designs before they are put into production, or architectural miniatures of proposed structures. In 3D Studio, this process can be taken much further—because size limitations are not a factor, you can add an animated tour of a building's halls and rooms.

Combining simple objects to create complex objects.

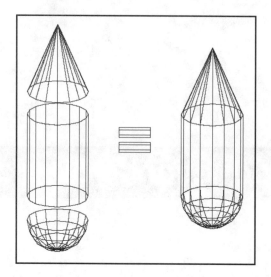

On a computer, the task of modeling an object can be much different from real-world modeling. Interacting with a three-dimensional program through a two-dimensional display using a mouse is a developed skill. Generally, you first draw one side of an object, representing the object's profile, and then, in a view perpendicular to the profile, you describe the object's depth. The technique is fairly straightforward on simple objects, but as the modeled object becomes more complicated in all dimensions, more time and skill are needed to get the job done. Some objects, such as a detailed, accurate skull, are so organic and irregular that they cannot be modeled practically. In such cases, the object is digitized directly to get its surface contours accurately into computer form—either the object itself or a clay model is scanned in some way to obtain enough points in space to describe the object in sufficient detail. After carefully applying materials, the rendered computer object can appear quite similar to the original subject.

Both the real-world modeler and the virtual-world computer graphics modeler must have good spatial skills. The modeler constantly compares his or her mental image of the desired model with the model in progress. Knowing exactly what the current model looks like can be difficult when a complex object's contour lines criss-cross everywhere in any view of the object on the computer. Luckily, some real-time viewers give you quick feedback about an object's current state. And by deft use of 3D Studio's capability to selectively hide any object, face, or edge, you can keep the viewports clear enough so that you can work. Still, while you are editing the object you constantly must combine in your mind the side, top, and front views of a shape and find the correct position for the edit.

High-precision modeling is similar to drafting. 3D Studio enables you to alter the generic *units* with which objects are measured, so that they define feet, meters, inches or some similar arbitrary measure. Then, with dimensional accuracy, you create and position the separate elements of a complex object. Note that 3D Studio is not (and does not attempt to be) a high-end CAD package. For complex 3D drafting requirements, you should use AutoCAD or a similar program designed for complex dimensioning, high accuracy, and other features appropriate to CAD. Nearly all drafting programs that are capable of 3D design allow for export to a file format called DFX. 3D Studio can import the 3D information of DFX format files.

In many cases, high accuracy is not necessary. When a modeled character is going to walk, bend, and sway across the monitor, you can get good results when the size of the objects is close enough. In fact, because of the inherent limited resolution of video playback, close enough and super-precision seem identical in most situations in which a collection of objects move around the screen.

For some people, modeling with 3D Studio is closer to sculpting than drafting. After assembling simple objects to define the rough appearance of an object, you reach the final modeled object by adding pieces to or cutting them from the object. 3D Studio can also bend, taper, and unequally scale any part of an object in any direction. To perform extremely complex object alterations, such as twisting or deforming, you can use one of many third-party utilities.

While modeling, 3D Studio gives you all the usual advantages inherent to a computer: the unlimited ability to edit, combine, save, and perform what-ifs without losing the capability to revert to an earlier version. 3D Studio includes a Hold feature that stores the entire state of 3D Studio when it is activated. Unfortunately, nothing performs a hold automatically. Before you try any procedure with uncertain results, you should save your file to a temporary name or click on the Hold button. As with any computer program, you must save your work frequently. The likelihood of a power outage seems to increase with the number of hours of unsaved work you've done.

CAUTION

Neither the 3D Editor nor Keyframer has an Undo button. Hold and Fetch buttons, however, are available in the lower right corner of both modules. Hold creates a temporary disk file that contains the entire state of 3D Studio, including meshes, materials, and views. Fetch retrieves the data from the last Hold action. A Fetch will not find data from a previous 3D Studio session's Hold action.

In Chapter 2, "Meet 3D Studio," you briefly practiced each of the tasks necessary for creating animations in 3D Studio: modeling, scene design, and animation. Each successive task is critical to creating a final animation, and each task—to succeed—relies on the quality of the work in the preceding task. Modeling is the first step in building any animation.

Modeling, in the paradigm of 3D computer graphics, means creating the matter of your world. Everything that is to appear in a 3D animation created by 3D Studio has to be modeled—including models you use that other modelers have created.

Modeling is sometimes described as 3D drafting, although it can be much more than that. At its simplest, modeling takes a shape and extrudes it, such as creating a tube from an O shape. More complicated modeling can begin with a two-dimensional floor plan and create a three-dimensional building for the rendering of an animated walkthrough. Modeling, however, can become more like sculpting, where an object can be roughed out in its basic forms and then pieces can be cut or added. When the modeler is creating irregular and organic-shaped objects, the sculptor mindset becomes uppermost. Thinking three-dimensionally as you add and subtract from the object will allow you to quickly build the object in your mind. In 3D Studio, areas of an object can be twisted or stretched like rubber, and every change can be undone easily if necessary.

Modeling is quite different from traditional drawing. When you draw in two dimensions, whether on paper or in a computer program like CorelDRAW!, all you need concern yourself with is the singular view of the image you are creating. In 3D Studio, all views are accounted for, because you must not only draw from a single viewpoint but also re-create the objects in question as virtual three-dimensional entities. Clearly, recreating an object in three dimensions can take more time than drawing a singular view, but you gain the advantage of having a virtual-world re-creation of your scene at your disposal. If the viewing angle is a bit off, and one of the objects should be deeper blue, the alterations can take only seconds to implement, and rendering the replacement image only a few minutes more.

Although modeling differs from drawing, modeling builds on the skills of drawing. The first step of many modeling jobs is to draw profiles of the object from various angles, which 3D Studio can create 3D objects from. Experience with any computer-based drawing package is helpful, because the same sort of drawing tools are used, such as rectangle, circle, and text. Additionally, 3D Studio can import shapes and curves from virtually any computer-based 2D draw package to be used as a starting point for modeling.

Learning More About the 2D Shaper

The 2D Shaper is similar to many computer drawing programs. Besides creating and editing all manner of polygons, the 2D Shaper can bring in shapes from other files. It can import shapes created in other 2D drawing programs, such as CorelDRAW!, and prepare them for use in 3D Studio. The 2D Shaper can also import any PostScript font for text creation. The 2D Shaper allows you to combine imported shapes with the shapes you create in the 2D Shaper, and prepare them for use in 3D Studio. When you have an appropriate shape, other modules of 3D Studio make use of that shape to create new objects.

The 2D Shaper enables you to create both closed polygons and open paths. After you create a closed polygon in the 2D Shaper, you can use that polygon to define the contours of a 3D object (which you extrude in the 3D Lofter). An open path is a straight or curved line that defines the direction(s) an object will be lofted in, but does not define the object itself. Paths can also be closed. A tublar capital B, for example, can be created by using a closed path that follows the capital B. You can also use the 2D Shaper to create flat objects that are not lofted, but are directly imported into the 3D Editor.

The following sections give detailed descriptions of polygons, paths, and flat shapes in relation to the 2D Shaper.

Polygons

A polygon is made up of two or more control points (called *vertices*) and a segment between each. (See fig. 3.2 for examples of different forms of polygons in the 2D Shaper.) The vertices in the Shaper are of a different type than those used to make up 3D faces in the 3D Editor. Vertices in the Shaper have unique controllers to adjust the curvature of the segments as they leave the vertex. These controllers are called direction arrows and they look like yellow and red arrows that point away from the vertex. Direction arrows appear only when you are adjusting a vertex (see fig. 3.3).

Figure 3.2

Polygons can be circles, text, lines, and other shapes.

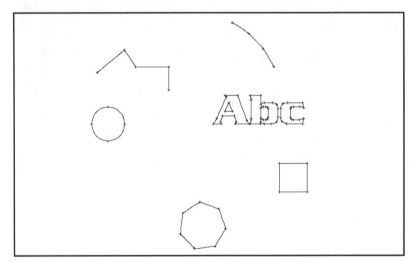

The 2D Shaper and 3D Lofter are different from the 3D Editor with regard to their most basic building block: In the 2D Shaper and 3D Lofter, lines can curve. Each vertex in the 2D Shaper is capable of adjusting the curvature of the line that enters and leaves that vertex. These types of lines are called *splines*. A complex curvy shape can be defined by relatively few vertices in the 2D Shaper, because the lines are splines. If the mouse button is clicked and held down when creating or moving endpoints in the 2D Shaper or 3D Lofter, two arrows appear as the mouse is moved. The red and yellow arrows adjust the curvature of the line as it enters and exits the vertex. Adjusting these spline controllers is discussed in more detail in Chapter 7, "Advanced Modeling Techniques."

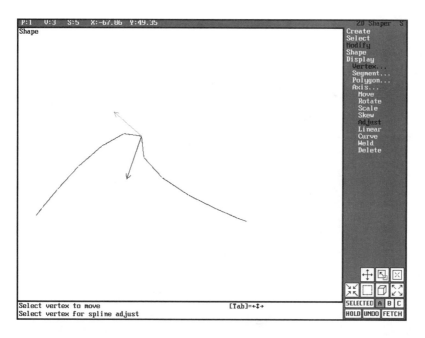

Figure 3.3

Direction arrows appear while the mouse button is held down in a modify/vertex/adjust operation.

Any closed polygon can be used as a shape. (*Closed* means that the end-points connect so that the shape is a closed loop.) It is possible for a shape to intersect itself, like a figure eight, but 3D Studio cannot work with such a shape (see the "Usable and Unusable Shapes" section later in this chapter). A closed shape is copied from the 2D Shaper module to the 3D Lofter module to define the contours of the object at some point along the path of extrusion.

3D Studio can loft closed polygons only; in fact, the 3D Lofter won't even accept an open polygon. A polygon is closed when it has no endpoints—the polygon loops around and connects with itself. A polygon's end vertices can lie atop one another and not be connected, which can be misleading—a polygon sometimes appears closed and ready to move to the Lofter, but 3D Studio displays an error when the shape is checked. The process of connecting the vertices is called *welding*. (For more information about this process, see the "Welding Vertices" exercise later in this chapter.)

Paths

Paths can be any shape at all. A path can intersect itself, and be open or closed. A closed path might take the form of a circle. A circle lofted along this path (figure 3.4) would create an object that looks like a doughnut or torus, as in figure 3.5. A path that looks like cursive writing might be used to extrude a circle shape to get a neon-tubing effect, as in figure 3.6.

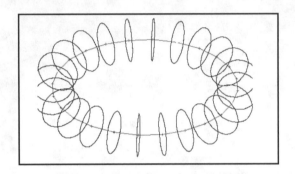

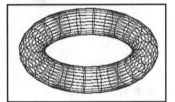

Flat Shapes

Sometimes it is desirable to have 2D objects in your 3D scene. These objects are, of course, flat and will disappear if viewed on edge. On rare occasions, a flat object can be used because the object modeled is flat—a sheet of paper, for example. More often, a flat shape is used as a decal. If a flat shape is placed slightly in front of a larger 3D object, the flat shape will appear like a sign stuck on a wall. Because the flat shape is against the wall, its flat nature will not be apparent during an animation.

In some cases flat shapes are used creatively. For instance, in an instructional animation, large text labels can appear to hover in the air over various objects, to point out a feature or focus attention on something important.

Flat shapes can also be used to save RAM. Your computer's RAM, or random-access memory, is a precious resource for 3D Studio. When RAM is exhausted, 3D Studio begins to substitute with space on the hard disk, which is many times slower. Images are most often applied (with materials) to create the effect of painted or decaled objects in a 3D Studio scene, but these image maps are RAM-hungry. If a needed decal for a flat area of an object is simple enough, a flat shape can be substituted for significant RAM conservation.

Usable and Unusable Shapes

Only certain types of polygons can be used in the 3D Lofter. The critical requirements are that the polygon be closed and that it not intersect itself. You can loft two or more shapes at the same time, provided that they don't overlap. For instance, two circles can be lofted together to form a 3D tube shape, provided that the two circles don't intersect anywhere. Figure 3.7 shows some examples of usable and unusable shapes.

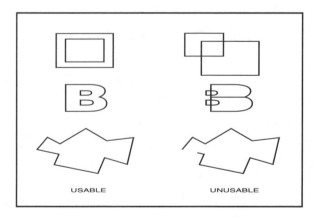

Figure 3.7

Usable and unusable shapes.

USABLE   UNUSABLE

To create a perfect-looking shape with its vertices in the right place, you need a little help from the 3D Studio. You could create, for example, two half-circle shapes near each other, move the endpoints around, and then weld them to create a closed shape. By moving the endpoints, however, you would ruin the shapes' perfect circular characteristics. To create new objects to exact dimensions, you can use 3D Studio's *snap* feature (described in the following section), which constrains the mouse so that it moves only between exact positions.

Using Snap and Grid

All of 3D Studio's modules (except the Materials Editor) are capable of displaying a grid and using snap to lock movements to a grid. The grid is a regularly spaced set of markers, like a ruler, that can be displayed for reference while creating a 3D scene. Whether the grid is visible or invisible, when Snap mode is on, the user's mouse actions will snap to fixed, evenly spaced positions, ensuring accuracy. You can turn Snap and Grid modes on and off by pressing S and G on the keyboard, respectively. When Snap is turned on, the character S is displayed in the upper right corner of the screen.

The following exercise explores 3D Studio's Snap and Grid features by activating each and adjusting their spacing.

Using Snap and Grid in the Shaper

Press F1	Displays the 2D Shaper module
Press **S** repeatedly	An S appears in the upper right corner of the screen
When the S character is deleted, move the mouse in the viewport	The mouse snaps from one coordinate to another, without permitting movement between the snap spacing. Note the mouse position's coordinates (listed at top of screen)

If the mouse seems locked in the viewport and won't move at all, the view may be zoomed to an area that has only one snapable point. Click on the Zoom Out button in the lower right corner of the screen to increase the number of visible snapable points.

Press **G**	Turns on Grid mode, displaying grid of regularly spaced points (see fig. 3.8)

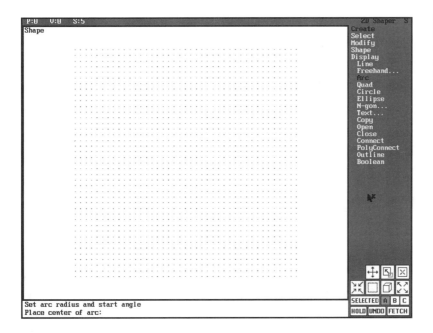

Figure 3.8

A grid of points appears when Grid mode is on.

The grid displays the snap-to points. Note that although grid and snap spacing are the same by default, the grid does not necessarily have to reflect the snap spacing. The spacing of either snap or grid is adjusted with the Drawing Aids option from the Views pull-down menu (the Views menu is shown in figure 3.9). Note that Snap and Grid can be turned on from this menu (as well as by pressing S and G). The asterisk (*) preceding the menu's Use Snap and Use Grid options indicates that these modes are currently active.

Choose Views/Drawing Aids	Displays the Drawing Aids dialog box (see fig. 3.10)

The Drawing Aids dialog box contains spacing settings for both Snap and Grid. The default value is 10 for both.

Replace the 10s in the Drawing Aids dialog box with 5s, and click on OK	The dialog box disappears. The pattern of grid dots displayed is now twice as dense as before (see fig. 3.11)
Move mouse in viewport	Mouse's movements are constrained to the Snap spacing
From the screen menu, choose Create/Shape/Quad	Highlights Quad on the screen menu

continues

continued

In the viewport, click at the 0,0 point
and drag the mouse to create a
square of 15 units on each side

A perfectly sized square appears in the
viewport (see fig. 3.12)

Choose File/Reset from the pull-down menu

The rectangle disappears and the 2D
Shaper is reset

Figure 3.9

The Views pull-down menu.

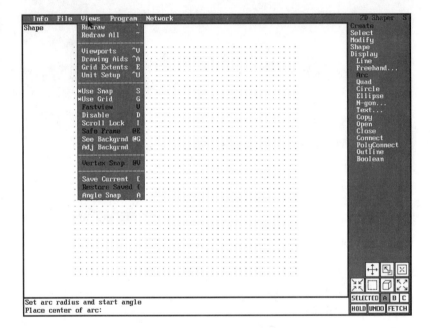

Figure 3.10

The Drawing Aids dialog box.

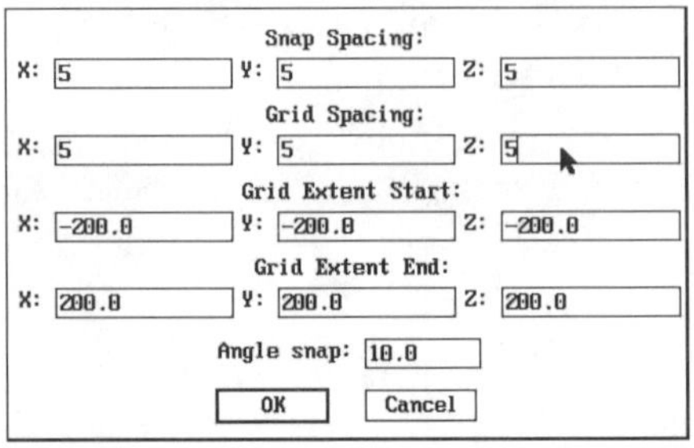

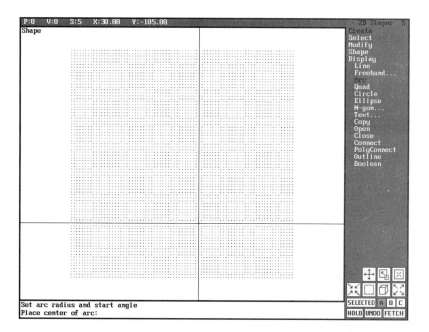

Figure 3.11

A more tightly spaced grid.

3

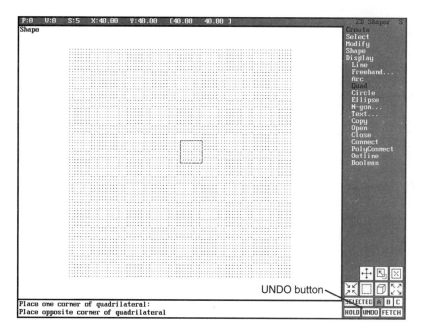

UNDO button

Figure 3.12

The square drawn in the viewport.

As you draw, the size of the square and the starting coordinates are displayed at the top of the screen. Most actions that create new polygons in the 2D Shaper will display size and position information at the top of the screen as the polygons are created.

Frequently, as you create shapes and objects, you need to go back one step. You can do so easily when you're using the Shaper because (unlike the Lofter, 3D Editor, and Keyframer) the Shaper has an Undo button. To undo a mistake, simply click on the UNDO button in the lower right corner of the screen (refer to fig. 3.12). Note, however, that the Shaper does not have a REDO button, so make sure you are positive about undoing an action.

Using Snap to Combine Polygons

The process of creating polygons in the 2D Shaper usually entails drawing lines, circles, and other simple geometric shapes, and then attaching the polygons (or pieces of them) to one another to create the complex polygon that you want. In the following exercise, you combine some simple polygons to create a shape that the 3D Lofter will accept. Snap enables polygons to be combined to create precise shapes.

In the following exercise, a square with a rounded top will be created by using the top half of a circle to replace the square's top line. Snap will enable you to line up the square and circle source objects exactly.

Creating a Unique Closed Shape

Start with the 2D Shaper empty. Use File/Reset to clear all the modules and any previous changes.

Confirm that Snap mode is on	Turns on Snap mode, displaying an S in viewport's upper right corner
If you don't see the S indicator in the upper right corner of the screen (to the right of the words 2D Shaper), press **S**	
From the screen menu, choose Create/Quad	Highlights Quad in the screen menu
Create a 20-unit square by clicking in the viewport at 0,0, moving	Displays square in viewport (see fig. 3.13)

the mouse down and to the right, and
clicking again. (Use the coordinate
readout displayed at the top of
the screen to monitor the size)

From the screen menu, choose
Create/Circle

Highlights Circle on screen menu

Now Create a circle centered in the
top of the square by first clicking
at 0,10 and then moving the mouse
to the right for a radius of 10 units, and
click again

The circle appears over the square,
as in figure 3.14

From the screen menu, choose
Modify/Segment/Delete. Click on ①
and ② (see fig. 3.15)

Deletes the segments

Save the drawing

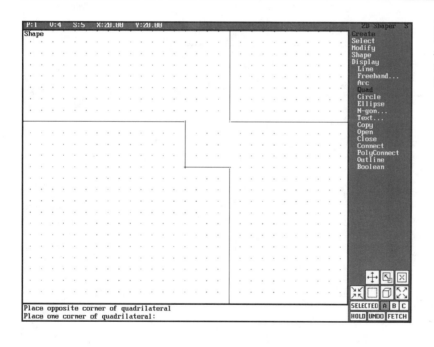

Figure 3.13

*A drawn square,
with corners
snapped to the grid.*

Figure 3.14

A circle centered at the top of the square.

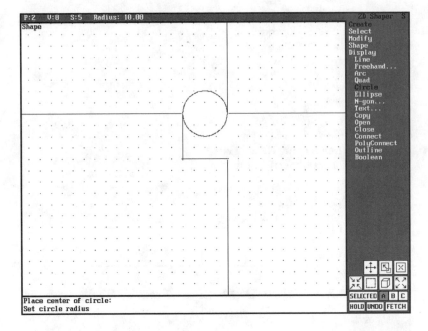

Figure 3.15

Deleting the segments.

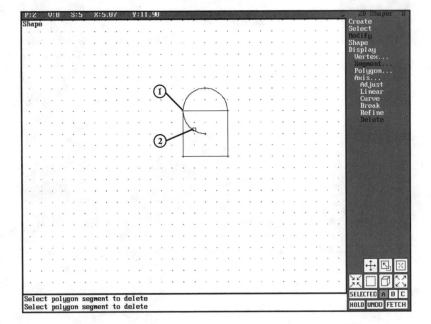

The shape that you created in the previous exercise is not yet ready to be imported to the 3D Lofter. The remaining parts of the square and circle are still independent, even though their endpoints overlap. Because the shape is not closed, you will follow procedures that will close the shape and make it acceptable to the 3D Lofter. To build shapes in the 2D Shaper that are acceptable to the 3D Lofter, you often assemble several basic arcs, lines, and polygons, then selectively delete segments and weld the connector points. The following exercise demonstrates welding to close a shape in the 2D Shaper.

Preparing a Shape for the 3D Lofter

Continue using the drawing you saved from the previous exercise.

With the deletions from the previous exercise, you've created what appears to be a new closed polygon from the first two shapes. The new polygon appears to be closed, but is not. This is easily determined by using the Assign function as this exercise demonstrates. Normally, you use the Assign function to flag a shape for the 3D Lofter or the 3D Editor. Because Assign selects only one polygon at a time, the function is useful also when you want to determine whether two polygons that appear to be connected are not.

From the screen menu, choose Shape/Assign	Highlights Assign in the screen menu
Click on the arc at the top of the new polygon (see fig. 3.16)	Only the arc turns yellow

The endpoints are not connected; instead of a single closed polygon, there are two open polygons. To create a single usable polygon, you must weld each side of the arc to the open-top square polygon.

From the screen menu, choose Modify/Vertex/Weld	Highlights Weld on the screen menu
Click on one of the vertices that coincide where the half-circle and open square meet	The mouse picks up one of the vertices that coincide at that point. Moving the mouse bends the leg of the polygon connected to the vertex, as in figure 3.17
With the Snap feature active, you can easily guide the mouse-controlled vertex until it is positioned on top of the other vertex. Click the mouse at that point	A yes/no dialog appears to confirm the weld
Click on Yes to create the weld	The dialog box disappears

continues

continued

Now the Shaper contains an open path that appears to be a closed polygon. The fact that the polygon is not closed is more difficult to detect, because the Assign function highlights the entire polygon.

From the screen menu, choose Shape/Assign	Highlights Assign on the menu
In the viewport, click on the shape	The entire shape turns yellow
From the screen menu, choose Shape/Check	Displays an error dialog box (because the shape is not closed)
Close the shape by welding the other vertex, following the procedure you used to weld the first one	Displays a Yes/No dialog box to confirm the weld
Click on Yes	Confirms the weld
From the screen menu, choose Shape/Check	Displays a dialog box to show that the closed shape is now OK

Figure 3.16

Assigning a shape.

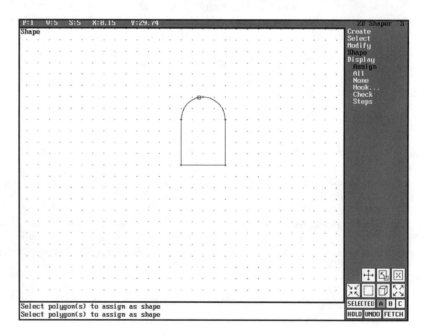

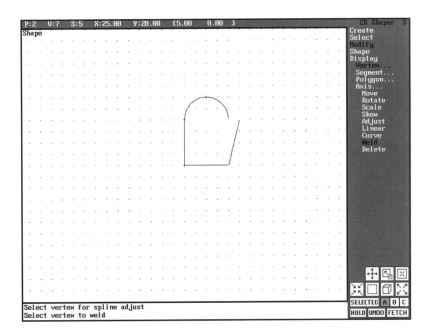

Figure 3.17

The first stage of welding a vertex.

Creating Flat Objects for Use in the 3D Editor

You can use the 2D Shaper also to create flat objects for use in the 3D Editor. Any valid shape that checks OK can be imported directly into the 3D Editor. This technique is often used for flat text labels. Using flat shapes to apply decals to objects not only conserves RAM, but often looks better close-up. This is because images used as decals can appear blurry at high magnification, but any flat object will have sharp edges due to the fact that it consists of faces.

Flat objects are created by first composing them in the 2D Shaper. Then, the shape is brought directly into the 3D Editor, bypassing the 3D Lofter. In the following tutorial, you will create some shapes to be used as flat objects in the 3D Editor.

Creating Some Flat Text Shapes

From the screen menu, choose Create/Text/Font, and select COBRA.FNT	Accepts the font
From the screen menu, choose Create/Text/Enter	Displays text-entry dialog box
In the dialog box, type **Clip,** then click on OK (see fig. 3.18)	Displays the text
From the screen menu, choose Create/Text/Place	Highlights Place on the menu
Press and hold Ctrl	Constrains outline shape to proper aspect
In the Shaper, draw a rectangle to define the boundaries of the text object	Displays text (see fig. 3.19)
Save the drawing	

Figure 3.18

Setting up text for the Shaper.

Figure 3.19

Displaying the text.

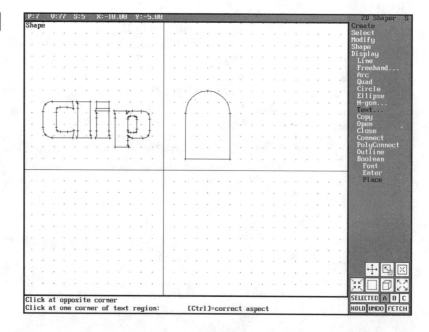

In the next exercise the shapes are brought directly into the 3D Editor.

Importing Shapes into the 3D Editor

Continue with the drawing you made in the previous exercise.

Choose Shape/Assign/Polygon to assign the text to be moved into the 3D Editor, one polygon at a time	Text turns yellow
Press F3 to switch to the 3D Editor	Displays 3D Editor
Activate the viewport in which the text will face forward (in this case, the front viewport)	Activates the front viewport
From the 3D Editor menu, choose Create/Object/Get Shape	The Shape Creation Control dialog box (see fig. 3.20) confirms the import

The Shape Creation Control dialog box offers several options for import of the flat shape. In this case, the default settings are appropriate except for the name of the new object.

Type **Flat**	The typed text appears in the object name area of the Shape Creation Control dialog box
In the Shape Creation Control dialog box, click on OK	Displays the new Flat text object in all viewports (see fig. 3.21)

Note that the flatness of the object is apparent in the front and left views, where it appears as a line.

Leave the new object in the 3D Editor

Save the project by choosing File/Save project and entering **Flat**	File is saved

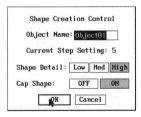

Figure 3.20

The Shape Creation Control dialog box.

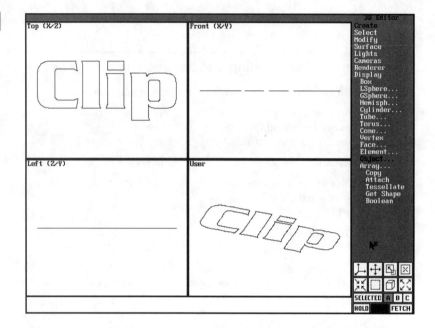

Figure 3.21

The flat shape is imported into the 3D Editor.

The simplest way to create an object type with the 3D Lofter is to extrude an object along a path. In the 2D Shaper, you create both the shape to be lofted and the path along which it is to be lofted. Then you import the shape and its path into the 3D Lofter, to create a new object. In the following exercises, you use this technique to create a paper clip shape.

Extruding a Polygon Along an Open Path

So far, you've used the 2D Shaper to create only the 2D outlines of objects. But you can use the 2D Shaper also as the source of the nonlinear path a shape follows as that shape is being extruded in the 3D Lofter. The path you create in the 2D Shaper is two-dimensional and flat. After you import the shape to the 3D Lofter, however, you can edit the 2D path into a 3D path. Because the path defines only a course for the cross-sectional shape of the lofted object, it does not have to be closed. The default path in the 3D Lofter is a straight line, which is not closed.

Most of your modeling in 3D Studio begins with the creation of the path and the shape in the 2D Shaper. Often, this is all you need to model the object, as is the case with a paper clip.

The first step is to create the cross-sectional shape of the paper clip. Paper clips are made from bent wire, and the cross section of a wire is a circle.

Creating a Shape for Lofting

Press F1 to return to the 2D Shaper	The 2D Shaper appears
Make sure that Snap mode is on by checking the upper right of the screen for the S indicator. Type **S** if necessary	Snap is activated
Choose Create/Circle	Highlights Circle in the screen menu
Create a circle in the 2D Shaper by clicking in the viewport and drawing a circle with a radius of 25	Displays a circle in the viewport at 0,0 (see fig. 3.22)

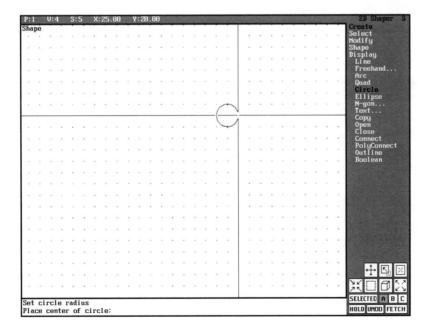

Figure 3.22

Creating a circle.

Next, you create the path for the paper clip (in this case, the looped shape of the paper clip). The path is constructed from three half circles connected by lines. The pieces of the polygons shown in figure 3.23 describe the construction of the paper clip path.

Figure 3.23

Diagram of paper clip segments.

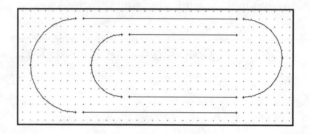

Creating a Path for Lofting

The first step in creating the paper clip path is to create the three turns. Each half-circle turn is created by drawing complete circles and deleting the unused half. The circles must have slightly different diameters because the paper clip path is essentially a stretched spiral

From the 2D Shaper menu, choose Create/Circle	Highlights Circle on the menu
In the viewport, draw a circle by clicking at –80,0 and define a circle with a radius of 40 units (see fig. 3.24)	Creates first circle
Click at 30,0 and define a circle with a radius of 35 units	Displays the second circle (see fig. 3.25)
Create the third circle—the last turn of the paper clip—so that it fits evenly inside the largest (first) circle. Click at 30, 5 and drag down and to the right to create a circle with a 30-unit diameter	Displays the new circle

With Snap, all three circles are at perfect coordinates (see figure 3.26).

Save the drawing

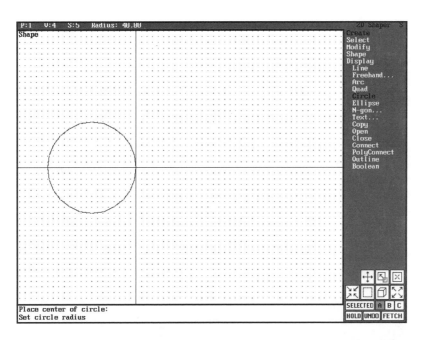

Figure 3.24

Drawing the first curve of the paper clip path.

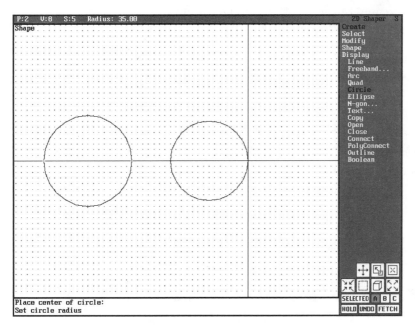

Figure 3.25

The second circle is drawn.

Figure 3.26

*Three circles
drawn.*

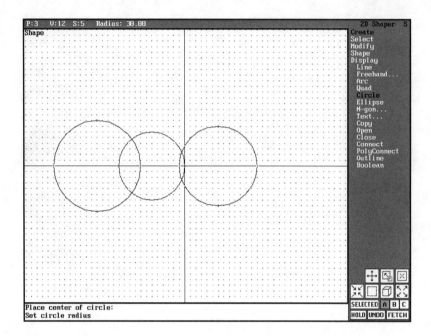

You have created the circles that will be the curves in the final paper clip. The next exercise takes the three circles and separates them to form the turns of the paper clip. You will delete the unnecessary parts of the circles, and then add line segments to connect the turns and form the basic paper clip shape.

Creating the Path

Continue with the drawing from the previous exercise.

You need to move the third circle to align it properly for the concentric-track shape of the paper clip.

Choose Modify/Polygon/Move and click on the rightmost circle	Circle moves as you move the mouse
Move the circle 50 units to the right and 5 units up, then click	Places circle, as shown in figure 3.27

Next, you're going to delete half of each circle, leaving three outer half-circles that approximate the paper clip's three turns.

From the 2D Shaper menu, choose Modify/Segment/Delete	Highlights Delete on the menu

Click the mouse on a segment between two vertices to delete it.

Delete the inner segments
of the circles, leaving the half-
circle shapes shown in figure 3.28

Three half-circles remain

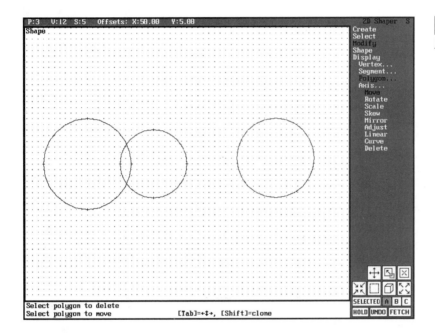

Figure 3.27

Moving a circle.

In the 2D Shaper menu, choose Create/Line

Highlights Line in the menu

Click at the top vertex of the
half-circle on the right and move
the mouse toward the top vertex of
the half-circle on the left

Draws a line between the vertex and the
moving mouse (see fig. 3.29)

Click the mouse again over the
top vertex of the half-circle
on the left

Connects the end of one half-circle to
that of the other half-circle. A Yes/No
dialog box is displayed when you click
over the vertex of the second half-circle

Click on OK (see fig. 3.30)

Confirms that the line end should be
welded to the end vertex. The dialog box
disappears

continues

continued

Figure 3.28

Unnecessary segments from the circles have been deleted.

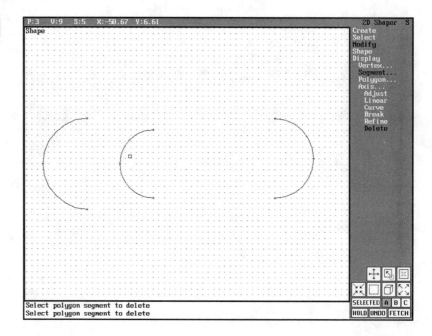

Figure 3.29

Adding a line to the curves of the paper clip.

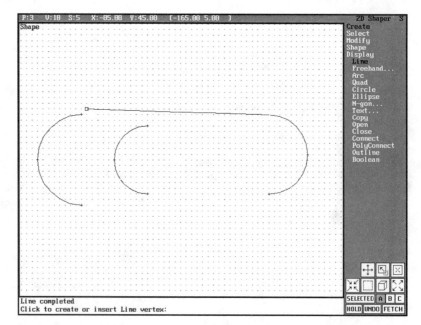

Figure 3.30

*The Weld Confir-
mation dialog box.*

Repeat the line-creation process
on the other half-circles

Creates the paper clip shape shown in
figure 3.31

The final paperclip path is perfectly horizontal, with a minimal number of vertices used
to describe its shape.

Save the drawing

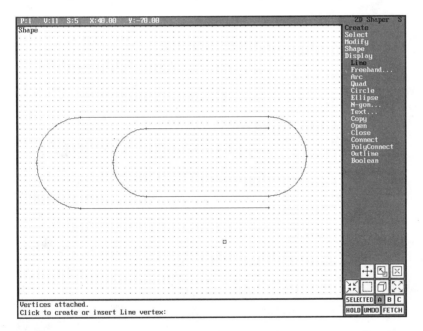

Figure 3.31

*The completed
paper clip path.*

The 2D Shaper now contains a circle shape and a paper clip path. The
next two exercises show you how to import the circle and the paper clip
path into the 3D Lofter.

Setting Up a Shape in the 3D Lofter

This exercise uses the paper clip path and shape created in the previous exercise. Load the project if necessary.

From the 2D Shaper menu, choose Shape/Assign and click on the circle	The circle turns yellow, indicating that it is assigned
Press F2	Displays the 3D Lofter
From the 3D Lofter menu, choose Shapes/Get/Shaper	Displays the circle in the 3D Lofter's Shape viewport (see fig. 3.32)
Choose Shapes/Scale	Scale is highlighted in the menu
Click in the 3D Lofter viewport labeled Shape (the viewport labels are in the upper left corner)	The circle shape scales to larger and smaller sizes as the mouse is moved
Adjust the circle down in scale until the top of the screen reads 15%, then click the mouse	The circle appears at the new size in the viewports

Figure 3.32

3D Lofter with circle shape.

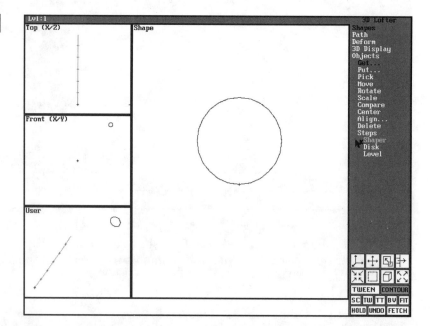

Now the shape is ready for lofting. The paper clip object will be created be lofting the circular shape along a paperclip path. In the next exercise, you transfer the paper clip path shape, as a path, to the 3D Lofter. With both path and shape correctly loaded in the 3D Lofter, the paper clip object can be created by the 3D Lofter.

Setting Up a Path in the 3D Lofter

From the 3D Lofter, press F1	Displays the 2D Shaper screen (Shape/Assign should still be highlighted in the menu)
Choose Shape/None	The circle's color returns to white from yellow, indicating that it is no longer assigned (Shape/Assign is still highlighted in the menu)
Click on the paper clip shape	Paper clip shape turns yellow
Press F2	Displays the 3D Lofter screen
Choose Path/Get/Shaper	Displays the path in the 3D Lofter (see fig. 3.33)

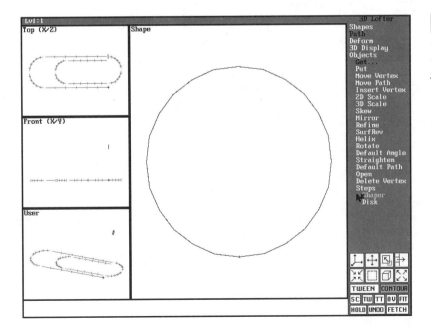

Figure 3.33

3D Lofter with both circle shape and paper clip path displayed.

Now the object is ready to be created in the 3D Lofter. The following exercise describes how to preview and create the object.

Lofting an Extrusion Along a Path

To get a better look at the effects of the preview, bring the user view to the large viewport by clicking on the user view to activate it, and then clicking on the top right icon in the icon panel. This is the swap viewport icon, and causes the view in the large viewport to change places with the currently selected small viewport.

Right click the zoom extents icon to be sure that all the parts of the loft are in view in the four viewports	The path and shape are centered in the four viewports
Choose Objects/Preview	The preview dialog reappears, with the same settings as before (see fig. 3.34)
Click Preview	The preview appears in all four viewports, as in figure 3.35

Note that a copy of the circle shape appears along the path at each point where a vertex exists. All the shapes are aligned in the same direction, and are not centered in the path. Although this preview is close to the desired effect, it looks horrible (and will yield a horrible 3D object). To get the proper paper clip model, you have to center the circle shape on the path, and activate Contour to cause the shape to turn with the path.

*The Preview
Controls dialog box.*

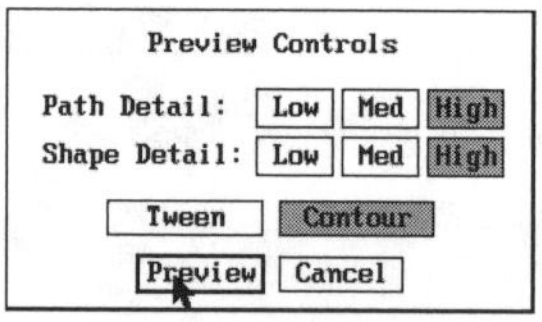

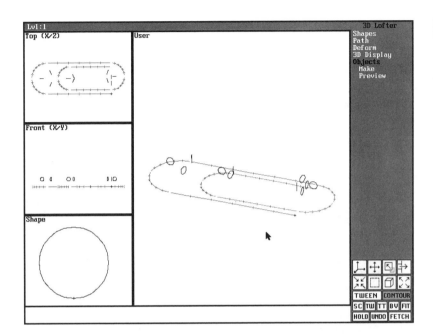

Figure 3.35

*The first preview,
without any
alignment.*

In the first previews of your circle shape lofted along a paper clip path,
the first circle did not appear as expected. This is because you expect
the round shape of the paper clip wire to be centered along the path the
paper clip follows. In the next exercise, you take the existing shape and
center it along the path in a single step.

Aligning the Shapes Along the Path

In the 3D Lofter menu, choose Shapes/Center	In the Shape viewport, displays a plus sign (+) in the center of the circle shape (see fig. 3.36)

This plus sign shape indicates the position of the *hook*, the point at which the path
passes through a shape to be extruded. The hook point can be altered in the 3D Lofter,
as you just did, or directly set in the 2D Shaper. To specify this point directly within the
2D Shaper, choose Shape/Hook/Show to display the hook position, then choose Shape/
Hook/Place to reposition it.

The shape must follow the path as it curves. That is, the circle shape should turn as the
path turns, to create an object that appears wire-like.

continues

continued

Click on the CONTOUR button in the lower right corner of the screen

The button turns red

Preview the adjustments by again choosing Objects/Preview from the 3D Lofter menu

The Preview dialog box shows the CONTOUR button already selected, echoing your change in the main screen

Click on Preview

A circle is now centered on each vertex of the paperclip path, with the orientation of the circle shape following the path (see fig. 3.37)

Figure 3.36

The centered shape.

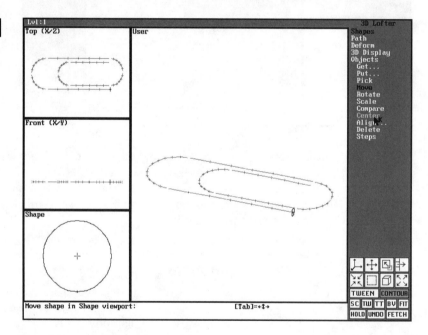

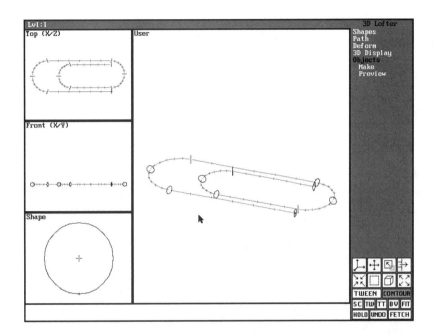

Figure 3.37

Preview, with centered shape.

3

If this object were lofted directly, it would have points instead of circular turns because of the lack of shapes around the rounded corners.

Because the 2D Shaper and the 3D Lofter allow curves and the 3D Editor does not, curves must be approximated with several straight lines. The number of straight lines used to approximate the curvature of a line between two vertices is called the step setting. With steps set to one, there will be a single point added to the center of a curving line between each pair of vertices. If more steps are used to approximate a curve, it will appear to be a true curve from some distance and only be apparent as a segmented curve up close. Therefore, the step setting should be adjusted based on how close the object will be positioned with respect to the camera at its closest point. Also, the zoom setting on that camera must be taken into account during the step-setting decision—a faraway camera with a highly zoomed lens will appear to be very close to the object.

If an object is being created for a variety of uses, modelers generally err on the side of higher complexity (and therefore slower rendering for the models user). You can save a Lofter setup at any time by using the File/ Save option in the 3D Lofter. That way, the file can be restored later to create higher or lower curve accuracy meshes.

In the next exercise, you adjust the path's step count so that the path has enough interim points in the curved areas of the paper clip path to appear round.

Adjusting Path Steps

From the 3D Lofter menu, choose Path/Steps	The Set Path Steps dialog box appears (see fig. 3.38)
In the Set Path Steps dialog box, set the slider to 10 and click on OK	The Path Steps is set to 6 and the dialog box disappears
Click on the TWEEN button in the lower right corner of the screen	The button turns red, activating the Tween function. This will place the shape at points between the vertices of the path during lofting
From the 3D Lofter menu, choose Objects/Preview	Displays the Preview dialog box, with both Tween and Contour active
In the dialog box, click on the Preview button	Displays a preview in which the shape appears 10 times between each vertex along the path (see fig. 3.39)
Save the project with File/Save project	The Save dialog box appears
Enter **Pclip** in the dialog box	File is saved and the dialog box disappears

Figure 3.38

The Set Path Steps dialog box.

Figure 3.39

The paperclip preview, with 10 shapes between each path vertex.

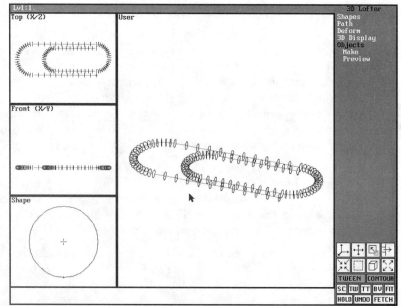

Switches in the Object Lofting Controls dialog box (see figure 3.40) control capping and smoothing. The Cap Start and Cap End buttons are used to create a surface at the start and end of the loft—in this case, placing a circle at the ends of the paper clip to close the wire shape. Usually, both buttons are left set to the default (On).

The Object Lofting Controls Dialog Box

The Smooth Length feature creates a smoothed appearance between faces along areas of the path that curve. The Smooth Width feature performs the same function for curved areas around the shape. Both buttons default to On.

You will also note two other options, Mapping and Weld Vertices. These options have special uses, and are discussed in detail in Chapter 7, "Advanced Modeling Techniques."

Type **PCLIP** to name the object	Displays the name in the Object Name box at the top of the Object Lofting Controls dialog box (see fig. 3.40)
In the dialog box, click on the Create button	Briefly displays the Object Creation Progress dialog box; then the 3D Lofter screen reappears, looking as it did earlier

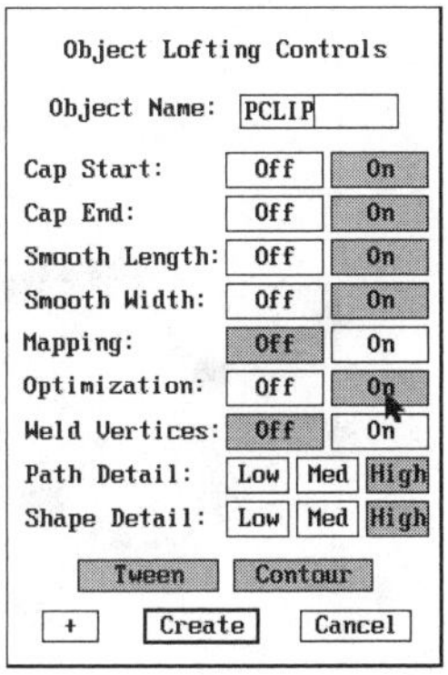

Figure 3.40

The Object Lofting Controls dialog box.

When the 3D Lofter creates an object, the newly created object is built in the 3D Editor and Keyframer modules. The 3D Lofter then returns to the same display it had before the object creation procedure. At this point, you can confirm what you've just created by switching to the 3D Editor. In the following exercise, you check the shape you've created, using the 3D Editor to make sure that the shape is correct.

Confirming Lofted Objects

This exercise picks up where the last exercise left off, with the 3D Lofter having just created an object. After the lofting process completed, the 3D Lofter screen reappears, and the created object is now in the 3D Editor module.

Press F3 to go to the 3D Editor	Displays the 3D Editor screen, with both the paper clip and the flat object previously generated. The paper clip has vertices only along its curvy areas and at its ends
Click on the Zoom Extents button to perfectly position the new object in the Top, Left, and Front viewports, thus making the object easy to inspect	Automatically adjusts the viewports to show the object full-screen (see fig. 3.41)

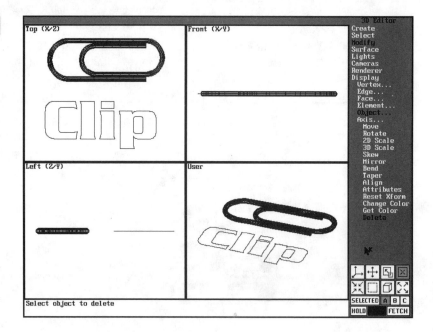

The 3D Editor, with created objects.

Previewing the Object with VIEW.PXP

Usually, previewing in the Lofter gives a reliable impression of the mesh complexity and contours. For a more interactive, visual check of your modeled object, however, you can use 3D Studio plug-in modules also called *IPAS routines*.

IPAS is an acronym for the different types of plug-ins (the P stands for *PXP*, or Procedural eXternal Process). With IPAS, you can use special external programs, designed for 3D Studio, to help model and refine objects. One amazing capability that external plug-ins have added to 3D Studio is a real-time shaded viewer.

To be able to access this utility that is external to 3D Studio, you must move it into the proper directory for 3D Studio to find it. The VIEW.PXP plug-in can be found on the CD-ROM that accompanies this book.

Although one PXP that comes with Release 4 is a fast preview, the viewer used in this section is a free IPAS plug-in that must be installed from the CD-ROM provided with this book. Although this IPAS doesn't include color, it can rotate and render an object in real-time much faster than the fast preview PXP. The result is smoother motion while you move the object about, so that you can easily and quickly analyze an object's structure and smoothing.

The next exercise takes you through the steps for installing the PXP plug-in, VIEW.PXP, from the CD-ROM.

Installing VIEW.PXP

PXP, IXP, KXP, and AXP IPAS modules all reside in one subdirectory, called PROCESS, of the 3DS directory, . By simply copying the PXP file to this subdirectory, you make the file available from the PXP selector in the 3D Editor.

Press F10 to jump to DOS	Displays a dialog box so that you can confirm that you want to use DOS
Type **OK**	Displays a DOS prompt on a blank screen

Use the following command to copy the VIEW.PXP file from the CD-ROM to the PROCESS subdirectory:

```
copy F:\IPAS\VIEW.PXP C:\3DS\PROCESS
```

where *C:\3DS* directory is your main 3D Studio directory, and the *F:* drive is the CD-ROM drive.

Type **EXIT** at the DOS prompt to return to 3D Studio	Displays the 3D Editor screen

---

Now that the VIEW.PXP plug-in program is in the proper directory, it can be activated by 3D Studio. F12 brings up the list of available external utilities in the 3D Editor and Keyframer. PXPs (used to add or alter your models) are only allowed in the 3D Editor, and KXPs (used to alter your animation) are allowed only in the Keyframer, so you must be in the 3D Editor to activate VIEW.PXP.

In the next exercise, you'll activate the VIEW.PXP plug-in that was just installed in the last exercise, and use it to view geometry created in previous exercises.

Using VIEW.PXP

This exercise follows directly from the last exercise, with the paper clip and flat text object still present in the 3D Editor. The VIEW.PXP plug-in was installed in the last exercise and is now available to run while in the 3D Editor.

Press F12   Displays the PXP Selector dialog box

This is the dialog box where all PXP IPAS routines are activated. The list contains all the PXPs present in your PROCESS directory.

In the list, find the VIEW entry, click
on the entry to highlight it, and click on
OK (see fig. 3.42)

The VIEW plug-in, like many of these routines, works on a single object. After the plug-in is activated, an object is selected before the plug-in proceeds. The plug-in initially communicates to the user at the bottom of the screen, requesting that you Pick an Object, as seen at the bottom of figure 3.43.

Click on the paper clip object in   Displays a special screen with a shaded
the viewport (see fig. 3.43)   version of the paper clip (see fig. 3.44)

You can rotate the object in the viewer. To rotate the object, click anywhere in the display window and move the mouse around. The shaded object will rotate based on the mouse movement. The instantaneous feedback on smoothing and object construction affords you an excellent confirmation of Lofter output.

Click on Dismiss   The View PXP disappears

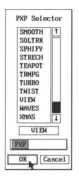

Figure 3.42

*The PXP Selector
dialog box.*

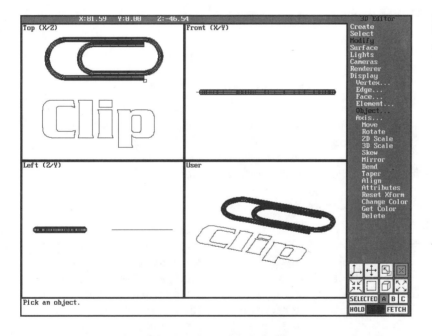

Figure 3.43

*Picking the object to
view.*

3

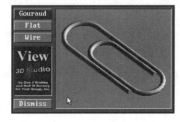

Figure 3.44

*The paper clip
object in the viewer
PXP.*

The 3D Editor should now contain both extruded and flat objects. With VIEW.PXP installed, you can more easily understand a concept important to the task of modeling—a task called *surface normals*, or often just *normal*.

The word *normal* is common in 3D work, especially in 3D Studio. The term describes the direction in which the flat face of a 3D triangle points. If you think of simple geometry, it might seem that a triangle, being flat, can be thought of as having two flat sides (and thus two normals). 3D Studio, however, creates each triangle with a single, inherent normal. Face normals describe the orientation of a face by defining which side of the face is considered the *inside* and which is the *outside*. 3D Studio saves rendering time by only rendering faces that have their outside visible in the view.

Viewing One-Sided Objects

Face normals are a critical part of 3D Studios approach to interacting and rendering 3D objects. In regular operation, a face is not shown if the viewpoint is on the far side of that face. When the 3D Lofter creates a capped 3D object, all of its sides are covered and all its normals will face out. Because most objects are covered on all sides, 3D Studio can both display and render an object twice as fast if it considers only faces whose *active* side faces the camera.

The VIEW.PXP plug-in that you have explored in the last exercise uses normals just the way 3D Studio does, and does not display any face that has a normal that points away from the viewer. The flat text shape now present in the 3D Editor is a one-sided flat object, which will only be visible from one side. Visualizing the way normals work is aided by using the VIEW.PXP plug-in to interactively view the flat object, and observing where the flat text object disappears. The following exercise takes you through the steps of viewing a flat object with the VIEW.PXP plug-in.

Viewing a Flat Object

This exercise uses the same objects created earlier in the chapter, the flat text object and the lofted paper clip object. You should be in the 3D Editor to begin.

Reactivate VIEW by pressing F12   Displays the PXP selector dialog box, with VIEW at the bottom; your last selection is ready for reactivating

In the dialog box, click on OK	Displays `Pick an object` message at the bottom of the screen
Select the flat text Clip object generated earlier	Displays the View dialog box containing the flat text object

The text object is made up of faces, as are all objects. However, the back side of the flat object is not covered, as it would be in a solid extruded object. As you rotate the flat text object, it becomes invisible when its back side turns to face the viewport (see fig. 3.45).

Figure 3.45

A flat object, turned to its back side, is invisible.

3

Viewing Multiple Objects with VIEW.PXP

Sometimes you need to view several objects simultaneously. In this case, simply copy all the objects to be viewed to a new, temporary single object that will be deleted when viewing is complete.

CAUTION

In some cases, copying several objects to a single object will not work because 3D Studio limits the size of single objects to 64,000 faces.

In the following exercise, you create a temporary new, single object that is a copy of several objects combined. This new object enables you to view the objects in proximity to each other.

VIEW.PXP with Multiple Objects

From the 3D Editor menu, choose Select/Object/Single	Highlights the three menu items
Click on the paperclip object	The object turns red

continues

continued

Click on the flat text object

> The flat text turns red, indicating that it is selected

Now, both objects are selected (see fig. 3.46). Actions taken on objects when the SELECTED button is active (red) affect all selected objects.

Figure 3.46

Both objects are selected.

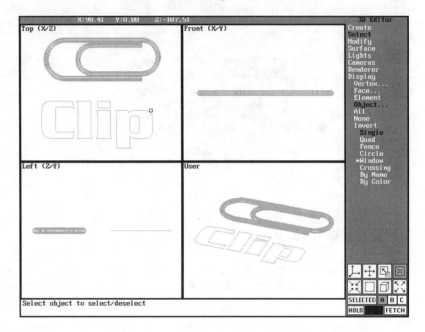

Choose Modify/Objects/Move

> Highlights the three menu items

Activate the SELECTED button in the lower right corner of the screen, either by clicking on it or by pressing the space bar

> The SELECTED button turns red

When you hold down Shift during any move, rotate, bend, taper, scale, or mirror operation, the original object remains unaltered. 3D Studio creates and modifies a copy of the object, naming the new object after the modifying action is complete.

Click in the Front viewport to move the selected objects

> The viewport becomes active

Press and hold Shift, then click in the viewport

> Displays a light-colored box surrounding the selected objects; the box moves as you move the mouse (see fig. 3.47)

Position the box so that the new objects are clearly above the original objects, then click the mouse button at this point

> The Copy Objects dialog box asks whether each object is to be copied (multiple) or whether all objects should be copied to a single object (single) (see fig. 3.48)

Choose the Single button object	A dialog box appears to name the new
Type **xxx** as the name of the temporary cloned object (see fig. 3.49). Then click on OK	The Name for new object: dialog box disappears, and the objects are displayed where the outline box was placed
Press F12 to bring up the PXP selector	Displays the PXP Selector dialog box
Click on the VIEW entry to highlight it, then click OK	The PXP Selector dialog box disappears and the `Pick an object` message is displayed at the bottom of the screen
Click on the xxx object just created in the active viewport	Displays the special View window with both objects visible
Interactively rotate the objects by clicking anywhere in the View window, and then moving the mouse	A shaded, 3D view of the just-created object moves about. The flat object disappears when it faces away from the window's point of view

Note how the one-sided normals of the flat object are apparent because it disappears when rotated so that it faces away from the viewer (see fig. 3.50).

Now that the xxx object has served its purpose, you can delete it.

Choose Modify/Object/Delete	Highlights the Delete option
Click on the xxx object. Click on OK when the Confirm Delete dialog box appears	The object disappears, and the scene looks just as it did when this exercise began

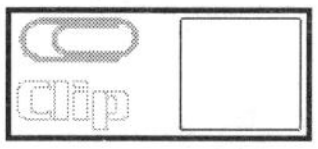

Figure 3.47

Copying an object with the Move option and Shift.

Figure 3.48

The Copy objects to: dialog box.

Figure 3.49

Entering the name for the new object.

Figure 3.50

Viewing both objects simultaneously.

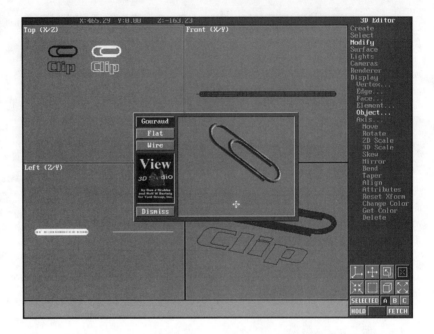

By viewing modeled objects attached to each other in this way, you can quickly check to make sure that the scene looks like what the animator expects.

Summary

In this chapter you have progressed through the most standard method that 3D Studio uses to create a new object: separately setting up a shape and a path in the 2D Shaper, then using each in the 3D Lofter to create new 3D objects. Variations on this include altering the shape as it travels along the path, or rotating the shape to create lathe-style objects. These more advanced forms of modeling are discussed in Chapter 7, "Advanced Modeling Techniques." However, no matter what type of object you've created, at present it is a flat, white object in the darkened room of the 3D Editor. Now that you've sculpted and modeled your objects, it's time to paint them, light them up, and place a camera in front of them. Chapter 4, "Lights, Camera, Set Design," describes how to add a camera and lights to your scene, and how to create and apply basic materials to the objects you create.

Chapter Snapshot

This chapter discusses the following topics relating to lights, cameras, and materials:

- The three types of lights

- Camera setup

- The Materials Editor

- Creating clear and wireframe materials

- Using texture maps

- Using reflection maps

Lights, Camera, Set Design

Completing your modeled scene involves lighting it, adding materials, and placing a camera. Like a set designer or a cinematographer, you combine lights, materials, and cameras to create a composition of appropriate mood. Besides illuminating the scene, lighting can add mood by coloring the light, casting shadows, or focusing on specific areas. Every face and object in a scene has some material applied to it, even if it is only the default flat white. Like wallpaper or paint, materials are applied to create the outward appearance of each face. Cameras complete the composition by establishing the point of view and perspective.

All the models created up to this point have been assigned the default material for the 3D Editor, flat white. The 3D Editor has no default camera or light. To get to a point at which you can begin to create test renders, you must add, at the very least, a light. Usually you will quickly add several lights, some standard materials, and a camera to a modeled scene to get the first rendered output of your work. Because the final form of your work always comes from the renderer, it is helpful to get feedback from the renderer as rapidly as possible. Tuning in the parameters of your animation is an interactive process, delayed by the time 3D Studio spends checking changes during each test render.

Lighting

Applying lighting in 3D Studio is quite different from applying lighting in the real world. The virtual lights of 3D Studio work very differently from real-world light. In 3D Studio, the lighting can very quickly become so bright that areas become over-illuminated, and the resulting renderings appear like an over-exposed photograph. The standard settings for 3D Studio lights create lights that illuminate equally from any distance. Two or three full-intensity lights with standard settings easily will overpower a scene, no matter how far away the lights are placed from the objects.

Another unique aspect of 3D Studio's lights is that only shadow-casting spotlights can be blocked. All the other types of lights used in a scene will illuminate right through objects to shine on other objects behind them. This effect has to be taken into account as you add the different types of lights to a scene.

Finally, lights in 3D Studio do not reflect from objects. Not only do they not reflect from mirror-like metal or chrome objects, but even more diffuse materials that would normally disperse light exhibit none of this behavior in 3D Studio. As mentioned in Chapter 1, "Three-Dimensional Computer Graphics," radiosity effects are not possible with 3D Studio. That is, no objects may cast light in 3D Studio, even if they have reflective or glowing materials applied. This might not seem like a major consideration, because we are not sensitive to the effects of the light that radiates from every surface. However, we do notice that we can easily see under a table that has only a single light source above it. Using sound as an analogy, consider the reverberation that occurs in an indoor handball court—the sound waves seem much louder than normal; they also bounce around the hard walls and hit every surface before dying out. Similarly, in a white-walled room a single light source illuminates broadly, and you can see clearly behind and under furniture, where light cannot shine directly. To compensate for 3D Studio's nonreflecting lights, you can add additional light sources—but you need to do so carefully. You can over-illuminate computer generated scenes very easily, causing washed-out colors and a flat appearance.

The many options possible with lights allow great flexibility in lighting complex scenes. Unlike reality, a light in 3D Studio can be set to shine only on certain objects. Lights and individual objects can be set to not cast shadows. Lights can even have negative values, acting like a light-vacuum in their area of influence.

When adjusting lighting in 3D Studio, three types of lights are listed: Ambient, Omni, and Spotlight. All scenes have a single ambient light setting that is an overall scene adjustment. However, to edit an omni or spotlight, you first must create the omni or spotlight in your scene.

The following sections describe ambient, omni, and spotlights in detail.

Ambient

The first type of light listed on the Light submenu is ambient light. This is more of an overall scene setting, designed to be the first level of compensation for diffuse light reflection. Ambient light falls equally on all objects, and sets the darkest level any object will render. You should adjust this setting carefully; too-high ambient light will brighten the shadow areas of a scene so much that there is no contrast.

The following figures illustrate ambient lighting effects. Figure 4.1 shows the screen shot of the scene to be rendered. In figure 4.2, the ambient light is boosted to maximum. This is done by displaying the Ambient Light Definition dialog box with Lights/Ambient, and adjusting each of the R, G, and B sliders to their 255 maximum. Now, all objects are fully illuminated, regardless of where they are. The result (see fig. 4.3) is almost cartoon-like, with depth implied only by perspective.

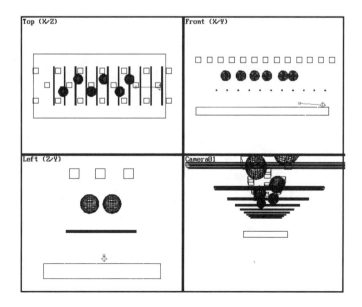

Figure 4.1

The scene as it appears in the four viewports.

Figure 4.2

*Boosting the
ambient light.*

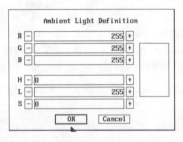

Figure 4.3

*The scene illumi-
nated by ambient
light only.*

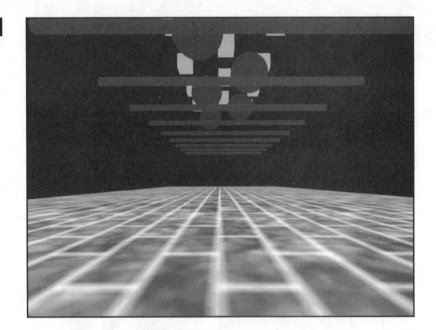

Omni

Omni lights are quite simple by nature. To use them, you simply define a
point in space from which light will emanate, and set a color and brightness level. The light hits all surfaces that are turned toward it, and are
not blocked by any object. The light level you set in the dialog box does not
diminish with distance unless the Attenuation button is selected in the
dialog box.

Four options are available at the bottom of the Omni Light Definition
dialog box: On/Off, Multiplier, Exclude, and Attenuation:

- **On/Off.** Provides a simple switch for disabling a light. It enables you to experiment with scene lighting by temporarily removing the effect of an omni light without deleting it or changing its settings.

- **Multiplier.** Enables a light to have an overall strength applied to it. When set between 0 and 1, it simply lowers the power of the light. When set to a negative value, the light becomes a light vacuum, darkening the lit areas that the omni light normally would illuminate. When set to greater than 1, the light illuminates more brightly than normal. This option can be used with the attenuation setting, which diminishes the light's power with distance (see the following section on attenuation).

- **Exclude.** Activates a list of all the objects within a scene. Any object you click will have an asterisk symbol placed by it, indicating that this omni light will not illuminate that object. Note that if you add new objects after setting exclusions for a light, the new object by default will be un-asterisked, and therefore illuminated by the light.

- **Attenuation.** Activates a mode where the light's power diminishes with distance from the light (this option works as an on/off switch). The ranges over which this diminishing effect occurs can be adjusted to any circular region around the omni light. The command for setting an omni light's attenuation range is Lights/Omni/Ranges. This option asks you to click on an omni light; you then will automatically be able to create one circle, and then another around the light. The smaller circle marks where the light's settings begin to diminish, and the larger circle marks where the light no longer illuminates. Note that although a circular range is drawn in a single viewport, the circle describes a spherical light falloff effect.

When creating scenes that require strong, dark shadows, omni lights must be carefully applied. Because they shine through all objects, they illuminate the cast-shadow areas of any object that the omni light strikes.

Omni lights typically are used to fill in broad areas with light from one direction. Most scenes are illuminated effectively with several omni lights and one or two spotlights. Because omni lights do not cast shadows, they rarely create the primary light in an outdoor scene.

In the following figures, the same scene as before is lit with a single omni light only, with a high brightness level (see fig. 4.4). Note that although the rendered image (see fig. 4.5) contains no shadows, it does have shading and highlights, with an apparent location of the source of light in 3D space.

Figure 4.4

Adding an omni light with maximum intensity.

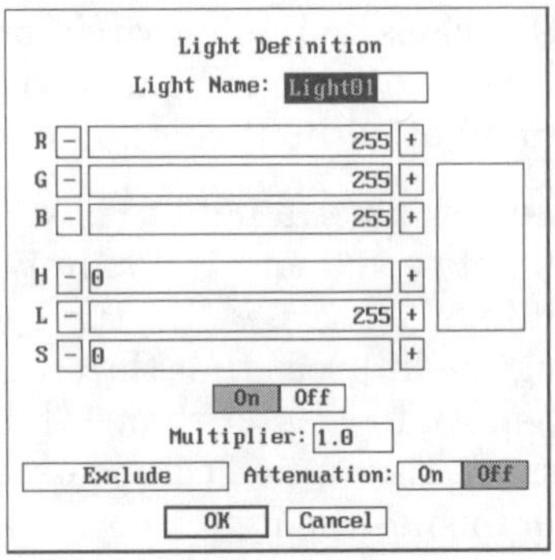

Figure 4.5

The rendered scene, illuminated only by a single omni light.

Spotlights

Spotlights focus an expanding, directional cone of light outward from a point. The cone of illumination outward from the point is constrained to open no larger than 175 degrees, to keep the cone from turning back on itself. The spotlight cone shape can be round or square, and can be rolled to any angle. All the features of the omni light type are available in the spotlight: name, color, multiplier, exclusions, on/off, and attenuation. In addition to these, spotlights have several other capabilities, including

Hotspot, Falloff, Roll, Shadows, Rectangle/Circle, Projector, and Overshoot.

- **Hotspot.** The spotlight has the capability to illuminate strongest at the center of the cone, and diminish to darkness at the edges of the cone. The cone of light expands at an angle from a point, and the area of illumination of the hotspot is set as an angle that is smaller than the overall illumination angle. The hotspot area is illuminated at the full value of the light. This value is best set interactively with the Lights/Spot/Hotspot command that displays an inner and outer ring at the end of the light cone, indicating the hotspot at the center of the overall spotlight area. Note that this is separate from attenuation, which diminishes light with distance from the point source.

- **Falloff.** This value works with the hotspot value to set the brightness falloff from the center of the cone. The falloff angle is constrained to 175 degrees or less, to keep the spotlight cone directional. The brightness of the spotlight will diminish from full intensity within the angle of the hotspot to zero at the falloff angle.

- **Roll.** This option rotates the spotlight. If the spotlight is circular and not projecting an image, it makes no sense to roll the spotlight. However, rectangular lights or projector lights can be rolled for various effects with this setting. Spotlight roll also can be animated.

- **Shadows.** This switch activates cast-shadow options. Two types of shadows are available, which are selected and adjusted with the Adjust button just below the Cast Shadows button. Cast shadows are discussed in more depth later in this chapter.

- **Rectangle/Circle.** These buttons select the shape of the light cone made by the spotlight. If the light is rectangular, the height and width of the rectangle can be adjusted with the Lights/Spot/Aspect option.

- **Projector.** Spotlights can project through an image to create a slide projector or movie projector effect (depending on whether a still image file or an animated image file is selected as the slide). The image to be projected is selected with the button just below the Projector button. When using the Projector option, think of the projector lightbulb as the colors set with the sliders at the top of the dialog box, which tint the projected image.

- **Overshoot.** This switch, when activated, causes the light to illuminate in areas outside the spotlight cone. The spotlight does not cast shadows in the areas outside the cone, but acts as an omni light in these areas. The spotlight becomes a combination omni and spotlight, in this case.

4

In figure 4.6, a spotlight is added with full brightness. Figure 4.7 shows the results of adding of the spotlight. The illumination is identical to that of a cone-focused omni light. In figure 4.8, shadows have been enabled, and a strong sense of depth and dimension is now becoming apparent. The dark areas are completely unilluminated, because ambient lighting is set to zero. A small amount of ambient light and some dim omni lights would bring out the completely dark areas and improve the final lighting of the scene.

Figure 4.6

Adding a full-intensity spotlight.

```
                    Spotlight Definition
              Light Name: Light01

      R  -                           255  +
      G  -                           255  +
      B  -                           255  +

      H  - 0                              +
      L  -                           255  +
      S  - 0                              +

   Hotspot: 43.75    Falloff: 54.5    Roll: 0.0
             Multiplier: 1.0
                   On    Off
  Cast Shadows  Show Cone   Attenuate       Exclude
    Adjust
      Type:     Rectangle    Projector
   Ray Trace    Circle                       Overshoot
                   OK      Cancel
```

Figure 4.7

The rendered image with shadows turned off.

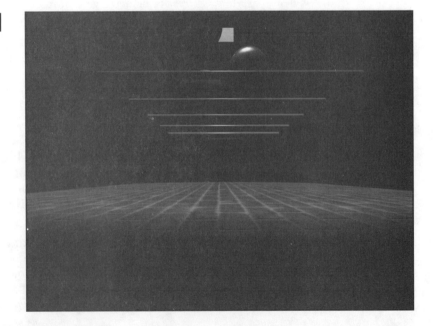

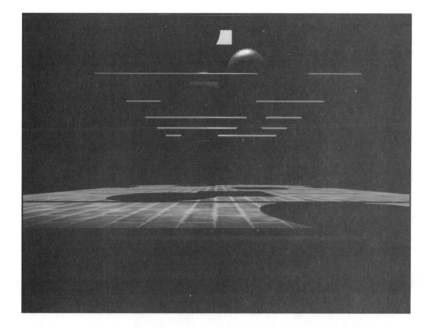

Figure 4.8

The same image with shadows turned on.

When you need a spherical light source that casts shadows, use two widely focused spotlights that point in opposite directions.

DESIGN TIP

4

Shadows

Two types of shadows appear in 3D Studio: mapped and ray traced. Shadow maps work by actually creating a special image from the perspective of the shadow-casting spotlight. You can adjust the bitmap size in the Shadow Parameters dialog box. The larger the image size, the tighter the shadows will appear. Because the shadow maps are effectively blurred to avoid a jagged-edge look, a shadow map that is too small often appears extremely soft-edged (see fig. 4.9). This type of shadow is extremely effective for indoor lighting, where shadows never have sharp edges. Keep in mind that a wider cone of the spotlight will spread the shadow map (whatever its size) over a greater area, given the same spotlight position. For sharper shadows, narrow the spotlight's coverage area, or increase the shadow map size (see fig. 4.10).

Figure 4.9

A small shadow map is blurred to create a very soft shadow.

Figure 4.10

Greatly increasing the map size results in tighter, almost hard-edged shadows.

If the lights, or any object, move at any point in an animated scene, the shadows are recalculated at each frame, speeding up rendering. Usually, unless you have specified a large shadow map size, and RAM is limited, shadow calculation is not very time-consuming. The mapped type of shadows requires more RAM than ray-traced shadows. This is especially true when large shadow-map sizes are used to get sharp shadows. Because ray-traced shadows require much less RAM, they actually can save rendering time if mapped shadows would cause paging to disk.

The other type of shadow is called *ray traced*. As its name implies, the spotlight's rays are traced through the geometry, taking transparency into account. These shadows always appear crisp and sharp-edged, and use almost no RAM (see fig. 4.11). In certain cases, however, the calculations required for ray-traced shadows can slow the rendering process dramatically. Ray-traced shadows are desirable where the shadows edges should not be soft-edged. In general, ray-traced shadows are ideal for outdoor scenes requiring the strong shadows cast by the sun. Ray-traced shadows are ideal for outdoor scenes requiring the strong shadows cast by the sun. Also, because only ray-traced shadows appear lighter when cast through semitransparent objects, they sometimes are required for realism. These shadows are only tints of gray, however. As mentioned in Chapter 1, "Three-Dimensional Computer Graphics," 3D Studio cannot render colored shadows caused by semitransparent colored objects.

4

Figure 4.11

Ray-traced shadows are perfectly hard-edged, and simulate the shadows cast by the sun.

In the following exercise, you will use the three types of lights to effectively light a chrome object. First, the unlighted scene is loaded from the CD-ROM. Then, each light type is added and adjusted to create a good lighting effect.

Lighting a Scene

This exercise starts with a ready-made scene that is on the CD-ROM. This exercise begins with loading this file.

Choose File/Load from the Top menu	Activates the File Selector dialog box
Set the appropriate drive letter in the dialog box for your CD-ROM, and choose the directory of the CD-ROM where the exercises are located	Activates a file list in the Selector box at the right of the dialog box
Click the entry LOGO-B.3DS and click OK	The dialog box disappears, and the scene file loads. After a moment, a simple scene with three walls and a logo appears
Adjust the scenes ambient light by choosing Lights/Ambient	The Ambient Light Definition dialog box appears. Soon, the ambient light in the scene is set to 0, which causes all unlit areas to be completely dark. Usually a small amount of ambient light is set, in order to cause these areas to be slightly visible.
Adjust the L slider to 20 for a low amount of ambient light (see fig. 4.12)	
Render the scene from the user view to see how the image will look with ambient lighting only. Choose Renderer/Render View	The Render Still Image dialog box appears
Set the Shading Limit button (at the upper left of the dialog box) to Metal, and click Render	After rendering, the image appears as shown in figure 4.13. The scene is very dark and has little depth, due to the lack of contrast

Next, you will add the primary light source to the scene—a spotlight. This light will cast shadows and create the highlights in the scene.

Choose Lights/Spot/Create and click in the top viewport	The top viewport becomes active
Click on the lower right of the logo object in the viewport, but do not click beyond the rightmost boundary where the wall is (see fig. 4.14)	A line from the click point appears when the mouse is moved

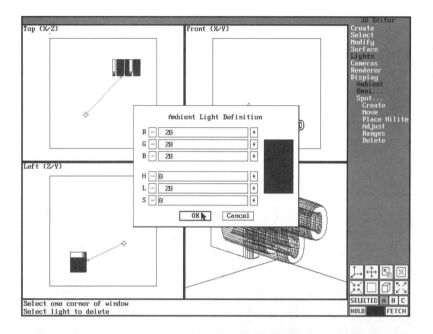

Figure 4.12

*Altering the
ambient-light
setting.*

Figure 4.13

*The rendered user
view with ambient
lighting only.*

continues

continued

Figure 4.14

Placing the spot-light.

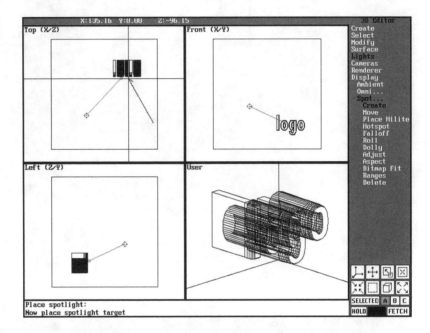

Move the mouse so that the end of the line is at the center of the logo and click	The Spotlight Definition dialog box appears
Click in the hotspot area, and replace the existing 44.0 value with 35. Click to activate the Cast Shadows option, and click to activate the Show Cone option. The dialog box should appear as in figure 4.15. Click Create to create the spotlight with these values	The spotlight symbol appears in the viewports as in figure 4.16

Because the spotlight was created in the top view, it is level when viewed in the front viewport. You should move the spotlight's source to a higher point, so that it shines down on the logo.

Choose Lights/Spot/Move	Move is highlighted in the menu
In the front viewport, click on the spotlight source (the pointed end of the cone)	The cone's point moves as the mouse is moved
Raise the spotlight's source to a point about two-thirds the height of the wall, and click	The new spotlight position appears
Click in the viewport labeled Left, and type the dollar sign (Shift+4)	The viewport becomes the spotlight view (see figure 4.17)

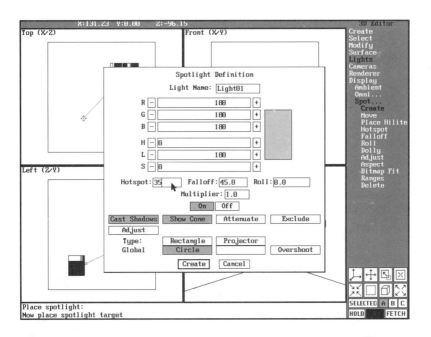

Figure 4.15

The spotlight parameters.

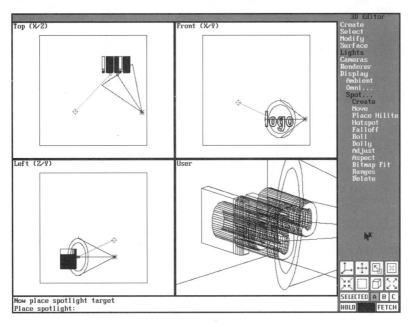

Figure 4.16

The spotlight symbol appears in the viewports.

4

continues

continued

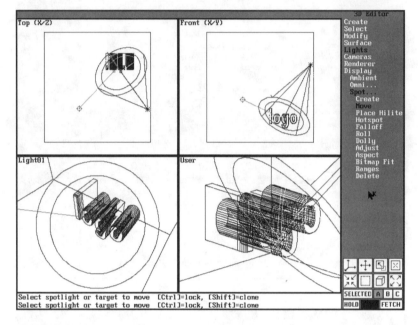

Figure 4.17

Moved light, with spotlight view in the lower left.

Choose Renderer/Render View, and render the user view to see the effects of the changes just made	The image appears with the spotlight area well lit and casting a shadow, as in figure 4.18

The unlit areas of this image are still too dark, and the logo would look better with additional highlights. To add this, you will apply a single omni light.

Choose Lights/Omni/Create	Create is highlighted in the menu
Click in the top viewport, and click to the left of and behind the logo	The Light Definition dialog box appears
Adjust the RGB sliders to 82, 50, and 50, respectively and click Create (see fig. 4.19)	The Omni light appears, as in figure 4.20. This light will create a dim, slightly reddish light that will illuminate the back areas of the scene somewhat
Render the scene from the user viewport a final time with Renderer/Render View	The image appears, with the backlight effect of the new Omni light apparent (see fig. 4.21). The final scene file is on the CD as LOGO-L.3DS, so you can load it if you want to check any of the settings

The results of this exercise are used in the camera-placement exercise that comes next. Save the file to the hard drive using the File/Save option.

Figure 4.18

Rendered User view with spotlight now added.

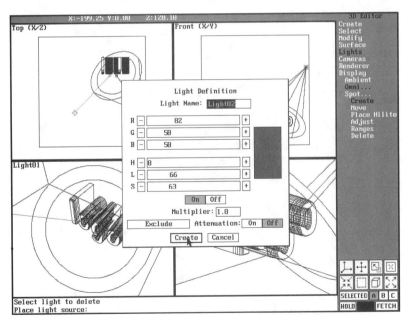

Figure 4.19

The Omni light settings.

4

Figure 4.20

*The Omni light
appears.*

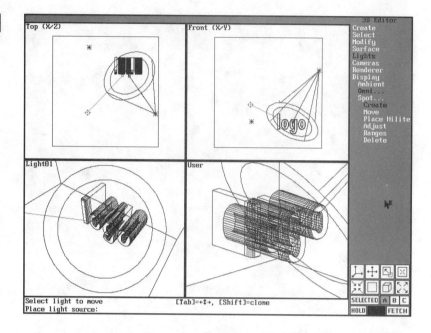

Figure 4.21

*The rendered scene
with omni and
spotlights added.*

Camera Setup

The 3D Studio scene is more than just a virtual stage; it is a studio that is photographed through the lens of a virtual camera. The position, perspective, and field of view of the camera play a major part in the final rendered animation. A low vantage point with exaggerated perspective might suggest that the object viewed is immense and important. A diminished perspective viewed from above might suggest that the viewer is looking down at the object as if through binoculars.

Note that 3D Studio's cameras always automatically stay level with the horizon. When a camera is placed so that it is looking straight down into a scene, its rotation can vary from the slightest change. In situations where the camera must be animated to fly over the top of an object while looking down on it, the entire scene must be rotated sideways 90 degrees, so that the camera does not rotate to compensate for the horizon.

Creating a Camera

Cameras should always be created in the Top viewport to ensure that they are oriented properly for keeping level with the horizon as the camera rotates around the 3D scene. The best technique is to position the camera quickly by clicking first at the camera's approximate viewpoint, and then clicking somewhere central to where the focus of attention should be. The dialog box will come up so that you can name the camera, but usually you can leave the length (in millimeters) setting as it is. The perspective and field of view are determined by the mm length of the lens, and both are interactively adjustable. That is, you can view your changes to the perspective and field of view (often abbreviated to *FOV*) as you make them, in the camera's viewport.

Adjusting the Placement of the Camera

After you place a camera, you usually need to adjust the placement. The best approach is to first center the subject in the viewport, and then use a camera dolly to move the camera closer to or farther from the subject along the target line of the camera. In addition, you can tweak the camera position directly from the camera viewport, by using Cameras/Move.

After a camera is placed, a dialog box with the camera settings appears. This dialog box enables you to adjust the camera Lens/FOV setting, Roll, and Cone On/Off. Descriptions of these settings follow:

4

- **Lens/FOV.** These two settings work with each other to set the camera's power and field of view (FOV). A higher lens setting means that you are using a higher magnification of lens, and thus the FOV is going to be narrower. The Stock Lenses section at the right of the dialog box contains nine presets for easy selection. Keep in mind that the human eye is roughly a 50mm lens, and those lenses smaller than 50mm tend to exaggerate perspective, while those larger than 50mm tend to diminish perspective. A custom value for lens or FOV can be set, but be sure to click the Calculate button afterward to set the corresponding value automatically for the other parameter.

- **Roll.** This setting enables the camera to tilt along the direction it is pointed, in order to create a banking effect. This parameter can be animated for effects such as animating the view from a dogfighting airplane's cockpit.

- **Cone On/Off.** This parameter switches on or off the lines that describe the view from the camera to the target. It functions like the Cone On/Off setting option in the Spotlight Definition dialog box.

CAUTION

> Sometimes the closest part (or even all) of an object does not appear in the camera viewport. The camera seems not to see all the closest faces. This problem, which also frequently occurs in previews, is caused by the proximity of the camera to the object. When the primary object's size (in units) is very small, such as 1 unit or less across, the camera is placed so close that 3D Studio has difficulty resolving which faces are in front of the camera. Usually, the best solution is to select all the objects in a scene and then scale them up so that the main scene elements are at least 20 units across.
>
> In some cases, a face does not appear in a viewport but renders correctly. This occurs in cases in which only part of a large face is in front of the camera, and the rest is behind. Suppose that you have a long box object with the camera in the middle, looking out to one end. Because of this placement of the camera, the long triangles that make the sides of the box do not appear in the camera viewport. Only the end caps of the plank are visible in the camera viewport.

In the following exercise, you create and place a camera. First, load the logo scene from the CD-ROM.

Creating and Placing a Camera

This exercise picks up where the lighting exercise ended, using the logo scene. A camera is placed and adjusted to view the scene.

From the 3D Editor menu, choose Cameras/Create

Activates Create option

Click in the Top viewport to select it

Activates the Top viewport

Click below and to the left of the logo

Tacks down the camera view-from point (see fig. 4.22). Right-click the mouse if you want to reposition this point

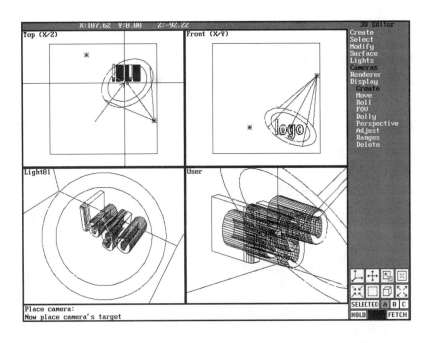

Figure 4.22

Creating a camera.

Move the mouse to the middle of the object, and click again

Displays the Camera Definition dialog box (see fig. 4.23)

In the camera definition dialog box, set the Show Cone button to on, by clicking the On button. Then click Create to create the camera

The camera symbol appears in the viewports

Click in the user viewport and press C

The user viewport becomes the camera view (see fig. 4.24)

continues

continued

Figure 4.23

The Camera Definition dialog box.

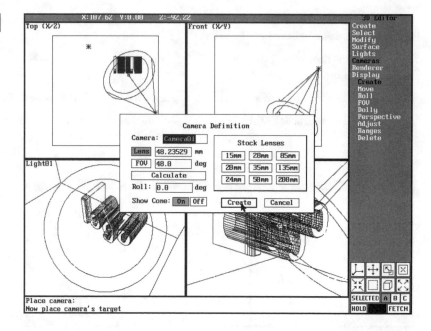

Figure 4.24

The camera symbol appears in the top, front, and light viewports, and the camera viewport displays the view from the camera.

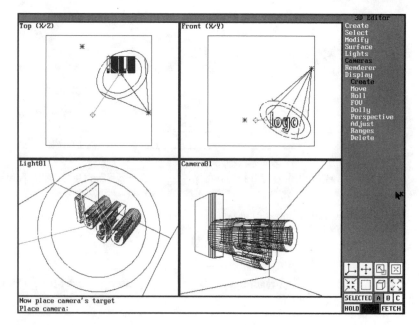

Again, the camera is perfectly level because it was placed in the top viewport. The camera should look slightly down on the logo object for this exercise.

Choose camera/move

Move is highlighted in the menu

In the Front viewport, click the camera symbol

The camera moves with the mouse, but the target remains focused on the logo. The camera viewport switches to box mode and reflects changes in camera position

Move the camera up roughly 150 units (the change in camera position is shown at the top of the screen during the movement; 150 units up means that these numbers should read 0, 150, 0) and click

The camera is placed at the new position (see fig. 4.25)

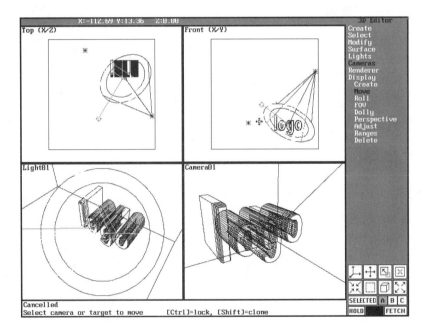

Figure 4.25

The final camera position.

Now, you will interactively adjust the FOV/Length of the camera for a more pronounced perspective.

Choose Cameras/Perspective and click on the camera in the top viewport

The camera moves closer and farther from the target as the mouse is moved, but the camera cone end stays the same size (see fig. 4.26)

continues

continued

Figure 4.26

Changing the camera's perspective.

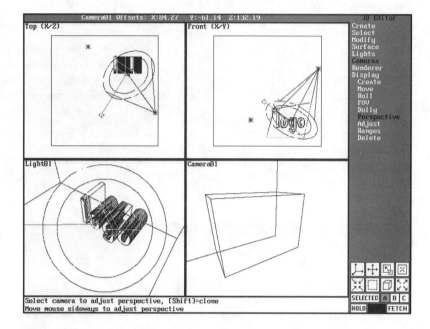

Adjust the perspective so that the top and sides of the l in logo are barely visible, and click the mouse

The new perspective appears in the camera viewport. This exaggerated perspective makes the logo look somewhat larger to the camera (see fig. 4.27)

Render the view in the camera viewport by choosing Renderer/Render view and clicking in the camera viewport

The Render Options dialog box appears

Click OK

The computer renders the image, as shown in figure 4.28

The final scene used in this exercise is saved on the CD-ROM as LOGO-C.3DS if you want to inspect it.

In the Stock Lenses section of the Camera Definition dialog box (refer to figure 4.23), you can directly set the lens to one of nine presets. The higher the mm setting, the more powerful the lens (and the less perspective evident). The effect of a 200mm lens, for example, is like that of a huge telephoto lens—to get all of the subject into view, the camera must be far away; and objects significantly in front of and behind the subject will appear only slightly closer or farther away. The human eye is considered to be comparable to a 50mm lens (the default lens length 3D Studio uses).

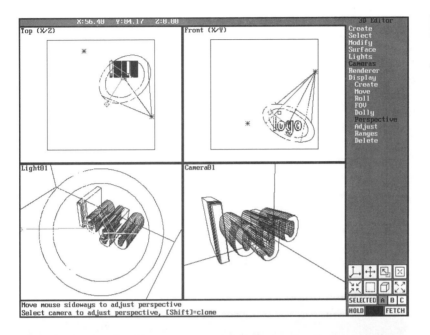

Figure 4.27

The final camera perspective.

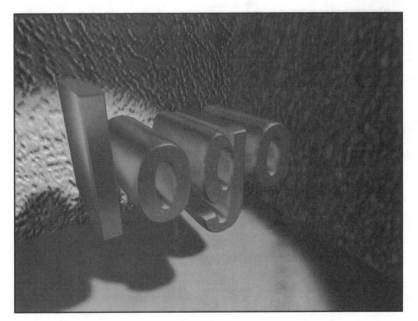

Figure 4.28

The final rendered scene.

continues

continued

Click the Create button, using the default settings	Redraws the viewports; now the camera icon is present (see fig. 4.29)

Figure 4.29

The camera icon in the Front viewport.

To make the lower right viewport a camera view, click in the window to activate it, then type **C**	Displays the view from the new camera

If there were more than one camera, typing C would display a list of the cameras so that you could choose one.

Cameras always are constructed to view straight ahead (horizontal to the ground plane). To view the underside of the logo, you need to adjust the camera.

Choose Cameras/Move from the menu	Activates the Move option

In the Front viewport is a line with a square icon at each end, representing the camera and its target. The larger icon is the camera, and the smaller icon is the camera target.

Click the camera icon	Displays the camera cone; the camera moves to track the mouse

Move the mouse down and farther to the left, leaving the camera target centered on the logo object (see fig. 4.30).

View the box-mode camera view as you adjust the camera for the correct position.

Click the mouse	Redraws the viewports with the new camera position

Choose Cameras/Dolly from the menu	Activates the Dolly option

Click in the Camera viewport, and move the mouse to alter the camera's closeness to the object. Note that the target is stationary, and the camera alignment is locked. Only the distance from the object is altered, which enables you to easily fill the frame with the logo (see fig. 4.31).

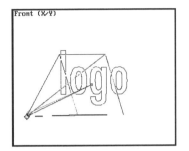

Figure 4.30

Moving the camera in the Front viewport.

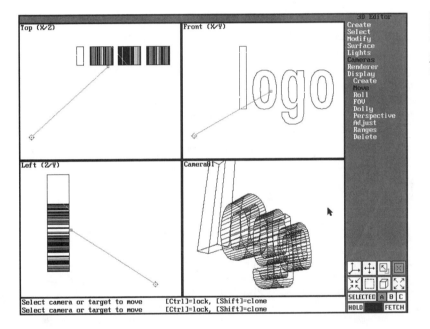

Figure 4.31

The final camera position as shown in box mode.

4

Materials

One of the most important decisions you make about how your scene will appear is the selection of materials for the parts of your scene. Materials are more than just a coat of paint that you apply to an object. Rather, they include every feature of the way a surface appears—including metallic, reflective, shiny, transparent, grainy, and bumpy. These and many other attributes are created in the Materials Editor, and can be applied to entire objects, single elements, groups of selected faces, or even a single face.

Materials can add detail and color to a scene by applying an image to an object in a manner similar to applying wallpaper to a real-life object. In 3D Studio, images exist as files on the hard disk. These images can be called up and included as part of a material to achieve a very realistic look. If a flat box object in a scene is supposed to be a plank of wood, for example, a material would be applied to it that contains an image of wood. This image would be stretched along the box object so that when the box is rendered, the wood image defines the colors in each of the faces of the box. However, an image can be used to define more than just the colors of an object—images also can be applied to define transparency, shininess, bumpiness, and other attributes.

For 3D Studio to be able to use images, it must know where to find them. When you create a material within 3D Studio, image files used in that material are not incorporated into your scene. Instead, the material merely points to the file on the disk. Because of this, you can edit the image file in a computer paint program and save it under the same name, and the scene then renders with the edited image file applied. However, 3D Studio requires that you supply a list of locations on the disk in order for the image files to be found. These are called *map paths*. You can alter this list by editing the 3DS.SET file, or by choosing Info/Configure and clicking the Map Paths button.

The Materials Editor

The Materials Editor (see fig. 4.32), a formidable surface-creation laboratory, can seem somewhat complicated to the new user. When you study each section separately, however, the Materials Editor's myriad parameters are fairly straightforward.

The menu options available at the top of the Materials Editor are critical to its use. You can see these options only when you move your mouse cursor to the top of the screen.

The options at the far left and far right are Info and Program, respectively. These options offer the same pull-down menus here as they do in the other modules. The following sections describe the other three options—Library, Material, and Options—and their pull-down menus.

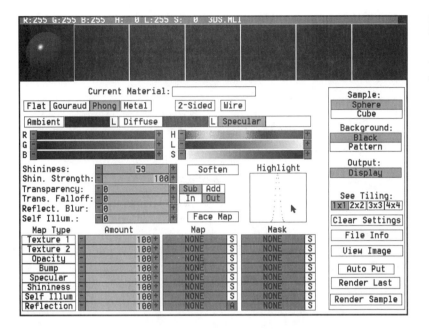

Library

You use the Library pull-down menu (see fig. 4.33) to manage your materials libraries. A library of materials is simply a collection of different surface attributes. Because the material library contains only the pointers to the texture map files they use, and the parameter values for all the different entries, each material library requires little hard drive space. Also, each material can be in several libraries at once.

Professional users of 3D Studio often develop multiple library files for their work, each with some overlap of content. 3D Studio comes with only one large library of files (the file 3DS.MLI), which is loaded automatically at startup. Over time, animators should develop their own libraries, with names like WOODS, MARBLES, CLOUDS, FAVORITE, BIZARRE, and GLASS. In this way, they can keep track of all the useful work included in previous projects, and not continually have to re-create each material.

With the library pull-down menu, you can load, save, merge, and delete your MLI files, each filled with any number of materials. To move only specific materials between libraries, you must load them temporarily into the Materials Editor, and then save them into a different library.

Figure 4.33

*The Library pull-
down menu options.*

A *material definition* contains the information describing how that one material will render. Maple, Red Metal, and Glass are examples of material definitions. A *materials library* is a file that contains groups of these material definitions. Materials libraries are tools for the animator to collect and organize useful materials as they are created or altered.

Anytime a new library is required, the Library/New command in the Materials Editor erases all the existing materials. This enables you to save materials currently in the Materials Editor to a new, empty library. Materials libraries do not automatically save the changes made to them, however. You always must save the materials libraries you have edited or added to by choosing the Save Library option on the Library menu in the Materials Editor.

Materials

Use the Materials pull-down menu (see fig. 4.34) to transfer materials into and out of scenes and libraries. The Get, Put, and Remove Material options deal with the currently loaded library, whereas the Get from Scene and Put to Scene options act on materials present in a loaded scene. 3D Studio always stores, in a mesh file with the 3DS file, all the materials definitions you are using. If you delete from a scene all objects that have a particular material, the Materials menu's Get from Scene option will no longer list that material. After you get a material from the active scene and edit it in the Materials Editor, you must use the Put to Scene option to update the new, edited version of the material in the scene. Use the Put to Current option to make the selected material the active material for future Material/Assign operations in the 3D Editor.

Figure 4.34

*The Material pull-
down menu.*

Options

The Options pull-down menu provides not only several settings for sample renders done in the Materials Editor, but also two utilities for working with images: View File Alpha and View Last Image (see fig. 4.35).

As you might recall, the Antialias option smoothes the pixelated, jagged edges of the sample rendered. With Antialias active, the rendering of the sample sphere or cube slows down somewhat.

The Backlight option activates a light behind the sample object, in addition to the always-present light in front and to the right of the sample object. This option can be useful when you are adjusting the shininess and bumpiness of a material, particularly in the case of metallic materials.

The Video Color Check option helps you tone down colors that are rendering too bright, by exposing colors that are over the limits of official television standards. 3D Studio is capable of creating too-intensive colors that cause problems when broadcast. When this option is active, the too-intense colors are shaded black.

Figure 4.35

The Options pull-down menu.

The View File Alpha option is useful while you use textures with masks. With this option, you can confirm that this usually invisible data is what you think it is.

View Last Image is useful for people with a single-monitor rendering system. By using this option to redisplay the last rendering of a scene made in the 3D Editor or the Keyframer, you have a reminder of the changes you need to make in materials.

The Control Panel

To change any frequently used settings, use the Control Panel—the boxed-in area at the far right of the Materials Editor screen (see fig. 4.36).

Figure 4.36

*The Control Panel
switches.*

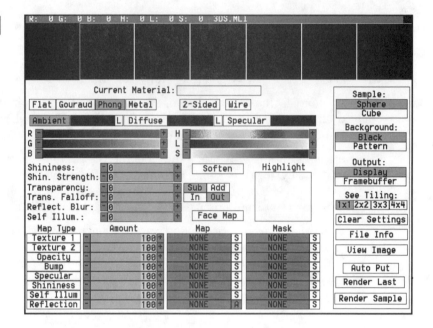

Descriptions of the switches follow:

- **Sample: Sphere or Cube.** Selects the type of sample object to be rendered in the seven mini windows at the top of the screen. Often, you'll render the sphere, then the cube, to check the appearance of both so that you have an idea of what the material will look like in the scene.

- **Background: Black or Pattern.** Use Pattern whenever transparency is part of a material. Otherwise, this switch usually is left set to Black.

- **Output: Display and/or Framebuffer.** If you have a *framebuffer* (an NTSC or PAL video-output hardware card) configured for 3D Studio's rendered output, you can render the sample squares to your workstation screen, your framebuffer, or both. If you have no framebuffer, only the Display button appears on-screen.

- **See Tiling: 1×1, 2×2, 3×3 or 4×4.** If a texture map is being used, this switch lets you see what the repeated bitmap looks like. Usually, you use this switch to study a texture map designed to tile without seams, and to confirm that it will cover larger areas effectively without revealing the bitmap's smaller size. See Tiling only affects the sample renders; it has no effect on the way the material is applied to objects in the scene.

- **Clear Settings.** This switch zeros or blanks out every Materials Editor setting for the active material slot.

- **File Info.** This button is both a switch and a drop point.

  To use it as a button: If you click on the File Info button, a file-selector dialog box is displayed (see fig. 4.37). When you select an image file in this dialog box, that file's statistics are revealed in a second dialog box.

  To use it as a drop point: You can press and hold the mouse cursor over the name of a texture map file displayed anywhere in the Materials Editor, drag the ghosted rectangle shape over the File Info button (see fig. 4.38), and release the mouse button to reveal that file's statistics (see fig. 4.39). This action is called a *drag and drop*. Analyzing the active textures is useful for dissecting complex materials from other animators.

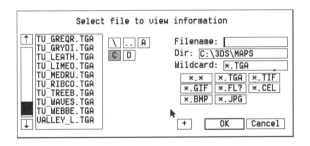

Figure 4.37

The file-selector dialog box for viewing information about an image.

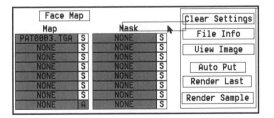

Figure 4.38

The drag-and-drop operation in mid-motion. The image file PAT0003.TGA is being dragged to the File Info button.

Figure 4.39

The Image File Information screen that describes this particular file. Note that Targa files contain comments, which are listed at the bottom of the dialog box.

```
                    Image File Information
        File: TU_TREEB.TGA          Type: TARGA 24 Compressed
                    Path:      .   C:\3DS\MAPS
            Date: 04/09/1995    Time: 00:57:32   Size:  74852
   Width: 190  Height: 130    Aspect Ratio: 1.0000 Gamma: 1.7990 Frames:   1
                        Comments:
    This is a quarter size sample image from the Organics directory of
    Autodesk's Texture Universe CD-ROM.


                       [    OK    ]
```

- **View Image.** This button works identically to the File Info button, except that instead of listing the statistics, it displays the image. For a quick check of any image you are working with, simply drag-and-drop it to the View Image button. Note that all images being used in the Materials Editor must be in one of the map paths, but the View Image button, when used as a button, enables you to view any image.

- **Auto Put.** The Auto Put button causes your edited version of a material to assign automatically to the faces in your scene that had the original material. A material must be put to a scene after it is edited for the changes to be effective. Auto Put only updates those materials that have the same name as the active material.

- **Render Last.** Render Last rerenders the last view rendered in the 3D Editor or Keyframer. This enables you to view your material changes as they are applied to your actual scene. The Auto Put button is left on while using the Render Last button, to force each edited material to be updated during the Render Last operation.

CAUTION

> The original material used in a scene is lost when you replace it with the edited version, unless the original material was saved in a library. To avoid losing an unsaved original material, you can leave it unedited in one of the materials slots. Then, using the drag-and-drop technique with the mouse, pick up the active render slot from the seven slots at the top of the screen, and drop it on an unused slot. This copies the material to the new material slot. Then, if a Render Last operation reveals that the edits made were not an improvement, the original copy can be put back.

- **Render Sample.** Use this button constantly to check the results of each edit. The render window will not rerender to reveal the changes you've made until you click on the Render Sample button. The spacebar is the key equivalent for this operation. You frequently will use the Render Sample button to keep the rendered sample object current with the changes you make.

This exercise shows you how to use the Control Panel and how to copy a material among the seven materials slots in the Materials Editor. The exercise starts with 3D Studio as it is when first loaded.

Copying Materials

To bring up the Materials Editor, press F5

Displays the Materials Editor with all seven slots black

Choose Materials/Get Material from the menu at the top of the screen

Displays the Get Material dialog box, which contains a list of materials (see fig. 4.40). These materials are included in 3D Studio's default library (3DS.MLI)

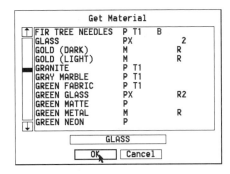

```
                Get Material
 [↑] FIR TREE NEEDLES  P T1    B
     GLASS             PX           2
     GOLD (DARK)       M         R
     GOLD (LIGHT)      M         R
     GRANITE           P T1
     GRAY MARBLE       P T1
     GREEN FABRIC      P T1
     GREEN GLASS       PX          R2
     GREEN MATTE       P
     GREEN METAL       M         R
 [↓] GREEN NEON        P

              [    GLASS    ]
         [  OK  ] [ Cancel ]
```

Figure 4.40

The Get Material option displays a list of all materials in the current library, sorted alphabetically.

Using the scroll bar at the right of the sorted list, find GLASS. Click on GLASS to highlight it, and click on OK in the dialog box

The dialog box disappears, and the active glass render slot begins rendering the texture

Note the nonzero transparency slider. Also note that the 2-sided option is selected. The sphere object in the window has highlights at the upper left and inside the sphere, in its lower right.

In the Control Panel, click on the Cube button

Turns off the Sphere button, and turns on the Cube button

Press the spacebar

Rerenders the material, this time in the shape of a cube (see fig. 4.41)

continues

continued

Figure 4.41

Using a cube as the render sample object.

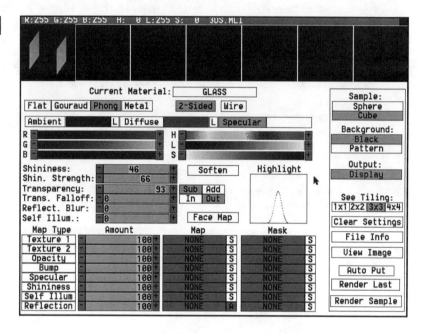

In the Control Panel, click on the Pattern button (under Background).

Press the spacebar	Rerenders the material, this time with a checkered background showing through the glass in some areas (see fig. 4.42)

The Pattern switch is useful when you want to see how an object's transparency will affect the appearance of objects seen through it. In this case, the glass material is so transparent that you see it largely because of the specular highlights made by the lights. Because cube objects do not generate well-defined specular highlights, the glass cube appears nearly transparent.

Figure 4.42

Checking transparency by using a background pattern in the sample render.

Click on the Sphere button	Turns off the Cube button, and turns on the Sphere button
Press the spacebar	Rerenders the material; the highlights are visible over the pattern, with the rest of the sphere faintly visible

Click over the rendered glass sphere image and hold down the mouse button. Drag the square outline that appears to the next render box, and release the mouse button

Choose Yes

The Copy Material dialog box appears (see fig. 4.43)

The image copies over, and the new render slot becomes the active slot. Note that the new copy is titled GLASS, just like the original (see. fig. 4.44)

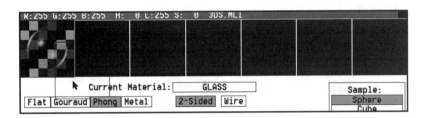

Figure 4.43

After drag-and-drop copying a material, a dialog box appears to confirm the copy.

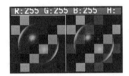

Figure 4.44

After you release the mouse button, the previously empty slot contains the copied material.

4

Materials from the default library are often a good starting point for new materials. In this case, the clear glass material loaded from the default material library is a good starting point for making a violet glass, which is the purpose of the next exercise.

As discussed earlier, the Ambient color swatch defines the shade of the object areas that are not directly lit (areas in shadow). With ambient light set to solid white, the sample render reveals that the contribution is small; the black object renders as a dark gray disk (see fig. 4.45).

The diffuse color is the primary solid color of the material. With a white diffuse and ambient color, the sphere looks like a sphere, with its dark areas somewhat illuminated (see fig. 4.46).

The specular swatch affects the material only when the Shininess and Shininess Strength sliders are set above zero. The specular color appears where the light sources cause highlights on a shiny surface (see fig. 4.47).

Figure 4.45

With Ambient set to white, and Diffuse and Specular set to black, the object renders as a dark gray disk.

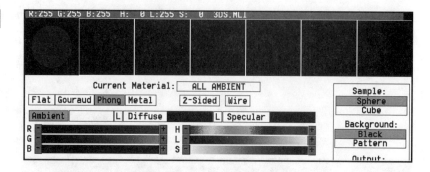

Figure 4.46

With Ambient and Diffuse both set to white, the sphere has some dimension.

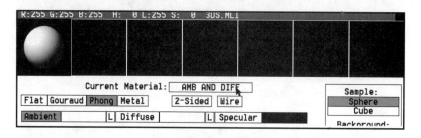

Figure 4.47

A black sphere with shininess and a white specular color renders like a black plastic object.

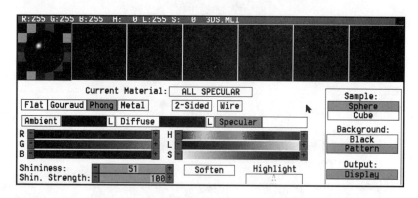

The existing glass is 93 percent transparent, as the transparency slider indicates, and is thus 7 percent opaque, as shown in figure 4.48. The Ambient, Diffuse, and Specular color swatches affect the glass, even though it is largely transparent. The specular color is the highlight color that appears on the shiny object. The ambient color describes the shaded areas of a material. The diffuse color, the main color of the object when illuminated, is usually the predominant color of the texture. If the glass material has a diffuse color of violet, it will appear as violet glass, as you will see in the following exercise.

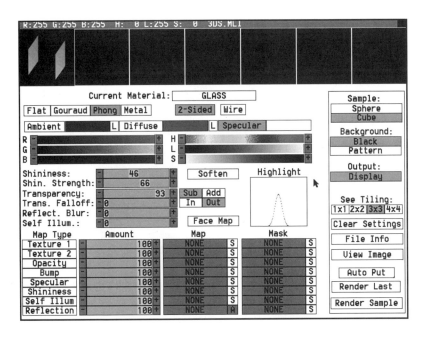

Figure 4.48

*Viewing the
transparency
percentages of the
glass.*

In this exercise, you will start with the existing GLASS texture supplied
with 3D Studio and alter the settings to create a purple-tinted glass. This
exercise picks up where the last exercise ended, with the GLASS material
loaded into one of the seven materials slots in the Materials Editor.

Editing Existing Materials

To adjust the diffuse color, first activate the diffuse swatch by clicking on the Diffuse button or the swatch next to it	Activates the Diffuse button
Adjust the Lightness slider (with an "L" to the left of the slider) to mid-range. Adjust the Saturation slider to fully up, at the far right	The color in the Diffuse swatch is bright violet

The HLS and RGB sliders are adjusted by either clicking in the color range sliders, or by
using the + and - buttons at the right and left of each slider.

There are two sets of color controls. One uses red, green, and blue (RGB); the other, hue,
lightness, and saturation (HLS). Note that adjusting the sliders on one side causes the

continues

continued

other side to readjust automatically to its recipe for the same color. Different animators often are more comfortable editing colors with one system rather than the other. Also, you might want to switch between the two color models for different tasks. The RGB model, for example, enables you to easily make a color warmer by adding red with the R slider. The HLS model, on the other hand, enables you to easily change the overall brightness of a color with the L slider.

Adjust the Hue slider to its violet area	The color swatch changes hue as the slider is moved
Press the spacebar to see the results of the editing	Rerenders the sample object in the active material slot; few changes are apparent because the object is so transparent that the added color intensity is barely noticeable (see fig. 4.49)
Reduce the transparency by adjusting the transparency slider down to a setting of 50. Press the spacebar to rerender	The sphere appears less transparent, but is tinted purple (see fig. 4.50)

Next, you make the center of the sphere more transparent than the edges by making the transparency fall off as the object's surface curves away from the camera. This gives the edges the deeper color you need, but keeps them fairly transparent in areas that are flat to the viewer's point of view. IN-type falloff causes the sphere's center to be more transparent, and the transparency falloff slider adjusts the strength of the effect. The OUT mode of falloff causes the sphere's center to be more opaque, and the edges to be more transparent.

To the right of the Trans. Fallout slider are two buttons for selecting In- or Out-facing normals for transparency to fall off across.

Adjust the Trans. Falloff slider to 90, then click on the IN button to make the center of the sphere more transparent, and press the spacebar	Rerenders the sphere

The sphere now has deep purple edges and a clear, slightly violet-tinted center area (see fig. 4.51).

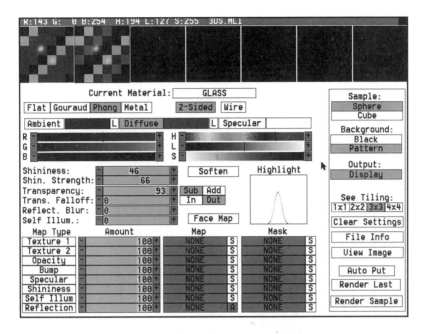

Figure 4.49

Although the diffuse color is now violet, the sphere is still so transparent that it renders clear.

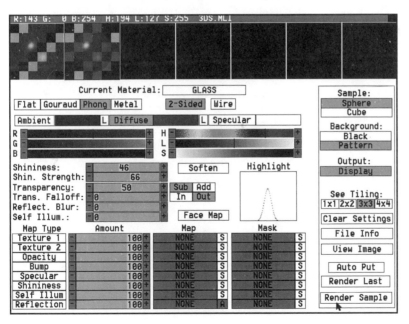

Figure 4.50

Now, with transparency reduced to 50, the tinting is more evident.

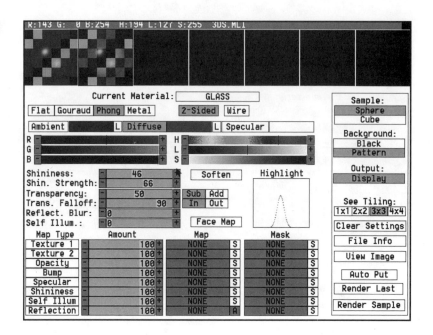

Figure 4.51

The purple glass is now especially evident in the sample sphere's edges, but the middle of the sphere is very transparent.

When the material you create is useful for future work, you should save it in a library. In the following exercise, you will create a new, empty library and place some materials into it.

DESIGN TIP

To remember how to use transparency falloff, just think of IN as meaning *transparent inside*, and OUT as meaning *transparent outside* edges. This effect is only as strong as the value to which you set the Transparency Falloff slider.

In the following exercise, you will create a new library and save the two glass materials in the new library. This library then will be saved as GLASS.MLI, for future additions of other useful glassy or transparent materials.

Working with Libraries

You will put the new material in a new library, called GLASS.MLI.

Create a new, empty library by choosing Library/New from the menu at the top of the Materials Editor screen	Displays a Remove all materials dialog box (see fig. 4.52)

Figure 4.52

Clearing out all the existing materials in order to begin a new library.

Click OK   The dialog box disappears

The loaded library contains no materials because the New command cleared it out. To start your GLASS materials library, you can save to the empty library the two materials currently held in the Materials Editor.

To save the texture, click the   Displays the Put Material dialog box
Put Material option in the Material   (see fig. 4.53); any existing materials
pull-down menu   in the current library are listed, and the
                                           name of the material to be added to the
                                           library is highlighted at the bottom

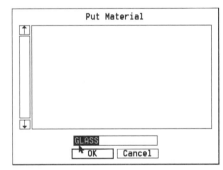

Figure 4.53

Adding a material to the empty list.

You need to change this material from GLASS to PURPLE GLASS.

Type **PURPLE GLASS**   Displays the typed name at the bottom of
                                           the dialog box

Click on OK to approve adding this   The dialog box disappears
material to the current library

Click on the original GLASS material's   Activates the selected window (indicated
sample render window to activate   by a white box around it) and all setting
the old material   in the material parameters area change
                                           to the original GLASS settings

continues

continued

To save this material to the library also, type **P** for the Put Material option in the Material pull-down menu

Displays the Put Material dialog box, this time with the PURPLE GLASS material listed in the main area and GLASS, the name of the current material, displayed in the slot at the bottom (see fig. 4.54)

Note that all menu commands with a hot key equivalent display the hot key to the right of the command name. Typing P is the same as using the Put Material option in the Material pull-down menu.

Figure 4.54

Adding the clear glass to the glass materials library.

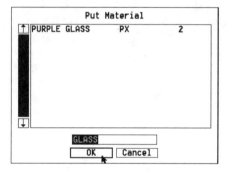

To more clearly differentiate this material from other glass materials you may add to the library later, type **CLEAR GLASS.**

Click on OK to approve adding the new material

The dialog box disappears

To confirm that the current, unnamed library contains the two added materials, try to retrieve one of them.

Click on Get Material in the Material menu

Displays the Get Material dialog box, with its a list of currently available materials: CLEAR GLASS and PURPLE GLASS (see fig. 4.55)

Click on Cancel

The dialog box disappears

To save the library, click on Save Library in the Library pull-down menu

Displays a dialog box in which you select a filename for the material you want to save (see fig. 4.56)

Type glass, and click on OK

The dialog box disappears as the library is saved

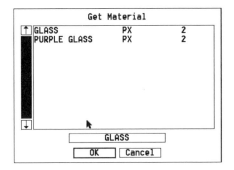

Figure 4.55

Using Get Material to survey the current library's available materials.

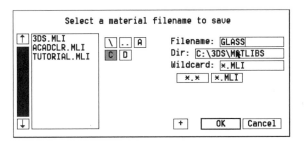

Figure 4.56

Saving the new library as GLASS.MLI.

CAUTION

Alterations to any library are not saved to the hard disk unless you save them by using the Save Library command in the Library pull-down menu.

Materials libraries are an important tool to using 3D Studio efficiently. As the preceding exercise illustrated, moving textures from library to library and creating new libraries is a simple, quick task.

Now that the basic operations and uses of the Materials Editor are better understood, some of the more specific sliders and variables can be applied.

Special Materials Attributes

Materials can be rendered in nonstandard ways for special effects or to serve a unique purpose. The following sections discuss wireframe, 2-sided, and self-illuminated materials. Wireframe materials render only the edges of the faces that make up an object, for a rendered appearance very similar to what is seen in the 3D Editors viewports. The 2-Sided option causes all faces to render, regardless of the direction of their normals, which is useful for glass and other objects where the back side of an object can be seen from its front. The Self Illumination setting causes an object to appear to be lit from within by a variable amount. This often is used to create neon effects, or to cause an object to have a minimum brightness.

Wireframe and Two-Sided Materials

In the last chapter, the one-sided nature of 3D Studio's objects became apparent during the use of the VIEW IPAS. As you rotated a flat modeled object, it was apparent that 3D Studio was taking into account only one side of the object. Although the VIEW.PXP program always displays faces as one-sided, it is possible to have materials that render from both sides, such as the glass material you just used. For a given object, the 2-sided option usually takes twice as long to render. Two-sided materials might be used on objects where the back faces of the object are visible due to transparent materials, or due to an opening in the objects mesh.

You also might recall that although all objects are made up of triangular faces, each face edge can be made visible or invisible. Edge visibility usually is altered while modeling, for the sake of clarity. In some cases, however, you can render only the active edges—a useful modeling approach or an interesting effect. Rendered in wireframe mode, a modeled dome shape can resemble a bird cage, or a gridded plane can be used as a fence.

The Wireframe button, when activated, brings up a dialog box that enables you to turn on the wireframe attribute. This dialog box also contains two important settings: Pixels/Units and Thickness:

- **Pixels/Units.** Chooses whether the thickness setting applied to the wireframe will be in an absolute pixel width, or in 3D Editor units. When Pixels mode is used, a wireframe objects lines will appear at the same width when rendered, regardless of their proximity to the camera. When Units mode is used, the edges will appear to have a physical size, and will render with perspective.

- **Thickness.** The thickness entry enables you to set the number of pixels or units wide at which the edges are to render. This number can be a fractional value in either mode.

The following exercise explores two-sided rendering and wireframe mode rendering.

2-Sided and Wireframe Attributes

Activate one of the seven slots in the Materials Editor by clicking on one of the render sample areas.

In the Control Panel, click on the Clear Settings button to blank out all the variables for the active material slot	Changes all nonzero settings to zero
Click in the Diffuse swatch and maximize the R slider in the RGB slider group	Changes the diffuse swatch color to a bright red

Use the drag-and-drop procedure to copy the color in the Diffuse swatch area to the Specular area:

While the mouse cursor is over the color, click and hold the left mouse button over the diffuse color swatch	On the screen, a rectangle representing the diffuse color follows the mouse cursor (see fig. 4.57)
Release the mouse button when the rectangle shape is over the Specular color swatch	Now the Specular color also is bright red
Raise the value in the Lightness slider	Changes the Specular swatch color from bright red to a pinkish off-white (see fig. 4.58)

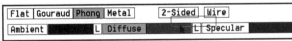
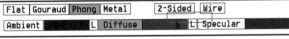

Figure 4.57

Copying the diffuse color to the Specular swatch.

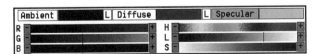

Figure 4.58

Lightening the Specular color from the bright red just copied from the Ambient swatch.

continues

continued

Press the spacebar to render the material   Renders a dull red sphere

Without shininess, Phong highlights are not visible on the sphere.

Adjust the Shininess slider to 70 and the Shininess Strength slider to 90

The Highlight window displays a spike that changes shape while you adjust shininess

Press the spacebar to render the material

Now the sphere has a highlight on one side (see fig. 4.59)

Figure 4.59

Red sphere with bright highlight.

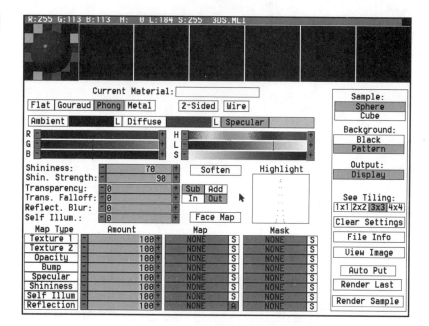

Activate the backlight option in the Options pull-down menu (see fig. 4.60), and hit the space bar again

The sphere re-renders with two highlights, one from the usual front light, and the other from the back light. See figure 4.61

Click on the Wire button

Displays the Wire Frame Mode dialog box so that you can set the wireframe parameters (see fig. 4.62)

Figure 4.60

*Activating the
Backlight option.*

Figure 4.61

*The rendered red
plastic sphere, with a
front light and a back
light.*

```
         Wire Frame Mode

    Thickness: 0.0

         in:  Pixels  Units

    Wire Frame:   On   Off
         OK       Cancel
```

Figure 4.62

*The Wire Frame Mode
dialog box.*

4

In this dialog box, the On switch must be set to activate a wire frame mode material.

Click over the On button to activate the   Activates the wireframe mode
wireframe button

In the thickness slot, type **1.0**, and then click the Pixels button and the On button. The
Wireframe dialog box disappears. Click OK.

Press the spacebar to rerender   The sphere is now made of a one-pixel-
                                        wide wireframe material (see fig. 4.63).
                                        Note that none of the lines visible in the
                                        rendering represent the back of the
                                        sphere

Click on the 2-Sided button to   Renders the sphere with both front
activate two-sided mode. Press the   and back wires visible (see fig. 4.64)
spacebar again to rerender

Figure 4.63

*Red plastic wire
grid material
renders with only
the front wires
visible.*

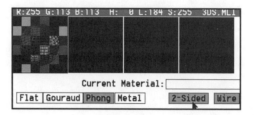

Figure 4.64

*Two-sided
wireframe material.*

In wireframe mode, only the visible edges render with wires present;
hidden edges are invisible as always. Whatever edges are displayed in the
viewports of the 3D Editor are good indicators of what that object will look
like with a wireframe material. Notice that even the sample sphere has
square-shaped holes in it, although it is made of triangular faces (as is
any 3D Studio object).

CAUTION

> If the Units or Pixels setting is too high in the Wire Frame Mode
> dialog box, the holes between the wires will close up, and the sphere
> will not look like a wireframe object at all.

In wireframe mode, use the Pixels setting for objects when no apparent
perspective is necessary, or when an object is likely to recede from the
camera's vantage point to such an extent that the wires would be too thin
to render. Use the Units setting to imply perspective, where the closer the
object is to the camera, the thicker the wires of the wireframe object.

Self-Illumination

Self-illumination is another materials attribute that can be useful in
certain cases. Instead of being on or off like 2-Sided or Wire Frame mode,
it is adjusted as a variable amount (although in release 2 it was simply an
on/off switch). Self-illumination is used to make an object appear to be lit
from within, like a neon tube or a street sign.

Self-illumination sets a minimum amount of light that all faces with the
self-illuminated material automatically receive. This is similar to, but
independent of, the ambient-light setting for a scene. Thus, an object with
a material that has self-illumination set fully on will render as though it
is glowing from within.

To the extent that an object is self-illuminated, it will not receive shadows or exhibit shading. For this reason, self-illuminated objects will seem to have less depth, for the same reason that scenes with high ambient-light values have less depth; with a minimum level of light forced on all sides of an object, an object's contrast will diminish.

In the following exercise, self-illumination is applied in stages to the sample sphere to show its effect.

Applying Self-Illumination

This exercise starts with an empty Materials Editor and creates a new material that is similar to a neon green. Before beginning to create a new material, the settings for the active materials slot can be cleared out with the Clear Settings button in the Control Panel.

Select a materials slot and click on the Clear Settings button in the Control Panel	Changes all settings to zero

Now you are going to create a green plastic material.

Select the Diffuse swatch, and raise the value in the G slider in the RGB color sliders group	Changes the Diffuse swatch to green
Use the drag-and-drop procedure to copy the green Diffuse swatch to the Ambient swatch	Changes Ambient swatch to the same shade of green as the Diffuse swatch (see fig. 4.65)
Darken the Ambient to near black by lowering the Lightness slider in the HLS group of color sliders	Changes Ambient to dark, dark green

Figure 4.65

Ambient and Diffuse are the same color after the Diffuse swatch is dragged and dropped into the Ambient swatch.

continues

continued

Select the Specular swatch and set it to white by raising the Lightness slider to maximum	Changes the Specular color to white (see fig. 4.66)
Add a specular highlight by setting the Shininess Strength slider to near maximum	A hump shape appears in the Highlight indicator (see fig. 4.67)
Adjust the Shininess slider to narrow the highlight shape depicted in the Highlight window	Makes a more pointed highlight shape in the Highlight indicator (see fig. 4.68)
Press the spacebar to test render the green plastic sphere	Renders the sphere, with proper highlights and shadow areas (see fig. 4.69)

Figure 4.66

The standard material starting point — a dark ambient value and a white specular value.

Figure 4.67

The Shininess Strength slider brings the highlight indicator peak to its maximum.

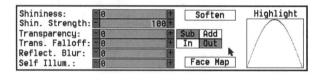

Figure 4.68

The Shininess slider changes the shape of the highlight displayed in the Highlight indicator window from a hump to a spike.

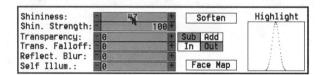

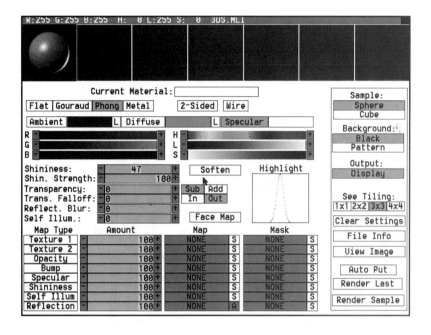

Figure 4.69

*The final green
plastic material.*

4

Self-illumination will cause the diffuse color to glow through the shadow and highlight areas.

Set the Self-illumination slider to 50, and press the spacebar to rerender

The green plastic sphere now seems to be glowing somewhat; some shadows and highlights are still visible (see fig. 4.70)

Maximize the Self-Illumination slider, then rerender the sample

Only a bright green circle with some white highlights is visible (see fig. 4.71)

With full self-illumination there is almost no depth at all, the object appears to be totally two-dimensional. Some uses for self-illumination are to simulate flat, illuminated objects such as an LED light, a TV screen, or a flat object used as a blue sky plane.

Figure 4.70

The Self Illumination slider at midpoint removes much of the darkness in the shadow areas, where the ambient swatch previously set the color.

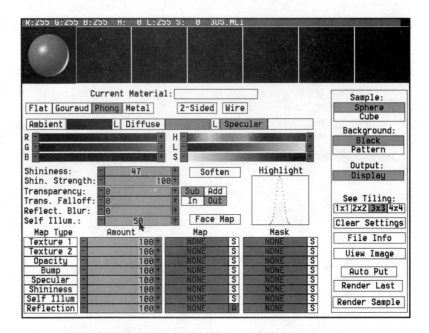

Figure 4.71

The fully self-illuminated material, with no shadow areas.

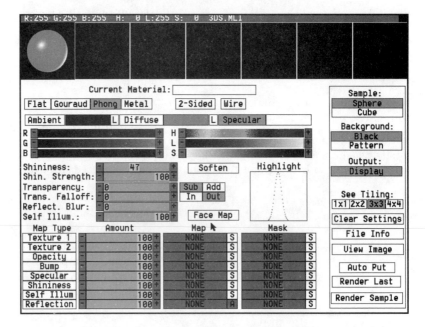

DESIGN
TIP

Although you can achieve a sort of glow effect with self-illumination, a self-illuminated material does not light nearby objects, which ruins the glow effect. Adding an omni light to the scene—just inside or in front of any self-illuminated geometry, adds greatly to the effect. The omni light should have attenuation turned on and the range of the attenuation set a short distance outside the object. Glowing objects also have a sort of aura about them that must be simulated in 3D Studio with an IPAS plug-in image-processing program (as this book is being written, the glow-aura-making plug-ins on the market for 3D Studio are LenZFX, from Digimation and Yost IPAS disk 1, from the Yost Group).

In addition to the uses listed earlier, sometimes self-illumination is applied to trigger certain special effects. Because some of the plug-ins work on only the final rendered image and are triggered by brightness levels, self-illumination can be used to force certain objects to trigger the plug-in. Crossed-twinkling highlights, for example, might be desired on a specific area, and if the twinkles are placed on areas above a certain brightness threshold, the self-illuminated option applied to a material can make certain that the object will be above the needed threshold.

Basic Texture Maps

As mentioned earlier in this chapter, a very powerful addition to materials is its use of images. Applied to an object to define its color, an image map is described as a texture map. Important facts to know about an image map before you apply it as a texture in a material include the images resolution and whether the image is tilable.

Images used as textures should be at an appropriate resolution for their use. A 6×6-pixel image applied as a texture map looks poor if applied to a large object within a scene, because the individual pixels are apparent. However, using extremely high resolution (greater than 640×480 pixels) images for every case is not helpful either. Image maps take a relatively large amount of your workstations precious RAM, so they should be used at a resolution no larger than necessary for the detail level that a rendered image will exhibit.

Images always are loaded into RAM in 24-bit color with no compression, so an image file's size is no indication of the amount of RAM it will use. Some GIF images that consist of large blocks of color may be only a few thousand bytes in file size, for example, due to the GIF formats internal compression and the fact that GIFs are paletted (8-bit color). That same GIF image requires nearly 1 MB of RAM if it is a 640×480 image. To calculate an images relative RAM requirements, multiply the width times the height, times three. In the example used here, this would be 640×480×3, or 921,600 bytes. Clearly, if you are limited on RAM, you can avoid disk swapping and speed your rendering by resizing needlessly large images.

Another important factor with any image used is its tilability. Many texture maps are designed to emulate repeating but varying patterns, such as wood, cloth, and marble. In order to save on memory requirements, many textures are designed carefully to appear natural and seamless when tiled to themselves. These sorts of textures are invaluable when creating materials for a brick wall, for example. A detailed brick texture to cover the entire wall would require a large amount of RAM. However, a well-designed tilable texture of only a few bricks could appear just as effective and use little RAM. Excellent tilable textures are included on 3D Studios world-creating toolkit CD-ROM, and on the CD-ROM that comes with this book.

Adding Texture Maps

In 3D Studio, the Materials Editor contains two positions at the lower left of the display under the Map Type label, listed as Texture 1 and Texture 2. Each of these contains an Amount slider, a Map indicator, and a Mask indicator. Clicking on the area below the Map label brings up a dialog box that enables you to select any valid image file for use as a texture map. Initially, the Map slots display NONE, but after selecting a texture map image file, the file name appears in the map area (see fig. 4.72). If the file type selected for the texture map is one of the animated file types (IFL or FL*), the texture changes over time.

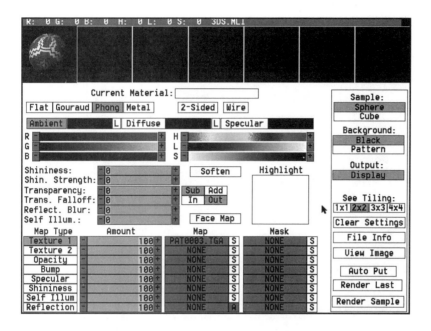

Figure 4.72

The image file PAT0003.TGA is applied to the Texture 1 map slot in this example.

After an image is selected, it appears in the Map slot. The Amount slider causes the Map color to override the diffuse color of the object as it is increased from 0 to 100. At 100, the diffuse color is covered totally by the texture map. Similarly, the Texture 2 map covers the Texture 1 map to the extent of the Texture 2 Amount slider. When a texture map is applied to Texture 1 or Texture 2, the button under Map Type turns red, indicating that the map is in use. You can click the Texture 1 and Texture 2 buttons to turn them off temporarily for experimentation.

Texture Map Options

After a texture map is applied, it can be modified in many ways by clicking the S setup button that appears to the right of the Map slot. When the setup button is activated, a Mapping Parameters dialog box appears, as shown in figure 4.73.

4

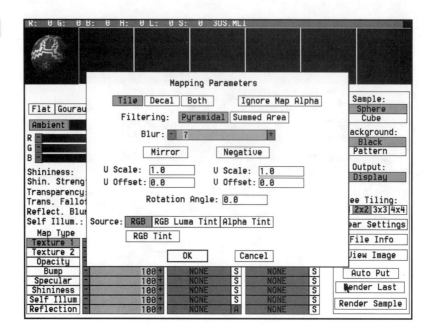

Figure 4.73

The Mapping Parameters dialog box.

This dialog box enables several options for the map, including the following:

- **Tile/Decal/Both.** Enables you to select whether the map appears once or tiles repeatedly. The Decal option also includes transparency, where it enables the diffuse or Texture 1 colors to show. This transparency is based on the color of the upper left pixel in the image. Whatever this color is, in decal mode, all pixels with this color are transparent. With Both active, the texture tiles and includes transparency.

  - Ignore Map Alpha

  - Filtering

  - Blur

  - Mirror

  - Negative

  - Scale

  - Offset

  - Rotation

  - Source

Ten Tips for Better Lighting

Lighting your 3D scenes is a skill that improves as you progress with 3D Studio. The following list presents some useful rules of thumb for most lighting situations.

1. Think of omni lights without falloff as a sun.

   As you apply multiple omni lights to brighten up areas of interest...

2. Don't saturate!

   Total up non-falloff light intensities should be less than 350 or so.

3. Limit the number of unattenuated lights. Three or so is plenty.

4. Limit the number of shadow-casting spotlights.

   Use only one or, at most, two shadow-casting lights in most situations; additional spots wash out shadows anyway.

5. Spotlights only stop if they cast shadows otherwise just like a constrained-area omni.

6. Touch up final lighting with exclusions. Use to fix final problems by lighting only problem objects.

7. Simulate light reflection with attenuated omni lights. Use high attenuated omni lights to simulate radiosity effects.

8. Use dim-colored lights to enhance metallic objects. Use low intensity, deeply colored lights to get interesting glints on metal objects.

9. Start with low ambient light levels near zero. Increase to bring out shadow detail after setting other light parameters.

10. Use several lights to enhance glass effect. To get lots of glints on glass surfaces, add lots of lights.

4

Summary

This chapter taught you the final stages of preparation before you can render a scene. Cameras and lights were positioned for a realistic look to the scene. Materials were added through the use of the Materials Editor. You learned how to apply and edit materials on different objects. The next chapter takes all of your scene preparation into the exciting realm of animation.

Animation is one of the most exciting and interesting parts of 3D Studio. There are many concepts and features to learn to help you produce crisp, clean, and exciting animations. This chapter deals with the basic issues, terminology, and methods necessary to generate simple animations. In particular, this chapter covers the following topics:

- The basics of animation

- Interpreting time

- The basics of the Keyframer

- Keys and keyframes

- Placing keys

- Previewing animations

- Rendering animations

- Basic animation rendering options

Directing the Show: Action!

N ow that you have learned a little about 3D Studio and how it works, it is time to take a closer look at one of the most important features of 3D Studio: animation. Animation is simply giving motion to objects over time. When, how, and where the motion occurs in the animation is completely up to you.

This chapter is an introductory chapter. If you feel you already know this information, Chapters 9 and 10, "Advanced Animation Techniques" and "Advanced Keyframing Techniques," cover advanced animation and advanced keyframing.

The Basics of Animation

Animation is nothing more than an illusion. Remember when you were young and you drew a series of images on different sheets of paper? Then, when you flipped back through the pages, the images seemed to come to life! Animation is the displaying of a series of still frames at a quick enough pace to give the illusion of motion.

3D Studio provides many animation capabilities never before possible without the use of a computer, especially because computer generated animation quality keeps getting better and better each year. Imagine what movies like *Star Wars* would be like with today's animation techniques. All you have to do is look at the *Jurassic Park* dinosaurs or *Casper, The Movie* to see the possibilities. Animation allows us to view scenes never before thought possible. This includes everything from walking through buildings that don't exist yet, to wild adventure rides through the depths of space. What you choose to do with animation is strictly up to you!!

Interpreting Time

The first important aspect to look at when dealing with computer generated animation is how you interpret the concept of time. In the real world, time is a constant; only your perception of time changes. In the animation world, time depends upon how you will play the animation back. Hardware and software limitations greatly affect how fast or slow you can play back an animation.

In general terms, animation is not considered smooth unless it is running at 15 frames or more per second (fps). To ensure absolute smoothness of the animation, 24 fps or greater is generally used. The common number animators have seemed to settle on is 30 fps. Twenty-four fps is still used for recording to motion pictures like *Jurassic Park*. Otherwise, for video tape rendering try to base all of your times on 1 second per 30 frames of animation.

As mentioned earlier, time is highly dependent upon the hardware and software used to play back the animation. 3D Studio provides an internal animation player, but it can only reach about 15 fps on the fastest machines available today. So, always keep in mind how you will be playing back the animation when you think about time.

The Basics of the Keyframer

All of the animation that is created in 3D Studio is created in the Keyframer module. No other module supports animation. The Keyframer provides you with all the tools necessary to create, layout, preview, and render any animations you want to create. The Keyframer also allows you to plug in IPAS routines to help you generate specific or difficult animation tasks.

Layout of the Keyframer

To access the Keyframer, simply choose Program/Keyframer from the
pull-down menus or hit F4. At first glance, the Keyframer, shown in figure
5.1, looks like the 3D Editor, with a couple of noticeable differences. The
most notable differences are the menu and the buttons in the lower right
corner.

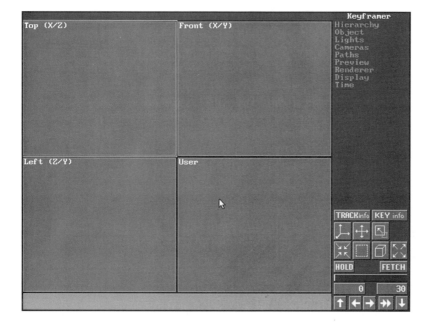

Figure 5.1

*The Keyframer
module.*

All of the pulldowns at the top of the screen are the same as those found
in the 3D Editor. As with the 3D Editor, you can arrange the viewports
on the screen in any way you like by choosing Views/Viewports from the
pulldowns. More important than the pulldowns, however, are the menu
items and buttons. The following describes the menu items and buttons
in detail:

- **Hierarchy.** This menu item allows you to create links between one
  object and another. This is very important for animation topics such as
  character animation (the animating of human motion). Chapter 9,
  "Advanced Animation Techniques," covers this menu in greater detail.

- **Object.** This menu provides you with a set of tools to manipulate
  objects in the Keyframer. Some of the tools include Move, Rotate,
  and Squash. Each of these tools works at an object level.

NOTE

As you will learn through the course of this book, you can create objects that are comprised of smaller elements. In the 3D Editor, you can manipulate objects, elements, faces, and even vertices. When animating, though, everything is dealt with at an object level. You cannot animate individual faces, vertices, or elements unless they are separate objects.

- **Lights.** This menu item allows you to control and animate the lights in the scene over time. Many of the commands found here are the same as those found in the 3D Editor.

- **Cameras.** The camera menu allows you to create animation of cameras. Again, many of the commands here are the same as those found in the 3D Editor.

- **Paths.** All motion in an animation in the Keyframer is based on paths. That is, each and every object that moves follows some sort of motion path. There are many ways to set up these motion paths. This menu allows you to set up and change motion paths in your animation.

- **Preview.** This menu item allows you to create preview animations. These animations are very simple animations that do not show shadows, materials, light, or other special tricks. These animations only show the animation of objects and the camera and are used to help you judge the motion of the animation.

- **Renderer.** This menu is just like the Renderer Menu in the 3D Editor. The only difference here is that this renderer allows you to render animations as well as still frames. Other than that, all the commands are the same.

- **Display.** This menu functions exactly as it does in the 3D Editor.

- **Time.** This menu item allows you to control the time frame that you are working on in the animation. In particular, you can set active segments of the animation to work on or even scale various segments of the animation.

Below the last menu item is a set of buttons, as shown in figure 5.2. Many of these buttons are the same as those found in the 3D Editor. By this point, most of these buttons should begin to look familiar to you. In the Keyframer, however, there are a few new buttons.

Figure 5.2

*The Keyframer
button controls.*

The first two new buttons you will notice are TrackInfo and KeyInfo.
These buttons bring up dialog boxes in which you can control the motion
of objects around their respective keys. (Keys are defined in the next
section.) KeyInfo and TrackInfo are lightly covered in this chapter. For
a more detailed look, refer to Chapter 10, "Advanced Keyframing Techniques."

The buttons to be most concerned about start at the long horizontal button
(red button on the screen) in the lower right corner of the screen and go
down from there. The horizontal button shows you the active segment of
the animation you are working on. Many times it is easier to work on an
animation in segments and piece them together. Clicking on the horizontal button brings up the Define Active Segment dialog box, shown in
figure 5.3. In this dialog box, you can type the start and end frames of the
active segment.

Figure 5.3

5

*The Define Active
Segment dialog box.*

Below the horizontal button are two buttons. The button on the left allows
you to set the current frame. Clicking on this button reveals the Set
Current Frame dialog box, shown in figure 5.4. The right button allows
you to set the total number of frames for the animation. The default
number is 30 frames or one second of animation, so you will generally
always have to change this number. Clicking on this button shows the Set
Number of Frames dialog box, shown in figure 5.5.

Below the frame buttons are another set of buttons. These buttons function like those on a VCR or tape deck. They are play buttons. The first
button on the left is an up arrow button. This takes the animation back
to the first frame. The next button is a left arrow button. This takes the

animation back one frame. The right arrow button takes the animation forward one frame. The double arrow button plays the animation back. When you choose this option, the active viewport takes over the screen and the animation is played back in Box Mode. (See the section on Preview for more about Box Mode.) The last button is a down arrow button. This button takes you to the end of the animation.

Figure 5.4

The Go To Frame dialog box.

Figure 5.5

The Set Number of Frames dialog box.

The last new feature of the Keyframer module is the time line. If you move the mouse to the bottom of the screen below the viewports, you will see a time line appear as in figure 5.6. This time line allows you to set the current frame. By clicking and dragging up and down the time line, you can also preview the animation in Box Mode. This is helpful because you can control the speed of the preview by how fast you move the mouse.

Figure 5.6

The Keyframer time line.

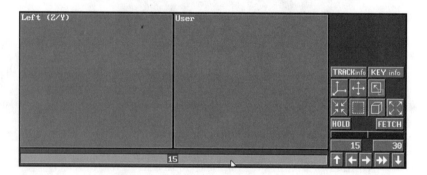

Keys and Keyframes

Now that you have been properly introduced to the Keyframer, it is time to look at how you actually create an animation in the Keyframer.

Animation is generated in the Keyframer by setting keys in specific frames. The motion between keys is then interpreted by the system. Say, for example, you have a block that you want to have move two feet in one second. To do this with keys, you simply set the current frame to 0, then place the block where you want it at frame 0. Next, set the current frame to 30 and place the block where you want it in frame 30. This sets a key in frame 0 and frame 30. When the animation is played back, the block will move from one key to the next with a consistent motion.

Frames 0 and 30 in the example are important frames. These frames are sometimes referred to as keyframes, or more simply as keys. The correct terminology is that frame 0 and frame 30 are keyframes because they have keys placed in them. A key is placed in an object to define a specific place or motion in the animation for the object in the keyframe. A key is a marker where and when animation is to occur in an object. Animation is then interpreted between keys. So, keys are at an object level and keyframes are at a frame level. A keyframe can have as many keys as you want in it.

Placing Keys

Placing keys is a simple process. All objects have a key in them at frame 0. So, when you switch to the Keyframer, it is generally set to a current frame of 0. If an object has a key applied to it, it turns white. Otherwise, the object will be black in the Keyframer. You can see this if you draw any object in the 3D Editor. Then switch to the Keyframer. It will still be white at frame 0. Then set the current frame to any frame other than 0. The object will turn black, telling you it does not have any key assigned in that frame.

There are several types of keys that you can place in objects, cameras, and lights. You can place Position, Scale, Rotation, Morph, and Hide keys. Position keys deal with the location of the object. Scale deals with the scale of the object. Rotation deals with how the object rotates, Morph deals with morphing options for the object, and finally, Hide deals with when the object is visible and when it is not.

5

Placing Keys in Objects

Placing a key in an object is very simple. Simply set the current frame to the frame you want the key to occur in. Then move, rotate, squash, or whatever you want the object to do. When you complete the command, the object will have a key assigned to it and the object will turn white.

The following exercise will step you through the process of creating a couple of keyframes in an object. In particular, the object will move from one point to another while rotating. Before starting this exercise, switch to the 3D Editor and create a box of about 20 to 30 units in size at 0,0. Then switch back to the Keyframer to start the exercise.

Placing Keys in Objects

Choose Set Number of Frames button	Enables you to set number of frames in the animation
Set length to 60 frames	Defines the length of the animation as 2 seconds
Choose OK	Returns you to the Keyframer
Choose Set Current Frame button	Enables you to set the current frame
Set current frame to 30	Sets the current frame to 30
Choose OK	Returns you to the Keyframer
Choose Object/Move	Enables you to move the object
Click in top viewport	Activates the top viewport
Choose the Object	Selects the object to move
Move the object down about 100 units	Moves object and sets the key

Notice at this point that the object has turned white to indicate a key has been placed in the object.

Choose the Play button in the lower corner of the screen	Plays back the animation

When the animation is playing, you will notice that the time line counts the frames as it plays. Because the top viewport was active when you started playing back the animation, that view of the animation was shown. Notice how the block moves from frames 0 to 30 and then stops for the rest of the animation. Also notice that when the animation passed frame 30, the block flashed white for a second. This indicates to you that a key was placed there. Now for a little more complex motion. From frame 30 to 60 the block will move and rotate.

Right Click	Stops the animation from playing
Set current frame to 60	Sets the current frame
Choose Object/Move	Enables you to move the object
Move the box to the right about 100 units in the top viewport	Moves the box and sets a key
Choose Object/Rotate	Enables you to rotate the object
Select the object in the top viewport	Selects object to rotate

At this point, a small explanation of the rotate command in the Keyframer is necessary. You can rotate the object around any of the three axes. Hitting Tab allows you to change the axis you are rotating around. The status bar at the top of the screen tells you the axis and the degrees of rotation you are applying.

Hit Tab until status bar says Axis: Z	Enables you to rotate the object around its Z-axis
Rotate the object 180 degrees	Rotates the object and places a second key in the object: a rotation key
Choose the play button	Plays back the animation

When you watch the animation playback, you will notice that the block begins to rotate almost immediately. This is not what was intended, is it? The reason this happens is that a rotational key was placed in the object at frame 60. The only other rotational key in the animation is at frame 0 (remember, all objects have a key at frame 0, marking their initial position, rotation, and so on), so the block begins to rotate from frame 0. Inexperienced animators might find that the easiest way to get around the problem of the block rotating from frame 0 to 60 instead of from 30 to 60 is to place a rotational key of 0 degrees at frame 30 to cause the block to stop rotating until it reaches frame 30. But, if you try this, you will find that the block still rotates from frames 0 to 30. So, the only other choice someone with little experience might make is to start over and place the rotational keys correctly. Sound inconvenient? It is, and there is another way to get around it. You can use TrackInfo to adjust the location of the first rotational key. The next part of the exercise will show you how to do this, but refer to Chapter 9, "Advanced Animation Techniques," for a detailed explanation of TrackInfo.

Choose the TrackInfo button	Enables you to use TrackInfo
Choose the box	The TrackInfo dialog box is shown in figure 5.7

continues

continued

Each black dot is representative of a key and is placed on a linear time line.

Choose Move	Enables you to move a key
Choose Dot in Rotation Row, Column 0	Selects rotation key at frame 0
Move key to column 30 and click to set new key position	Moves key to frame 30
Choose OK	Returns you to the Keyframer and implements the changes
Click in top viewport	Activates the viewport
Choose Play button	Plays back the animation

Now, the animation plays back correctly, as stated in the description.

Right Click	Stops the animation
Choose File/Save	Enables you to save the project
Save the file as CH5TUT1.3DS	File will be used in a later exercise

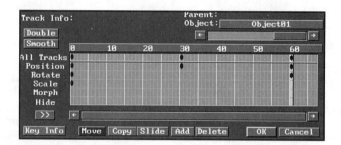

Figure 5.7

The TrackInfo dialog box for this exercise.

You should realize that during this exercise you can place more than one key in a single object in a single keyframe. But, you need to be aware of what types of keys you are placing and where other keys occur. An amateur would have done the exercise as is and would get frustrated because the animation did not come out correctly. Just take your time and think about what you are doing before you do it.

Placing Keys in Lights

Placing keys in lights is as simple as placing keys in objects. You can place keys in the light, or if the light is a spotlight, you can place keys in the light and its target. When you place a key in the light, a small white dot will show up in the light or the target, depending upon which you are animating. Generally, you need to show the cone of the light to be able to see this.

Use the options under the Lights menu to adjust the light. Any option you can adjust under this menu can be animated over time.

Placing Keys in Cameras

Cameras work just like lights. You can place keys in the camera and its target as well as animate camera properties, such as lens length, over time. When you place a key in a camera, a small white dot shows in the center of the icon for the camera and its target. The camera cone needs to be showing to be able to see the key indicators.

As with lights, there is a Camera menu. Any item under this menu can be animated over time.

The Path

The path is a line that is generated between each position key of any object. This path is what the object will follow when it is animated. 3D Studio treats the key positions as vertices of a spline. So, the results of placing several position keys might not result in the motion you would expect.

You can see and adjust the motion path of an object with the tools found under the Paths menu in the Keyframer. These commands allow you to adjust the path or even to import a 3D line as a new path.

The following exercise walks you through the motion path, and how to adjust this path. Some of the topics of this exercise are discussed fully in Chapters 9 and 10, "Advanced Animation Techniques" and "Advanced Keyframing Techniques." These topics will be briefly touched upon here. For this exercise, you need to load the animation from the last exercise. The animation should be saved under CH5TUT1.3DS. Load this file and switch to the Keyframer before beginning this animation.

Working with Motion Paths

Choose Paths/Show-Hide	Enables you to see the motion path for an object with animation
Choose the block	Shows the path for the block. Figure 5.8 shows the motion path for the block

continues

continued

You will notice that a red and yellow line appears on the screen. This is the motion path. Along this line, you will see three white blocks. These are representative of the position keys assigned to the block. Notice that the block is showing on the path and a yellow dot is in the center of the block. This is the current position of the block on the motion path.

The motion path doesn't look quite like you would expect, does it? You probably expected the motion path to be a straight line from one key to the next. Because the line type is a spline (defined in Chapter 7, "Advanced Modeling Techniques") a curve is produced instead of a straight line. For this exercise, the line will be adjusted to be perfectly straight in and out of each key.

Choose Paths/Adjust TCB../Continuity	Enables you to adjust the continuity of a key
Choose the middle key	Selects the key to adjust
Adjust Continuity to 0	Adjusts the continuity. Watch the top of the screen
Click mouse	Accepts new continuity value

Notice how the lines are perfectly straight at this point. That is the effect of continuity around that particular key. Now play back the animation to see how it looks.

Figure 5.8

The Block with its motion path.

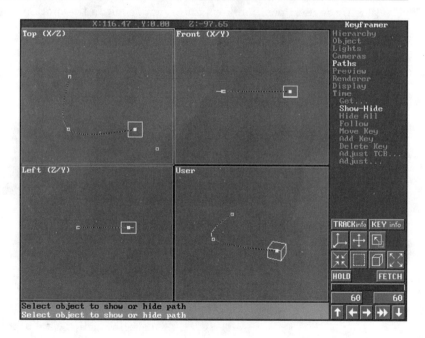

As you can see, you can display and adjust the motion path that is generated from the placement of position keys. This is a very important capability considering that the effect of more and more position keys in an animation can become unpredictable.

Previewing Animations

Now that you have seen the basics of keyframing, there are several things you should know about previewing an animation. Animations take a long time to generate. Nothing is worse than wasting days of rendering time to find out you have an error in the animation. There are several methods of previewing an animation before rendering it. These methods include:

- Box Mode playback
- Fast Preview
- Preview Animations
- Test rendering every *N*th frame

Box Mode Playback

Box Mode playback is where you set the display of geometry to Box Mode. You can do this by choosing Display/Geometry/Box or pressing Alt+B. Box Mode only shows the bounding box or outer extremities of the objects. Thus, the objects redraw very quickly.

When Box Mode is combined with the Play button, you can play back animations at close to 30 fps depending upon your hardware. Because Box Mode playback takes advantage of the current active viewport, you can check the animation from the view of the camera, or any other view on the screen.

Generally, this type of playback is used to check the basic motion of the animation. Some basic collision detection can be done with Box Mode previews, but the bounding boxes prevent you from seeing the details of the geometry, so it is hard to see if two objects are hitting each other when they should not be.

You should utilize Box Mode previewing as much as possible to help reduce the amount of errors in your animation. It is the quickest and easiest way to check animation for errors.

5

Fast Preview

Fast Preview is one of 3D Studio Release 4's new features. In this mode, all the geometry in the scene is rendered in any of four rendering modes that you choose. These modes include wireframe, flat, gouraud, and phong shading modes. No materials or mapping are used in the Fast Preview. Fast Preview only works with camera views.

You can access Fast Preview by first activating the viewport you want to preview and then choosing Program/Camera/Prevu from the pulldown menus or pressing F7. This displays the Fast Preview dialog box shown in figure 5.9. The command only works if your display supports 256 or more colors.

When this command is chosen, 3D Studio loads the geometry into a quick draw buffer and displays one of the four shading modes available, depending upon which mode you choose. Phong shading is the default rendering mode for Fast Preview. A single light is also lighting the scene. This light is a part of the Fast Preview and is constant. The dialog box allows you to set the various parameters of the preview, including shading mode, playback speed, and actually playing the animation in preview mode with the play buttons.

Figure 5.9

The Fast Preview dialog box.

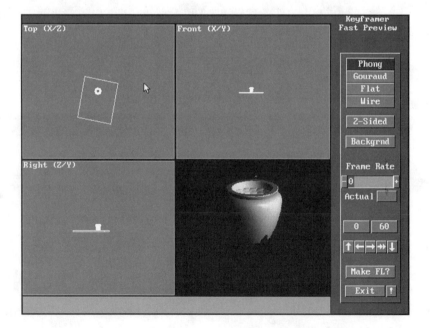

A button of interest in this dialog box is the Make FL? button. Choosing this button enables you to create a Flic of the Fast Preview animation. This Flic then can be played back at a high rate of speed so that you can judge how the animation will look. When you choose the button, the Make Flic Options dialog box is displayed, as shown in figure 5.10.

The Make FLI/FLC dialog box.

In this dialog box, you can set the shading mode, resolution, and file type for the resulting Flic animation. When you choose Render, you are given the option to name the file; then 3D studio will proceed to generate the preview animation.

The following exercise shows you how to create a Fast Preview of the marble vase file with animation. Before starting this exercise, you will need to load the CH5TUT2.3DS file from the included CD.

5

Creating a Fast Preview Animation

Switch to the Keyframer (F4)	Switches to the correct module
Click in Camera Viewport	Activates the Camera viewport
Choose Program/Camera/Prevu	Load the Fast Preview module
Choose Make FL?	Enables you to create a fast preview animation
Choose OK	Accepts the default rendering values
Name the file **CH5TUT2.FLC**	Names the output animation
Choose OK	Accepts file name and 3D Studio begins to generate the animation

The generation of the animation should take less than five minutes. When it is done, you will have a Flic file in the FLICS subdirectory of your 3D Studio directory. Now, to play back the animation:

continues

continued

Choose Exit	Exits the Fast Preview module
Choose Renderer/View/Flic	Enables you to view a Flic
Switch to FLICS Directory	Switches to the directory
Select CH5TUT2.FLC	Loads the file and begins playback

You will notice the quality is not very high, but the animation shows you a lot more than the Box Mode preview mentioned previously.

Preview Animations

Preview Animations can be created by choosing Preview/Make animation. This displays the Make Preview dialog box, shown in figure 5.11.

Figure 5.11

The Make Preview dialog box.

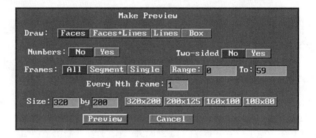

This dialog box allows you to set the various options associated with a preview animation. You can choose to display just faces, faces and lines, just lines, or render the animation in Box Mode. Below these buttons is a helpful option—the Numbers option. This option will place a frame count in the upper right corner of the animation so you can see which frames have errors. To the right of this button is the Two-sided button. Enable this if you would render the final animation in Two-sided mode. The other buttons in the box should look like standard rendering buttons.

Preview Animations are simple shaded animations of the motion of objects. No lights, colors, or materials are applied. All objects are white. This is one of the quicker methods of previewing the animations, but is rather limited in what it can show you.

The following exercise shows you how to create a Preview Animation. Be sure to compare this preview animation with that of the Fast Preview animation from the previous exercise. Before beginning this exercise, load the CH5TUT2.3DS file from the CD and switch to the Keyframer.

Creating a Preview Animation

Choose Preview/Make	Enables you to create a preview animation
Click in Camera01 Viewport	Select view to render
Choose Preview	Accepts the default values
Name the File CH5TUT2A.FLC	Names the file and begins to generate the animation
Choose Renderer/View/Flic	Enables you to play back a Flic
Choose FLICS directory	Switches to correct directory
Choose CH5TUT2A.FLC	Loads the file and begins playing it

As you can see, this preview is a simple flat shaded preview of the object. On large datasets, a preview animation will generate much quicker than a Fast Preview animation.

Test Rendering Every Nth Frame

The last and most accurate method of testing an animation is to actually render parts of the animation. A good way to check is to render every Nth frame of the animation and then check those frames for errors. You should be able to detect any errors if they appear.

You can render every Nth frame by choose Renderer/Render View. This displays the standard Render Animation dialog box shown in figure 5.12 Simply set the Every Nth Frame field to the interval of frames you want to render. For example, if you wanted to render every fifth frame, you would set the value to 5.

Figure 5.12

The Render Animation dialog box for Nth Frame rendering.

Then, just save the file to disk as a Flic file. When the rendering is done, check the Flic file for errors. If there are any errors, fix them and repeat the process.

The following exercise shows you how to create an *N*th frame rendering. Load the CH5TUT2.3DS file and switch to the Keyframer before beginning.

Creating an Nth Frame Rendering

Choose Renderer/Render View	Enables you to render the view
Set Every Nth Frame to 5	Sets rendering to every fifth frame
Choose Disk	Saves the file to disk
Choose Configure	Enables you to configure the renderer
Choose Flic	Selects output file size
Choose 320×200	Selects output resolution
Choose OK	Returns you to Render Animation dialog box
Choose Render	Starts the rendering process
Name file **CH5TUTB.FLI**	Names the output file

The system will render for a while. Depending upon your hardware, it could take between a couple of minutes to an hour or so.

Choose Renderer/View/Flic	Enables you to play back flic files
Choose Images	Switches you to Images subdirectory
Choose CH5TUTB.FLI	Selects file
Choose OK	Starts playback

Compare this animation with the other forms of preview animation. You should be able to see the value of each type.

The other nice advantage of rendering every *N*th frame is that the total rendering time of the animation can be calculated. For example, in the case of rendering every tenth frame, simply take the amount of time necessary to complete that task and multiply it by ten. The resulting time will not be an extremely accurate number, but it will be the most accurate guess on the amount of time to finish the animation that you can get.

Rendering Animations

Rendering animations is the same as rendering a still frame, except for the fact that you are rendering multiple frames to individual files or an animation file. When you choose Renderer/Render View and select a viewport to render, the Render Animation dialog box is displayed (see figure 5.13).

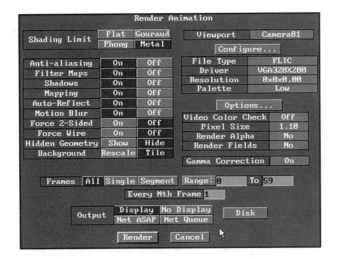

Figure 5.13

The Render Anima-tion dialog box.

The only difference between this dialog box and the Render dialog box in the 3D Editor is the Frames section of the dialog box. Here, you can choose the various ranges of frames that you want to render. You can choose All to render every frame, Single to render the current frame, Segment to render the current active segment, and Range to render a range of frames that you must provide in the key-in fields. Below these buttons, you can choose the interval of frames to render. Otherwise, most everything in this dialog box is the same.

Simply choose the output file type, render, any render options you want, and then render the animation. If you save the animation to individual files, each file will be numbered in succession so you will know which file belongs with which frame. Chapter 12, "Output Issues," has more on output file types and methodologies.

Tips and Techniques on Basic Animation

The following are some tips on basic animation:

- Be aware of the different types of keys you place in your animations and where they occur.

- Always remember that the motion path generated between frames is a spline and not a straight line. This line can always be adjusted if necessary.

- Always preview your animation until you are sure the animation is correct before generating it. This will save you an enormous amount of time when it comes to the final rendering.

- Utilize all three preview types to help you visualize your animations.

Summary

As you can see, even the basics of animation encompass a lot of work. If you work at it, you can create nice animations using just the tools introduced here. Add in the tools in Chapters 9 and 10 and you can do anything you want!

The next chapter introduces you to more advanced topics of 3D Studio, including customization and hints on usage.

Since the first chapter, you have been introduced to the basic definitions and functions of 3D Studio. This chapter takes you through another level of 3D Studio—a more advanced level where you combine several of the techniques you have previously learned. This chapter presents some overall important techniques as you progress from a casual user to a higher level. The techniques discussed in this chapter are as follows:

- Customizing 3D Studio

- Solving problems using the 3D Editor

- Setting up backgrounds

- Rendering resolutions

- Saving your files

3D Studio on a Higher Plane

At this point, you've applied the primary tools of 3D Studio and progressed through the phases of developing an animation. Now you will begin to take steps toward becoming an advanced user. You will improve your editing techniques through various editing tools and functions. You will learn how to speed up your rendering time through various tips and tricks. This chapter takes you through some more advanced features of 3D Studio, increasing your drawing and animation power, making your organization more efficient, and speeding your end results.

Customizing 3D Studio

Already, perhaps, you've discovered certain techniques for keeping organized and efficient. 3D Studio is a very user-configurable program that you can customize in many ways. If you find that some minor part of the way 3D Studio works is not natural to the way you work, checking the original manual's discussion of that feature can yield a way to customize the feature so that it is more to your liking. Many of the customizable features are set up in the 3D Studio configuration file, called 3DS.SET. To this end, if you have yet to study the 3DS.SET file for 3D Studio, follow the exercise in this chapter for loading and examining it.

In the 3DS.SET file, note that any line that begins with a semicolon (;) is a comment and not a 3DS.SET parameter. These comments give explanations, and are not for the computer to try to read. You can make notes to yourself in the file by starting a line with a semicolon.

The following exercise will introduce you to the basics of configuring 3D Studio to suit your needs. When you choose Renderer/Setup/Configure you are presented with the Device Configuration dialog box. In this dialog box, you can set your output file resolutions. If you have specialized hardware, you might need a resolution that is not listed in the 4 preset buttons. A PAR board from DPS, for example, uses a resolution of 752×480 with an aspect ratio of .85. In this case, you would probably want to have a button with that preset. The exercise will show you how to modify the 3DS.SET file to accomplish this modification. As you learn about 3D Studio, you probably will find other settings you want to modify to suit your needs.

Customizing 3D Studio through the 3DS.SET File

Press F11 to switch to the 3D Editor	Starts the 3D Studio Text Editor
At the top of the screen, Choose File, Load	Displays the Load Script dialog box, with several filters listed on buttons in the lower right
Click on the *.SET button extension (See figure 6.1)	Enables you to choose files with a SET extension

The Load Script dialog box.

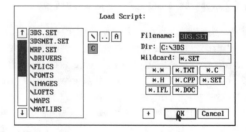

Click on 3DS.SET then click OK   Loads the 3DS.SET file

This file is broken down into several distinct sections allowing you to quickly find the set of options you are looking for. Each section is defined by a set of horizontal lines and a title such as Keyframer Parameters. For this exercise, find the section titled Renderer Parameters. You can use the page up or page down keys or the scroll bars at the right to find this section. The Renderer Parameters section of the 3DS.SET file allows you to modify parameters specifically associated with the Renderer. In the Renderer Parameters section, find four lines that start with the words RES. These allow you to customize the four render resolution buttons in 3D Studio.

Edit RES3 to the following:

RES3 = 752,480,.85   Sets the RES3 button to
752×480×.85 resolution

Choose File, Save   Enables you to save the file

Choose OK   Saves the file

Choose OK   Tells 3D Studio to overwrite the previous file

Quit and restart 3D Studio   Reloads 3D Studio with the new 3DS.SET file

Choose Renderer/Setup/Configure   Displays the Device Configuration dialog box

The changes made to the 3DS.SET file should show on the third resolution button. Figure 6.2 reflects the changes you just made.

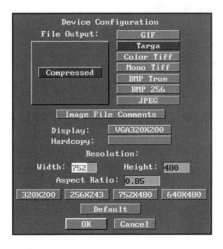

Figure 6.2

The Device Configuration dialog box after modification.

6

After you edit a version of the 3DS.SET file that you will need for certain uses only, you can save the new SET file in DOS, as follows:

1. Load the 3DS.SET file.

2. Use the Save command to save the file as NEW-FILE.SET.

3. Make any changes you want to the file.

4. Save the file again with the same filename.

This creates a second file called NEW-FILE.SET. Then, when you load 3D Studio, you can specify a specific SET file to use in the session, like this: 3DS SET=NEW-FILE.SET. This will load 3D Studio with an alternate 3DS.SET file. Examples of why you might want alternate SET files include: different display resolutions and color depths, different rendering parameters, or others.

To become a more advanced user, you must learn how to work efficiently in 3D Studio and how to solve your problems quickly. Editing the 3DS.SET file allows you to customize 3D Studio, but it does not help you to solve problems.

Divide and Conquer: Solving Problems, One at a Time

Many problems that crop up as you go about creating new animations are not immediately obvious. Some problems are not apparent until an image is rendered, and others don't become evident until the entire animation has been rendered. Rendering a still, or the entire animation, takes a substantial amount of time. The time it takes to render an animation, check the animation for errors, correct the errors, and re-render the animation can be enormous.

To help speed the process of detecting and correcting errors in your animations, you must adopt a divide and conquer philosophy. Each part of an animation should be proven separately from the rest of the scene. Avoid the temptation to render a test Flic animation with all the objects in the scene, at least until you reach the very end of the tuning-in work.

Instead, check each portion of the animation separately in the most time-effective way. If you are going to use a Flic file as an animated texture map on a wall, for example, and you are concerned about what part of the Flic texture plays as the animation progresses, you can use Renderer/Render Object and render only the single object that has the Flic texture. You can render this object to a Flic of 320×200, with no anti-aliasing. The animation will render out much more quickly, yet still have enough detail for you to make decisions on new changes to the animation. The following sections describe various techniques for helping to pinpoint problems in the early stages of your animation.

Clarity in the Editor

Creating an animation in 3D Studio can quickly become confusing when the scenery in your animation is complex. Clarity often is lost as object wireframes overlap each other to the point where you can no longer clearly discern individual objects while you edit. Certainly, the higher the resolution at which you can set the display in your 3D Editor and Keyframer, the finer the lines displayed. (If you must use a resolution of 640×480, wireframe lines will seem to merge together with simpler meshes than if you can work at resolutions of 800×600 or 1024×768.) Many more methods can and must be used, however, to keep your work-in-progress clear and easy to work with.

Using Different Object Colors

By default, the 3D Editor displays objects as white wireframe lines. The color of the wireframe lines drawn in the editor has no impact on the way the objects render. Many people leave all their objects to be drawn in this default white wireframe color. If you prefer another color for an object, however, you have 64 colors to choose from. To recolor an object, choose Object/Change Color from the 3D Editor menu (see fig 6.3). After you select an object, the palette of available colors appears. Sometimes, when the mesh complexity obscures the objects whose color you want to change, you can make the separate objects very clear by switching to Box mode (see fig. 6.4). To turn Box mode on and off, press Alt+B.

6

Figure 6.3

*The Recolor
Object(s) dialog box.*

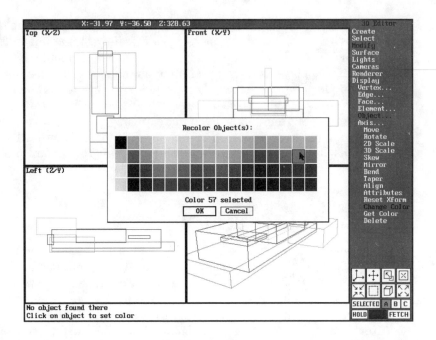

Figure 6.3

*The Recolor
Object(s) dialog box.*

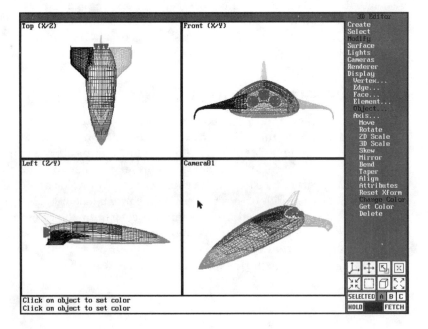

Figure 6.4

*Switching to Box
mode provides
different views of
the same object.*

> **USAGE TIP**
>
> Remember—when 3D Studio prompts you to select an object, you can always press H (for *hit* by name) to get a list of all available objects. Whenever several objects overlay each other and make choosing the intended object difficult, use the hit shortcut.

Using Fewer Lines to Represent an Object

When you look at objects in the 3D Editor, you see many lines. These lines represent and describe the object for you. In 3D Studio, it does not matter if the lines are visible or not, as they will have no impact on the final rendered image or animation. The lines are there to help the animator see the objects. As you generate more and more objects, there will be more and more lines on the screen. This will cause your display to get cluttered and 3D Studio to slow down. Each line on the screen must be redrawn every time you change views or change the model. If there are a lot of lines, this can take a long time. 3D Studio provides three tools to help you reduce redraw times, the number of lines, and the resulting clutter on the screen: fastdraw, fastview, and autoedge.

Fastdraw

Fastdraw speeds up redraws in 3D Studio by displaying only some of the lines in an object. When fastdraw is turned on, it is on for all viewports. You can access the fastdraw command by choosing Display/Speed/Fastdraw. The opposite of fastdraw is fulldraw, which draws all lines in the objects.

The number of lines drawn in the objects is controlled by Display/Speed/Set Fast. When this option is chosen, a dialog box with a slider appears, see figure 6.5. Higher values in this box will result in less lines being drawn on the screen, and lower values result in more lines. Fastdraw is actually a ratio of displayed edges over total edges. When you set the Set Fast dialog box, you are setting the ratio of lines that will show on the screen. The default is 10 where one line will show for every ten lines on the screen.

6

Figure 6.5

The Set Fastdraw Speed dialog box.

Fastdraw can also work on an object-by-object basis instead of the whole viewport. In this case, you can turn fastdraw on for complex objects you are not working on. These objects will then redraw on the screen much faster than normal while you work on other parts of the model. The advantage here is that you can still see the boundaries of the complex object while you are working on the other objects, but the complex object does not reduce your redraw speed. See figure 6.6.

Figure 6.6

The effects of Fastview on an object.

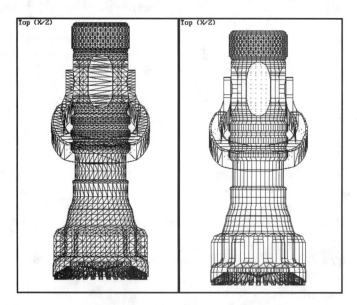

Fastview

Fastview creates the same effect as fastdraw, but on a viewport-by-viewport basis. Fastdraw can be turned on for all viewports or any specific object. You can access the fastview command by choosing Views, Fastview. Because this is a toggle, an asterisk will appear next to the command in the pulldown when it is activated for the current viewport.

You use fastview when you are primarily working in one viewport and do not want to have the other viewports wasting your time redrawing objects.

Using fastview allows you to do this while seeing the effects of your work in the other viewports.

Again, fastview also works with the Set Fast parameter in the same manner that fastdraw does.

Autoedge

Autoedge is a command that lets you permanently reduce the number of edges displayed in an object. Fastdraw and fastview are just different methods of viewing the object. You can access the Autoedge command by choosing Modify/Edge/Autoedge. When you choose this command, you are prompted to choose the object on which you want to reduce the number of edges. After choosing the object, a dialog box is displayed that allows you to choose the autoedge angle.

The angle in the Autoedge dialog box determines how many of the edges will be removed from the object. Remember, removing edges does not affect the rendering of the object. The angle is the angle between two faces. For example, two faces next to each other, such as two faces on a wall, are coplanar and have an angle of 0. Two faces that face each other have an angle of 180. This is the full range of the Auto Edge command. When you specify an angle in the dialog box, 3D Studio will then look at all the faces in the object and calculate the angle between each face. If the angle is less than the number specified in the dialog box, the edge between the two faces will be removed.

An example of when to use this command is when you import an object from another program such as AutoCAD. These objects will generally import with every face in the model showing. This can create a huge amount of confusion. When 3D Studio creates a box, it creates the box out of 12 faces, two on each side. The edge between the two faces on each side of the box is not shown by default. Imported objects will show this edge. Auto Edge can remove this line to help simplify the look of the geometry. On planar elements such as walls, you will want to use an Auto Edge value of 1. Any others, you can experiment with the value to see what works best for you.

USAGE TIP

If the file you load contains certain objects that seem to have missing faces, it is possible that those objects are not flawed but are instead switched into fastdraw mode. No matter how often you press V, you cannot view the full object; you must switch it out of fastdraw mode by choosing Display/Speed/By Name from the 3D Editor menu, and then (in the Select Fastdraw Objects dialog box) click on any objects in the list with names preceded by an asterisk (*). If no asterisks mark objects in the list, when the dialog box appears, the object is not in fastdraw mode. Auto edge may have already been applied to the object at too high an angle producing the same results. You can always confirm that a viewport is not in Fastview mode by making sure no asterisk appears next to the Fastview option in the Views pull down menu.

Box Mode

Box mode, already mentioned as an aide for assigning object colors, is helpful also in many other situations, for moving, copying, and other operations.

In animation editing, box mode is critical for playbacks that approximate the full video rate (30 frames per second). In some cases, certain objects are not useful in box mode. A large, bumpy landscape with prominent features, for instance, becomes a featureless slab in box mode, and box mode is of no help for previewing a tour of the landscape in an animation. In these situations, you can create temporary objects to point out the key features of the complex object so that box-mode animation playing makes more sense. In the case of the landscape, you can generate small cube objects in the 3D Editor and place them in important areas of the topography past which the camera will travel. With these reference cubes, you can use box-mode playback to quickly check the fine-tuning of camera motions and other animation. When the final animation is rendered, the reference cubes can be deleted (choose Modify/Object/Delete) or hidden (choose Display/Hide/Object).

Avoiding Screen Clutter

Objects, elements, and faces can be selectively hidden in the 3D Editor. To easily focus in on key areas, you can temporarily get rid of the clutter caused by the many other objects in the scene. By using Display/Hide, you can also hide lights and cameras temporarily, so that the zoom extents can fully fill each viewport with the important object. Lights can also be hidden with Alt+L and cameras with Alt+C.

You can isolate parts of objects by first selecting the faces to be hidden, and then hiding them by choosing Display/Hide/Face. Unless you hide all the faces behind the front layer of a shape such as a tube as you try to select faces on the front of that shape, you are bound to select faces you don't mean to select. The next exercise illustrates this procedure.

The following exercise will step you through the process of hiding selected faces on a sphere. The exercise also gives you the bonus of seeing how to apply materials to specific faces on the same object. Selection sets are used fairly heavily in this exercise. Make sure you are familiar with selection sets before starting this exercise.

Hiding Selected Faces

From the 3D Editor menu, choose Create/LSphere/Smoothed	Enables you to create a smooth sphere
Click in the center of the Front viewport and move the mouse to the right	Displays a circle to describe the size of the sphere being created
Create circle that fills half the viewport	A sphere appears in the four viewports (see fig 6.7)

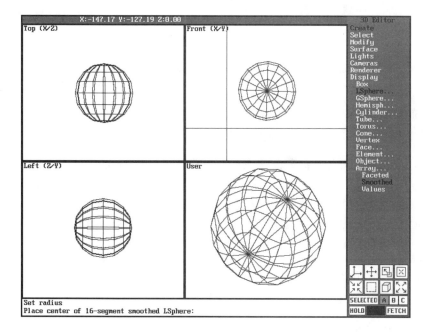

Figure 6.7

A sphere in the four viewports.

6

continues

continued

Choose Lights/Omni/Create and click in the lower right corner of the Top viewport to place a light there	Displays the Create Omni dialog box
In the dialog box, click Create	Accepts the default settings, and Create Omni dialog box disappears
Choose Select/Face/Window	Sets the Face Selection Window Type and enables you to select faces with Quad Selection Window
In the Top viewport, click at the upper right of the viewport and move the mouse to create a rectangle that covers the top two-thirds of the sphere (see fig. 6.8), then click again	The faces within the selection rectangle change to red because they are now selected

Figure 6.8

The Selection Window in the 3D Editor.

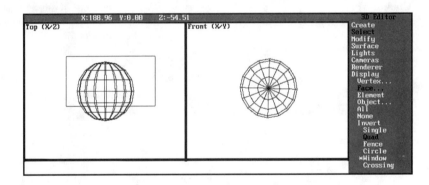

From the 3D Editor menu, choose Display/Hide/Face, and press the space bar	Highlights the Face option and activates the SELECTED button
Click anywhere in the Top viewport	The selected faces disappear (see fig. 6.9)

Now you can select other faces of the sphere in the front viewport without the selections affecting faces behind the front faces of the sphere.

From the menu, choose Select/Face/Circle	Enables you to select faces with a circular selection window
In the Front viewport click in center of sphere and draw a circle around the center faces	
Click to draw a rectangle around the centermost faces in the Front viewport (see fig. 6.10)	Selects the center faces, changing their color

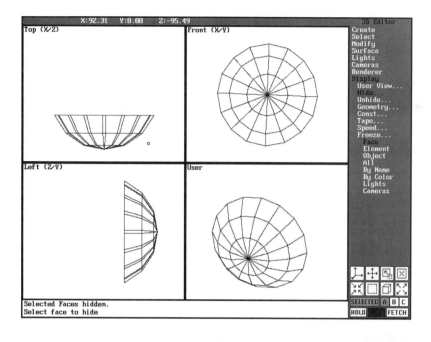

Figure 6.9

*The selected faces
are hidden.*

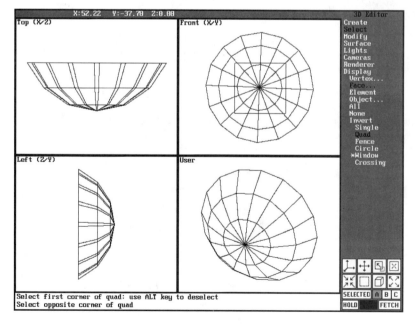

Figure 6.10

*Selected faces in the
Front viewport.*

continues

continued

Select every second square of the faces of the next ring by using Select/Face/Fence and drawing a line across the outer edge of each face you want to select.

Choose Surface/Material/Choose	Displays the Material Selector dialog box
Choose the Blue Metal texture from the list (see fig. 6.11), and click on OK	Makes Blue Metal the current material

Figure 6.11

The Material Selector dialog box.

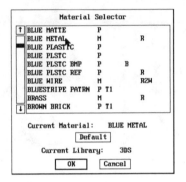

Choose Surface/Material/Assign/Face, and press the space bar	Enables you to assign the material to the selected faces
Click anywhere in the Front viewport	Displays dialog box so that you can confirm application of the Blue Metal material to the selected faces only
In the dialog box, click on OK	Applies texture to selected faces
Choose Renderer/Render Object, and click on some part of the sphere	Displays the Render Still Image dialog box (see fig. 6.12)

Figure 6.12

The Render Still Image dialog box.

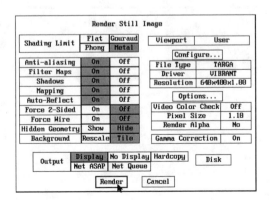

Click on OK to approve the standard
settings. You do not need to activate
the DISK button because this test render
does not need to be saved for future use

Renders the image

Note that the hidden faces are included in the sphere because you used Render Object.
Actually if any portion of an object is visible when any rendering command is invoked,
all faces of that object will be rendered. Note also that there is no seam between the
displayed and hidden faces, they are just hidden temporarily.

As you can see, using selection sets and the Display/Hide/Face command
can provide you with a lot of control over how you work with the objects
for assigning materials.

Freezing Objects

When you are working on a model, you generally work on small portions
of the model at a time. After a while, you will end up with portions of the
model that are the way you want them to be and you do not want to
change them. 3D Studio has a command that can help you to accomplish
this. You can freeze objects so they cannot be altered. When an object is
frozen, it stays on the screen, but it is greyed out to reflect its frozen
state.

You can access the freeze command by choosing Display/Freeze. There are
three options to this command: freeze by name, by color, or select the
object. When you select the object, it turns grey and the object is treated
like it does not exist by 3D Studio. This is helpful because you can still see
the object to work around it, but you can not accidentally modify the
object or delete it.

6

Setting Up Backgrounds

3D Studio allows you to setup a background behind your model. The
background is a bitmap, gradient color, or solid color that appears behind
all the objects in a scene. For example, you might do an architectural
rendering of a building and want to place the building in a realistic
setting. Many times, this can be accomplished simply by putting a bitmap
background of the setting behind the rendering. If you use Perspective
matching, you can even match the perspective of the background.

To set the background, use the Renderer/Setup/Background menu option. The solid color is set like any color in 3D Studio, with a set of sliders for RGB and HLS.

The Gradient option uses three colors, with one at top, one at the bottom, and one somewhere in between. A smooth horizontal gradient is produced between the three colors. You can choose the center color's position by clicking anywhere in the gradient preview box in the Define Gradient Colors dialog box (see fig. 6.13).

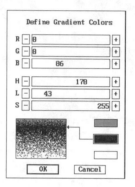

With the Bitmap option, any image or animation can be used as the background. This image can be tiled repeatedly to fill the rendered resolution, or it can be rescaled to fit at rendering time. The Tile/Rescale background option is set at rendering time, with the switch labeled Background, in the Render Still Image dialog box (refer to fig. 6.12).

The critical thing to remember about backgrounds is that they are just images behind the geometry.

USAGE TIP

For faster test renders with a rescaled background, manually rescale the background once to create a background of the correct size. This one-time action will take 5 to 30 seconds off each test render you create. It can also save time on any and all renderings you create.

Saving Your Files

You can save five types of files (SHP, LFT, MLI, 3DS, and PRJ) in 3D Studio. Clearly, you should save your work frequently. You should also use the different file types for their strengths:

- **SHP files.** These 2D Shaper files can have any number of open and closed polygons. SHPs are most useful for saving the contents of the 2D Shaper before you clear important and complex parts out of the 2D Shaper to begin lofting a new object. Also, frequently used shapes can be archived as SHP files.

- **LFT files.** These files, which store the contents of the 3D Lofter, are useful when you have created a complex loft that you might later want to tweak, or use as the starting point for a new loft.

- **MLI files.** These files contain material definitions. They contain only the data from the slider settings in the Materials Editor and the names of the actual image maps used. Because of this, MLIs are very compact (in terms of disk space consumed). You should organize your collection of materials, perhaps breaking them into multiple MLIs for metals, marbles, and other commonly used types of materials. You can use the Materials Editor's seven slots as a holding space to load a material from one library and then save it in a different library.

- **3DS files.** These files contain all the data of the 3D Editor and Keyframer. 3DS files do not contain the renderer settings or the Video Post module's data. (Video Post is discussed in Chapter 11.) The 3DS files contain only the meshes, the animation, and the viewport configuration. Material assigned to meshes are stored as part of the mesh data in the 3DS file, but again, the only things stored are the Materials Editor settings and file names used for the texture and other maps.

- **PRJ files.** These files contain virtually every setting in 3D Studio. When you load a PRJ file, all five modules are restored to the exact way they were when the file was saved. PRJ files are the most common way to hold works in progress. (Some animators use 3DS files to save their animation work after the objects are modeled, because of the simpler format of the 3DS file, and its greater reliability.)

6

Besides the five formats available for saving your files, you can also create ZIP archives directly from within 3D Studio. The original PKZIP program does not come with 3D Studio; you must obtain it separately from a BBS or other on-line service. This utility, which compresses groups of files into an archive file that can be extracted later, is ideal for sending animation files to other animators. 3D Studio can activate PKZIP with the File/Archive option in the File pull-down menu, and will include all maps related to the project currently loaded. You can also use your favorite compression program by modifying the 3DS.SET file.

Why and When to Limit Rendering Quality

Before rendering occurs, a list of options is displayed on the left side of the Render Still Image dialog box (see fig. 6.14). The default options are usually the Shading Limit option is set to Metal, and the five other options are set to On, a combination that produces 3D Studio's best quality rendering. To create test renders and images efficiently, however, you can selectively scale back these options.

Figure 6.14

The options list in the Render Still Image dialog box.

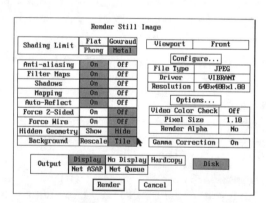

- **Shading Limit.** Alters the appearance of your materials. With any mode other than Metal, any metal objects will look washed out and dull. Because Phong and Metal take about the same amount of time to render, you get faster render times by limiting shading to either Flat or Gouraud. These settings alter smoothing within an object—shiny highlights look angular with Gouraud, and faceted with Flat shading. If you've perfected your materials and are only trying to work out motions and interactions, Flat shading improves rendering speed.

● **Anti-aliasing.** As explained earlier, *aliasing* is the pixelated, jagged edges associated with computer graphics. 3D Studio's built-in anti-aliasing perfectly blends the stairstep edges of object boundaries, but there is a price for the computation involved. When Anti-aliasing is not activated, 3D Studio speeds up dramatically.

● **Filter Maps.** Each texture map used in a material is filtered to make it look smoother and more natural in the final animation. Feel free to switch this setting off for test renders.

● **Shadows.** When this setting is turned off, no shadows are calculated. Ordinarily, shadows are time-intensive only when you use raytraced shadows (see Chapter 8, "Advanced Lighting/Materials Techniques"). Unless you are certain that shadows are falling correctly in your animation, you should leave this setting on.

● **Mapping.** When this setting is turned off, no maps are applied. Only the diffuse color of an object is used. If you are certain of your materials, and your scene contains so many maps that 3D Studio needs a significant amount of time to load each material, you can disable this setting for animation tests. Usually, map loading time is not significant. When the renderer is setting up, it displays a `Readying Materials` message while it loads the maps. You can gauge the time required to load maps by this prompt.

CAUTION

With many materials that use texture maps, the map slider is set to 100 so that the texture maps totally cover the diffuse color. Because diffuse color does not show through, the material designer often does not bother to adjust the diffuse color, and leaves it black. In such cases, the object renders as a black object when the maps are not used. Objects will also render as black objects when you use the 3D Studio's Quick Preview feature, which uses only diffuse color and ignores all texture maps.

● **Auto-Reflect.** Having a material calculate a new reflection map at each render, for effects such as shiny floors and mirrored objects, is possible. Doing so can often take nearly as much time as a full render, however, because 3D Studio essentially creates a full-color texture map on-the-fly by relocating the camera to the center of the reflective object and rendering the reflection map from this vantage. Turn this button OFF when a scene contains materials with Automatic Reflections and you are not concerned with reflections for this test render.

In sum, when materials have been adjusted and the test render is for motion and placement, you typically will render in Flat shaded mode, with Anti-aliasing and Filter Maps switched off. In this way, you render your work 2 to 5 times faster.

Batch Rendering and Stand-Alone Network Rendering

Like many DOS-based programs, 3D Studio can *batch render* a scene file. That is, from the DOS prompt, you can type some parameters after the 3DS, which starts the program, causing 3D Studio to immediately load and begin rendering a specific animation. To get the parameters available for command-prompt batch rendering at any time, simply type **3DS RENDER** at the DOS prompt. This form of batch rendering works especially well when you are in a situation in which the hardware lock is not present, but a 3DS or PRJ file requires immediate rendering. In most cases, however, a feature of the network rendering option—called *stand-alone network rendering*—replaces the need for command-prompt batch rendering.

Note that you can use Stand-alone Network approach without network software or hardware. You can do stand-alone network rendering on any PC that can run 3D Studio and has R3 or R4. An added benefit is that you can get familiar with the way network rendering works before you actually deal with a real networked *rendering farm* (a collection of PCs networked to cooperatively render the frames of an animation).

The procedure for network rendering is relatively easy. Instead of rendering to the display, you render to the Net Queue device. When you click on Render in the Render Still Image dialog box, instead of the machine prompting for the file name of the image or animation, a different dialog box appears, from which you can select the active machine and file directory. In this dialog box, you simply click on Any, and then type a file name for output. After you click on the OK button in this dialog box, the computer does not start rendering immediately; rather, it pauses briefly and returns to 3D Studio. The computer has simply saved your project file and placed it in a list of projects to be rendered. The project file contains all the parameters set for rendering, pallette, lights, and so on. When the machine is idle, all queue entries will render in order after you put the machine into slave mode with the Network/Slave option from the top menu.

The following exercise illustrates this procedure.

Working with Stand-Alone Rendering

In this exercise, you use the 3DS file BIRDSHOW.3DS, from the \Meshes subdirectory. This file includes a short animation of a bird hopping on a pedestal. The BIRDSHOW.3DS file is installed in this directory when 3D Studio is initially installed. If this file is not available, you can substitute a different animation.

Choose File/Load from the top menu · · · · · · · Displays the Select a mesh file to load dialog box (see fig. 6.15)

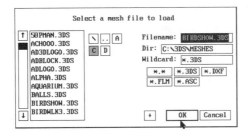

Figure 6.15

Selecting BIRDSHOW.3DS from the Select a mesh file to load dialog box.

Click over BIRDSHOW.3DS, and click on OK · · · · · · · Loads the birdshow mesh

Press F4 to switch to the Keyframer · · · · · · · Displays the Keyframer

Choose Renderer/Render View and click in the camera viewport in the lower right of the dialog box · · · · · · · Displays the Render Animation dialog box. Because the camera is named rolli, instead of the default Camera01, rolli is displayed in the Viewport slot at the upper right of the dialog box

Click on the Disk button at the lower right of the dialog box to save the rendering. If this button is not selected, you are not prompted for a filename as rendering starts, and the animation is only rendered to the screen. Usually, you leave the Disk button off only when rendering a single frame as a test · · · · · · · Activates the Disk button

6

continues

continued

Choose Configure	Displays the Device Configuration dialog box (see fig. 6.16)

Figure 6.16

*The Device Configu-
ration dialog box.*

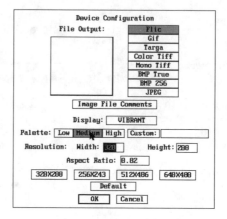

Click on the 320×200 button, click on the Medium button to ensure the optimal medium pallette for Flic creation, and make sure that the Flic file format is selected for output.

Click on OK at the bottom of the dialog box	The Render Animation dialog box re-appears; the values under the Configure button reflect the changes made (see fig. 6.17)

Figure 6.17

*The values under
the Configure
button reflect
changes made.*

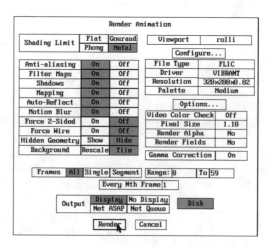

At this point, if you clicked on the Render button, the animation would begin rendering with the settings you have just activated. Because the Display/No Display buttons are set with Display active, the animation could be monitored as it rendered. You gain a slight speed advantage by choosing No Display. In this case, however, the rendering will be done later, because the animator is not finished working for the day.

Click on the Net Queue button to set up this animation rendering for later	Deactivates the Display button, and activates the Net Queue button
Click on the Render button	If this is the first network render you've done, a dialog box is displayed so that you can confirm creation of the MCS file; click on Yes. (This dialog box will not appear again.) Then the Network Queue Entry dialog box is displayed (see fig. 6.18)

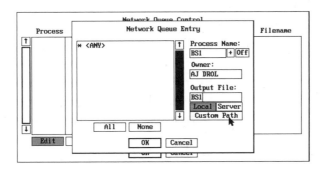

Figure 6.18

The Network Queue Entry dialog box.

At the left of the dialog box, a box contains the list of computers on the network. Because there is no network, the only entry is the word <ANY>.

Click over <ANY>	Displays an asterisk to the left of <ANY>

The Process Name entry at the upper right of the dialog box is the name of this particular project during the network rendering. If several versions of the BIRDSHOW animation were to be rendered together, this first version might be called BS1.

Type **BS1**	The new text replaces the highlighted text, UNNAMED

In the Output File slot, you must type the name of the final output file, in this case a Flic file, just as you would type it in the file prompter for a normal rendering. Usually, when several variations of the same animation are being rendered, the best way to keep things straight is to give output Flic animations the same name as the process name.

continues

6

continued

Type **BS1** in the Output File slot	The changes are reflected in the Network Queue Entry dialog box
Click on OK	Displays the Network Queue Control dialog box (see fig. 6.19), which lists all the animation projects (awaiting rendering) in the queue

Figure 6.19

The Network Queue Control dialog box.

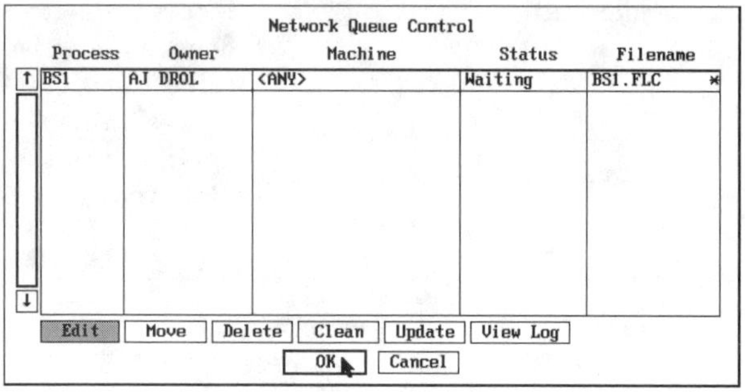

When the machine renders these projects, it starts at the top of the list. To reorder the animation projects, you use the Move button at the bottom of the dialog box.

Click on OK	The dialog box disappears

At this point, your rendering request is waiting for a machine on the network to be placed into slave mode before 3D Studio will begin sending out the frames of this project for rendering. Because there is no network, the only computer available is the one you are working on at this moment. At the end of the day, however, you can place your computer into slave mode. When you do, the machine will immediately start processing every rendering job in the queue. You can place the machine into slave mode in two ways: Either by choosing Network/Slave from the pull-down menu at the top of the screen, or by starting 3D Studio from the DOS prompt by typing **3DS SLAVE** instead of the usual 3DS. Starting slave mode from DOS usually is the better approach, because you ensure that 3D Studio is starting with a clean slate.

The animation file for each network queue entry is saved on the hard drive in the \NETWORK subdirectory. If necessary, you can load this file easily into 3D Studio by using the File/Load Project command from the pull-downs. In the case just described, the file is called BS1.PRJ.

To begin network rendering, exit 3D Studio; enter **3DS SLAVE** at the DOS prompt in your main 3D Studio directory	3D Studio starts up; a message displayed in the middle of the screen tells you 3D Studio is in slave mode. The project file is then loaded and the animation

begins to render. Even though 3D Studio
is in the 3D Editor, it will render the
animation as though 3D Studio were in
the Keyframer

The output files are placed in the /IMAGES subdirectory by default,
even if the output file is a Flic animation. You can choose a different
place on the hard drive for your output by clicking on the Custom
Path button in the Network Queue Entry dialog box.

Occasionally you will need to press Esc to halt the slave-mode rendering.
When this happens, 3D Studio considers the job incomplete; you can
restart the job later by simply resetting the entry in the network queue.

Creating a Flic is a special case, because the animation is first
rendered to individual frames as a series of temporary files, after
which an optimal 256-color pallette is applied and the Flic is compiled. If you interrupt a Flic that is rendering in normal mode or in
slave mode, your only choice is to create a Flic file from the frames
that have been created up to the point at which rendering was
interrupted. When you restart slave-mode rendering (as explained in
the following exercise), the Flic rendering begins from the interrupted frame, and previous frames are lost. When you render to any
format other than Flic, the rendering picks up at the frame at which
it was interrupted.

A Pre-Rendering Checklist

Nothing is so disappointing as returning to your computer to view what
you had thought would be rendered perfectly over a night or weekend,
only to find an error message that occurred at frame 5, just after you left
the room when you initiated the rendering. Or you might find a completed
animation with an error in the motion of a prominent object, or with an
improper material. The machine might still be rendering, but at a snail's
pace (due to an unintended effect). If you methodically check your project

before you begin the final rendering, you can confidently expect complete and perfect work in the shortest time possible.

Map Paths Order

Map paths are one of the main reasons for a halted or slowed rendering. 3D Studio looks for textures it needs only when it needs them, and only knows to look in the list of file directories you provide. Therefore, if a hidden object appears at frame 30, and that object requires a texture map that can't be found, 3D Studio halts. The best approach is to keep all your textures for the current project in a working subdirectory that you know is listed in 3D Studio's map paths. The map paths themselves can be edited and added to at any time. You can add a map path permanently in the 3DS.SET file, or add a map path temporarily while you are working in 3D Studio. To adjust the map paths, first choose the Info/Configure options from the pull-down menu to display the Program Configuration dialog box (see fig. 6.20).

Click on the Map Paths button at the bottom of the dialog box to bring up the Specify Map Paths dialog box shown in figure 6.21.

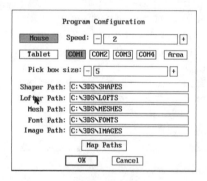

Figure 6.20

The Program Configuration dialog box.

Note that the paths are listed in the order in which 3D Studio will search for a particular image file. Because 3D Studio knows only the file's name, if it needs an image called SAND.TGA and finds one in a higher C:\3DS\MAPS directory, it will use that SAND.TGA image, even though the animator may have intended a texture with the same name that is listed in a lower directory.

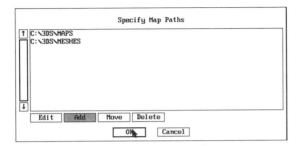

Figure 6.21

The Specify Map Paths dialog box.

Also, as the list of map path directories grows, 3D Studio must search longer for textures in the lower directories. Animators who have 30 map path directories can save hours of rendering time by simply sorting the map path list so that the most frequently used paths are at the top of the list. To do so, simply click on the Move button in the Map Paths dialog box; then you can click over each path and move it to any spot in the stack.

Preview Checks: Single Frame, Motion

Previews are an important tool for finalizing your work before you commit to a lengthy full-quality rendering. These previews usually are for one of two purposes: checking your set design or checking your motion.

Checking Set Design

Checking the set design is simply making sure that all of your lights, cameras, and materials are rendering the way you want them to, before you render the animation. The best way to check your set design is to render selected frames individually throughout the animation.

Still renders in the 3D Editor usually are enough to get to a point where the materials, lights, and shadows seem correct. All the properties or lights, cameras, or materials can be animated, however, and if your lights are moving or changing color, or if a material is animated, you'll need to test the animation somehow. First, you need to choose important frames in the animation and render them (in the Keyframer, with Single selected) to the display.

After you spot-check individual critical frames, the best way to achieve a test render of your set design is to use the Every Nth Frame option in the Keyframer, and forego anti-aliasing. Usually, you'll want to use full resolution for these tests to ensure that details are not missed.

The Every Nth Frame option appears above the renderer output buttons in the Render dialog box. You can check your set design at, say every 10th frame of a 600-frame animation, and be reasonably certain that if this collection of frames is correct, the final animation will be also. With anti-aliasing turned off, the time necessary for a final test animation should be considerably less than the final rendering time.

Checking Motion

3D Studio has a variety of tools for testing motion, each with its own strengths and weaknesses. Box mode playback with all paths hidden should provide a reasonable preview in real-time in the Keyframer. When you are almost finished, press F7 to bring up the Fast Preview feature, which enables you to make a relatively detailed preview animation very quickly. Note that this feature also has an Every Nth Frame option for faster animation generation (see fig. 6.22). Note, however, that for motion tests, if you render only every 2nd frame, you must play back the animation at half speed to get a reliable idea of what the final animation will look like.

Figure 6.22

The Make FLI/FLC dialog box.

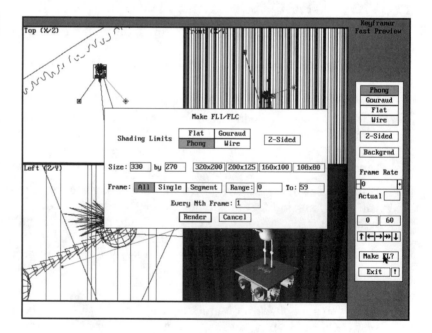

If your animation uses AXP IPAS stand-in objects, only the renderer will allow a preview that you can rely on. You cannot rely upon Fast Preview when dealing with IPAS routines. Assuming that your materials are correct, however, you can improve speed by rendering with virtually all settings turned off. And you can hide, from box or Fast Preview tests, all objects that are known to be animating properly.

The divide-and-conquer rule is very important here. For example, with flat shading and anti-aliasing turned off, you quickly can render a fireworks AXP object by itself to a Flic. Then, knowing that (for example) a certain firework fills roughly the upper right fourth of the screen for frames 30 to 55, you can adjust the camera angle accordingly.

Speeding Up Render Times: Ten Important Tips

Frequently, animators who ignore the things that slow down their computers, and instead invest in machines with higher horsepower (more random acces memory, or *RAM*), find that they still hit brick walls at render time. An animator who casually uses a dozen textures of 800×600 in size consumes 16.5 megabytes of RAM. The difference between the animator who tunes and tightens his system like a race car, and the animator who drop-kicks his project into a system he treats like a wood chipper, is often enough to make or break a production deadline. To maximize your final rendering performance, follow these 10 tips:

1. **RAM: Don't be Face-thrifty and Texture-wasteful.** A face in 3D Studio requires 60 bytes at render time; a vertex, 34 bytes; and a texture map, 3 bytes per pixel, regardless of the image file format and color depth. Therefore, don't be so stingy with faces that curved objects have faceting on their silhouettes. The extra 3,000 faces an object needs to appear beautifully round will cost you only 231 KB of RAM—the equivalent of a tiny texture map, 277 pixels square. If a large stripe or some bold text is to appear on an object, consider using a mesh item (rather than a large texture map) to create the decal, especially if the camera is to zoom close to the decal. Textures in 3D Studio cannot help but appear blurry at close range, whereas a flat mesh object of, for example, a numeral 2 will be sharp and clear at any range.

6

2. **Don't Use FLIs for Animated Textures.** Many utilities exist for breaking a FLI or FLC animation into a numbered group of GIF or TGA files. You can then replace the FLI or FLC animated texture with an IFL file (an *IFL* file is a text list of files to be used). The original FLI animation is certainly useful for previewing how the animated texture will work, but if the animation has more than a few dozen frames, 3D Studio needs a great deal of time to set up the texture from the animation. The reason is that the FLI and FLC formats create animation as a series of differentials, in which only frame one is completely there, and all subsequent frames are described in data that lists the differences between it and the preceding frame. Because it would be prohibitive for 3D Studio to try to remember all the information about how to create each frame in a FLI texture map, the program must instead re-create the desired frame by starting with frame one, and essentially playing the animation through to the needed texture. This is not a problem at frame one (or even frame 20) of the FLI or FLC texture map, but at frame 300, things slow down dramatically. Breaking a FLI or FLC into its constituent frames, and then using the MAKEIFL utility to create the replacement IFL, is a fairly quick procedure.

3. **Sort Map Paths According to Use.** As mentioned earlier, map paths are searched in the order in which they are listed in the Info/ Configure/Map Paths dialog box. If 3D Studio must search through 12 directories and 4,000 files whenever it needs a texture map, rendering setup will take many seconds longer than necessary. Sort the map paths so that most of the textures needed for your project are at the top. (You can sort the map paths just before you begin the final render, if that's easier.)

4. **Optimize Swap Space on Disk with DOS Utility.** Unless you are rendering fairly simple scenes or have an extremely large amount of RAM (such as 64 MB), 3D Studio inevitably requires a swap file during rendering. As your projects become more ambitious, you might find that swap files are simply a given for your work.

Hard drives are organized so that they have a limited number of fixed-size spaces, which are used up as files are stored. When a file is later deleted, its spaces are opened up. When a new, larger file is stored, it may fill up the newly opened spaces of the old deleted file, and also need some new spaces (in another part of the disk) in which to store the rest of the file. Then, when that file is read from the drive, the disk must find the file in two noncontiguous areas, which slightly slows down the file-reading process. Over time, as files are written and erased thousands of times, a disk becomes *fragmented*— files are not in two pieces, as in the preceding example, but are in dozens of pieces all over the drive. Clearly, fragmentation can slow disk access dramatically.

When 3D Studio uses the disk as RAM in a swap file situation, the file is written and read to thousands of times a minute. If the disk's open spaces are not contiguous, this process can slow greatly.

MS-DOS comes with a disk defragmenter, called DEFRAG, that you run from the DOS prompt. (See your DOS manual for more details about how to use DEFRAG.) Be sure to use this utility on your swap drive before you begin large animation renders.

5. **Separate Swap and Render-to Drives.** If 3D Studio is writing files to the drive you are using for swapping, any defragmenting work you might have done before rendering will be undone some-what as free space is filled with rendered images. You can create multiple logical drives, called *partitions*, on a single hard drive. You should create a partition of perhaps 30 to 120 MB, and keep it com-pletely empty. This gives 3D Studio an empty workspace to swap to when it runs out of RAM, and helps speed up the rendering process. Also, if the space is empty, you have nothing to defragment, and can ignore the preceding tip. Even if the partition you choose to swap to contains files, swap speed should improve (provided that the drive is first defragmented, and 3D Studio is not creating new files on the disk). Use CF16386 to tell 3D Studio where a swap drive is.

6. **Resize Maps for Minimal Space.** Many of the objects that appear in your scene will stay in the background. For example, a car tire may never appear more than a few pixels in diameter in a final rendering if the car the tire belongs to is far in the background. If a large, elaborate texture map is applied to the tire object, however, all the usually required RAM will be taken to hold the texture. (For example, a 640×480 JPG texture may take only 45 KB on the hard disk, but require 900 KB of RAM at render time.) Virtually no benefit to your final render is gained, however, because the object is never close enough for the viewer to see any of the detail in the map. Therefore, by creating a smaller version of the map or leaving the map out altogether, you can regain most of the RAM taken by the texture map. Utilities such as Image Alchemy are excellent for creating a smaller map, but you can also resize the texture in

6

3D Studio. In a case such as this, you could resize a 640×480 map to 64×48 (9 KB of RAM required) or 128×96 (36 KB of RAM required), regaining nearly all of the previously used RAM.

7. **Reuse Texture Maps where Possible.** If a texture map is used in multiple places, it is loaded only once into RAM. You can use this to your advantage, especially with generic textures used for reflection and bumpiness. Every chrome or brass object in a scene can use the same reflection map, with no loss of image quality, and a great savings of RAM.

8. **Hide or Delete Unseen Geometry and Lights.** If complex geometry is completely hidden from the camera view at certain points in an animation, you can save RAM and rendering time by hiding the objects during those frames. Many animators simply delete the unseen geometry, render the frames in question, then reload the original project and render the other frames.

9. **Minimize Number of Shadow Map Casting Spotlights.** A shadow is not much of a shadow when six shadows are all going in different directions. Good lighting rarely requires more than one shadow-casting light. Because each shadow cast requires a moment to render, and a fair amount of RAM, you can conserve a great deal of RAM and rendering time by using omni lights and spots that don't cast shadows for most of your side and back illumination. These lights can exclude certain objects where necessary, to achieve much more efficiently the lighting effect you wanted originally.

10. **Use Render-time Killers Only When Necessary.** Certain 3D Studio options cause long rendering times, no matter what you do. The biggest offenders are motion blur, raytraced shadows, transparency, SXP textures, and multiple reflection maps set to generate automatically. A description of each option follows:

    Motion blur. A neat effect, when an object is moving so fast around a scene that it appears strobed. Because this option always adds significantly to render time, however, be sure to use it only when you can afford that extra time.

    Raytraced shadows. This option produces sharp, crisp shadows like those cast by the sun. For outdoor scenes, raytraced shadows are fairly necessary, but if your shadow silhouettes are the result of thousands of faces (such as a tree object, with all its leaves, might cast), rendering time will rise dramatically. Use large shadow-maps instead. (Set the cone as narrow as possible and increase the Map Size parameter.) Test rewind single frames with both shadow types and determine which will save you time versus quality in the final render.

Transparency. Transparency is not a serious issue unless you have many layers of it, as can happen when light-beam objects are extruded from complex objects, as well as with the FLAME and VAPOR IPAS routines that can create thousands of overlapping semitransparent objects. The more layers of transparency you have, the slower the progress of the render. If only a few pixels on the screen have many layers of transparency, the cost will be unnoticeable, but if you fill the screen with layer upon layer of transparent objects, plan on extraordinarily long rendering times.

SXP textures. These solid, procedural textures work on complex objects that display smeared or pinched edges when mapped with traditional textures, using planar, cylindrical, or spherical mapping. They can provide natural stone, marble, wood (and other) textures in a seamless, easily applied way. They usually take about twice as long to render as a texture map, however. When multiple SXPs are used in the same material (as for color and bump), unless the parameters are exactly alike, separate calculations must be performed for each of them, and rendering time will be quite slow in areas of the screen with these textures.

Automatic Reflections. Automatic reflection maps are much slower than shadow maps, because more than a silhouette must be generated. Essentially, by strategically relocating the camera and rendering the scene from the reflecting object's perspective, the renderer is creating a new texture map on-the-fly for the scene it is about to render. When used on many different objects, automatic reflection maps can slow rendering significantly. Try to confine this effect to the areas in which it will be noticed, such as a shiny floor (as opposed to a chrome doorknob).

6

USAGE TIP

Sometimes 3D Studio will not list the CD-ROM's drive letter among the available drives in the file selector list. This can be easily fixed by forcing 3D Studio to wake up that drive. In a file selector dialog box (for example, during a file load, or in a material texture slot), click over the listed directory slot. 3D Studio highlights the text. As soon as you begin to type, the existing text disappears, and is replaced by what you type. You should simply type the drive letter and a colon (if your CD-ROM drive is the D drive, for example, type **D:**), and then press Enter. When the dialog box disappears, bring up the file selector dialog box again. The files and directories in the box on the left of the file selector dialog box should be those of the CD-ROM.

Summary

As you can see, careful use of your resources and skills can help you increase your productivity and reduce your frustration when creating animations and renderings. Many of the tips in this chapter—customization, reducing redraw times, quality tips—can help you to increase the productivity and quality of your final product.

The next chapter introduces you to advanced techniques for modelling. In particular, the 2D Shaper, 3D Lofter, and 3D Editor are explored in more detail.

Chapter Snapshot

3D Studio provides you with a broad variety of tools that you can use to create just about any object you want. These tools include the 2D Shaper, the 3D Lofter, and the 3D Editor. By combining one or more of these modules, you have all the tools necessary to be as creative as you like.

This chapter introduces you to the following concepts:

- Interaction between the 2D Shaper and the 3D Lofter

- Creating a variety of shapes in the 2D Shaper

- Lofting shapes into objects with a variety of methods

- Advanced modeling techniques for the 3D Editor

Advanced Modeling Techniques

Most complex shapes can be created using the 2D Shaper in combination with the 3D Lofter. In this combination, you draw the outline or profile of the shape in the 2D Shaper and loft or extrude this shape along a path in the 3D Lofter, ending up with an object in the 3D Editor. You can also create many of these shapes using just the 3D Editor. The most important factor for the success of the modeling project is the technique you choose for building the more difficult objects.

Interaction between the 2D Shaper and the 3D Lofter

The 2D Shaper and the 3D Lofter work together to create complex objects. Shapes, outlines, profiles, and even lofting paths can be created in the 2D Shaper. The 2D Shaper objects are then imported into the 3D Lofter where they can be extruded along a path. That is, an extruded shape travels along a path generating a skin or surface as it goes. The shape can rotate, scale, or change form along a path that follows any direction in 3D space. The only limitation to an extruded object is that it might not fork or branch along the path.

The technique for using the Lofter-Shaper combination is always the same. Create all the necessary shapes and paths in the 2D Shaper. Shapes created in the 2D Shaper must always be closed objects or they will not import into the 3D Lofter. A path generated in the Shaper can be open or closed depending upon what you want to do. Most of the paths you will use will be generated in the 3D Lofter, though. These paths include helixes, straight lines, and circles. Paths that are not planar are created in the 2D Shaper and edited in the 3D Lofter to create a 3D path.

Once you have the shapes and paths, you simply import the shape into the 3D Lofter, then set any loft parameters you like. Loft parameters can include beveling, scaling, rotating, and deforming the shape as it is extruded along the path. The resulting 3D object appears in the 3D Editor. This process is repeated as many times as necessary to create the objects you need for your scene.

Now that you have an idea of the process of using the Shaper-Lofter combination, it is time to take a closer look at the components of this process. First, take a closer look at the workings of the 2D Shaper.

A Detailed Look at the 2D Shaper Tools

The 2D Shaper allows you to create just about any 2D shape you like. If you cannot create the shape you want with the existing tools, you can import the shape from another program such as CorelDRAW! or AutoCAD. This section takes a detailed look at the 2D Shaper, including the following:

- 2D Entity Creation and Editing
- Vertex Editing
- Text Issues
- Importing from other programs

2D Entity Creation and Editing

The 2D Shaper provides you with the basic set of tools necessary to create and edit any type of shape you want. This section addresses how you go about creating and editing the shapes using the tools provided to you. Some of the tools covered here include the following: line, freehand, arc, quad, circle, ellipse, N-Gon, text, outline, and Boolean editing.

Line

There is more to the Line tool than meets the eye. At its simplest, you click in the viewport after choosing Create/Line—each click of the mouse places a line vertex. These line vertices are all spline points, however, and the spline attributes for each vertex can be adjusted while you draw.

A spline is a curve that has control points, known as vertices. Each point on the spline affects the curve of the other points on the spline. Splines are generally used when you need a non-uniformly curved line. Thus, every line drawn in the 2D Shaper is a spline of sorts.

Adjusting a spline is simple. Instead of just clicking the mouse to place a vertex, press and drag the mouse from the click-point; the control arrows will follow, while the arc of the line reflects the control arrows' positions (see fig. 7.1). The Alt and Ctrl keys have special functions during control-arrow editing: With Ctrl pressed, the placed point can be moved from its original placement point. While the Alt key is pressed, only the red arrow is adjusted. (The red arrow determines how the line enters the vertex; the yellow arrow influences how the line leaves the vertex.) Therefore, you can smooth or cusp (make pointed) the vertex.

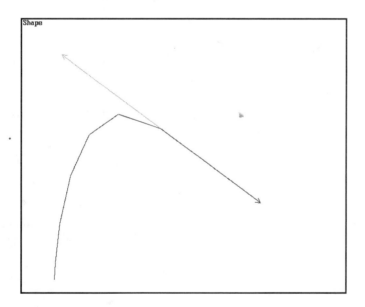

Figure 7.1

A vertex showing control arrows.

7

Freehand

With this tool, you can draw as though you were using a pencil. The Smoothness setting determines how accurately 3D Studio tries to reduce your sketching to lines and vertices. The results of a low smoothness setting are more vertices but less curvature (see fig.7.2). Lower settings also more exactly follow the mouse's movements. This tool is used rarely—usually to model organic shapes.

Figure 7.2

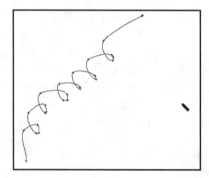

A freehand curve.

Arc

An arc is defined as a segment of a circle. It is often used to create smooth turns where two lines meet. You draw an arc in the 2D Shaper by defining it with three points: the center point, the radius of the arc, and the length of the arc. The first click determines the center point of the arc, and the second click starts the arc drawing at a locked radius (see fig. 7.3). Details about the arc parameters are displayed at the top of the screen. For large arcs, you may prefer to use N-Gons or circles with more vertices, and then delete the unneeded segments.

Figure 7.3

Creating an arc.

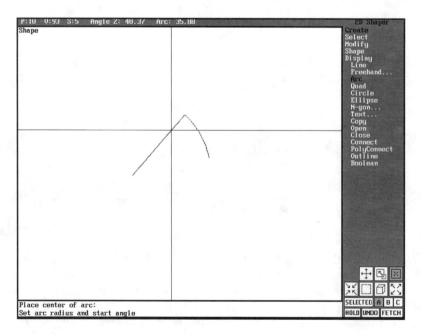

Quad

The Quad option creates any sort of square or rectangle. By pressing Ctrl, you constrain movement to a perfect square (see fig. 7.4). The coordinates and overall rectangle size are displayed at the top of the screen.

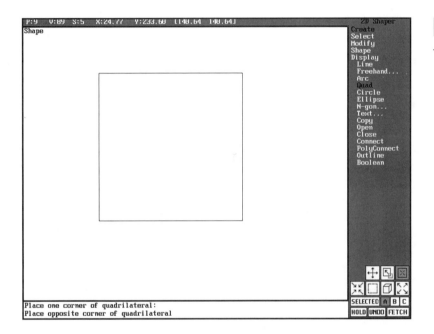

Figure 7.4

A square created using Quad.

Circle

The Circle option always creates a 4-vertex circle. The center point is determined at the first click, then the mouse is moved to the radius of the circle. The top of the screen reflects the center coordinates and radius value.

Ellipse

An ellipse is defined by three points. The first two points on the ellipse define the major axis of the ellipse. The last point defines the length of the minor axis and the overall width of the ellipse (see figure 7.5). The ellipse, like a circle, has four vertices in it.

7

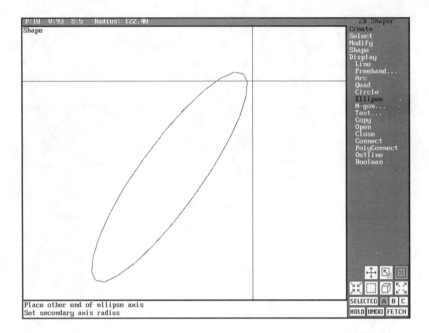

Figure 7.5

*An ellipse created
with the ellipse tool.*

N-Gon

The N-Gon command enables you to create polygons with any number of sides equal in length. There are two types of N-Gons you can make: flat and circular. A flat N-Gon can be used to create polygons such as hexagons and octagons. A circular N-Gon can be used to create circles with any number of vertices. Circular N-Gons are important when dealing with the 3D Lofter (see section later in this chapter), because the 3D Lofter is very particular about different shapes along a path having the same number of vertices. Figure 7.6 shows the Set N-Gon Sides dialog box where you can set the numbers of sides for the N-Gon. Figure 7.7 shows a flat and a circular N-Gon with the same number of vertices.

Figure 7.6

*The Set N-Gon
Sides dialog box.*

```
          Set N-Gon Sides
 ┌─┐┌────────────────────────┐┌─┐
 │─││ ▯                      ││+│
 └─┘└────────────────────────┘└─┘
              Sides: 8
          ┌──────┐ ┌────────┐
          │  OK  │ │ Cancel │
          └──────┘ └────────┘
```

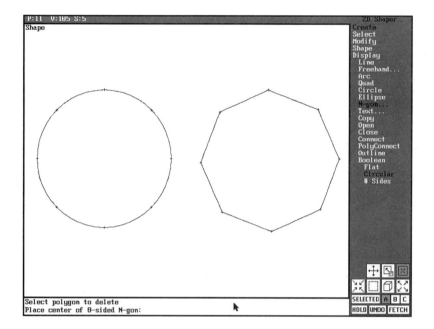

Figure 7.7

Circular and flat N-Gons with the same number of vertices.

Text

One of the most useful Shaper tools is the Create/Text tool. Before you can place the text shapes, you must select a font (see fig. 7.8) and type some text. Note that although the default font type and directory are 3D Studio's FNT file type and FONT directory, you can also use PostScript fonts from any directory. 3D Studio includes 100 additional fonts on its CD-ROM, and thousands of fonts are available from commercial BBSs and other CD-ROMs. In order to see PostScript font types, you must click on the *.PFB button to display files with the PFB extension.

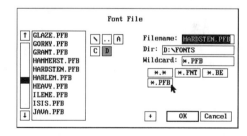

Figure 7.8

The Font File dialog box.

7

When you place text in the 2D Shaper, you click and drag a box that defines the outer limits of the text you are placing. Unfortunately, this box will, many times, not match the aspect ratio of the font you are using. This can create text that is too tall, too short, too fat, or too thin. You can get around this problem by holding down Ctrl while you are drawing the placement box. This forces the 2D Shaper to use the aspect ratio of the font for determining the size of the box. Figure 7.9 shows text that has already been placed in the 2D Shaper.

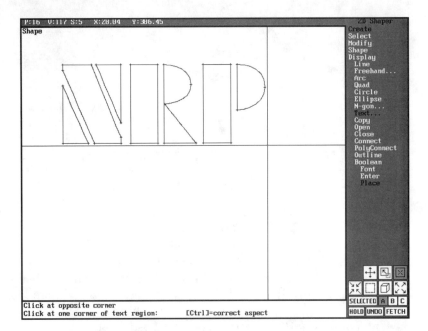

Outline

This tool works on existing shapes. On an open shape, the outline tool creates a closed shape that surrounds the line at a fixed distance. On a closed shape, two outlines are created, one smaller and one larger than the original shape. Note that in both cases the original shape is deleted (see fig. 7.10).

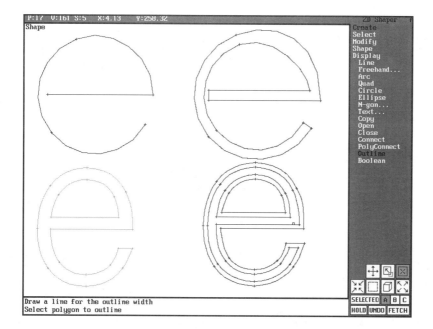

Figure 7.10

Source objects on the left, and resulting outlines on the right.

A good technique to use when dealing with outlines is to first create a copy of the shape to be outlined. You can use Create/Copy to make a copy of the shape. You do this because when the outline is created, the original shape will be deleted. This way, you will not lose the original shape if the outline does not come out correctly. If you create the copy of the shape in the same place the original shape is located, the shape will seem to disappear when the outline is created. Simply redrawing the screen using the tilde (~) key will show you the original shape again.

Boolean

A powerful way to create complex shapes is simply to combine several simple shapes with the Boolean tool. Booleans act on overlapping shapes, and combine them in one of three ways: union, subtraction, or intersection. A *union* of two shapes joins them into a single shape. A *subtraction* uses the second object to "take a bite" out of the first selected object. The *intersection* creates a shape from the overlapping parts only (see fig. 7.11).

When you create a Boolean shape, a dialog box is shown (figure 7.12) that enables you to choose which type of Boolean operation you want to perform. There are two other important options in this dialog box: Weld

Polygons and Hold. Weld Polygons tells the Shaper to weld the vertices of the resulting polygon together so there aren't any duplicate or overlapping vertices. Generally, welding polygons is a good idea. The second option is the Hold button. The Hold button saves the current state of the 2D Shaper in a storage buffer. It is always a good idea to choose Hold before performing Boolean operations. If something goes wrong with the Boolean operation, you can simply choose Fetch from the lower right part of the 2D Shaper to retrieve the shapes from the hold buffer. This way, you do not have to redraw any shapes if something does go wrong.

Figure 7.11

Original shapes and resulting Boolean operations.

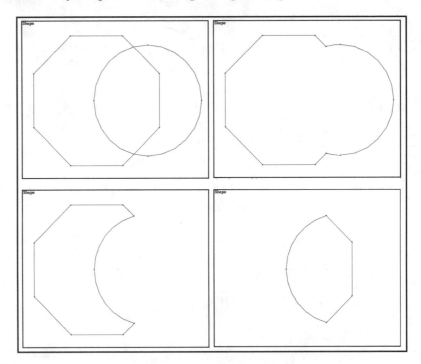

Figure 7.12

The 2D Boolean Operation dialog box.

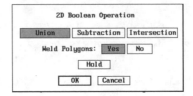

The following exercise shows you how to use some of the aforementioned tools to create a shape. This shape should be saved to disk as it will be used in a later 3D Lofter exercise.

Creating a Shape

In the 2D Shaper, create a circle

Choose Create/Circle, and click-and-drag from the center of the viewport to about 100 units	A circle appears in the viewport
Choose Create/Quad, and place a square of about 7 units at the top of the circle	The square appears (see fig. 7.13)
Choose Modify/Polygon/Move, and click on the square while you hold down the Shift key	Clones the square; the mouse moves the new copy
Place the square at the bottom of the circle	The square appears
Choose Create/Circle, and draw a small circle of about 15 units at the right of the large circle	The small circle appears (see fig. 7.14)
Using the same technique as before, choose Modify/Polygon/Move and hold down the Shift while you click over the new circle. Copy the small circle to the left side of the large circle	Small circles are now at both the left and right sides of the large circle

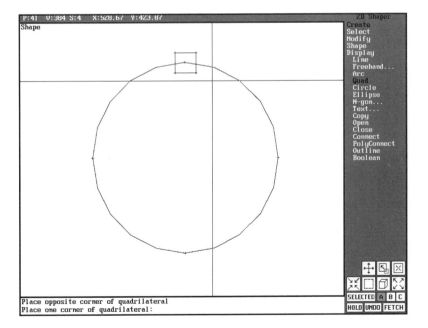

Figure 7.13

Circle with the small square.

7

continues

continued

Figure 7.14

Circle with square and smaller circle.

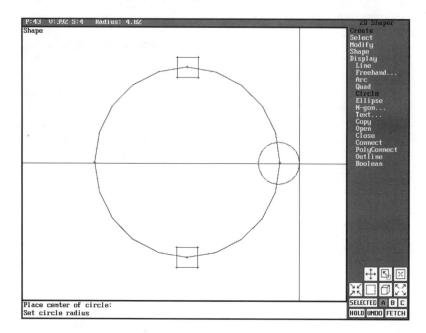

You use these new shapes to cut from the large circle.

Choose Create/Boolean	Activates Boolean
Click on the large circle, then on the small circle at right	The 2nd Boolean Operation dialog box appears (see fig. 7.15)
In the dialog box, choose the Subtraction button, and click on OK	The small circle is gone; in its place is a cut in the large circle (see fig. 7.16)
Using this same procedure, cut out the other three small shapes	The circle has four cuts (see fig. 7.17)
Choose Shape/Assign, and click on the new shape	The new object becomes yellow, indicating that it is the chosen shape for the 3D Lofter to accept
Save the shape as **CH7TUT1.SHP**	Saves the shape to disk

Figure 7.15

Settings for the 2D Boolean Operation dialog box.

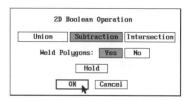

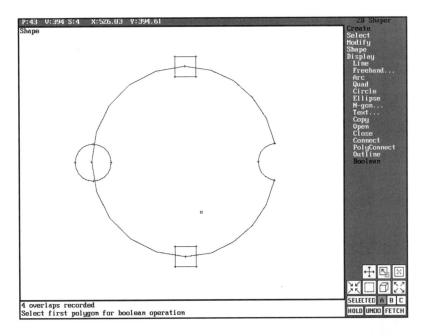

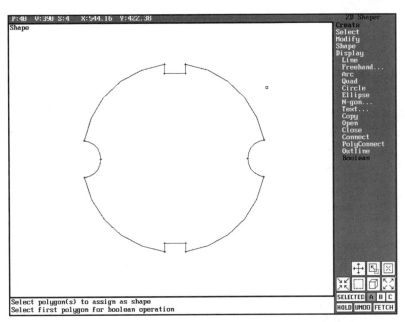

Vertex Editing

While you work in the 2D Shaper, you'll make much of the final adjustment by using the tools described in the following sections.

Vertex/Adjust

Each vertex of a shape can be adjusted along a spline. Even if you've drawn a rectangle, you can use Vertex/Adjust to make the vertex "curvy" (see fig. 7.18). After a shape is drawn, you can adjust each vertex by adjusting the control arrows (as with Create/Line): Click and hold the mouse button over the vertex, and move the mouse to modify the spline control arrows. To edit only one arrow, press Alt, and use Ctrl to move the vertex.

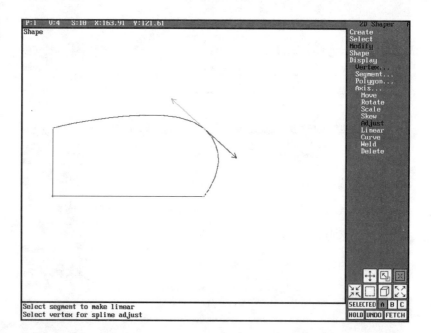

Figure 7.18

A rectangle with an adjusted vertex.

Vertex/Linear/Curve

With the Vertex/Linear command, you can instantly change a chosen vertex from a curved spline to a flat corner (see fig. 7.19). Similarly, the Vertex/Curve command switches a corner of a polygon into a smooth curve. Depending on how the adjacent vertices curve, the default curve conversion is a smooth turn instead of a hard corner.

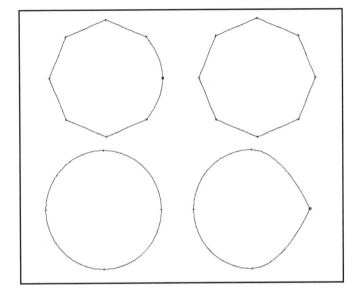

Figure 7.19

Linear and curve vertex editing.

Vertex/Weld

The Weld command closes shapes by welding loose vertices. The Weld function first picks up a vertex, which is placed over a second vertex to be welded. The single vertex that remains is left in the position of the second vertex. Sometimes two unwelded vertices are right on top of each other, and the reason Shape/Check gives an error for having an unclosed shape is not clear (see fig. 7.20).

Unlike other 2D Shaper errors, open shapes that are nearly closed do not display where they are closed. The Create/Close command often takes care of any unclosed shape, but some imported shapes may have breaks in many places along the shape, and this option will not include all the pieces of the shape. The best approach to fixing multiple barely open points on a shape is to select all the vertices and use Vertex/Weld, with the SELECTED button active. In this case, the weld is a one-step process. Any vertex within a threshold distance of another vertex is welded automatically at the center point. To set the threshold, choose System Options in the Info pull-down menu to bring up the System Options dialog box, in which you can set the Weld Threshold (see fig. 7.21).

7

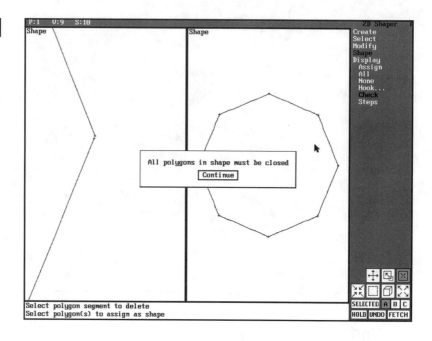

Figure 7.20

An unclosed polygon with an error message.

Figure 7.21

The System Options dialog box.

Segment/Linear/Curve

The Segment/Linear option works just like the Vertex/Linear tool, except that instead of zeroing the control arrows for the two sides of a vertex, the two vertices at the end of a segment have their control arrows zeroed on the side that faces the segment. The result, of course, is a straight line between those two vertices. This tool is especially usefully for making sure that certain segments are perfectly straight and not slightly curved.

The Segment/Curve option changes a line segment into a smooth curved line between the segments at each side.

Segment/Refine

The Refine tool shows up in many places in the 3D Lofter, where it functions the same as it does here in the 2D Shaper: a vertex is added at the clicked-upon point, without disturbing the shape. Because each vertex adds a new control point and ultimately results in more complex objects in the 3D Editor, the Refine option is used often. When you need a gap at a special place in a shape, use Segment/Refine to add a vertex, and delete the segment in the gap with Segment/Delete.

In the example shown in figure 7.22, the rectangle is supposed to smoothly join the circle. First, arcs are made that roughly curve between the rectangle and the circle. Next, vertices are added to the circle in the join points, with Modify/Segment/Refine (see fig. 7.23). Then the unneeded segments are deleted with Modify/Segment/Delete (see fig. 7.24). Finally, the pieces are connected with Modify/Vertex/Weld (see fig. 7.25).

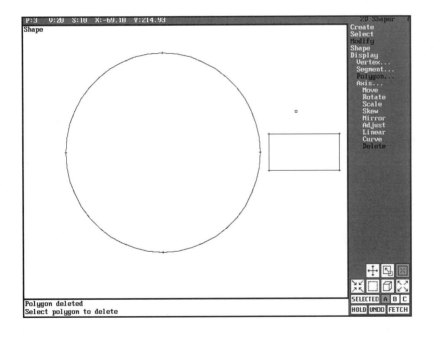

Figure 7.22

A circle and a rectangle.

7

Figure 7.23

A circle and a rectangle with arcs and refined segments.

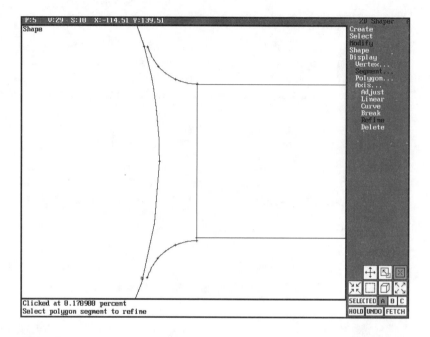

Figure 7.24

The deleted segment.

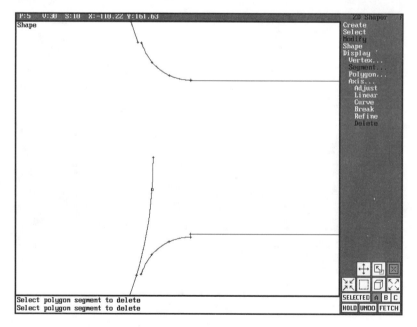

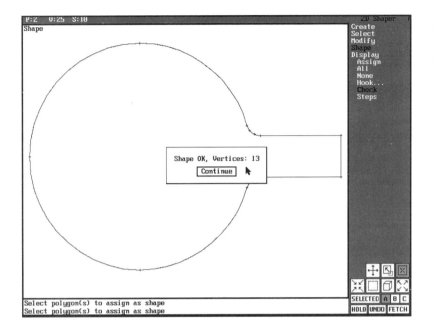

Figure 7.25

The final shape with welded vertices.

Vertex/Delete

Normally, this is a simple tool used to delete a vertex. The adjacent vertices still have a segment between them; only the vertex is deleted. Because the adjacent vertices' curvature remains, however, this tool can be used in conjunction with the Modify/Segment/Refine command to achieve perfect fillets and chamfers. In the following figure, the corners of a rectangle were refined at precise distances from each corner by using snap-to-grid. When the corner vertex is deleted, the two new vertices force a perfect smooth corner (see fig. 7.26).

Segment/Delete

As in the earlier example used to illustrate Segment/Refine, segments are deleted to create gaps for shape design. This tool is often used closely with the Shape/Refine tool to create precise openings onto which new shapes can be "grafted."

7

Figure 7.26

*The shape after a
vertex is deleted.*

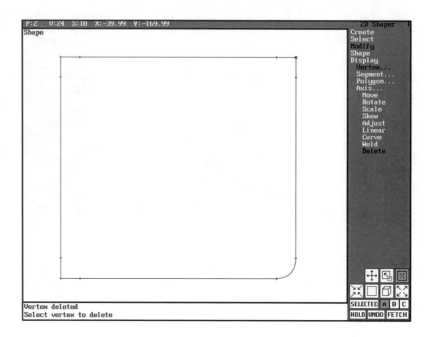

Adjusting Shapes

From the 2D Shaper menu, choose Create/Quad	Highlights Quad in the menu
Using figure 7.27 as a guide, create three rectangles, making sure that they overlap a little	The rectangles appear
In the 2D Shaper menu, choose Modify/Polygon/Rotate	Highlights the Rotate option in the menu
Make sure that the local axis icon is turned on (to activate it, either click on it or type **X**)	Local axis is on
Click on the far right rectangle, rotate it counterclockwise about 15 degrees, and click again to place the rectangle	The rectangle is rotated
In the 2D Shaper menu, choose Modify/Polygon/Move	Highlights the Move option
Click on the far right rectangle, and move it so that it overlaps the top right end of the flat rectangle	Moves the rectangle (see fig. 7.28)

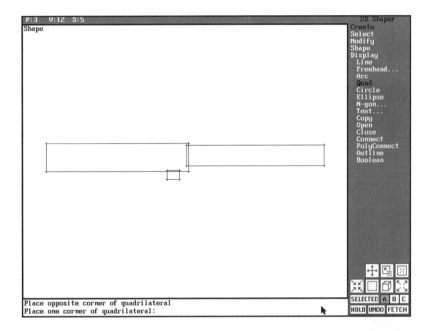

Figure 7.27

Three quads in correct position.

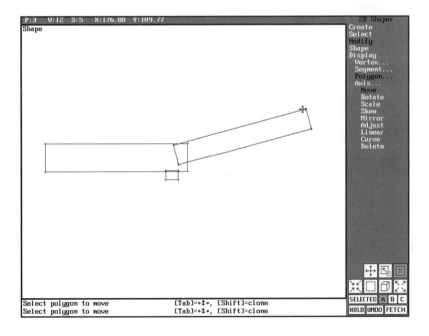

Figure 7.28

The rotated and moved polygon.

continues

continued

In the menu, choose Create/Boolean	Highlights the Boolean option
Click on the two long rectangles	Displays the Boolean dialog box
In the dialog box, choose Union, then click on OK	The two rectangles now form one complex polygon
Click on the two remaining shapes	The Boolean dialog box appears, still in Union mode
Click on OK	Joins all the polygons into a single shape (see fig. 7.29)

Figure 7.29

The shape after Boolean operations.

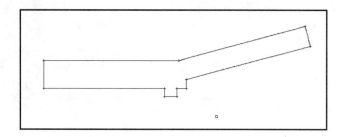

Now you are going to fillet (smooth the corners of) the shape by adding vertices around each corner, then deleting the center corner vertex.

In the 2D Shaper menu, choose Modify/Segment/Refine	Highlights the Refine option
Click to the left and right of the top center vertex, on the joining segments that form the flat and slanted parts of the plate. In each case, click about one fourth of the way to the far edge	New vertices appear (see fig. 7.30)
Now, click a slight distance from each of the bottom rectangular shapes' top two corners	The four vertices appear
In the menu, choose Modify/Vertex/Delete	Highlights the Delete option
Delete the four corner vertices, as indicated in figure 7.31	When the vertices disappear, the newly created vertices at each side have curves between them
Choose Modify/Vertex/Move	Highlights the Move option

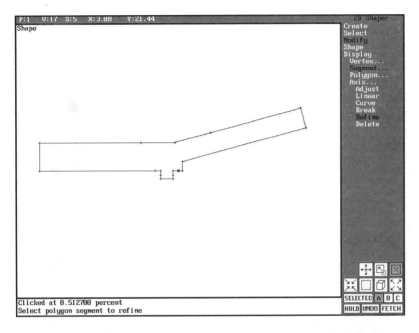

Figure 7.30

Shape with new vertices.

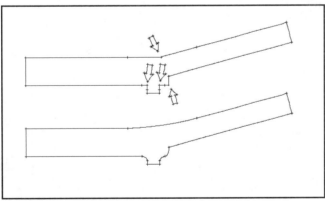

Figure 7.31

Shape with deleted vertices.

Click on the lower right vertex of the rightmost half of the plate shape, and move the vertex up so that the plate's lip is thinner than the plate's center (see fig. 7.32)	Moves the vertex
Choose Modify/Segment/Adjust	Highlights the Adjust option
Click and drag the segment between the two rightmost vertices	Control arrows appear at both vertices at the ends of the segment (see fig. 7.33)

continues

continued

Figure 7.32

Shape after moved vertex.

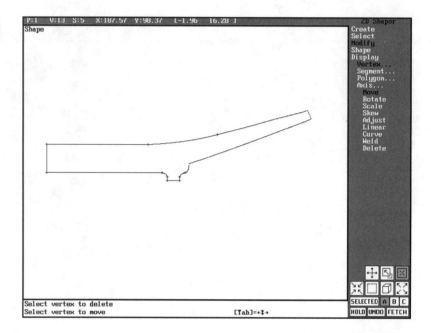

Figure 7.33

Vertex adjustment on the shape.

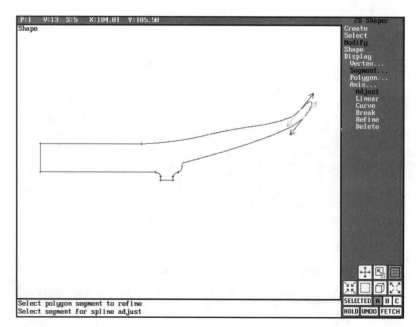

Adjust the mouse so that a slightly rounded edge replaces the blunt flat edge (see fig. 7.34); if you need to readjust, use the UNDO key to reset the adjusted segment

The curve is set when you release the mouse button

Now, you will add two decorative ribs to the top of the plate.

In the 2D Shaper menu, choose Create/Circle	Highlights the Circle option
Create two small circles at the right top of the plate shape; they should overlap the top segment	The circles appear
Choose Create/Boolean	Highlights the Boolean option
Click on the plate, and on one of the circles	Displays the Boolean dialog box, as before
In the dialog box, leave Union mode selected, and click on OK	Joins the two shapes
Click again on the plate and the remaining circle	Again, the Boolean dialog box appears
In the dialog box, click on OK	The second circle joins the main shape (see fig. 7.35)
In the 2D Shaper menu, choose Shape/Check, and click on the shape	Checks the shape; if the shape is OK and ready for the 3D Lofter, a dialog box is displayed
Save the shape as **CH7TUT3.SHP**	Saves the shape

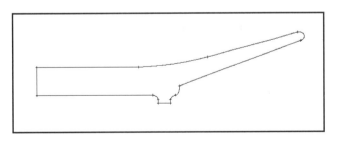

Figure 7.34

The adjusted shape.

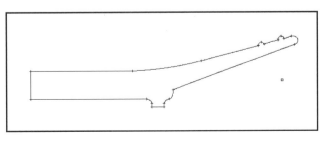

Figure 7.35

The final shape.

7

Text Entry

Using text in the 2D Shaper is a valuable tool, especially if you create a lot of logos or 3D text for use in your animations. This section deals with topics associated with using text in the 2D Shaper.

Using Fonts

Because modern digital fonts are described by lines and curves and not bitmaps, they can have smooth, perfect curves at any size, whereas bit-mapped fonts become jagged at a certain magnification. These fonts are designed to be used in printing, and are not intended for 3D usage. They may need some editing in the 2D Shaper before they are accepted into the 3D Lofter.

TrueType versus PostScript versus FNT

As a result of the revolution in desktop publishing over the past decade, two types of font files have become standard: PostScript and TrueType. PostScript was the standard until recently, when Microsoft implemented TrueType into its Windows software. Now, most freely distributed fonts are TrueType format.

Unfortunately, 3D Studio imports only PostScript (and the rarely seen, URW-formatted BE and FNT fonts). Therefore, TrueType fonts must be converted to PostScript, or used in a drawing program that can export AI files for importation as a complete shape into the 2D Shaper.

Although the shareware and public domain fonts found on BBS systems are usually in TrueType format, most commercial fonts are available in either format. CD-ROMs that include hundreds or even thousands of PostScript fonts (and cost less than $50) are available, and should satisfy your need for a basic font library.

Converting Fonts

When you need a font that is not in a usable format, it usually can be converted to PostScript or the FNT format with a commercial font-conversion utility, such as Ares' Fontmonger. Running under Windows, this type of utility can read a TrueType font and export to FNT, PFB, or several others. With the common usage of TrueType in company logos, the minor investment in a conversion utility is worthwhile.

Sizing Text on Multiple Lines (Descenders, Ascenders)

When you place text in the 2D Shaper, the rectangle displayed reflects the actual size of the active text string (see fig. 7.36). For this reason, problems arise when you enter separately several lines that must line up. Characters such as p and g contain only downward-extending *descenders*, and characters such as d and b contain only upward-extending *ascenders*. If a line of text that contains only ascenders is placed next to a line of text that contains only descenders, the bounding rectangle will cause misalignment (see fig. 7.37).

To avoid this, add characters to one end of the text line that contains the other type of characters. A good technique is to just put the letters Ip at the end of each line, so that the scaling rectangle will cover the full maximum vertical range of the font (see fig. 7.38). The extra characters can be deleted later.

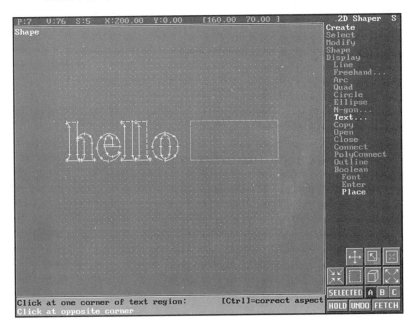

Figure 7.36

Text with placement box.

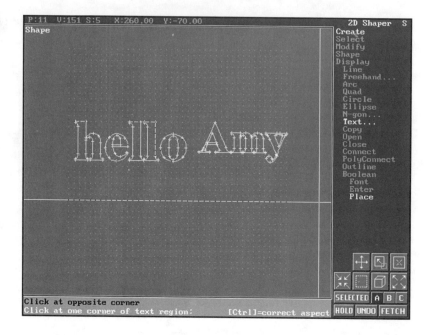

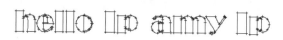

Importing from Windows' Drawing Programs (Corel, Illustrator)

Although the 2D Shaper is a useful utility for creating new shapes and preparing them for use in 3D, it is not nearly as sophisticated and complex as dedicated Windows-based drawing programs, such as CorelDRAW! and Illustrator. Some people are more comfortable creating shapes or tracing scanned artwork in these dedicated drawing programs. Also, clients sometimes provide original artwork (such as logos) in one of these formats. Getting these shapes into 3D Studio is a straightforward process.

If you have access to the program in which the file was created, make sure (before exporting the file) that it is not needlessly complex. Detach the shapes and convert text items to curves. Always export from the drawing program in Adobe Illustrator (AI format) file types. If several flavors of this format are available, use the Illustrator 88 format.

In the 2D Shaper, load the AI formatted file. Certain programs export in "stripes," as shown in figure 7.39. The stripes in the text are just lines from one vertex to another that are left over from the importation process. Sometimes there is more than one line in the same place also.

When this happens, delete all the stripes that appear (see fig. 7.40). Be sure to press the accent (`` ` ``) key repeatedly (this key, also called the *tilde* (~) key, is to the left of the 1 key on the keyboard) to redraw the screen after each deletion. You need to do this because, if two lines fall on top of each other, deleting one makes it appear as though both are deleted, until the screen is redrawn.

At this point, the shapes look correct but are disconnected. The disconnected vertices are not apparent because they fall directly on top of other vertices. Many exported shapes exhibit this problem, which sometimes is not detected until the shape is checked. Luckily, each vertex does not have to be hand-welded. Because the vertices are directly on top of each other, the entire shape can be welded in one step, and should then be complete. First, use Select/All, then choose Modify/Vertex/Weld, with the SELECTED button activated. At this point, the shape checks OK (see fig. 7.41), and is ready to be lofted or moved to the 3D Editor.

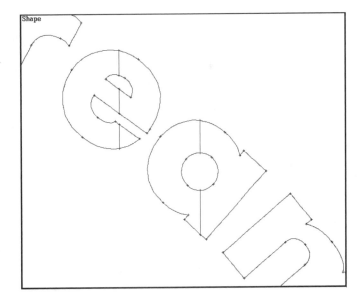

Figure 7.39

The striped imported text.

7

Figure 7.40

The deleted stripes.

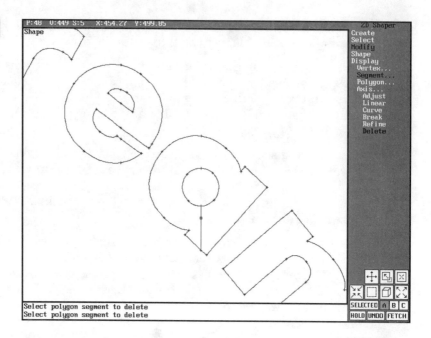

Figure 7.41

The final version of the imported text.

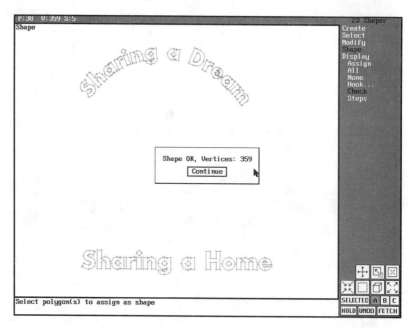

More on the 3D Lofter Tools

The 3D Lofter is a powerful tool that enables you to create objects from shapes that have been extruded along a path. These shapes can undergo any of several transformations along this extrusion path. This section deals with some of these transformations, in particular, the following:

- Lofting Different Shapes Along a Path
- Scale Deformation
- Twist Deformation
- Teeter Deformation
- Bevel Deformation
- Fit Deformation
- Unique Paths
- Lofting with Mapping Coordinates
- Surface of Revolution Paths
- Deform/Fit Lofting

Learning how and when to use each of these tools will provide you with the capabilities to create just about any object you can think of.

Lofting Different Shapes Along a Path

When you create a path in the 3D Lofter, a series of tick marks is displayed along the length of the path. These tick marks represent levels of the path. Each level can have a different shape assigned to it. The only restriction on the shapes is that they must have the same number of vertices. Then, the shape at the beginning of the path is extruded to match the form of the other shapes along the path. The Lofter simply connects one vertex of one shape to the same vertex on the next shape. Thus, having the same number of vertices is crucial or you will not get a correctly lofted shape.

One thing to watch out for is the orientation of each shape. When a shape is created in the 2D Shaper, it has a start vertex and an end vertex. When placing shapes along the path, you want to make sure the first vertex of each shape is aligned with the others. This helps to ensure correct lofting of the final 3D object. Figure 7.42 shows a loft with a series of varying shapes. Figure 7.43 shows the resulting lofted 3D object.

7

Figure 7.42

A loft path with varying shapes.

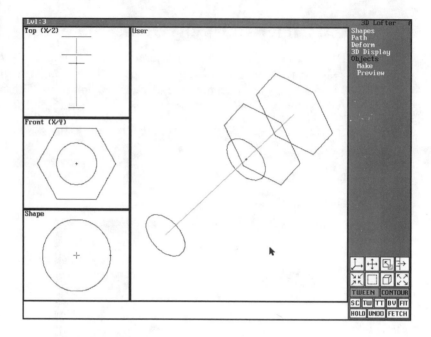

Figure 7.43

The resulting 3D object.

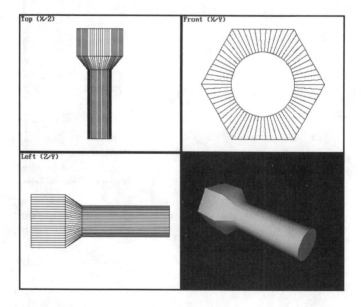

Before introducing you to the basic deformation tools provided for you in the 3D Lofter, an introduction to some of the common elements of these tools is necessary. All of the deform tools come with a Deformation grid through which you define how that deformation tool will affect the final shape.

Each of the graphs you will encounter have several basic properties about them. Most are compromised of white, blue, and yellow lines. The white lines are the graph levels themselves. The yellow lines represent the levels in the current path in the Lofter. The blue line is the deformation line that is similar to the path in the Lofter. Adjusting the blue line using the tools provided for each deformation type enables you to control where and how much deformation occurs. Figure 7.44 shows you a Scale Deformation grid with the shape at 100% at one end of the path and at 50% at the other end.

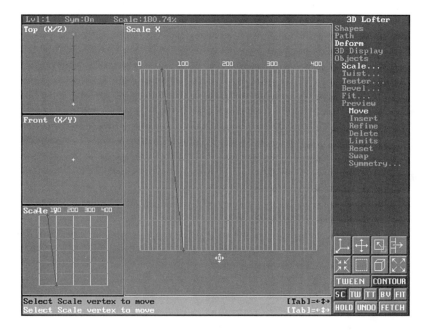

Figure 7.44

The Scale Deformation grid.

Under a scale grid, you can cause the shape that is being extruded to change scales as it moves along the length of the path. Adjusting the control line (the blue line) is as simple as adjusting or refining a line in the 2D Shaper. Many of the tools are the same for adjusting the line. Say, for example, you want an object that starts out with a scale of 100% at one end of the path and ends up with a scale of 50% at the other end. You would simply choose Deform/Scale.../Move to adjust the top end of the blue line to 50%. Then, make your object. It will have a consistent slope from the original shape to the scaled down version of the shape.

All of the deformation tools also take advantage of symmetry. The tools can deform the shape along the X or Y axes, or both in the case of symmetry. You choose Deform/*Tool you are using*/Symmetry to enable or disable this feature. Remember that shapes are extruded along the path. Therefore, the X and Y axes are always perpendicular to the path.

All the deformation grids use a similar methodology. The only difference is the scales the grid is using. For example, a Scale deformation has percentages across the top of the grid representing different scales for the shape, whereas a Rotation deformation will have rotational degrees across the top. Otherwise the tools are the same, except for the Fit Deformation tool (covered in greater detail later in this chapter). It requires a little more work but is much more powerful than the others.

Manipulating the blue path line is accomplished through several tools that are common to each deformation type. Some of these tools are Move, Insert, Delete, Refine, Limits, and Reset. Move allows you to move any vertex in the path line. As with a normal vertex move operation, the Tab controls, snap, and grid can all be applied to provide precise movement of the path line. Insert allows you to insert a vertex in the line. Most of the time, if you are moving some point other than an endpoint, you will have to insert a new vertex to move first. Delete allows you to delete a vertex. Refine works just like it does in the 2D Shaper—it enables you to add a vertex to the line and help refine the shape of the line. Limits enables you to define how much or how little the deformation tool can effect. You could limit, for example, the Scale Deformation tool to a maximum of 200% scale. Reset simply resets the graph to its default form. These tools are located in the deformation menu for each deformation type.

Finally, all deformation types have a Preview function. The preview command enables you to see a wireframe preview of the object before it is created. This helps you to catch errors in the lofting process before you create the object.

Each grid type will be discussed in more detail when the matching deformation tool is discussed. Now that you have been introduced to the basics of the deformation tool grids, it is time to look at the tools themselves and see how each works.

Scale Deformation

The Scale Deformation command is located under Deform/Scale... When you choose this option, the Scale Deformation grid will be displayed in the viewport. The Scale Deformation tool works by scaling the shape as it is lofted along the path. Notice that the Scale Deformation grid goes from 0% scale to 400% scale (see figure 7.45). This can be controlled with the Limits command.

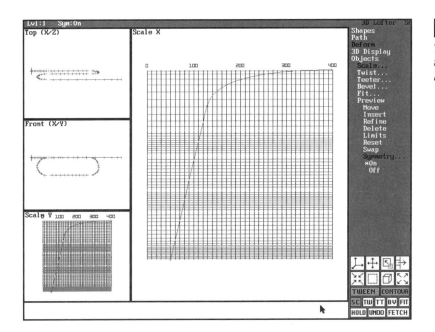

Figure 7.45

*The Scale Deforma-
tion Grid with
Symmetry On.*

You control where and how the Scale Deformation occurs by adjusting the blue line in the graph. This blue line is representative of the path and runs from bottom to top. The yellow lines represent the levels of the path. So, you can simply move the blue line at the appropriate level to the scale you want at that level. For example, if you place the middle of the blue line at 200% on the grid and leave the endpoints at 100%, you will have a bow shaped line. This will result in a shape that scales up 200% as it approaches the middle of the path and then back to 100% as it approaches the other endpoint.

Adjusting the path line in the deformation grid is accomplished through several tools. These tools are very similar to the drawing tools provided in the 2D Shaper, so you should not have any problems picking these up. The tools are located under Deform/Scale... Here, you will find Move, Insert, Refine, Delete, Limits, Reset, Swap, and Symmetry. The two commands here that are not common are Symmetry and Swap. These two commands relate to the X and Y axes of the deformation command. You can deform the shape along its X or Y axis, or both. Symmetry allows you to keep the deformation symmetrical. Otherwise, you have both an X and a Y deformation grid to work with. Swap will swap the X deformation grid for the Y deformation grid.

Figure 7.46 shows you a preview of an object using Scale Deformation. The resulting object is a trumpet. This is simply a linear scale of the shape along a custom curved path. Figure 7.47 shows the resulting shape.

Figure 7.46

Preview of Scale Deformation object.

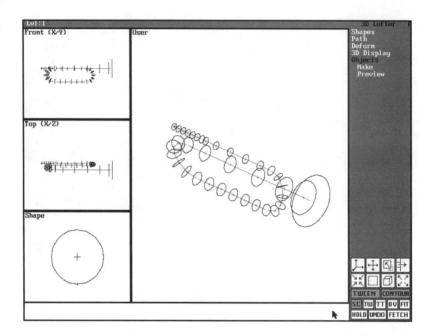

Figure 7.47

Object after lofting.

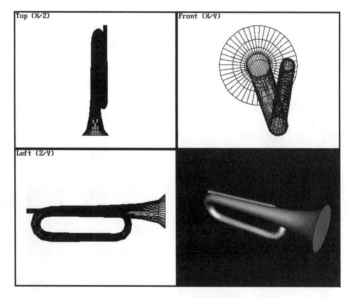

Twist Deformation

Twist Deform spins the shapes around the path as they travel along the path. The path always acts as the center of rotation or the axis of the twist. The command can be accessed by choosing Deform/Twist... Screw and helix type shapes are most often created with this type of deformation. Be-cause the shape need not be centered in the path it is traveling, a wobbling spin or even a helix can be created with Twist. The Twist grid lists rotation in degrees across the top (see fig. 7.48). Twist does not support symmetry because it has only one axis. Figure 7.49 shows a preview of the Twist deformed object, and figure 7.50 shows the final Twist deformed object.

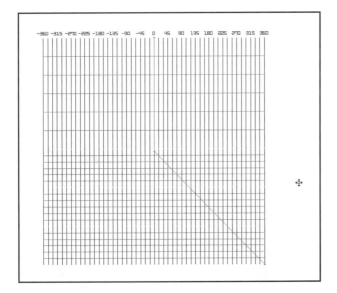

Figure 7.48

The Twist Deformation grid.

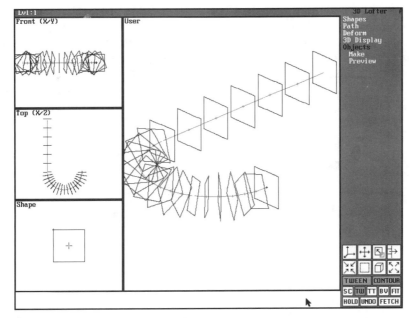

Figure 7.49

Preview of a Twist deformed object.

7

Figure 7.50

The final object with Twist Deform.

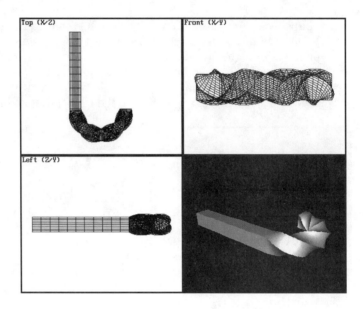

Teeter Deformation

Teetering is where the shape rotates about the two axes perpendicular to the path it is traveling. Both X and Y teeter are available (see fig. 7.51), pertaining to the rotation of the shape about the path, which is considered the center point. Symmetry is available in the Teeter Deformation, but be careful using the Symmetry option for this deformation type as it can yield unexpected results. As the shape travels along the axis teetering from one side to another, symmetry can cause it to teeter differently to match both axes instead of how you wanted. Explore the command and use it when you need it. Figure 7.52 shows a preview of an object with a Teeter Deformation applied to it. Figure 7.53 shows the final object with Teeter Deformation.

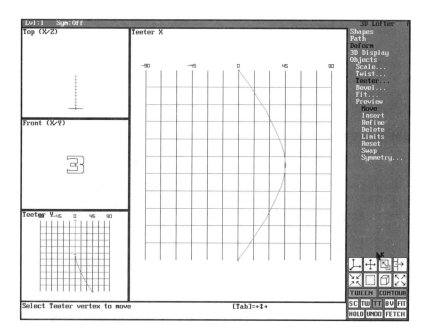

Figure 7.51

The Teeter Deformation grid.

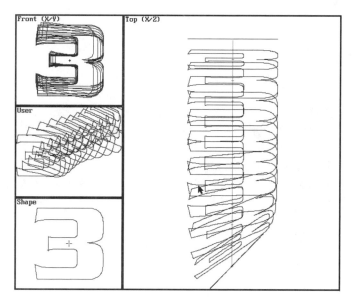

Figure 7.52

Preview of a Teeter deformed object.

7

Figure 7.53

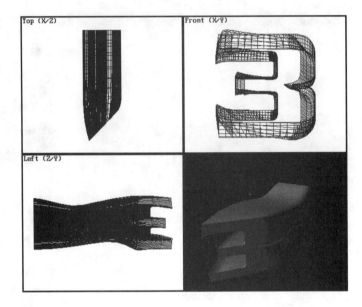

Final Teeter deformed object.

Bevel Deformation

The Bevel Deformation command is accessed by choosing Deform/Bevel... This displays the Bevel Deformation grid (see figure 7.54). A bevel deformation is similar to a scale deformation, except that it bevels the shape as it goes, making the shape smaller. The Bevel Deformation grid uses actual drawing units instead of percentages to determine how much bevel you use in the loft process. This enables you to precisely determine how large or small the bevel will be, instead of having to guess at scale percentages. Too much bevel can result in a shape that crosses itself. This results in an invalid shape and you get a warning message (see figure 7.55).

Be careful using curved or complex shapes, especially text, with a bevel deformation. These types of shapes are difficult to bevel and may not always bevel correctly. If it does not bevel correctly, you may try a scale deformation instead. Figure 7.56 shows a preview of a beveled shape. Figure 7.57 shows the final beveled shape.

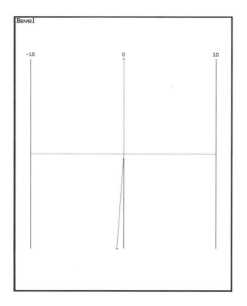

Figure 7.54

The Bevel Deformation grid.

Figure 7.55

Beveled shape is invalid warning.

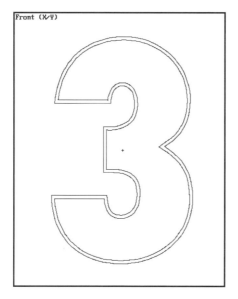

Figure 7.56

Preview of a Bevel deformed object.

7

Figure 7.57

Final Bevel deformed object.

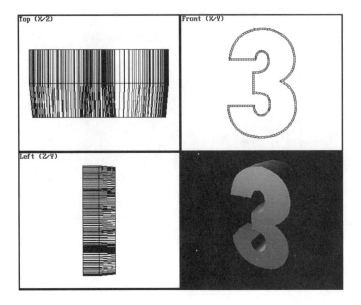

Fit Deformation

Fit Deformation is one of the more powerful and complex tools you will run across in 3D Studio. You can access the Fit Deformation command by choosing Deform/Fit... Fit Deformation works on the principle of profiles. In Fit Deformation, you can assign a profile (shape) to the X-axis, Y-axis, or both. Then, as the shape is lofted, it is forced to fit the profile in one or both axes. For example, imagine a phone handle. The shape that is to be lofted can be either a circle or a square. For the profile in the X-axis, you would draw the profile of the top of the phone. Then, you could place a profile of the side of the phone in the Y-axis. When you loft the shape, you will get a phone.

There are a few limitations on the shapes that you can use as profiles. The top and bottom of the profiles must be either flat or come to a point, and the profile cannot branch or backtrack onto itself from top to bottom. Otherwise, you will get an invalid shape or object.

Figure 7.58 shows the Fit Deformation grid. Because there are two axes, symmetry is used in this type of deformation. You import shapes into the fit grid by first activating the viewport you want to place the shape in, then choosing Deform/Fit/Get... You can load the shape from the 2D Shaper or from a disk. Each of these shapes can then be modified using the commands found under Deform/Fit...

A new command for 3DS Release 4 in Deform/Fit is Gen Path. This command looks at one or both the shapes you have loaded and generates a

3D Studio
❹ BEGINNERS

The church image printed from a laser printer (see Chapter 12).

The church image printed from an inkjet printer.

The church image printed from a thermal wax printer.

The church image printed from a dye sublimation printer.

Image created by Steven D. Elliott as seen in New Riders' 3D Studio Special Effects.

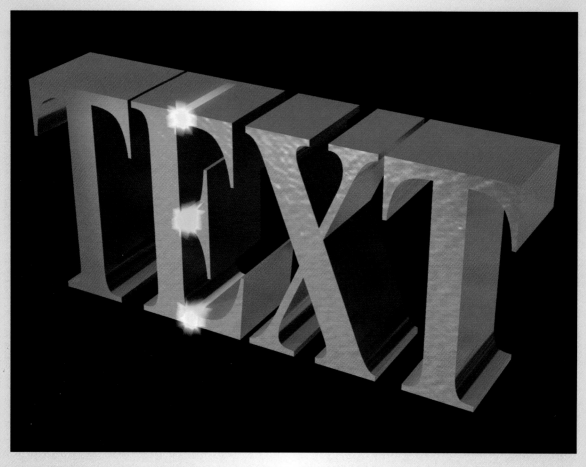

Image created by Richard Sher as seen in New Riders' 3D Studio Special Effects.

Image created by Gregory Pyros, AIA, as seen in New Riders' 3D Studio Special Effects. *Image shows 3D Studio's zooming capabilities.*

*Four still frames from a logo-animation sequence created
by Eric Peterson.*

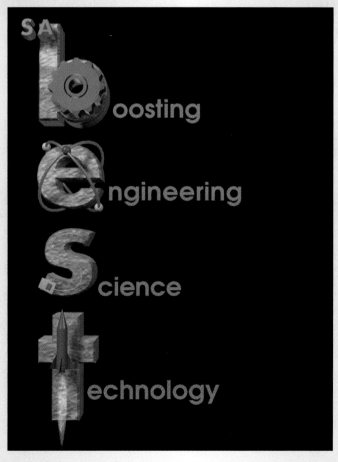

A laser burning a logo into a piece of wood. Four still frames from an animation created by Eric Peterson.

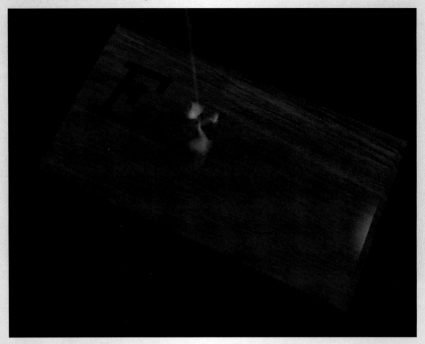

Engineering Spectrum Inc.

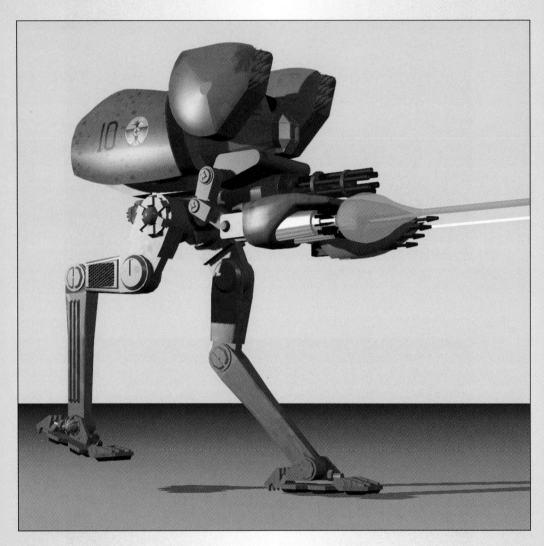

Image created by Eric Peterson using 3D Studio Release 4 .

Using multiple lighting techniques. Image by Eric Peterson.

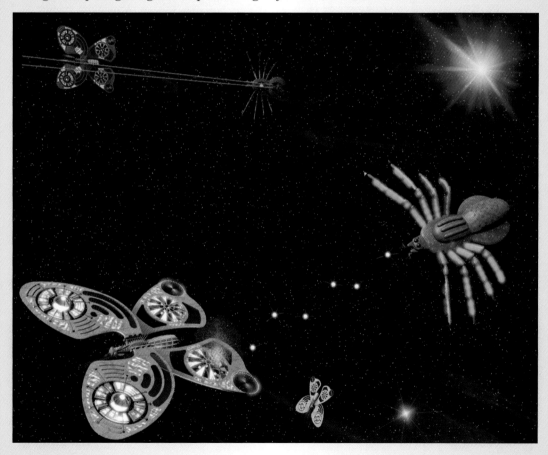

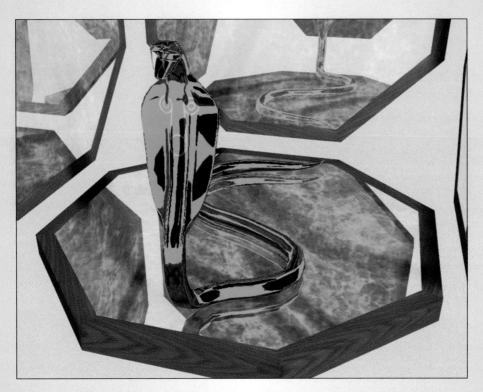

Image by Eric Peterson.

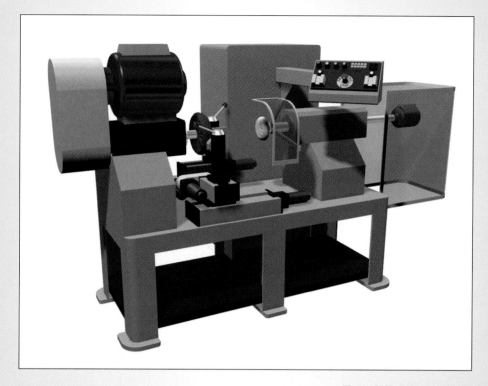

*Two different views of
the same object. Images
by Eric Peterson.*

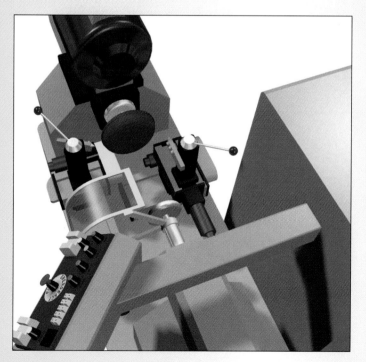

The simulation of backlit and self-illuminated signage. Image taken from Inside 3D Studio Release 4 *from New Riders.*

The simulated illumination of free-form neon. Image taken from Inside 3D Studio Release 4 *from New Riders.*

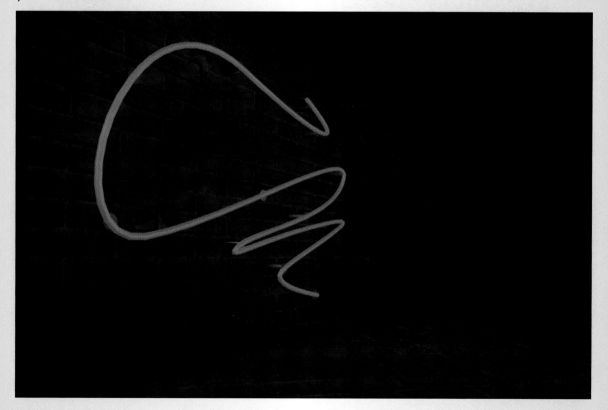

Textures image by Tim Forcade as seen in 3D Studio Special Effects *from New Riders.*

new path based on these shapes. This enables you to see how many new vertices will be created due to the parameters set by the profiles you are using.

Figure 7.59 shows a preview of an object that is using a Fit Deformation. Figure 7.60 shows the final Fit deformed object.

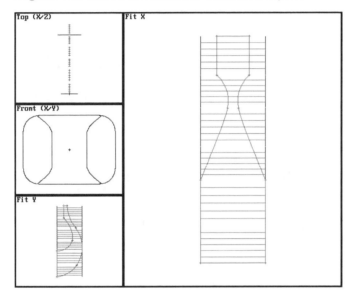

Figure 7.58

The Fit Deformation grid.

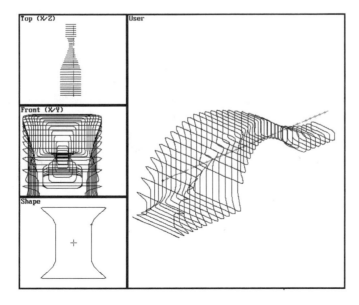

Figure 7.59

Preview of a Fit deformed object.

7

Figure 7.60

The final Fit deformed object.

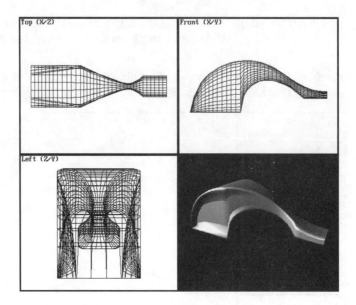

Using More than One Deformation Type

3D Studio enables you to use more than one of the deformation types mentioned previously at the same time. Simply set up the deformations you want to use. In the 3D Lofter there is a set of buttons in the lower right corner of the screen. Five of these buttons have two letters on each button. They are SC for Scale deformation, TW for Twist deformation, TT for Teeter deformation, BV for Bevel deformation, and FT for Fit deformation. By clicking on each button, you can enable or disable each type of deformation.

An example of using multiple deformation might be an object that uses Scale deformation to change scale from one end to the other. A second deformation using Twist deformation can be added to make the shape twist as it changes scale. You should be careful in choosing which deformations to use together. For example, a Fit deformation might not work well with the others because it uses profiles for both axes. You will have to explore and decide for yourself which deformations work well together and which don't.

Unique Paths

Any shape can be a path. Even a path that doubles back on itself or crosses itself is legal. Two types of paths can be generated automatically in the 3D Lofter, with the Path/Helix and Path/SurfRev commands. The Helix option allows for a spring-like path with definable start and end diameter, height, and total number of turns (see fig. 7.61). *SurfRev* stands for *surface of revolution*, which is in essence a circular path (see fig. 7.62). Any object that might be lathed in real life is a candidate for modeling with a surface of revolution path. Such objects might include plates, vases, tires, and any other object with a single axis about which a shape rotates.

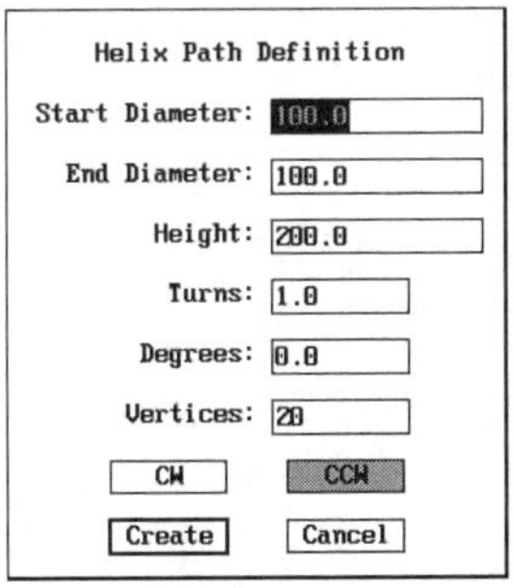

Figure 7.61

The Helix Path Definition dialog box.

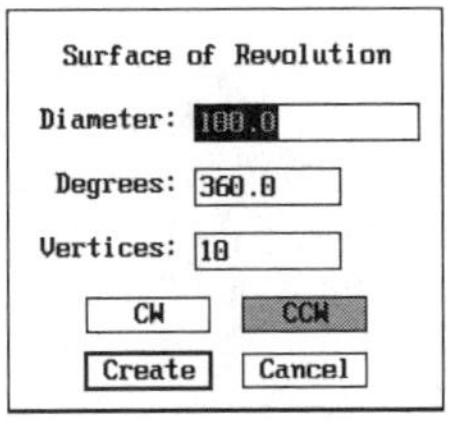

Figure 7.62

The Surface of Revolution dialog box.

Lofting with Coordinates

Chapter 8, "Advanced Lighting/Materials Techniques," explains mapping coordinates. Whenever one of the materials that uses a texture map is applied to an object (except for Reflection Maps), 3D Studio needs to know how and where to apply the texture map. In many cases (a helical shape, for example), none of the three types of mapping will yield satisfactory results. In the shapes shown in figures 7.63 and 7.64, a certain amount of smearing is evident. *Smearing* occurs when a texture is stretched unnaturally along an area of an object. It is most evident when a planar texture is applied to the front face of an extruded shape, and the sides of the extruded shape show a striped pattern where the texture crosses the edge.

7

Figure 7.63

Three helixes with incorrect mapping.

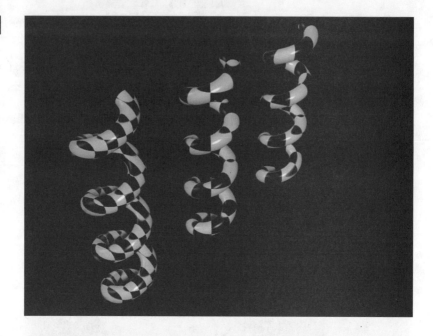

Figure 7.64

Letter with material smearing.

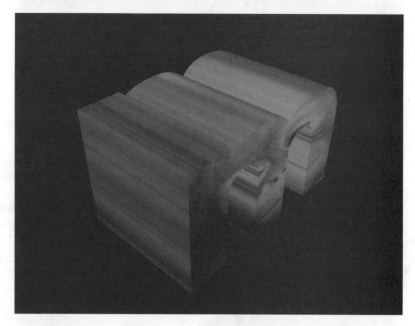

When an object is created in 3D Studio, the Lofter can apply coordinates as the object is lofted. In this way, you can easily apply appropriate mapping to complex shapes. Applying mapping is accomplished through the Mapping on/off button in the Object Lofting Controls dialog box that appears when the 3D object is created. In figure 7.65, the same checkered material is perfectly applied by this technique.

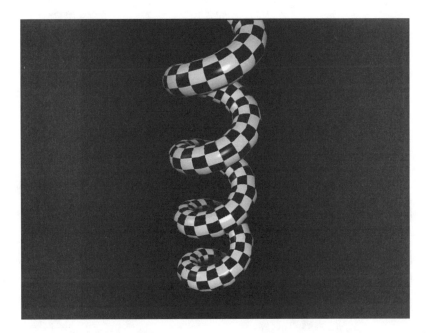

Figure 7.65

Correctly mapped helix.

In the following exercise, you use the mapping coordinates to create a perfectly mapped helix.

Using Mapping Coordinates

Switch to the 3D Lofter by pressing F2	The Lofter appears
Create a helical path	
Choose Path/Helix	The Helix Path Definition dialog box appears
Set Height to 500, Turns to 4, and Vertices to 60	The dialog box reflects changes made (see fig. 7.66)

continues

continued

Figure 7.66

*Helix Path Defini-
tion dialog box.*

```
┌─────────────────────────────┐
│    Helix Path Definition    │
│                             │
│  Start Diameter: [100]      │
│                             │
│    End Diameter: [100.0]    │
│                             │
│          Height: [500.0]    │
│                             │
│           Turns: [4.0]      │
│                             │
│         Degrees: [0.0]      │
│                             │
│        Vertices: [60]       │
│                             │
│      [  CW  ]   [  CCW  ]   │
│      [ Create ] [ Cancel ]  │
└─────────────────────────────┘
```

Click on the Create button

A confirmation dialog box appears
because you are destroying the
existing path

Click on OK

The new path appears (see fig. 7.67)

Figure 7.67

The helix path.

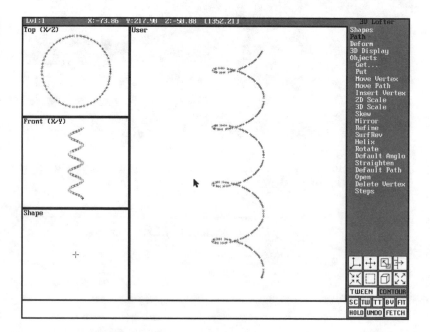

Choose Shapes/Get.../Disk

Enables you to load a shape from the disk

Select CH7TUT1.SHP from your disk

Loads the shape file

Choose Shapes/Center	Centers the shape on the helical path; note that it now is in the correct place in all viewports
Choose Objects/Make dialog box (see fig. 7.68)	Displays the Object Lofting Controls
In the dialog box, click on the Mapping On button, then click on the Tween button	Activates both buttons (see fig. 7.69)
Name the object **Helix1**	Gives the object a name

Figure 7.68

The Object Lofting Controls dialog box.

Click on the Create button	The Mapping Coordinate Repeat Values dialog box appears
Set Length Repeat to 40.0, and Perimeter Repeat to 4.0 (see fig. 7.69)	The dialog box reflects changes made; with these settings, the map can go around your circular shape four times, and repeat 40 times along the sides of the helix

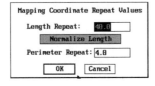

Figure 7.69

The Mapping Coordinate Repeat Values dialog box.

7

Click on the OK button	The object is created in the 3D Editor
Press F3 to switch to the 3D Editor	Displays the 3D Editor

continues

continued

Right-click on the Zoom Extents icon (see fig. 7.70)	Centers the new object in all viewports
Save the file as **CH7TUT2.3DS**	Saves the object

Figure 7.70

The final object.

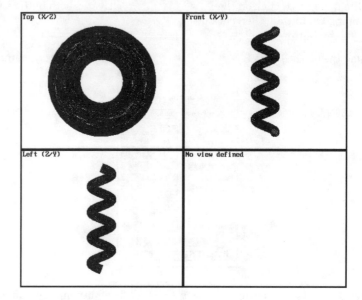

In the next exercise, you add a material so that you can view the mapping coordinates. First you create the material, then you apply it, add lights and camera, and, finally, you render the object.

Adding Materials to Lofted Helix

Load CH7TUT2.3DS	Loads file
Switch to the Materials editor by pressing F5	Displays the Materials Editor
Click on the Map slot in the Texture 1 row of texture map slots	Displays the Select Texture Map dialog box
Click on the *.CEL button on the right side of the dialog box	Displays a list of all images with the CEL file extension
From this list, choose CHECKER.CEL and click on OK	

Press the spacebar to render the new image	Displays a ball with one check
In the See Tiling area at the right of the Materials Editor, click on the 4×4 button, and again press the spacebar	Renders the sphere with the checkers (see fig. 7.71); note the pinched effect at the top of the sphere, caused by a forced spherical mapping on the render sample

4×4 enables you to get a better idea of how the material looks. It does not affect the material definition.

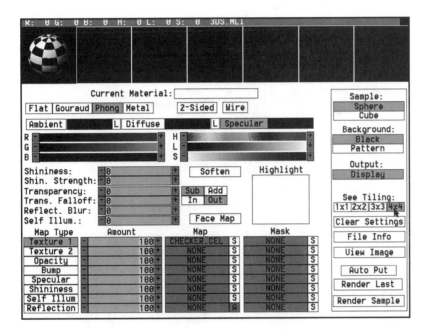

Figure 7.71

The Checker material.

In the Materials Editor, choose the Specular color button	Activates the Specular button
Click in the luminance slider (in an area at its far right)	The specular swatch turns white
Adjust the Shininess to 50 and Shin. Strength to 90 to get a moderate bump in the Highlight window	The Highlight window reflects the changes made
Type **C**	Displays the New Current Material Name dialog box, in which you can simultaneously name this new material and make it active

continues

continued

Type **CHECKS**, and click on OK	Names and activates the new material
Switch back to the 3D Editor by pressing F3	Displays the 3D Editor
Choose Surface/Material/Assign/Object	Highlights Object in the 3D Editor menu
Click on the helix	Displays a dialog box in which to confirm application of the material
In the dialog box, click on OK	Assigns material to helix
Press Alt+B	Switches the viewports to Box-mode display (Zooms are much faster, but you can still see where to point the light and camera)
Right-click on Zoom Extents	Resets all viewports
Right-click on the Zoom Out icon three times	All the viewports zoom out three times
In the 3D Editor, choose Lights /Omni/Create	Highlights Create in the menu
Click at the bottom center of the top viewport	Displays the Light Definition dialog box
In the dialog box, click on Create	A light icon appears in the viewports
Click at the top left of the Top viewport	The Light Definition dialog box appears again

Make this light dimmer by setting the luminance slider to 60 (see fig. 7.72).

Choose Create	Creates light
In the 3D Editor menu, choose Lights/Omni/Move	Highlights the Move option in the menu
In the Front viewport, adjust the two lights so that they are somewhat above the object	Moves the lights (see fig. 7.73)
In the 3D Editor menu, choose Cameras/Create	Highlights the Create option in the menu
Now you need to create a camera	
Click in the top viewport	Activates the viewport
Click at the lower left of the Top viewport, and again just below the object	Displays the Camera Definition dialog box

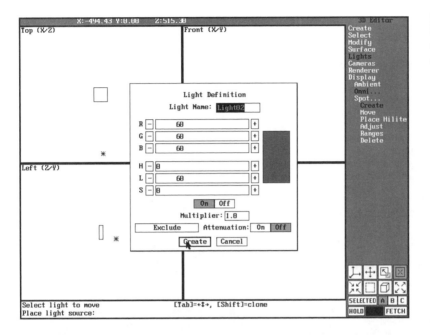

Figure 7.72

Scene with two lights.

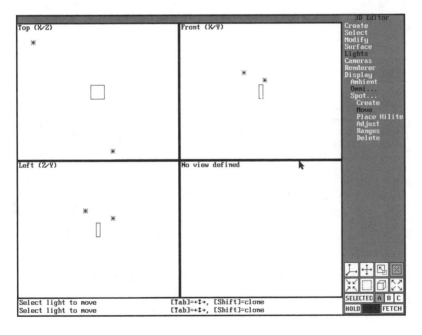

Figure 7.73

Scene with two lights correctly placed.

continues

continued

In the dialog box, click on Create	The camera icon appears in all viewports
Choose Cameras/Move	Highlights the Move option in the menu
In the Front viewport, move the target to the center of the object, and the camera slightly higher	Repositions the camera
Click in the lower right viewport and press the C key	The viewport becomes the camera view (see fig. 7.74)

At this point, the helix is ready to be rendered.

Choose Render/Render View, and click in the Camera viewport	Displays the Render Still Frame dialog box
Click on Render	Renders the image (see fig. 7.75). The mapping is perfect, and slots are evident in the sides of the helix where the shape had cuts

Figure 7.74

Scene with lights and a camera.

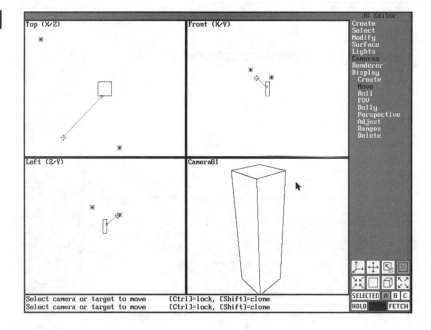

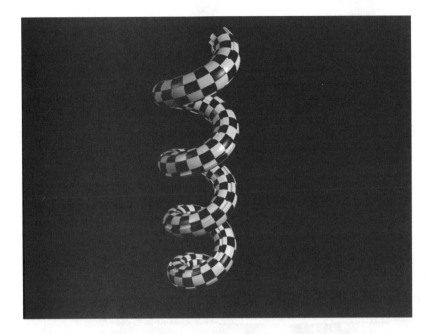

Figure 7.75

Final rendering of helix.

Paths: Surf-Rev

One special type of object creation is the Surface of Revolution. You use this approach to create objects, such as vases and wheels, that are symmetric about one axis. Objects (such as wheels) that have a hole in the center are lofted like regular objects, with a circular connected path.

Objects such as vases—the sort of objects created by a lathe—are different. To create these sorts of objects, instead of just extruding a shape along a path, you create only one half of the object in the Shaper, and spin this shape about an axis. The flat side must be perfectly centered, and all the center vertices are welded to complete creation of the object.

In the following exercise, you use a Surface of Revolution to create a plate object.

7

Using a Surface of Revolution

Because Surfaces of Revolution rotate a cross section about a center axis, only the right half of the cross section is created as a shape. In the case of a plate, imagine cutting the plate in half down the center to view its cross section, then discarding the half to the left of the plate's center point. First you'll create the basic shapes of the plate. Then, using the techniques covered in this chapter, you'll smooth some of the edges.

Press F2 to switch to the 3D Lofter	Displays the 3D Lofter
Choose Path/SurfRev	The Surface of Revolution dialog box appears (see fig. 7.76)

Surface of Revolution
Diameter: 100.0
Degrees: 360.0
Vertices: 18
CW   CCW
Create   Cancel

Because the default settings work well for this case, which is a standard Surface of Rwevolution, click on Create	Displays a dialog box in which to confirm the path replacement
In the dialog box, click on OK	The dialog box disappears; a ring-shaped path is now evident in the viewports
In the 3D Lofter menu, choose Shapes/Get/Disk	Displays the 2D Shaper shape; note that assigning the shapes in the 2D Shaper was not necessary because only one shape exists in the 2D Shaper
Choose CH7TUT3.SHP from your disk	Loads the shape (see fig. 7.77)

Note that the shape appears centered in the circular path, but not aligned with its flat left edge at the center point.

To align the shape, choose Shapes/ Align/Left	Moves the shape so that its flat edge is at the center of the circular path

Using a perfectly flat left edge of your shape in the 2D Shaper, and aligning this shape left in a counterclockwise path (counterclockwise path rotation was set in the SurfRev dialog box) is critical to proper surfaces of revolution with a solid center.

Choose Objects/Preview	The Preview Controls dialog box appears
In the dialog box, activate the Tween button and click on Preview	The preview appears in the viewports (see fig. 7.78); note that the flat left edge of the shape is placed at the center of the previewed object

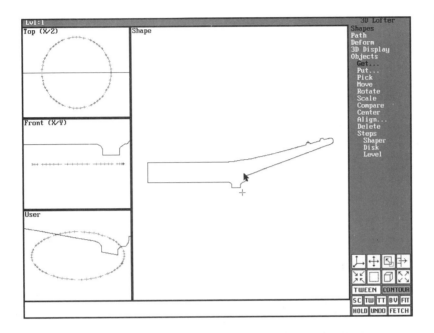

Figure 7.77

Shape loaded in the Lofter.

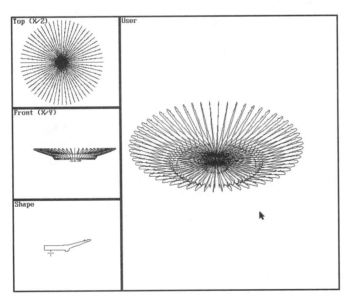

Figure 7.78

Preview of the object.

7

continues

continued

In the 3D Lofter menu, choose Objects/Make

Displays the Object Lofting Controls dialog box

In the dialog box, switch the Weld Vertices button to On to combine all the center vertices created by each shape that appears around the circular path; Name the object **Plate1**. Leave the other buttons in their standard position, and click on Create

The Object Creation dialog box appears briefly; then the message Welding Object, please wait appears for a while at the top of the screen

Press F3 to switch to the 3D Editor

Displays the 3D Editor, with the newly created plate (see fig. 7.79); because of the lofting process, the center of the plate renders smooth; the rim displays the ribs added with the Boolean circles

Figure 7.79

The final 3D plate.

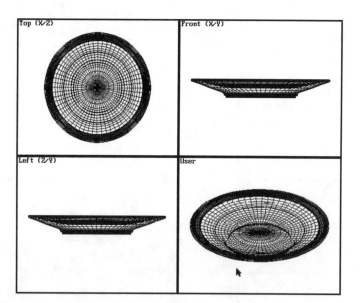

3D Editor Modeling

Many objects are easier to create in the 3D Editor (instead of creating them in the 2D Shaper and then importing them into the 3D Editor).

Simple shapes are often combined to create a final object. Also, for special cases, the 3D Editor's Array and Boolean tools enable you to create new complex objects from existing objects.

Object Creation Tools

Tools used for object creation are discussed in detail in the following sections. These tools include: Array, Boolean, Box, L/G/Hemisphere, Cyl/Tube, Torus, and Cone.

Array

This tool copies an object many times. You can create the array in a linear or radial manner. In Linear mode, the new copies are placed in a line. The linear array can be created by using either the Create/Array/Linear or the Create/Array/Move commands. Using the Create/Array/Move command is often a more intuitive procedure, because the object spacing and direction of the line of copies is set graphically. The Create/Array/Linear command brings up a dialog box with spacing controls, for exact numerical entry.

If you take a closer look at the Linear Array dialog box shown in figure 7.80, you will see a number of useful options. First, you can key-in the number of objects that will be in the array. Then, you can define how the array is to occur. The first way is to define the distance between each object. Alternatively, you can define the overall length of the array. One of these two parameters will be the controlling parameter, depending upon which you choose. Finally, you can determine how 3D Studio interprets the distance from object to object. The distance can be calculated from the center of one object to the center of the next or from the end of one object to the end of the next object. This allows you precise control over how the array is created. Clicking OK creates the array.

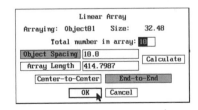

Figure 7.80

The Linear Array dialog box.

7

You would use a linear array to create objects that are repetitive and equally spaced like columns in a building or a grove of trees or even a set of parking lot spaces.

When you are working in Create/Array/Linear mode, the icon exhibits a single-pointer shape. As usual, you use the 3D Editor's TAB key to switch the directional options of the arrow. The arrow in this case points in the direction of the array's creation.

The Create/Array/Radial and Create/Array/Rotate commands are similar in operation, but place the rotated copies in a circle instead of a line. The center point of the rotation is set by the Modify/Axis/Place command.

The Radial Array dialog box shown in figure 7.81, like the linear version, provides you with precise control over the creation of the array. First, you can set the total number of objects in the array in a key-in field. Then, you can set the degrees between each object in the array or the arc length between objects. As with linear, these are the two controlling options on the distance between each object. Finally, there is a Rotate Objects button. Activating this button causes the arrayed object to rotate as it is copied, keeping the object correctly aligned toward the center of the array. Click on OK to create the array.

Radial arrays can be used in any circumstance where you have a number of objects spaced equally in a circle. An example might be the lights around a helicopter landing pad.

Figure 7.81

The Radial Array dialog box.

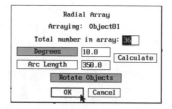

The following exercise steps you through the process of using the array commands to create a simple fence. This fence will be comprised of very simple objects. From it, you can see how easy it is to create complex looking objects from a set of simple objects that have been arrayed.

Creating a Fence

In the 3D Editor menu, choose Create/Cylinder/Values	Displays the Set Cylinder Values dialog box

The default setting in this dialog box is a six-sided cylinder, which usually is too coarse.

Adjust the Sides slider to 18, and click on OK	The dialog box disappears
Choose Create/Cylinder/Smoothed	Highlights the Smoothed option
Click in the Top viewport, draw a small circle about 5 units in size, then click again	Displays the crosshairs
Click once to begin drawing a line, then move the mouse to indicate a line roughly 8 times as long as the circle shape was wide	Displays a dialog box in which you name the new shape
In the dialog box, click on Create	Displays the cylinder in the viewports
To gain some space, right-click on the Zoom Out key	All viewports zoom out
In the menu, choose Create/Box, and click in the Front viewport	Highlights the Box option
Click a rectangle in front and to the right of the cylinder, near the top. (The rectangle should be roughly the size of a wood plank, used as a fence board)	The box disappears and the cross hairs reappear
You are prompted for this board's depth; click to draw a short line, and click again to accept	Displays a dialog box in which you can name the new box shape
In the dialog box, click on Create	The dialog box disappears, and the box shape appears in the viewports (see fig. 7.82)
Choose Modify/Object/Move	Highlights the Move option
In the Top viewport, move the box so that it rests in front of the cylinder, just touching it	The box shape is moved (see fig. 7.83)

continues

7

continued

Figure 7.82

A cylinder with a box.

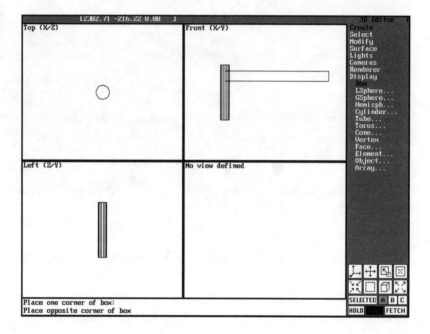

Figure 7.83

The cylinder with the box correctly placed.

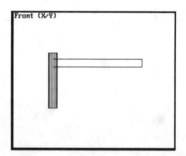

Click in the Front viewport to activate it, then press Tab until only up- and down-arrows are evident in the cursor	Only up and down pointer are on the cursor
Press and hold the Shift key while you click on the box object	A copy of the box, constrained to moving up and down only, follows the cursor
Place the box near the bottom of the cylinder, and click	Displays a dialog box in which you can name the new object

Click on Create to approve the default name	The dialog box disappears, and the new box is displayed in the viewports
While holding down the Shift key, copy the box object again, to the middle of the cylinder; approve the default name	Now three horizontal slabs are beside the post (the cylinder object)
Choose Modify/Object/Rotate, and activate the local axis button if it is not already on (either type **X** or click on the icon)	Highlights the Rotate option; the local axis icon is active
Click on the middle box, and rotate it about 9 degrees	Rotates the board (see fig. 7.84)
Choose Select/All	All the objects turn red to signify that they are selected
Choose Create/Face/Detach, and press the spacebar to activate the SELECTED button; click anywhere in any viewport	Displays a dialog box in which to confirm detaching the selected faces
In the dialog box, click on OK	Displays a dialog box in which to name the new object
Type **fence01**, and click on CREATE	The dialog box disappears, and the selected objects are deselected
In the 3D Editor menu, choose Create/Array/Move	Highlights the Move option
Click in the Top viewport, and press Tab until only the left and right arrows are visible on the cursor	The cursor has only left and right arrows
Click on the single fence object and slide it to the right, until it is almost at the right extreme of the original object (see fig. 7.85)	Displays the copy as a bounding box, which moves with the mouse
Click to place the copy	A dialog box appears, in which to enter the number of copies in the array
Type **25**, and click on OK	Copying is evident in the viewports
Right-click on the Zoom Extents button	The complex fence is now quite long (see fig. 7.86)

continues

7

Figure 7.84

Fence with all boxes.

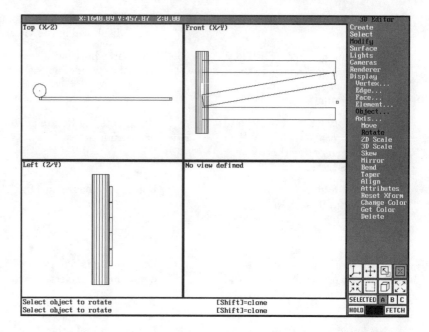

Figure 7.85

The array location.

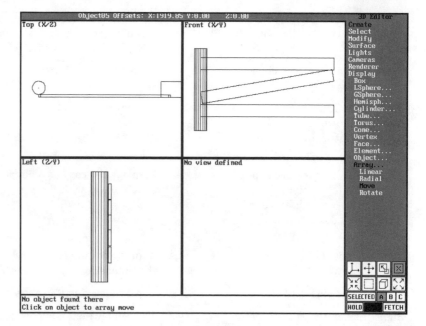

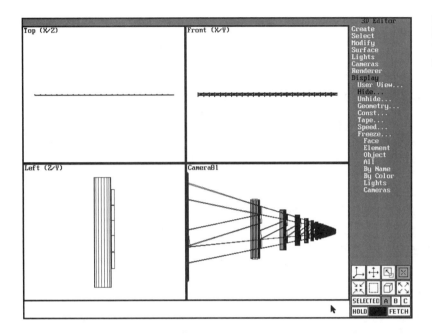

Figure 7.86

The final version of the fence.

Boolean

The 3D Editor's Boolean option works identically to the Boolean operations in the 2D Shaper. Two overlapping objects can be attached, subtracted, or intersected. 3D Booleans are fairly reliable, but can be problematic—sometimes they fail, or produce undesirable results. They always result in a higher face count, which slows rendering and consumes RAM. Therefore, use Booleans only when necessary.

Sometimes, Boolean modeling is the only way to quickly model an object. Imagine an assembly of wood. Your job is to animate how to put it together. More than likely, you will have some blocks with holes in them. How would you create these blocks? Well, if the hole goes all the way through the block, you can simply create a 2D shape of the block and loft it with the hole in place. If the hole does not go all the way through the block, you would have to loft the object and create a second block to cover the hole in the first block. Boolean operations simplify little problems like this by enabling you to simply draw a cylinder and subtract it from the block.

Boolean operations don't always work correctly, however, or even the way you would expect them to. Always make sure you hold the objects in a save buffer before you perform a Boolean operation. This will enable you to quickly recover your information if the Boolean operation fails.

Box

The Create/Box command creates a box shape by accepting first a drawn rectangle to define the box boundary, followed by a drawn line to define depth. If you hold Ctrl before you start the box shape, the box is drawn as a perfect cube after a square shape is defined, and you are not asked for a depth line.

L/G/Hemisphere

Two types of spheres are available in the 3D Editor: the L-type and the G-type. The L-type, which has longitudinal and latitudinal faces, is useful when some of the faces will be deleted to create a partial spherical shape. Otherwise, use the G-type of sphere. The G-type is made up of faces arranged in a geodesic pattern. The pattern does a good job of avoiding faceted silhouettes with a minimum of faces.

Note in figure 7.87 that the two full spheres have roughly the same number of faces, but the geodesic sphere (far right) has a smoother outer border. The object at the left is a sphere from which a group of faces was deleted, to create a new object from an existing L-sphere. A selection of faces like this would be impossible in the G-sphere.

Figure 7.87

Different types of spheres.

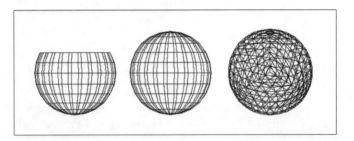

To define the total face count of a G-sphere, you use the Create/G-Sphere/ Values command. To adjust the total number of segments in an L-sphere, use the Create/LSphere/Values command.

The Create/G-Sphere command offers both smoothed and faceted versions. The faceted version looks like cut crystal, and the actual flat faces are visible. Usually you will use the smoothed version of this and other round objects, so that highlights within the object appear as though an infinite number of faces make up the object, and only the edges reveal a coarser face count.

Also available is a hemisphere option that creates half an L-sphere.

Cyl/Tube

The Tube object is a Cylinder object with a hole in the center. When you create a cylinder, a circle is drawn to define the end of the cylinder, then a line is drawn for the length. You create a tube object in the same way, but you must add a second circle to define the diameter of the tube wall.

Note that the Values dialog box for the tube and cylinder objects enables you to have multiple segments of tubing, as well as to set the number of faces for the circular part of the object. Multiple segments of tubes and cylinders are useful when the object will be bent or twisted after you create it.

Sometimes you will want to create cylinders with many segments. This enables you to easily modify or bend the cylinder using any of a number of editing tools found in the 3D Editor or the Keyframer. The Set Tubes dialog box enables you to create multiple segments.

Torus

The Torus creation tool simply takes two circles to define the object. Because this donut-like object is assumed to have a circular profile, only the inner hole and outer diameter are required. The Torus, like the tube and cylinder, has a Values Adjustment dialog box in which you set the fineness of the Torus's cross section, as well as the fineness of the Torus' overall O shape. When you adjust these settings, you should consider how close the object will get to the camera, and how much detail is necessary to avoid faceting at the edges.

Cone

This tool is identical to the Create/Cylinder tool, except that two circles are drawn, one for each end of the cone.

Combining and Separating Multiple Objects

When you deal with objects you create in 3D Studio, you will probably end up with quite a few objects in a scene. Many times, it is easier to turn

7

multiple objects into one object so you can move all the objects with one command. 3D Studio provides a tool for this called Attach. It is located under Create/Object/Attach.

This tool enables you to attach one object to another object and they become one object together. The object name then becomes the name of the second object you choose because it had the first object attached to it. The original objects then become elements of the larger object. You can attach as many objects together as you like, as long as the total number of vertices in the object is not greater than 65,000. There are several ramifications to attaching objects, though.

When the objects are attached to each other, they retain any mapping coordinates and material assignments they had as separate objects. Be careful, because assigning any new mapping or materials to the attached object will override any existing mapping or materials. You can choose to assign mapping and materials to each individual element in the object, or even each individual face in the object. Once you combine two objects into one, be very careful about how you assign materials to that object. Also, once the two objects are combined, the center of the object and its bounding box will change as well.

3D Studio provides you with a set of tools that enables you to manipulate elements. Elements of an object can be manipulated much like an object itself can be. Just look under the Modify/Element menu in the 3D Editor. As you can see, most of these commands are the same commands you can use with standard objects.

An example of a good time to attach objects is a door. When creating a door, you create the door and the handles as separate objects. If you want to animate the door opening and closing, though, you will want the door and the handles to be one object. After assigning materials and mapping, simply attach the handles to the door. They then become one object with correct materials and mapping that should not have to be changed.

By the same token, there will be instances when you want to separate one object into smaller objects. You can accomplish this by choosing Create/Element/Detach or Create/Face/Detach. Both will create new objects that you can freely name. The only difference between the two is that Element can detach any individual element in an object. Because it cannot work on multiple objects, it can become very tedious to detach many elements from a larger object. In this case, you might want to choose Create/Face/Detach where you can detach any face or any group of selected faces. The selected faces are then detached into a single object that you can name.

As with elements, Faces also have their own modification menu where you can freely modify any single face in an object. This menu is located under Modify/Face... Here, you will find the same set of tools you have under Element. These tools work only with faces though. The last option you have for modify objects, elements, and faces is to modify their vertices. Each vertex of an object, element, or face can be modified using the tools found under Modify/Vertex... Again, these are the same tools as under Element, but on a vertex level.

As you can see, with careful thought and planning, you can manipulate 3D objects in any of a variety of methods to help you achieve everything you want to. You can also work with objects from the basic level of a vertex all the way through the higher level of object-element relationships.

Other Modeling Methods

In a beginner's book there are many things that need to be covered. As you can guess, only some of the more advanced modeling techniques have really been covered in this chapter. There are other methods worth mentioning, but are really beyond the scope of this book. Some of these methods include the following: modeling with IPAS routines, advanced editing tools, and others.

Modeling with IPAS routines is one of the most interesting options you might choose to explore. Here, you can find an IPAS routine that will create objects for you. An example of this is Schreibers Nursery routine, a PXP modeling routine that can be purchased separately from 3D Studio. This routine enables you to create any of 50 or 60 highly detailed trees. Some of these trees have over 100,000 faces in them!! Can you imagine how long it would take you to model something like that by hand?

IPAS routines like Nursery are loaded by choosing Program/PXP Loader from the pull down menu or pressing F12. The actual use of each IPAS routine is specific to that routine. You are encouraged to find demos of modeling IPASs and see what they can do. One of the more popular IPAS types now available is the Metaballs Blob Modeller. Here, many spheres are placed close to each other. Then, a tension value is assigned between the spheres. Like mercury, the balls will seem to meld together into an amorphous object. This is an easy way to create complex shapes such as the human body.

7

Of course, once you have created geometry, you will want to change it. Many of 3D Studio's commands are geared toward editing objects at varying levels of complexity. You are highly encouraged to explore these commands in a greater detail than covered in this book. The more you know about these commands, the more you can do and the more creative you will eventually be.

Summary

This chapter has introduced you to more advanced techniques of modeling using the 2D Shaper, the 3D Lofter, and the 3D Editor. Each of these modules provides a unique set of tools for the creation of geometry in 3D Studio. You might have found some of these modules confusing and frustrating. Don't give up. Remember, you are just learning. When you are able to create the objects you envision in your mind at will, you will enjoy 3D Studio more than you can imagine.

The next chapter introduces you to advanced methods of materials and lighting, in particular, using mapped materials and spotlights.

Chapter Snapshot

This chapter, which introduces you to some of the more advanced concepts of materials and lighting, covers the following topics:

- The relationship between lighting and materials

- Color systems for lighting and materials

- More on the Materials Editor

- Mapping coordinates and controls

- Advanced texture mapping

- Tips and techniques on materials

- More on lighting

- Tips and techniques on lighting

Advanced Lighting/Materials Techniques

As you progress with your learning of 3D Studio, you will eventually find that one of the most important aspects of the rendering process is the creation of your materials with the appropriate attributes for what you are trying to achieve. This chapter introduces you to some of the more advanced topics and techniques that will speed you along toward your mastery of materials creation.

The Relationship between Lighting and Materials

The relationship between the lighting and materials in a scene is very important to the overall look of the final rendering or animation. An understanding of the key relationships here can only help you in your quest for a good-quality rendering.

For example, when you render a scene in which the lighting is too bright, you wash out the colors of the materials, or they look too light to be suitable. The opposite happens if the light is too dark. Shiny surfaces, such as highly polished wood, may not look right if too much light is on them, or if the light hits the surface at the wrong angle in relation to the camera. Both cases cause the surface to wash out.

Shadows also are very important to materials. Material definitions include an ambient light definition that helps to define the color of the material when it is shaded from lights. You can also control the color of the specular light, or bright spot, on a material. All of these subtle things combine to create a realistic rendering.

When you place the lights in a scene, you can control the color of the light. The color of light is very important when you look at the color of the materials in the final rendering, just as it is when you look at surfaces in real life. The choice of the wrong color light on a material can produce a bad result in your final rendering.

Be aware of the relationship between the lights and materials. This relationship includes the position of the light relative to the material surface and the camera, the color of the light, the ambient and specular colors of the material, and the strength of the light. Forethought, and careful adjustment of these elements, help produce higher quality renderings.

Color Systems for Lighting and Materials

Before taking a look at some more advanced material options, you need to have a good, solid understanding of the three color systems used to create renderings or animations: RGB (Red, Green, and Blue), HLS (Hue, Luminance, and Saturation), and CMYK (Cyan, Magenta, Yellow, and Black). The RGB and HLS color systems are used in 3D Studio to create all the colors you use in your renderings. CMYK is used when you print the colors, using a color printer. Fortunately, you do not have to learn a great deal about CMYK, because most of today's printer drivers handle the conversion to that color system.

RGB is the most commonly used color system, and the easiest to understand. Each color is based on a mix of red, green, and blue. By varying the percentage of each color, you can create just about any color. Each of these three colors has a value between 0 and 255. By varying the value of each color, you can create just about any color you like. With all three colors at 0, you have black; and with all three colors at 255, you have white. 3D Studio uses 256 levels of red, green, and blue—the equivalent of 24-bit color (8 bits of red, 8 of green, and 8 of blue).

The HLS color system is related to the RGB color system in that any color you can find in the HLS system can be found in the RGB system. HLS just provides you with a higher degree of control over colors, and is a little more intuitive than RGB. In HLS, you have three factors to work with: hue, luminance, and saturation. You select the basic color by choosing the hue of that color. (In 3D Studio, you can choose any of 256 hues.) After you have chosen the hue, or base color, you can adjust the luminance and saturation of that color. The *luminance* of a color is the brightness of that color. High luminance values produce washed-out colors, whereas low values produce dark colors. The *saturation* controls the intensity of the color. Luminance and saturation give you control over slight variations in the color you are working with.

A good way to look at this relationship is to look at how 3D Studio creates these colors. When you create a spotlight, you can use the Spotlight Definition dialog box to change the color of the light, using HLS or RGB systems (see fig. 8.1).

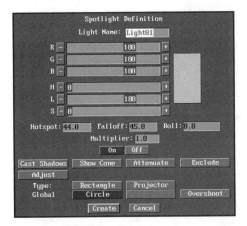

The Spotlight Definition dialog box.

At the top of the dialog box are six sliders, three for each color system. To the right of the sliders is a color swatch that reflects the changes you make. You should take this opportunity to play with the colors until you understand the relationship between the color systems.

The CMYK color system is used almost exclusively in the printing process. The output files that 3D Studio produces are encoded in RGB colors. When you print these files, using any program, the RGB colors are converted to CMYK to better match the printing inks used in the print

8

process. CMYK is also the color system used in photography. The thing to remember here is that because of this color-conversion process, the color of your materials and lights, when printed, might not look exactly the same as those on the screen.

As you can see, the main color systems are not difficult to understand. Understanding the relationship between colors themselves is more difficult. One of the many available books on color theory can help you in this area.

A Closer Look at the Materials Editor

Now it is time to take a good, close look at the Materials Editor (see fig. 8.2). You will use it a great deal in this chapter.

Figure 8.2

The Materials Editor.

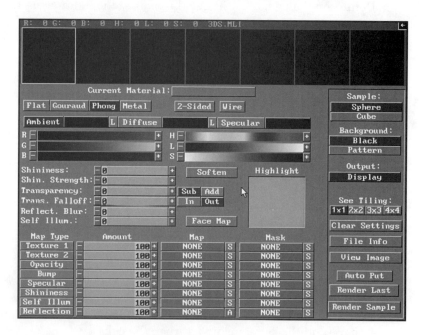

Notice that the Materials Editor looks much busier and more complex than the other 3D Studio modules. Fortunately, the Materials Editor is not difficult to get used to.

At the top of the screen is a series of windows, each of which can display sample renderings of materials you create. You can create a material and then interactively change the properties by using these windows. Your video configuration directly affects the look of these materials. Generally, the Materials Editor should stay at a resolution of 640×480, but with the highest color depth your video card can display.

On the right side of the screen is a column of buttons. The top half of these buttons control the appearance of the material preview, and the bottom half enable you to create the material preview, as well as to render the last scene.

The Auto Put and Render Last buttons are particularly useful. Often you cannot get the full sense of a material without it being in the environment in which you envision it. Well, the Materials Editor can help you with this. If (in the 3D Editor) you have just assigned a material, and that material is still current, you can switch to the Materials Editor and modify that material. Then activate the Auto Put option by clicking on the Auto Put button. This automatically puts the new material changes back into the scene. Then click on the Render Last button, which renders the last scene you rendered in the 3D Editor. In this way, you can change material properties, click on Render Last, and see how the changes affect the outcome of your rendering.

All of the other buttons and sliders on the screen enable you to control and change various properties of the materials. Some of these properties you might never have a use for; others you will always have a use for.

At the top of the Materials Editor are four buttons (Flat, Gouraud, Phong, and Metal) that enable you to define the shading mode for each material. Having already looked at shading modes, you should understand what each of these will do to the material. Just remember that a material that is set to a flat shading mode will always render flat, no matter what shading mode you use for the final rendering. To the right of the shading-mode buttons are two buttons that enable you to control another aspect of shading. As its name implies, the 2-Sided button creates a two-sided material. You should use two-sided materials whenever you turn on two-sided rendering. The Wire button forces the material to render as a wire frame. This feature can be handy when you are looking for that effect.

Below the shading mode buttons are the color sliders. Because color is essentially nothing more than reflected light, the colors in a material are treated similarly to light, but with color sliders. There are three basic

8

types of color in a material: Ambient, Diffuse, and Specular. Ambient is a general overall level of illumination for the color of the material. Ambient also affects how the material looks when it is in shade or shadow. Diffuse is the general color of the material. Specular is the color of the highlight of a material, assuming the material has a highlight. Each of these colors can be adjusted individually, or you can lock them together by using the L button located between each color type.

The L button allows you to lock two or more of the material colors so you cannot adjust them. This can be handy if you are constantly changing the color of a material in search of the perfect color setup. Locking the colors prevents you from inadvertently changing a color setup you already like.

Below the light types are the color sliders—an RGB set and an HLS set—through which you can change the colors of the materials. These sliders work the same as those in the Spotlight definition dialog box, mentioned earlier. The only difference here is that the sliders are colored, to give you a better idea of the color you are looking at. When you want to adjust the color of the Ambient, Diffuse, or Specular light of a material, simply highlight that button and adjust the colors. A sample of the adjusted color appears to the right of the button.

In the area below the color sliders, you really begin to control the material properties. Here, a set of six sliders enables you to adjust the material's shininess, shininess strength, transparency, transparency falloff, reflection blur, and self-illumination.

You use the Shininess slider to control how shiny the material is. Higher values produce brighter highlights. With the Shin. Strength slider, you control how strong the shininess is. Both of these sliders affect the Highlight box, located to the right. This box displays a graph of the highlight when you adjust either the Shininess or Shin. Strength sliders.

The Transparency slider defines how much light can pass through the material. Glass has a very high transparency. The Trans. Falloff slider controls how the transparency of a material is interpreted, according to the object's orientation to the view. Modification buttons to the right of both of these sliders enable you to change the type of transparency and the type of falloff.

With the Reflect. Blur slider, you control the blurring of any reflections in the material. This feature is handy because most reflective materials have a slight bit of blur in the reflection. You use the Self Illum. slider to control how bright the material is.

All the other controls in the dialog box are related to mapped materials. The Face Map button, located to the right of the Self Illum. slider, overrides all other mapping settings, and centers the texture map of the material on each and every face of the object to which it is assigned.

The following exercise leads you through the process of creating a simple glass material that is slightly shiny and not quite clear.

Creating a Glass with the Materials Editor

Load 3D Studio and go to the Materials Editor	Starts the program
Choose Current Material button	Enables you to name the material
Enter **Glass1**	Names the new material Glass1
Choose Phong	Sets the current shading mode to Phong for this material
Set Shininess to 25	Sets the material's shininess to 25%
Set Shin. Strength to 25	Sets material shininess strength to 25%
Set Transparency to 90	Sets transparency to 90%
Choose Diffuse	Enables you to set diffuse color
Set Diffuse color to a light gray	Gives glass a smoky quality
Choose Render Sample	Renders a sample of the material in the current review window

Because this is an almost clear glass, and might not show up on a black background in the preview window, change the background.

Choose Background/Pattern	Sets the background to a color pattern, instead of black
Choose Render Sample	Renders a sample of the material

Now that you have a new material, it is time to save the material to the material library. You must always do this, or you will lose the material definition.

Choose Material/Put Material from the pull-down at the top of the screen	Displays the Put Material dialog box (see fig. 8.3), so that you can save the material definition
In the Put Material dialog box, choose OK	Saves material in current library

continues

8

continued

Choose Library/Save Library from the pull-down at the top of the screen	Displays the Save Library dialog box
Choose OK in the Save Library dialog box	Saves the current library
Choose OK	Verifies that you want to overwrite the previous library

Now, what if you wanted to make a small change to this glass, and save it as another material? In the next section of the exercise, you make a copy of the material, and make the glass darker (like sunglasses).

Click on the Preview Window that contains the Glass1 material, and drag the material to the next window. When you release the mouse button, answer Yes to the Copy material? prompt (see fig. 8.4). Choose Material Name and name the material Glass2.

Set Transparency to 50	Sets new transparency to 50%
Set Diffuse color to a dark gray	Changes overall color of glass
Save material as before	

Figure 8.3

The Put Material dialog box.

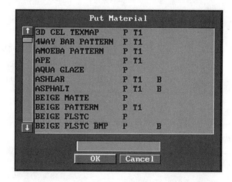

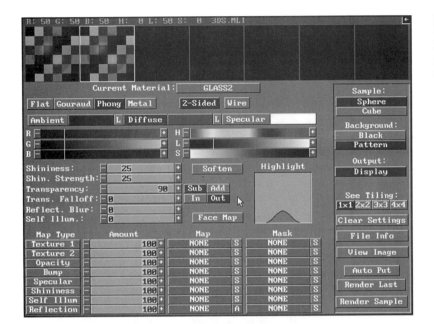

Figure 8.4

The Material Editor after copying material.

DESIGN TIP

Creating your own material libraries is always a good idea. For example, you might create a library of different wood materials or marble materials that you need for a particular project.

Now you have two glass materials to work with. Setting up a simple material is a fairly easy task. Mapped materials, on the other hand, are not as easy.

Mapped Materials

A *mapped material* is a material that physically places a bitmap on the surface of the object. The placement of the bitmap is accomplished through the use of mapping coordinates that tell the system how to place the map on the surface.

The mapped material definition determines how the material is placed on the surface. There are two types of map placement: tiled and decal. A *tiled* map is repeatedly placed across the surface of the material, rather like a checkerboard (see fig. 8.5). The only problem with this type of map is that the seams between the copies of the texture map are easy to see if the map

8

is not a seamlessly tileable map. *Decal* mapping, on the other hand, places the map on the surface of the object only once, rather like a label on a soda bottle (see fig. 8.6).

Figure 8.5

Tile texture mapping.

Figure 8.6

Decal texture mapping.

The eight types of mapping that you can use in any material are texture (two texture maps), opacity, bump, specular, shininess, self illumination, and reflection mapping.

Texture Mapping

Texture mapping applies a texture or material to the surface of an object. The texture is actually a photograph of a real-life material, such as wood or marble. This photograph is then trimmed in such a manner that when it is placed next to itself, you cannot see the seam between the two bitmaps.

3D Studio supports several file formats for texture maps, including GIF, Targa, Tiff, JPEG, Cel, and Flic. A Flic file produces an animated texture map. (See the "Animated Textures" section, later in this chapter, for more information about Flic files.)

Creating a textured material is fairly simple to do — placing that material correctly on the surface of an object requires a little more work. Placing the material requires mapping coordinates to tell the system where to place the map on the surface of the object. (This is covered later this chapter in the section titled "Mapping Coordinates.")

The following exercise shows you how to make a material that uses a single texture map.

Making a Single Texture Map Material

Load 3D Studio, and switch to the Materials Editor	Loads program and appropriate module
Choose Material Name button located below the Material Preview window	Enables you to name material
Name the material **Marble1**	Names material
Choose the None button under Map next to Texture 1	Enables you to choose the material (see fig. 8.7)
Choose *.GIF	Enables you to select .GIF files
Choose GrayMarb.Gif from Maps subdirectory	Chooses file to use
Choose OK	Displays Materials Editor, with Graymarb.Gif now the current material
Set Amount Slider to 75	Sets the Strength of the bitmap
Choose S button next to Graymarb.Gif	Enables you to set up the material and its mapping (see figure 8.8.)

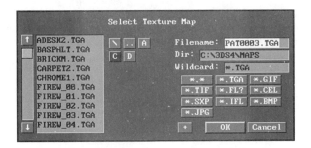

8

Figure 8.8

The Mapping Parameters dialog box.

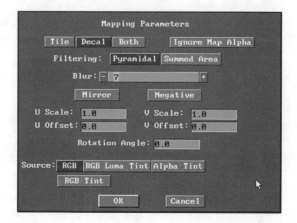

Before you go any farther, you need to take a closer look at this dialog box and learn how to control the mapping of the texture at a material level. The Mapping Parameters box is the same for all mapped materials.

You use the first three buttons (Tile, Decal, and Both) to select the type of mapping. (The Both button simply combines the Tile and Decal methods.) The Ignore Map Alpha button is used to create transparent sections of the material. Say, for example, that a bitmap of a label has a black background. In tile mode, the label appears on a black background, whereas in decal mode, the label is on a transparent background. This transparency comes from the Alpha channel of the bitmap, if it has one.

Filtering enables you to control how the bitmaps are anti-aliased. The Summed Area button produces better results, but requires more memory than Pyramidal.

With the Blur slider, you control how blurred the texture map is on the surface of the object. Simply adjust the slider to suit your needs.

The Mirror button uses a flipped, or mirror, version of the bitmap, and the Negative button uses a negative of the bitmap as the map.

U and V Scale enables you to control the scale of the map at a material level. U and V are similar to X and Y coordinates in the 3D Editor, but correspond to the orientation of the material, not the 3D Editor coordinate system. Also, to help keep you from confusing the coordinates, U and V are used instead of X and Y. Adjusting the U and V Scale of the map will determine the size of the map as it is repeated across the surface of an object. With U and V Offset, you can control where the map starts tiling or is placed on the surface of an object. Of course, Rotation Angle controls the rotation of the map.

You use the last four buttons (the Source buttons) to specify which source of the bitmap to use in the texture for various operations, such as Transparency mapping. (For more information about the alpha and RGB sources, see Chapter 11, "Video Post.")

Single Texture Map Material

The following steps will finish the previous exercise.

In the Mapping Parameters dialog box, set mapping type to Tile	Sets the mapping type
Choose OK	Displays the Materials Editor

The strength of the bitmap was intentionally left at 75%, to enable you to control the color of the marble.

Choose Diffuse	Enables you to change the diffuse color
Set diffuse color to anything you like	
Choose Render Sample	Enables you to render a sample

At this point, you might find that the strength of the bitmap was set too high or too low, which caused the colors you chose to render incorrectly. Feel free to play with those two settings until you are comfortable with the material, then save the material to any library you like.

Opacity Mapping

Opacity mapping, a very powerful form of mapping, uses the intensity of the colors of a bitmap to create varying degrees of transparency in the bitmap. An example of how you'd use an opacity map might be a complex window, such as stained glass. Instead of physically creating all of the lead lines, you can use a photo of the stained glass as an opacity map. The window then becomes a simple face in the 3D Editor. With the stained glass bitmap, you get varying degrees of translucency. If you use raytraced shadows, you can even get the opacity map to cast shadows (see the section on spotlights, later in this chapter).

In the following short exercise, you apply an opacity map to the gray marble material you created earlier.

8

Applying an Opacity Map

Load 3D Studio, and switch to the Materials Editor	Loads the program and appropriate module
Load Marble from last exercise	Loads a material
In the Map column of the Opacity row, choose the NONE button	Enables you to choose an opacity map
Choose *.cel	Enables you to choose a *.cel as a map
Choose Grid.CEL from Maps subdirectory	Chooses a file
Choose OK	Displays the Materials Editor
Choose S next to Grid.CEL	Enables you to set up the Grid.CEL map
In Mapping Parameters dialog box, choose Tile as mapping type	Sets the mapping type
In the Materials Editor menu, choose Render Sample	Renders a sample of the material
Save material as Marble2	

You should end up with a rendering of the marble material, with sections missing, in a grill pattern (see figures 8.9 and 8.10). Play with the mapping parameters and see what happens. Try changing the map to a negative map and see what the results are.

Figure 8.9

Material with an opacity map.

Figure 8.10

Material with a negative opacity map.

Imagine the possibilities of opacity mapping and how much time it can save you. Always remember, though, you want to keep the number of texture maps you use in a scene as small as possible.

Bump Mapping

Bump mapping is a mapping type that can really save a great deal of time and reduce the complexity in your models. Bump mapping takes the texture map assigned to it and adjusts the colors in the final rendering, to give the illusion of 3D mapping. The limitation of effect is apparent at the edges of the object. A popular example of bump mapping is brick. Instead of actually creating each brick and the mortar, you can simply use a brick bump map, which gives the illusion of 3D surfaces. Unfortunately, at corners and other edges, you will not see the mortar cracks, as you would in real life. In many cases, this trade off is more than worth it.

A bump map interprets the intensities of the colors in the images as heights, with black being 0 height and white being full height. The height is dependent upon the strength assigned to the bump map.

In the following exercise, you add a brick bump map to the marble1 material. Normally, you would not do this, but it will show you how bump mapping works.

Adding a Bump Map

Load 3D Studio, and switch to the Materials Editor	Loads the program and appropriate module

continues

8

continued

Load the Marble1 material	Selects current material
In the Bump row, choose None in the Map column	Enables you to select a file
Choose *.CEL	Enables you to choose a .cel file
Select brnbrick.CEL from Maps subdirectory	Selects file to use
Choose OK	Displays the Materials Editor
Set strength to 100 by adjusting the strength slider in the Bump row	Sets bitmap strength
Select Render Sample	Renders a sample

Your sample rendering should look like a brick pattern with a marble surface as illustrated in figure 8.11. If the mortar of the brick is raised instead of the bricks, simply choose S to start the Mapping Parameters dialog box and change the map to a negative map.

Figure 8.11

A marble material with brick bump map.

As you can imagine, bump mapping is very powerful. An even more powerful form is displacement mapping. Yost Groups disk #7 has a routine called displace. Displacement mapping uses a map that is similar to a bump map to alter a specific piece of geometry. Instead of providing the illusion of a 3D surface like a bump map (Remember how a brick bump map looks at the edges!) displacement mapping physically alters the geometry so it really has a true 3D look. You can then apply any materials to that surface. Exploring IPAS routines like Yost Groups can help you to reduce the amount of memory necessary to render a scene, thus decreasing your rendering times.

Self-Illumination Mapping

Self-illumination mapping is used to make a material appear to produce its own light. When using a self-illumination map, the Self-Illumination slider is not used. The Self-Illumination slider is used to give self-illumination to materials that do not have a self-illumination map. Otherwise, the self-illumination map takes precedence over the Self-Illumination slider. As with other mapped material types, you have a strength slider where you can control the strength of the self-illumination map. Higher intensity values produce brighter areas in the material. You can apply the self-illumination map exactly like the other mapped material types.

Shininess and Specular Mapping

Shininess and specular mapping are similar to each other. Both use bitmaps to modify the highlight or shininess of a material. Shininess mapping is used to give some noise to the highlights of a material. Again, these maps are applied like the others.

Reflection Mapping

Reflection mapping is a necessity because of the method 3D Studio uses to create its renderings. Say, for example, that you have a nice shiny silver teapot in the middle of a table. The teapot reflects all the environment around it. If you have used a raytracing program in the past, you know that the reflections are automatically done for you. Because 3D Studio uses raytracing only for shadows, you have to manually create the reflections maps. What you would do in this instance is render the environment with a camera where the teapot is. Use Renderer/Setup/Make.cub to create a six-sided bitmap that can be used as a reflection map. When you assign the bitmap, use the CUB file as the bitmap. This type of reflection mapping is good for still images, not animations. 3D Studio provides three other types of reflection mapping: Spherical, Automatic, and Flat mirror. Those are assigned in the Reflection Mapping Parameters dialog box.

Spherical reflection mapping is as easy to assign as a bitmap texture. When using this type of map, the bitmap is treated as a sphere and applied to the object, giving the illusion of the surrounding scenery. This works very well when the background bitmap is used again as the reflection bitmap.

8

To use an automatic reflection map in 3D Studio, click on the A in the Map column of the Reflection row. Because using automatic reflection mapping slows the rendering process considerably, be cautious when using it.

If you click again on the Automatic button, you display the Automatic Reflection Map dialog box (see fig. 8.12). Flat mirror is one of the options in this dialog box. This option works very well with, and should be used only for, flat surfaces.

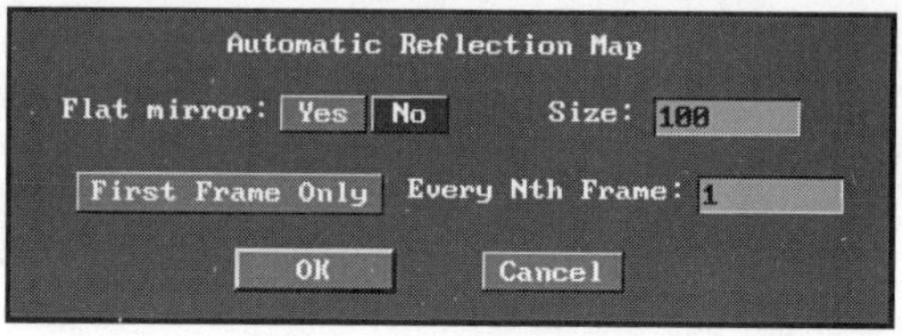

Figure 8.12

The Automatic Reflection Map dialog box.

A reflection map is just about as easy to create as other mapping types. In the following exercise, a reflection map is added to the Marble1 material created earlier. By adding a reflection map, you make the marble look like a highly polished piece of marble.

Adding a Reflection Map

Start 3D Studio, and switch to the Materials Editor	Loads program and appropriate module
Load Marble1 material created earlier	Loads material
In the Map column of the Reflection row, choose NONE	Enables you to assign a reflection map
Choose *.tga	Enables you to use Targa files
Choose Valley_1.TGA	Choose a reflection map
Choose OK	Displays Materials Editor
Set strength to 25	Sets strength to 25%
Choose Render Sample button	Renders a sample

Most reflections are a subtle addition that adds life to a scene. Unless the material is intended to be highly reflective, like a mirror, you probably will use fairly low-strength values. Feel free to adjust the strength of the reflection map and re-render the sample to see how it works.

As you can see, reflection mapping adds a measure of realism to scenes.

Mapping Coordinates

Now that you have a good idea of the mapping types available to you in 3D Studio, it is time to look at the way you tell 3D Studio to use the mapped materials on individual objects. Basically, you have to tell 3D Studio how to apply the maps to the objects, using mapping coordinates.

The four basic types of mapping in 3D Studio are Planar, Spherical, Cylindrical, and Box mapping. A fifth type of mapping is available by turning on mapping in the 3D Lofter, to produce lofted mapping. Mapping is handled in the 3D Editor, where all mapping is applied and adjusted. These mapping types apply mapping coordinates when assigned to any object.

The mapping coordinates project the bitmap(s) of the material onto the surface of the object. Planar mapping, for example, rotates the bitmap(s) into whatever plane you specify, and then tiles the maps across that plane. If the object does not intersect the plane, the maps are projected up or down, perpendicular to the plane, until they hit the surface of the object. You can imagine how the other types are handled. Figure 8.13 shows the result of using the four mapping types in 3D Studio.

Figure 8.13

Different types of mapping coordinates.

8

All mapping commands are accessed under the 3D Editor's Surfaces/ Mapping menu. When you choose this option, a yellow mapping icon appears in the 3D Editor window. This icon is roughly equivalent to one copy of the bitmap used in the mapped material. If you choose the Type option, you can choose the type of mapping to use. Box mapping is located in Surface/Material/Box.

Under Adjust is a series of commands that are worth looking at. These commands allow you to have better control over how the mapping coordinates are applied to an object.

The Find option rescales the mapping icon to fit the viewports, making it easier to find. This can be helpful with meshes that are complex or contain many colors.

The Scale option is very important to control the overall scaling of the mapping. Region fit makes the mapping fit a region you specify in a viewport, with the mouse. This option can be very helpful with decal mapping. Bitmap fit allows you to scale the proportions of the mapping icon to the bitmap you are using in the material. This option helps to ensure that a map will tile correctly.

When you choose View Align, the mapping icon aligns to the current view. This can be helpful for creating certain special effects, such as a camouflaged object. Face Align aligns the mapping icon with a specific face you choose, and Center centers the icon on any object. Finally, you can use the Acquire option to retrieve mapping coordinates from existing objects. Most of the other common commands are self explanatory.

After you have set the options, choose Apply Object or Apply Element, and choose the object or element to which you want to assign the mapping coordinates.

Box mapping is essentially a planar mapping with which you can assign a different material for each side of a box. When you choose Surface/Material/Box from the 3D Editor menu, and then select the object to which you want to apply box mapping, the Assign Box Materials dialog box appears (see fig. 8.14). In this dialog box, you specify a different material for each side of the box

Box mapping is used frequently in architectural applications where different materials have to be assigned to different surfaces on the same object. Because most buildings are comprised of planar surfaces, box mapping works well to apply the different materials.

Figure 8.14

The Assign Box Materials dialog box, used for box mapping.

The only disadvantage to box mapping is a loss of control over the scale and rotation of the mapping. The only way to control the scale of box mapping is to set the U and V scales in the material definition.

More on Materials

When you get beyond basic mapped materials, there are several other material options that you can use to produce certain effects. These include: masking mapped materials, procedural materials, and animated textures.

Masking Mapped Materials

When you use any of the mapped materials mentioned earlier, you can use a mask option. A *mask* effectively blocks out part or all of the bitmap. Masks are based on the same methodology as transparency maps: the higher the intensity, the greater the area of the map you can see. Masks can be useful for creating a variety of effects.

Masked materials are used when you want to block out a material. Say you want to create a material that has two textures that repeat in a specific pattern. You can use two texture maps in the material, and one mask map to produce the pattern (see fig. 8.15). Granted, this type of effect does not occur often, but you can use your imagination to see where else you can use this capability.

8

Figure 8.15

A Masked Material.

Procedural Materials

Procedural materials (also referred to as *photorealistic* materials, or *solid* materials) are materials generated by mathematical algorithms. When you use these types of materials, you can cut out part of the mesh object, and the material will still look correct (which is not always true with a mapped material). Procedural materials have the advantage of using much less memory than mapped materials, but can take longer to render because of the overhead necessary to use the material.

Procedural materials have an SXP file extension, and can be used in place of any bitmap in any type of mapped material. Generally, woods, marbles, and granites are some of the more popular procedural materials. A disadvantage of procedural materials is that they sometimes have many little parameters, and setting all those parameters correctly (to produce the look you want) can be a slow process.

Procedural materials are used when you have an object to which it is very difficult to apply mapping coordinates (such as a block of wood with a piece carved out), or when you need to save some memory. Procedural materials use less memory, but take a little longer to apply. These materials can also be used when you cannot find a bitmap that is exactly the colors you want. What do you do, for example, if you need a light blue marble and only have dark blue? A procedural material can be used because you can control the colors in the material easily.

Animated Textures

Animated textures can be some of the more interesting texture types you can create. Imagine you want to create a TV with something showing on it. You would use an animated texture map as the television screen.

There are two ways to create an animated texture map: assign an animated bitmap or use a projector spotlight (see the section on spotlights later in this chapter.) An animated texture map is created the same way as a regular texture map. You just use a series of still images or an animated file as the texture map.

An animated file is a FLI or a FLC file that can be created in 3D Studio or any of a number of other programs. You can also use an IFL file, which is essentially a series of still images. In most cases, it is best to use a series of still images instead of a FLI or a FLC file.

You can use animated texture maps in any of the standard mapped material types, including bump, self-illumination, and opacity to produce an enormous variety of animated effects. Imagine the effects of an animated bump map. Use your imagination again, and try to see how many different ways you can use an animated texture map.

IFL Files

An IFL file is an *image file list*. This is a simple text file that lists a series of individual maps to bring up and use as texture maps. A DOS-based utility, called Makeifl, is provided with 3D Studio to assist you in the process of creating IFL files.

Tips and Techniques for Materials

The following tips and techniques are handy when you use some of these more advanced materials:

- Use as few texture maps as possible, to reduce the amount of memory needed to render the model.

- Be inventive with the different mapped material types. By using one or more combinations of mapped material types, you can produce very nice results.

- For animated textures, use IFL files, when possible. They are easier to use than FLC files, and produce much better results.

8

- Be inventive in how you use your texture mapping. For example, to correctly map a box with the same material, you could use Box mapping. Or, you could rotate a planar map so that it is perpendicular to two opposite corners of the box. This works, and you will not lose all control over scale and rotation.

- Be careful in your use of automatic reflection maps and procedural materials. Both can dramatically increase rendering times.

- Use bump maps and opacity maps instead of modeling difficult meshes. If the face counts on a mesh get very high, opacity or bump maps may be quicker to use. The trade off is in the amount of memory used. A little experience will help show you which to use in what situations. It is better, for example, to use a bump map than model each individual brick on a brick wall, or use an opacity map instead of modeling a complex piece of stained glass.

Lighting

Lighting is a very important part of the rendering process. This section deals with some of the more advanced features of spotlights.

Spotlights

Spotlights are the only lights in 3D Studio that can cast shadows. Hence, they are the most flexible. An important aspect of spotlights is the way they interpret shadows. Two methods are used for generating shadows: shadow maps and raytraced shadows.

Shadow Maps

Shadow maps produce a bitmap for each and every spotlight that uses shadow mapping in a scene. If any object is moving in an animation, every spotlight regenerates the shadow maps for every frame. You can use several options to control the shadow maps. When you create a spotlight, you can choose the Casts Shadows button in the Spotlight Definition dialog box (see fig. 8.16) to tell 3D Studio that this light will cast shadows.

Choosing the Adjust button below the Casts Shadows button displays the Local Shadow Control dialog box (see fig. 8.17), in which you can adjust the properties of shadow maps and of raytraced shadows.

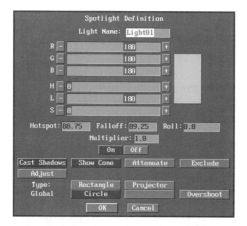

Figure 8.16

The Spotlight Definition dialog box.

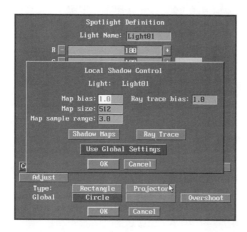

Figure 8.17

The Local Shadow Control dialog box.

In this dialog box, you can choose between raytraced, shadow maps, and global shadow settings. Global settings are defined in the Renderer/Setup/Shadows controls.

The three options for controlling shadow maps Map bias, Map size, and Map sample range. The Map bias option controls how far beyond the object casting shadows a shadow will appear. The Map size option controls how large each shadow map will be. The larger the shadow map, the more accurate the shadows. Valid sizes are 0 to 4096. Be careful, because file sizes can grow rapidly. A 4096-size shadow map takes 67 MB of memory.

8

Raytraced Shadows

Raytraced shadows work in a slightly different way, and take much longer to compute. With raytraced shadows, a ray is cast from the camera view through each pixel. If the ray hits an object, another ray is cast toward each spotlight that uses raytracing. If an object is between the intersection point and the light, there is a shadow. This produces very crisp, solid shadows. Unfortunately, you cannot create nice soft shadows by using raytracing.

To use raytraced shadows, choose the Ray Trace option in the Local Shadow Control dialog box. The raytrace bias works just like the shadow map bias: it controls how far beyond a shadow-casting object a shadow will appear.

Be very careful in your use of raytraced lights. They can increase rendering time dramatically. If you are careful in adjusting your object properties, especially the capability to cast and receive shadows, you can reduce the amount of time a raytraced shadow rendering takes.

Projector Lighting

Projector lighting is one of the newer features in 3D Studio. This option enables you to assign a bitmap to a spotlight. The spotlight then projects the bitmap, like a projector. This can be very handy for producing effects like the shadows from a stained glass window or a projector.

Setting up a projector light is fairly easy. Simply create a standard spotlight and choose Projector in the Spotlight Definition dialog box. The blank button below the Projector button enables you to assign a bitmap to use. Generally, you will also set the light cone to rectangular, instead of the default circular type (see fig. 8.18).

Figure 8.18

The Spotlight Definition dialog box for a Projector light.

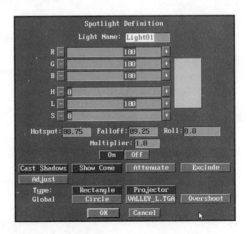

After you have created the spotlight, you probably will need to make one more small adjustment to the spotlight to get a correct projector light. In the 3D Editor menu, choose Lights/Spot/Bitmap Fit. Just like the bitmap fit function for mapping, this command will change the spotlight cone to match the proportions of the bitmap you are using.

The following exercise shows you how to create a simple projector light. Load the file CH8TUT1.3DS before you begin the exercise. This file has a prebuilt model that enables you to adjust the spotlight into a projector light.

Creating a Projector Spotlight

Load 3D Studio, and stay in 3D Editor	Loads program and appropriate module
Load CH8TUT1.3DS from the CD	Loads a prebuilt model
In the 3D Editor menu, choose Lights/Spot/Adjust	Enables you to adjust a spotlight
Click on light in scene	Chooses a light to adjust
In the Spotlight Definition dialog box, choose Rectangle	Changes cone type to rectangular
Choose Projector	Tells light to be a projector light
Choose blank button below Projector	Enables you to select a bitmap
Choose Valley_l.tga	Selects a bitmap to use
Choose Show Cone	Make sure that cone is displayed in model
Choose OK	Displays 3D Editor
In the menu, choose Light/Spot /Bitmap Fit	Enables you to change ratio of cone
Choose Valley_l.tga as Bitmap	Selects bitmap from which to obtain ratio
Choose OK	Displays 3D Editor
Choose Renderer, Render View	Enables you to render a viewport
Click in the User viewport	Renders that viewport

As you can see in figure 8.19, the bitmap image is projected onto the ground with some degree of transparency.

8

That's about all there is to projector lighting. When you use a projector light to cast shadows from a stained glass window, correctly aligning the light with the window can be very difficult. Projector spotlights are a powerful feature of spotlights that provide you with a neat special effect.

Tips and Techniques for Lighting

The following are some tips and techniques for the use of lighting in 3D Studio:

- Be careful when you use raytraced shadows. They can increase rendering times substantially, sometimes as much as tenfold.

- When using a projector light, always use a rectangular cone and perform a bitmap fit on the light to make sure that the proportions are accurate.

- When using shadows maps, be careful of your shadow map size. Generally, a map size of 512 is sufficient for most applications. Only on large renderings, such as 2048×1536, should you increase the shadow map size.

Summary

As you can see, there is much to learn about materials and lighting. Always remember that the two work together, hand-in-hand. This chapter introduced some new techniques. Use your imagination, and see what you can create when you use one or more of these techniques.

The next chapter introduces you to advanced animation techniques including path based animation, character animation, and IK.

8

Chapter Snapshot

Animation is one of the fun aspects of 3D Studio. This chapter discusses advanced methods of animation that will enable you to create a variety of animations with relative ease. The following topics are covered:

- Path-based animation

- Hierarchical linking

- Inverse kinematics

- Character animation

Advanced Animation Techniques

Combining the techniques learned in this chapter—path-based animation, hierarchical linking, inverse kinematics, and character animation—with advanced keyframing techniques (see Chapter 10, "Advanced Keyframing Techniques") will enable you to create just about any animation you can imagine.

Path-Based Animation

Path-based animation is the following of a path by an animated camera, light, or object. Path-based animation gives you the advantage of precise control over the motion of objects, cameras, and lights. Keyframing, on the other hand, is not as precise. When you place keyframes, 3D Studio creates a spline through the keyframe locations you specified. When you create many keyframes, the motion might not be exactly what you expect because of how 3D Studio interprets the curve. You can, however, combine both keyframe animation and path-based animation in the same animation.

3D Studio enables you to create the path that an object will follow in any of a variety of programs outside of 3D Studio. Inside of 3D Studio, any 2D shape or 3D loft can be used as a motion path. Otherwise, simply import a DXF file from whatever program you want to create the path in. This can be especially nice if you created your original geometry in a program such as AutoCAD. You then can create a 3D Polyline in AutoCAD and import that as the motion path.

When using a path to control the motion of an object, light, or camera, 3D Studio treats the vertices of the path as keys in the motion of the object. Therefore, the number of vertices in the path directly reflects upon how many keys will be produced in the motion. These keys can then be treated just like any other key you create.

All of the controls for path-based animation are located in the Keyframer under the Paths menu item (see fig. 9.1).

Figure 9.1

The Keyframer with the Paths menu.

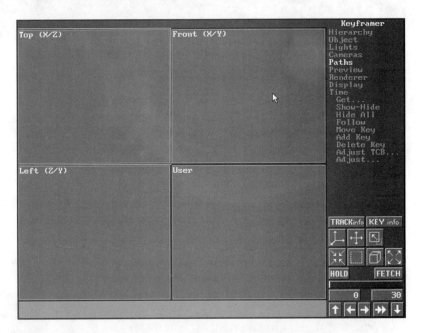

When you look at the menu items, you see there are a few options for paths in the animation. The first option is "Get...". This option enables you to retrieve any path for use as an animation path in the keyframer. Choosing Get... displays a subtree that enables you to tell 3D Studio where to get the path. There are three options here: Shaper, Lofter, and Disk. Disk enables you to load either SHP files that have been previously saved from the 2D Shaper, or DXF files that can come from any program that can write to a DXF file.

Below the Get... option is the Show-Hide command, which enables you to show the motion path on the screen or to hide it. When you select Show-Hide, you are prompted to choose the object that is attached to the motion path, then the motion path will be displayed or hidden. Motion paths are shown as a red line on the screen with white squares representing the individual keyframes on the motion path. The next menu option is Hide All which, as you can guess, hides all the motion paths in the Keyframer.

The next option, Follow, enables you to control whether the object following the path will bank around the corners, and if so, at what angle the object banks.

The last four options enable you to control the keys that are created in the path. Remember, each vertex in the path is a key, and you can add, delete, or move any key. You also can adjust the Tension, Continuity, and Bias of each key by choosing Adjust TCB. (See Chapter 10, "Advanced Keyframing Techniques," for more on these topics.) Finally, you can adjust the Ease To and Ease From values by choosing "Adjust...".

The following exercise shows you how to create a couple of motion paths and assign an object and a camera to these paths. Before beginning this exercise, load the CH9TUT01.3DS file from the accompanying CD. This file has an object, camera, and light already created in it. No animation has been assigned yet, though.

Creating Path-Based Motion

Load CH9TUT01.3DS from the CD	Loads the appropriate file
Press F1 and switch to the Shaper	Loads the Shaper Module
Type **S** then **G**	Turns on Snap and Grid
Choose Create, Circle from Menu	Enables you to create a 2D circle
Choose center of circle at **0,0**	
Set Radius of circle to **120** units	Chooses size of circle
Press F4 and switch to Keyframer	Loads Keyframer Module
Set animation sequence length to **60**	Sets length of sequence
Choose Paths, Get..., Shaper	Tells Studio to retrieve path from the 2D Shaper

continues

continued

In Top Viewport, choose the Camera   Applies the path to the camera

At this point, you are prompted for three options about the path (see fig. 9.2). The first option asks if you want to relocate the object to the beginning of the path. The second option asks if you want to reverse the direction of the path. The third asks if you want 3D Studio to automatically adjust the keys that will be created, to produce smooth motion along the path.

Figure 9.2

The Get Path dialog box with three options.

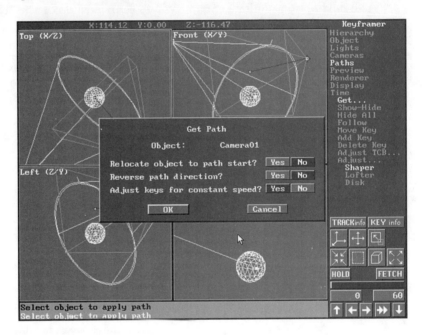

Choose Yes to Relocate Object   Moves object to start of path
to Start of Path?

Choose No to Reverse Path Direction

Choose Yes to Smooth the motion

Click on OK   Imports the path according to the parameters you set and attaches the camera to
the path

Choose Paths/Show-Hide   Displays the motion path

Figure 9.3 shows the Keyframer after assigning the motion path to the camera.

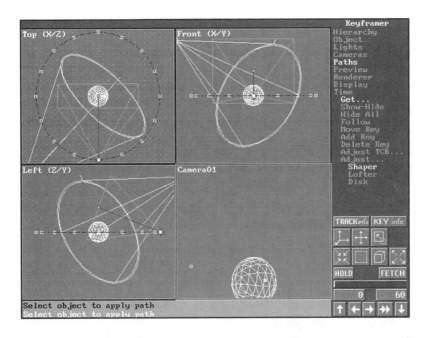

Figure 9.3

The Keyframer after applying the motion path.

9

| Click in Camera Viewport | Activates the Camera Viewport |
| Click on the Play button in the lower right corner of the Keyframer | Plays back the animation on the screen |

At this point, the only motion in the animation is the camera moving around the ball at a constant pace. Notice that the path automatically assigned itself the length of the current active segment of frames in the Keyframer.

Right Click	Stops the animation playback
Press F2 to switch to the Lofter	Switches you to the 3D Lofter
Choose Path/Helix	Enables you to create a Helix path

3D Studio displays for you the Helix Path Definition dialog box where you can choose various helix options (see fig. 9.4).

Set number of turns to **5**	Causes the helix to rotate 5 times
Click on OK	Accepts the options you chose
Click on OK	Tells 3D Studio that you want to change the present path

Figure 9.5 shows the Helix path after it has been created.

continues

continued

Figure 9.4

The Helix Path Definition dialog box.

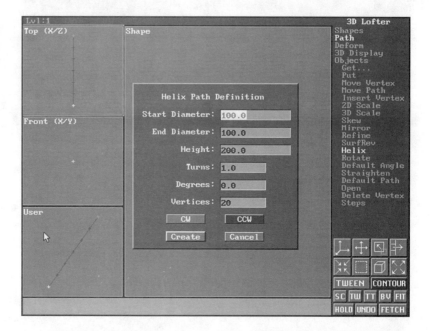

Figure 9.5

The Lofter with the Helix.

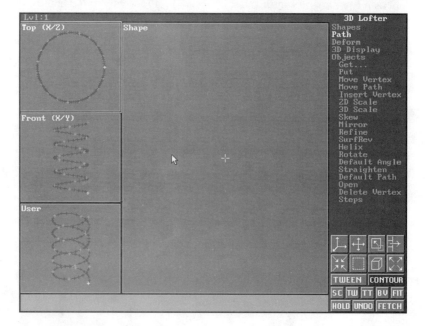

Press F4	Loads the Keyframer
Set current frame to **0**	Sets the current frame
Choose Paths/Get.../Lofter	Enables you to load a motion path
Choose the ball	Selects the ball to which the motion path is applied
Choose Yes to Relocate Object	
Choose No to Reverse Path	
Choose Yes to Smooth Keys	
Choose OK	Accepts the path parameters
Choose Paths/Show-Hide	Enables you to display or hide motion paths
Choose the ball	Displays the motion path for the ball

Figure 9.6 shows the Keyframer after applying the second motion path.

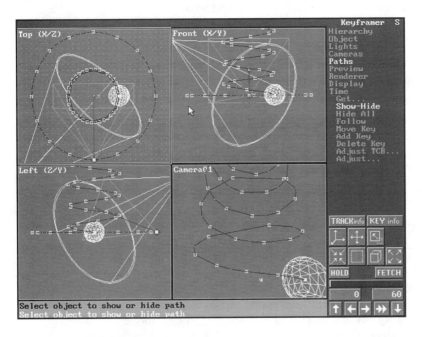

Figure 9.6

The Keyframer with both motion paths.

Choose the Play button in the lower right corner of the Keyframer	Plays back the animation

As you can see, creating a motion path is a simple thing to do and can make your life a lot easier. Use motion paths when you need to—otherwise, just use standard keyframes. Remember, you can apply a motion path to any object, camera, camera target, light, or spotlight target. Also remember you can use keyframes in the same animation in which you use motion paths.

Character Animation

Character animation is the process of animating a person or animal, or any object that can be animated like a character. This is much more complex than traditional cell animation techniques. Here, all characters are in full 3D with arms, legs, and so on. All parts of this character must be animated, and they must be animated in such a way to produce realistic motion to give the character life. This might sound difficult, but it is not. Character animation does, however, take a long time and requires a lot of patience. Many examples of character animation are provided on the 3D Studio World Creating Toolkit, and some are provided as example files with 3D Studio.

3D Studio provides you with two built-in sets of tools to enable you to create character animations: hierarchical linking and inverse kinematics. Inverse Kinematics is provided to you in the form of a Release 4 IPAS routine.

In hierarchical linking, various parts of the character are linked to other parts. For example, a hand is linked to a forearm which is, in turn, linked to an upper arm. This way, if you move the upper arm, the forearm and hand move as well.

Inverse Kinematics (IK) takes this one step further. IK assigns a skeleton to the linked parts. This skeleton can then have joints assigned. The power of IK lies in these joints. You can limit the motion of any or all joints to force that joint to behave as it would in real life. For example, take your elbow. How can you move it? Obviously, you can curl your arm in one axis. But the length of this curl is limited by your upper arm on one side and your elbow on the other. This limits how you can use your arm. These same types of limitations can be applied to a character in the animation, so the character cannot do anything you don't want the character to do.

9

Unfortunately, to be able to use IK, you must understand how hierarchical linking works. IK makes use of the links you create to help define the joint connections in the character.

For the rest of this chapter, use the CH8TUT02.3DS file provided on the accompanying CD. This file contains a very simple character that you will animate through a series of tutorials. By the end of this chapter, you will have a good idea how to go about creating character animations, but it will probably take a while before you are good at it. Just to give you an idea of how complex the IK can get, it took ILM (Industrial Light & Magic) 2 months to get the IK animation of the T-Rex in *Jurassic Park* correct! But, if you have seen the movie, it was well worth the effort!

The CH8TUT02.3DS file is a simple ball-like figure with two white eyes, one open mouth, and two legs. The character animation concentrates on making this character walk with some degree of realism.

Hierarchical Linking

3D Studio provides a menu entry, Hierarchy, for hierarchical linking in the Keyframer (see fig. 9.7). Under this menu, you will find all the tools you need to create hierarchical linking.

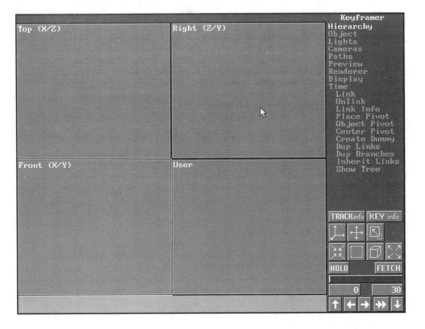

Figure 9.7

The Keyframer.

The first option, Link, enables you to link one object to another. When you do this, the first object you choose is the *child* object and the second object is the *parent* object. From this point on, if you move the parent object, the child object moves with it. If you move the child object, the parent object will not move. This is the nature of the link. The parent object has control of the child object.

You can create another link from the parent object to a third object, creating a tree structure of the objects. This relationship is very important. Make sure you take note of it. In this case, the parent becomes a child of the third object, and so on.

The second option on the menu is Unlink, which unlinks one object from another. If you unlink two objects in a hierarchical tree, you will be asked if you want to unlink the subtree as well. This will unlink any objects below the parent and child you just unlinked. See figure 9.8 for a diagram explaining this relationship.

Figure 9.8

Objects in a hierarchical link.

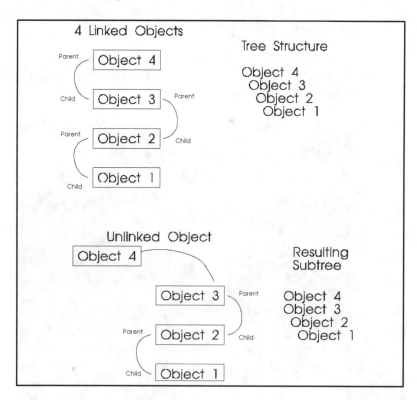

The next command in the menu is Link Info. This option lets you decide how the two objects are to be linked together. After linking two objects together, choose Link Info, then select one of the objects. This displays the Define Link Type dialog box (see fig. 9.9).

In the Define Link Type dialog box, the first thing you will notice is that it shows you what the parent object for this object is. Below this are two columns of buttons allowing you to control just how strong the link between the two objects is. You can control the rotation and scale in the x, y, and z planes. By highlighting each button, that link is turned on. You might, for example, have a situation where you have two objects linked together. When you scale the parent object, you do not want the child object to scale. Simply turn off all the scale links in this dialog box.

The next three menu items enable you to control how an object rotates in the Keyframer. You must use pivot points because the Keyframer has no axis you can control like you can in 3D Editor. The first option is Place Pivot, which enables you to place a point around which all objects will pivot. Object Pivot allows you to control pivoting on an object-by-object basis. The last option, Center Pivot, centers the pivot point in any object you select.

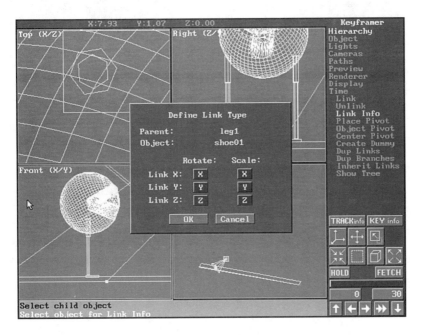

Figure 9.9

The Define Link Type dialog box.

The next option, Create Dummy, is one of the most important options. It enables you to create a dummy object. A *dummy* object is linked to other objects, then, when you move the dummy object, the other objects move as well. Dummy objects do not render and appear as dashed cubes. They become very important in inverse kinematics because dummy objects can be used to create extra joints when necessary.

The next three options enable you to copy or duplicate links and branches of the hierarchical tree. Inherit links enables you to inherit all the links from another object.

- Dup links enables you to duplicate any links that you have between two objects.

- Dup branches enables you to duplicate any branches in the hierarchical tree and assign the duplicated branches to another object.

- Inherit links enables an object to inherit a link from another object.

Finally, the Show Tree option displays a dialog box that shows you the links between all the objects in the scene (see fig. 9.10).

Figure 9.10

The Object Attachment Tree dialog box.

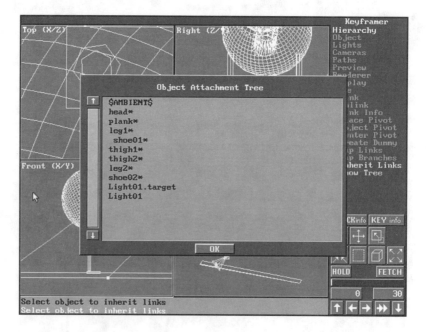

In this particular figure, there is only one link that has been created between the objects. Shoe01 is a child of leg1. All other objects, lights, cameras, and so forth, are not linked. This tree diagram will prove to be invaluable for finding mislinked objects.

The following exercise takes you through the basics of linking objects together and then animating the objects. Load the CH9TUT02.3DS file before beginning this exercise.

Linking and Animating Objects

Choose F5	Loads the keyframer
Choose Display/Hide/All	Hides all objects on the screen
Choose Display/Unhide/By Name	Enables you to selectively unhide objects
Unhide Leg1, Thigh1, Shoe01, and Plank	Unhides these four objects

Three of the objects that were just unhidden compromise one leg of the character. Given, this is a very simple leg, but it will enable you to learn how to create the links and animate the leg. The plank object serves as a ground plane.

Choose Hierarchy/Show Tree	Shows the link tree

Figure 9.11 shows the hierarchy tree before any links are made. Notice that even hidden objects are shown in the tree, helping to ensure that you do not break a link with a hidden object by accident.

Choose OK	Closes the Tree window
Choose Hierarchy/Link	Enables you to link objects together
Select the shoe object	Selects the child object
Select lower part of leg	Selects the parent object
Select lower part of leg again	Selects the child object
Select upper part of leg	Selects the parent object
Choose Hierarchy/Show Tree	Shows the link tree

Figure 9.12 shows the tree after linking the objects together. The object with the highest priority is the upper leg object.

Notice how shoe01 is below leg1, which is below thigh1. This is precisely the order in which you chose to make the links.

continues

continued

Figure 9.11

The hierarchy tree without any links.

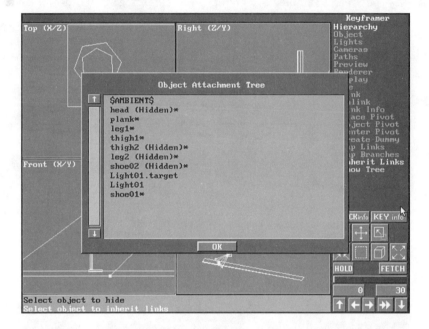

Figure 9.12

The hierarchy tree after linking.

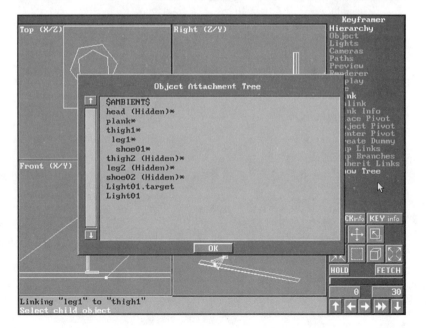

Choose OK	Returns you to the Keyframer
Choose Hold	Saves current settings to a buffer
Click in Front Viewport	Activates the viewport
Choose Object/Move	Enables you to move an object
Move the upper part of the leg to a new position on the screen	Sets a new position key

Notice how the rest of the leg moves with the upper part of the leg. This occurs because the upper leg is a parent of the lower leg and therefore takes precedence. The shoe moves because it is a child of the lower leg and must move when the lower leg moves.

Choose Fetch	Restores the buffer
Choose Hierarchy/Object Pivot	Enables you to place the pivot point for a specific object
Choose the lower part of the leg	Selects the object on which to place the pivot point

When you choose Object Pivot, notice how the geometry disappears and you are left with the lower leg and the upper leg showing on the screen. This happens because the lower leg is the child and the upper leg is the parent. When you choose Object Pivot, the child object is chosen and the parent object is displayed as well. Notice the black crosshairs now showing. These represent the current position of the pivot point. Because the joint between the upper and lower leg is the knee, a pivot point should be placed there.

Click in the Top Viewport	Activates the top viewport
Click in the middle of the joint between the two parts	Places the pivot point

Figure 9.13 shows the Keyframer after placing the pivot point. Notice that even after you have placed the pivot point, the missing geometry has not returned. Simply choose any other command to return the geometry to the screen. Now that you have placed a pivot point, it is time to animate the leg.

Set animation length to **30**	Sets the length of animation
Click in front viewport	Activates the viewport
Set current frame to **15**	Sets the current frame
Choose Object/Rotate	Enables you to rotate the object and place a key
Choose the upper part of the leg	Selects object to rotate
Rotate the leg **30** degrees	Places the key

continues

continued

Choose the lower part of the leg	Selects object to rotate
Rotate the lower leg **-60** degrees	Places the key
Set current frame to **30**	Sets the current frame
Choose Object/Rotate	Enables you to rotate an object and place a key
Choose the lower leg	Selects object to rotate
Rotate the lower leg **60** degrees	Places the key
Choose Object/Move	Enables you to move an object and place a key
Choose the upper leg	Selects object to move
Move the leg to the right **1** unit and down **1** unit	Moves the object
Choose the play button in the lower right corner of the Keyframer	Plays back the animation
Save the projects as **CH9TUT2A.3DS**	Saves the project

Figure 9.13

The Keyframer after placing the pivot.

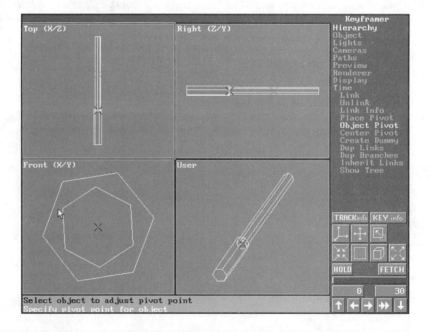

As you can see, you have at this point a very rough animation of a segment of a walk. The timing looks a little slow on the step, but this was done intentionally to help you see how the motion works. By adding more keyframes and carefully observing how the motion is supposed to look, you can create a smooth animation of a leg walking.

Using only hierarchical linking and your basic rotate and move commands can be tedious and difficult to use to create a smooth animation of a character in motion. But it can be done and done very well. For an example of this, look at Humanoid figures from Crestline. These are a series of high detail human bodies that already have the motion attached to them.

After you get beyond hierarchical linking, you will be in the world of inverse kinematics.

Inverse Kinematics (IK)

Inverse kinematics is the process of placing real world physical constraints on a series of joints to produce life-like motion with ease. 3D Studio implements its IK routine as an IPAS routine. You can start IK by choosing Program/IK from the pull down menus or by choosing F8 in the Keyframer. Because the IK module is a KXP IPAS, it can be accessed only when you are in the Keyframer. Starting IK brings up the IK Plug-in dialog box shown in figure 9.14.

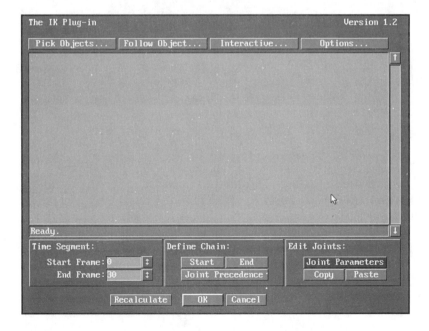

Figure 9.14

The Inverse Kinematics Plug-In dialog box.

When the dialog box first comes up, it looks fairly simple. Most notably, there aren't any objects selected. You must choose Pick Objects to select objects for use in the IK module. The objects that you pick must already be hierarchically linked together. When you pick an object, its tree will show in the window. If any objects that are picked already have animation assigned to them, that animation will appear in the IK module.

To the right of the Pick Objects button is the Follow Objects button. If you press it, a dialog box appears that enables you to select an object that will follow the last object in the chain (see fig. 9.15). There are two check boxes in this dialog box worth mentioning.

Figure 9.15

The Pick Follow Object dialog box.

The Solve for orientation check box tells IK to adjust the orientation of the follow object to match the orientation of the IK chain it is attached to. The "Follow object motion is relative" check box enables you to determine whether the follow object follows absolutely or relative to the chain. An object follows another absolutely when wherever the first object goes, the second object goes. For example, your hand absolutely follows your wrist. When an object follows another relatively, the second object starts from a position relative to the first object and then begins to follow the first object. Kind of like a bouncing basketball is relative to your hand, it follows the motion, but is not attached. When you choose an object, IK will automatically begin processing the new joint positions for the follow object.

An example of a follow object might be a bouncing ball. Say you have created an IK animation of an arm bouncing the ball. Instead of setting keyframes for the ball, you can assign the ball as a follow object to the hand, then the ball will follow the hand absolutely or begin moving from its original position, which is relative.

To the right of the Follow Object button is the Interactive button, which is used to assign the animation keys using IK. Selecting this option loads the objects that you have previously loaded into IK into an interactive editing box (see fig. 9.16).

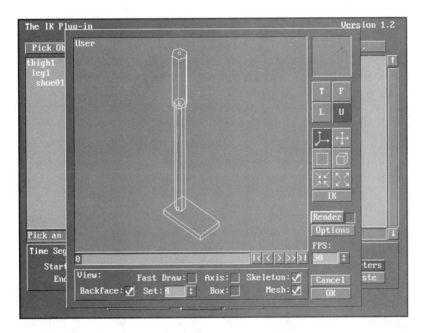

In the interactive window, you will see the object you have selected to work with. In this case, the leg from the previous exercise is loaded into IK at this point. Notice the blue line with the light blue boxes running through the object. This line represents the IK skeleton and each box represents a joint.

At the bottom of the dialog box are a set of buttons and sliders that should look familiar to you by now. First, you have a frame slider and a set of playback buttons, just like you do in the Keyframer. Below these are a set of View buttons that work just like the standard View buttons in the Keyframer and the 3D Editor.

To the right of the interactive window is a set of buttons that enables you to control the view of the object. Most of the buttons should look familiar to you because they are the same as those used in any of the other modules in 3D Studio. The only new button is the IK button, which allows you to change the position of IK joints and set keyframes in the animation.

Below the IK button is a Render button. This does not render the scene with the materials you have already applied to the model. Instead, it renders all the objects as a flat gray. This is good enough to see how the model will look. You can use this mode to play back the animation in real time, assuming your model is not too complex. Below the Render button is an FPS field where you can set the playback speed of the interactive playback.

Returning to the main IK dialog box, you next see the Options button. This allows you to set many of the IK modules preferences. Most of these are beyond the scope of this book. Refer to the Release 4 Add-on guide for more information. The button also allows you to save the IK animation and remove all follow objects from the animation.

At the bottom of the screen on the left, you will see a time segment box. This allows you to define where and how long an animation segment will be in the IK module. When working with character animation, it is best to work on small segments at a time.

To the right of the Time Segment box is the Define Chain box. This allows you to automatically set joint precedence. Joint precedence helps you to determine which joints will have the most influence.

The last option in the base dialog box is the Edit Joints box. Here, you can define the individual joint parameters necessary to fully constrain and control the motion of that joint. Selecting the Joint Parameters button and choosing an object from the list will display the joint parameters dialog box. See figure 9.17.

For the most part, you will make heavy use of the Joint Parameters box and the Interactive window to control the IK animation.

Now that you have a basic overview of the IK module, it is time to look more closely at the types of joints you can create with IK. This will be followed by an exercise that will step you through the basics of the IK module.

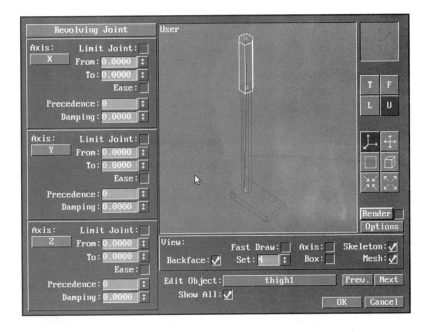

Joints

The basis of IK is the joints and how you constrain the joints you create in
your character. These joints will enable you to emulate real life motion
much easier than when using hierarchical linking and basic move and
rotate commands. Because joints are such an important part of IK, they
warrant a closer look than any other part of the IK module.

Joint Parameters

The IK in 3D Studio uses two types of joints: revolving joints and sliding
joints. Revolving joints allow the joint to rotate in the x, y, and z directions. Sliding joints do not allow the joint to rotate, but to move in the x,
y, and z directions. The default joint type is a revolving joint.

Revolving Joints

To access the joint controls, choose the Joint Parameters button in the IK
dialog box. Then click on the name of the object you want to work with.
This displays the Joint Parameters dialog box (see figure 9.18).

Figure 9.18

The Revolving Joint Parameters dialog box

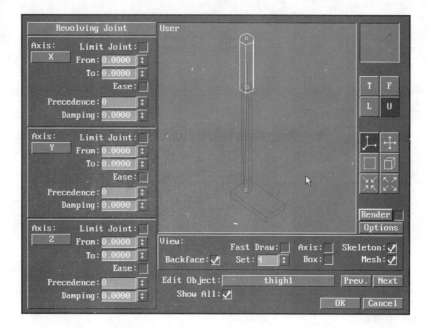

Notice how the model is displayed in the view window. The white part of the model represents the current joint you are going to work with. Also notice that the skeleton and joint locations are available as well.

The first thing you will notice in this dialog box is that all of the joint parameters are currently set to 0. In this case, the leg from the previous exercise is loaded in the dialog box. As you can see, you can access the x, y, and z rotations of the joint.

The x, y, and z rotations referred to here are the local axis of the joint, not the global x, y, and z of the keyframer. You can view the axis of each joint by choosing Axis from the view section of the dialog box. You can also see how the joint moves by adjusting one of the limit fields for an axis. The view window will show you the range and direction of motion for the model for that axis. So, worrying about the orientation of the local x, y, and z axes is not that important.

If you take a closer look at the X rotation section of the dialog box, you will see several parameters that you can adjust. First, there is a Limit check box. When you turn this on, you can limit the motion of the joint. The two fields following this check box allow you to key in the start and end limitations of the rotation of the joint in degrees. The next check box is Ease. Ease allows you to simulate restriction in the movement of the joint as the joint approaches its limits.

The next set of fields are also important. The first field is joint Precedence. This field determines how important this particular joint is relative to the other joints in the model. The other field, Damping, allows you to create resistance across the range of motion that the joint has.

Again, in this dialog box, you have an assortment of tools to allow you to view the model in different ways. You should be familiar with these options by now.

Sliding Joints

Sliding joints are similar to revolving joints and have a similar set of constraints placed on them. To set up a sliding joint, simply click on the revolving joint button. This will switch the joint to a sliding joint (see figure 9.19).

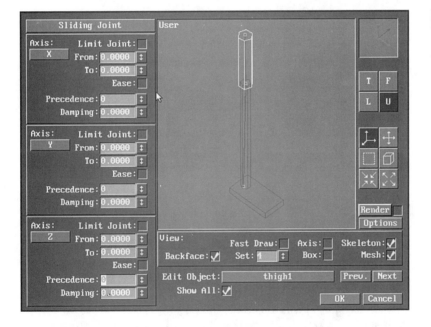

Figure 9.19

The Sliding Joint Parameters dialog box.

As you can see, all of the individual parameters are the same. When you adjust the limits of a joint, you are not adjusting rotation degrees in a sliding joint, but linear motion. Values can range from –9999 to 9999.

Revolving joints are used in situations where the joint has to have a rotation in one or more of the axes, such as a knee joint or a wrist joint. Sliding joints are used when the joint does not rotate, but does move in one or more of the axes. An example of a sliding joint is a piston in a car engine. This piston only moves up and down; the shaft of the piston is what rotates.

Now that you have a basic idea about joints and how they work, it is time to run through an exercise. This exercise will use the CH9TUT02.3DS file. Again, the exercise will focus on animating one leg of the model. This exercise will also utilize the creation of a dummy object for increased control over the animation.

Character Animation with IK

Load CH9TUT02.3DS into 3D Studio	Loads a file
Press F5 to switch to the Keyframer	Loads the Keyframer
Choose Display/Hide/All	Hides all objects in the scene
Choose Display/Unhide/By Name	Unhides objects in the scene
Choose Shoe01, Leg1, Thigh1, and Plank	Unhides these objects
Choose Hierarchy/Link	Enables you to link objects
Choose shoe01, then leg1	Links two objects together
Choose leg1, then thigh1	Links two objects together

At this point, nothing new has been explored. The next section of the exercise will briefly enter the IK module to look at how the joints are placed at this time.

Press F8	Loads the IK module
Choose Pick Objects	Enables you to choose objects to work with in IK
Choose the Thigh1 object	Selects object to work with
Choose Interactive	Enables you to view the object and associated joints

At this point, you can see the model with the skeleton and joints displayed. Figure 9.20 shows the model as it should look in the IK module at this point. All the joints appear to be in the correct position. If a joint is not in the correct position, use Object Pivot in the Keyframer to reposition the pivot point. This has the effect of repositioning the joint in IK.

Choose OK	Returns you to base IK Screen
Choose OK	Returns you to the Keyframer

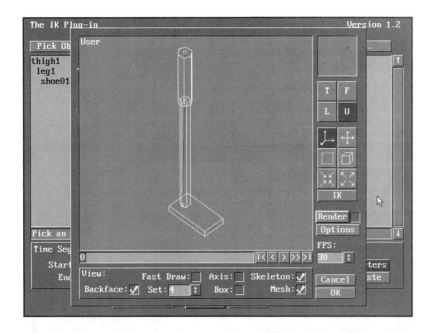

Figure 9.20

The Interactive IK screen with the model loaded.

9

At this point, a dummy object will be created at the toe of the shoe. This will give a greater sense of control over the motion of the foot. You are asked to choose a scale for the dummy object when you place it. All dummy objects are squares.

Click in Top Viewport	Activates the top viewport
Zoom out so you can see the foot	
Choose Hierarchy/Create Dummy	Enables you to create a dummy object
Click in the middle of the toe area of the foot	Places dummy object
Scale the dummy object so you can see it	Scales the dummy object

Check all viewports to make sure the dummy object is located at the toe of the foot. Sometimes it may be correct in the top viewport, but be above or below the foot in the front viewport. It just depends upon the location of the active plane. If the dummy object is not in the correct position, choose Object/Move and move it into position as if it were any other object.

Choose Hierarchy/Link	Enables you to link an object to another
Choose dummy object, then the shoe	Links the dummy object to the shoe
Choose F8	Starts the IK Module

continues

continued

Choose Pick Objects	Enables you to choose objects to use in IK
Choose the thigh again	Selects object for use in IK
Choose Interactive	Allows you to view the model interactively

The interactive screen now shows the dummy object and a new joint at the location of the dummy object. Using dummy objects to create new joints is a very powerful feature of IK. Take an ankle for example. An ankle can only rotate in one direction, forward and backward. But, rotating the leg can rotate your ankle left and right. If you create a dummy object at the toe of the foot, as in this exercise, you can rotate the dummy object around the ankle to produce that motion that you could not otherwise produce. Figure 9.21 shows the IK screen with a dummy object and the resulting joint shown.

Figure 9.21

The Interactive dialog box with the dummy object.

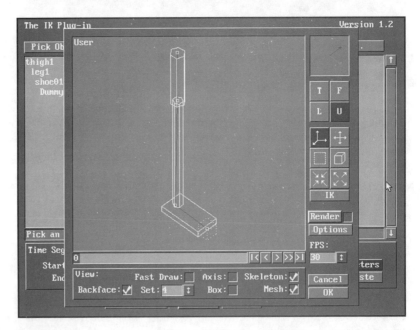

Choose OK	Returns you to the base IK screen
Choose Joint Parameters in Edit Joints	Enables you to edit the joint parameters
Choose Thigh1 from list on screen	Enables you to edit the thigh1 joint

At this point, you are ready to start setting joint parameters for the model. All joints will be set in succession during this exercise. You may do them in whatever order you like when you are working on your own model. First, you need to see how the joint will work. Because this is the thigh joint, the leg will swing back and forth, but not right or left. So, you need to find out which axes to use.

Choose double arrow next to From in the X section	Enables you to limit the joint
Move the mouse up and down	Rotates the joint

The leg should not move in this manner, so you do not need the x-axis.

Right-click	Cancels the From field
Choose double arrow next to From in the Y section	Enables you to limit the joint
Move the mouse up and down	Rotates the joint

The leg should not move like this either. So, Y is not needed.

Right-click	Cancels the From command
Choose the double arrow next to From in the Z axis	Enables you to rotate the joint

The leg should move like this, so Z is the correct axis.

Set From to 30	Limits the movement of the joint
Set To to –30	Limits the movement of the joint

The values 30 and –30 are chosen to limit the range of the motion of the leg to help approximate real world motion. Each value was chosen by adjusting the rotation sliders back and forth until a correct-looking range of motion was determined. The numbers were then rounded to the nearest 10 degrees for simplicity's sake. When you create your own joints, you should explore the range of motion of each joint and limit that joint to approximate real world motion.

Click in Limit field	Enables limits for this axis in this joint
Click on the Z button	Turns on the Z axis
Choose the Next button in the lower right corner of the screen	Moves to next joint in scene, which is the knee joint

Repeat previous process to find correct axis of movement. You should find that Y is now correct.

Choose Y	Turns on Y axis for this joint
Click in Limit field	Enables limits for this axis in this joint
Set From to 0	Limits the joint
Set To to –45	Limits the joint

As with the first joint, these numbers were generated through the use of the rotation sliders to best approximate the motion of a knee joint.

Choose Next to move to shoe joint	Moves to next joint—the ankle

Again, repeat the process for finding the axis. Again, this joint will use axis Y.

Choose Y	Turns on Y axis for this joint

continues

continued

Click in Limit field	Enables limits for this axis in this joint
Set From to 10	Limits the joint
Set To to -45	Limits the joint

As with the first joint, these numbers were generated through the use of the rotation sliders to best approximate the motion of an ankle joint.

As you can see at this point, the dummy object created earlier is not really needed and serves no purpose here. It was used in the tutorial to illustrate how to create a dummy and how it affects the rest of the model.

Choose OK	Returns you to base IK screen
Choose Interactive	Enables you to work interactively with the model
Choose IK button on the right	Enables you to set the IK motion
Choose Shoe Joint	Chooses a joint to move

Simply swing the joint left and right and notice how the model behaves according to the restraints you have placed on the joints. As you can see, the IK allowed you to limit the motion of the leg until you were able to easily adjust the animation for real world motion. When compared with using hierarchical linking and pivot points, IK is a lot easier and has more control. Using IK is the easiest method for generating character animation; it just takes time and patience.

Choose F button	Switches view to front view of model
Move frame slider to 15	Sets current frame to 15
Choose IK	Enables you to move the joints
Choose Shoe joint	Enables you to move the shoe joint

Move the joint until you have the model looking close to figure 9.22 (the knee joint is at approximately 30°.

Move frame slider to 30	Sets current frame to 30
Choose IK	Enables you to move the joints
Choose Shoe Joint again	Enables you to move the shoe joint

Move the model into a position close to figure 9.23.

Choose the Double Arrow Play button	Plays back animation
Choose OK	Returns you to the base IK box
Choose OK	Returns you to the Keyframer and saves the animation
Save the file as **CH9TUT2B.3DS**	Saves the file

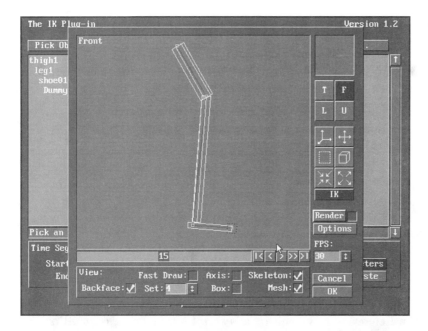

Figure 9.22

Interactive IK position at frame 15.

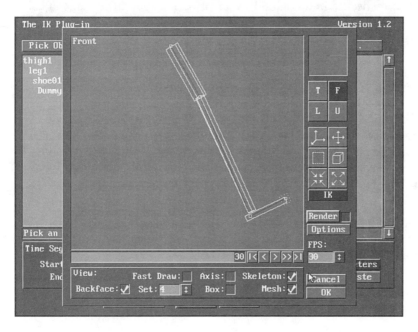

Figure 9.23

The Interactive dialog box at frame 30.

In a short amount of time, with a higher degree of control, you were able to recreate the hierarchical motion in the IK module. Obviously, to achieve realistic motion, much more work must be done on the model. For an exercise on your own, see if you can link both legs to the head of the model and animate the model walking down the plank!

Other Options

Beyond IK, there are very few options for creating realistic character animation. One option that does come up is digitized motion. Schreiber Instruments and other companies have created a software and hardware combinations that allow you to digitize human motion. The hardware is a suit that a user wears. The suit is covered with motion sensors. As you move around in the suit, the motion data is translated into keyframes in 3D Studio. Unfortunately, these kind of setups are expensive and might not suit the motion that you are looking for.

The only other option for animation control is Keyscripting, which is available in Release 4. Keyscripting is a script language for controlling how animation occurs in a model. Keyscripting is beyond the scope of this book. You are referred to the New Features book provided with Release 4 for more information on Keyscripting.

Summary

As you can see, character animation is not difficult, but is a very time-consuming task. But, it can be accomplished through the use of hierarchical linking and IK. The IK module does provide some other functionality not covered here, and you are encouraged to explore the module fully, as it is your best bet for producing good character animation inside of 3D Studio.

Next, you will be introduced to Advanced Keyframing—in particular, how to control keys using TrackInfo and KeyInfo dialog boxes in the Keyframer.

Chapter Snapshot

Now that you have been introduced to the basics of animation, it is time to look at some of the more advanced keyframing techniques available. Animation is a complex task that requires a great deal of thought, patience, and work. Some of the tools introduced in this chapter simplify much of the work necessary to achieve good animation skills.

This chapter introduces you to the following:

- The KeyInfo dialog box

- The TrackInfo dialog box

- Using KeyInfo and TrackInfo together

- Basic morphing, using keyframes

- Morphing materials, using keyframes

- A quick look at other animation techniques

- Tips and techniques for keyframing

Advanced Keyframing Techniques

Imagine an animation of a bouncing ball. Inexperienced animators might think that they could create the animation with three keyframes: the ball at a start position, the ball at the top position, and the ball returned to rest. This example assumes the ball is bouncing vertically. Well, the default keyframe setup will create a very smooth animation of the ball from the ground to the top of the motion and back. The problem is that, in real life, the motion is not smooth and even. If you think about it, one important element of realism is missing from an animation of this type: gravity. As the ball nears the top of the motion, it actually slows down, and then speeds up as it heads back toward the ground. Right now, the only way you know to create this animation effectively is to add more keyframes. But by using the tools introduced in this chapter, you can create this animation with a high degree of realism—using the same three keys.

First, a quick review of assigning keyframes to various objects.

Assigning Keyframes

Fortunately, assigning keyframes is a very intuitive approach to animation—an approach that simplifies the task of learning how to animate. Basically, you can assign keys to three types of studio objects: cameras, lights, and mesh objects. You cannot assign animation to any faces or elements unless you first separate them into individual objects.

Before you begin assigning keyframes and creating an animation, you need to understand a little about how time is interpreted in 3D Studio. Animation is nothing more than the process of displaying a series of still frames at a high enough speed to produce the *illusion* of motion. Generally, you need to display the frames at a rate of 24 frames per second or higher to achieve smooth motion. What is critical here is how you are going to play the animation and what you are going to play it with. Ordinarily, if the animation is going to be recorded to videotape, you use 30 frames per second (fps). If you record the animation to a Flic file, your hardware determines how fast you can play back the animation. You might only be able to play back the animation at 15 fps or less. (This number depends also on the output resolution.)

NOTE

All animation exercises in this chapter are based on a frame rate of 30 fps. If you cannot play back at 30 fps, the only result is the animation will just be slower.

Now that you have a better understanding of time, take a look at assigning a total number of frames to the animation. This is done in the Keyframer (see fig. 10.1).

In the lower right corner of the Keyframer, at the bottom of the Keyframer menu area, is a set of buttons that look like the controls on a tape deck or VCR. Directly above these buttons are two others: the one on the left represents the current frame, and the one on the right represents the end frame of the animation. You can set the total length by clicking on the button on the right, and then using the Set Number of Frames dialog box to set the total length of the animation in frames (see fig. 10.2).

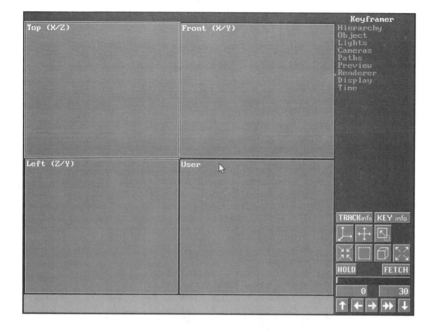

Figure 10.1

The Keyframer.

Figure 10.2

*The Set Number of
Frames dialog box.*

When you move the cursor to the bottom of the Keyframer a time line
appears. You simply click and drag along this time line to select a specific
frame number to set a key in (see fig. 10.3).

Figure 10.3

*The time line in the
Keyframer.*

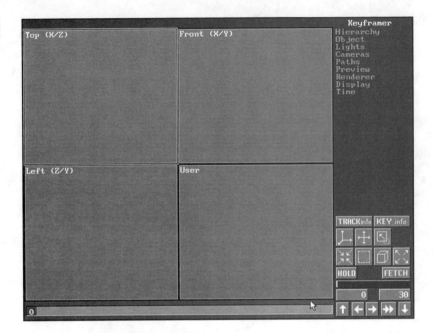

Assigning Keyframes to Objects

Assigning keyframes to objects is a very simple task. First, to move to the
frame in which you want to set the key, you either click and drag on the
time line at the bottom of the screen or set the current frame by clicking
on the current frame button. When you move to a frame other than zero,
all the geometry changes to black. Simply move the object you want to
animate to its new position by choosing Object/Move from the Keyframer
menu. When you place the object in a new position, it becomes white in
the current frame (indicating that you have assigned a key to this object).

The following short exercise demonstrates placing a keyframe.

Placing a Keyframe

In the 3D Editor, create a box	
Switch to the Keyframer	Enables you to set up animation sequences
Leave number of frames at 30	Creates a one-second animation
On the time line at bottom, drag the marker until you are at frame 30	Sets current frame to 30

Select Object/Move, and move the object to a new position	Moves the object and sets the key

Notice that the object turns white in frame 30.

Click on the double-arrow button	Plays back the animation
Save as EX1.3DS	Saves the file

You now get a slow rendition of the animation on your screen. Notice that as the animation passes scenes where keys are set, the appropriate objects turn white.

Assigning Keyframes to Lights

Assigning keyframes to lights is also a simple task. You can assign a key to two parts of a light: the light itself, and its target. Simply follow the procedure you used to assign the keyframe to an object. When you set a key in the light or its target, a white dot shows up in the center of the icon to let you know that a key is assigned to the light.

Assigning Keyframes to Cameras

The process of assigning keyframes to cameras is the same as that used to assign keyframes to lights, and also displays the same white dots to indicate that the key is set.

If you want a light or camera to move, you must either assign keys or a path. The following exercise demonstrates the use of keys in lights and cameras.

Animating Lights and Cameras

Load the EX1.3DS file from the previous exercise. This file should contain the animation of a block from one position to another. In the 3D Editor, add a spotlight shining on the block and a camera looking at the block. Feel free to place the camera and spotlight where you like, but make sure the targets are on or near the block.

Switch to the Keyframer	Enables you to assign keys
Set current Frame to 30	Moves to frame 30 to set keys
Choose Camera/Move	Enables you to move the camera or its target

continues

continued

Move camera to a new position	Sets the camera key
Choose Light/Spot/Move	Enables you to move the spotlight or its target
Move the spotlight to a new position	Sets the spotlight key
Render the animation	

Adjusting Keyframes with KeyInfo

Frequently, when you create an animation with keyframes, you want to control what happens at each key and around each key you have assigned in the animation. 3D Studio's KeyInfo dialog box gives you that control. To activate the KeyInfo dialog box (see fig. 10.4), click on the KeyInfo button located in the lower right corner of the Keyframer window, and then select an object to which a keyframe is assigned. (Remember, you know a key is assigned because it is white.)

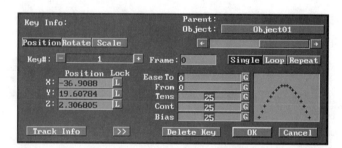

The KeyInfo dialog box lets you control three aspects of the key you selected—position, rotation, and scale—as well as the frame position around the keyframe. To select the type of key information you want to control, you use the set of buttons in the upper left corner of the KeyInfo dialog box. When you select one of these buttons, the contents of the dialog box change slightly. The default selection, Position, is a good place to start.

When the Position button is highlighted, you can control the position of the object at this key. Below the Position button is a Key# slider. This slider enables you to move back and forth between the keys assigned to

10

this object. Because many keys can be assigned to objects at various times during the animation, this is a handy tool.

Below the key slider are three fields, one for each coordinate. These boxes will contain the location of the objects for this key. The L button to the right of each field enables you to lock that field in this key, so that it cannot be changed. If the position of the object in this key is critical, lock each coordinate to keep it from changing.

Below the coordinate boxes is a TrackInfo button. (The TrackInfo button is discussed in the next section.) To the right of the TrackInfo button is a double-arrow play button. This button enables you to make changes to a key and then automatically play back those changes to see how they work.

In the upper right corner of the dialog box, you will see the name of the object you selected. If the object is hierarchically linked to another object, the name of the parent object is displayed in the Parent slot. The slider below the object name enables you to move to the next object in the scene. When a scene contains many objects, this can be a difficult way to reach another object to work with in the KeyInfo dialog box.

Below this slider is a Frame field. This box shows you the frame this key is located in. To the right of the frame field are three buttons that affect the pattern of the motion for this key: Single, Loop, and Repeat. The default key type is Single. In this case, the motion is based on each individual key in the animation. The Loop button copies the values of key #1 to the last frame of the animation to create a loop in the animation. The Repeat button establishes a pattern of keys that cycles throughout the animation. None of these buttons adds any keyframes to the animation.

Why Spline Paths?

In 3D Studio, all motion is handled with spline paths. To create a smooth, natural movement between each specified position (or key), 3D Studio adjusts the position of the object, camera, or light so that it can pass into and out of each key without abruptness. Although the settings certainly can be adjusted for occasions in which some linear motion or jerky behavior is necessary, the usual mode is to keep motions smooth and even.

To better visualize the splined-motion animation of 3D Studio, think of a thick metal wire, like those on the bass side of a piano. If you attach the ends of the wire to two pegs, the wire stays unflexed, and draws a straight line between the pegs. If you then add a third peg, away from the present path of the wire, the wire flexes so that it curves smoothly through this new center point. When you apply tension to the wire by pulling it at its two endpoints, the curve tightens at the center point. At some extreme level of tension, the wire draws tight to the peg, and the curve becomes two straight lines. In this analogy, the pegs represent keyframes, and the wire represents the path of an object over time.

Because the splines are created on a computer, a great deal of control over the way a spline is drawn is available through parameters listed in the KeyInfo dialog box.

Below the motion pattern buttons are five important sliders: Ease To, From, Tens, Cont, and Bias. To the right of these sliders is a graph, which shows a series of black ticks and one red tick. The red tick represents the current key and the black ticks are the frames that surround the key. By adjusting the shape of this curve, you can control the motion of the animation around each keyframe. For example, if you shift the number of frames closer to the key, you slow down the animation as it approaches the key. You adjust the graph by using the five sliders at the left of the graph (see fig. 10.5).

Figure 10.5

The KeyInfo graph and sliders.

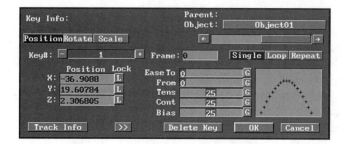

If you consider the graph as a motion, things are easier to understand. The closer you move to the keyframe in the animation, the closer you get to the red key on the graph. The Ease To slider enables you to ease closer to the keyframe by moving more of the frames that precede the keyframe closer to the Keyframer. Compare figure 10.6, which shows the graph with Ease To set at 50, with figure 10.5, which shows the default graph position. Notice how the position of the frames preceding the key has changed.

Figure 10.6

The graph, with Ease To at 50.

The From button has the same effect, but on the other side of the key (see fig. 10.7). Compare figure 10.7 to figures 10.6 and 10.5. To slow the animation on both sides of the keyframe, adjust both Ease To and From to the same value.

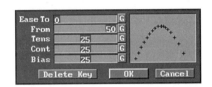

Figure 10.7

The graph, with From at 50.

10

The last three sliders are not as easy to understand as the Ease To and From sliders. The tension, continuity, and bias controls for the motion graph are all set at a median value of 25 to produce a smooth motion through the keyframe. The Tension button controls the curvature of the graph around the keyframe. Higher values of tension create a flatter graph that looks like a triangle (see fig. 10.8). Lower values create more of a circular shape at the keyframe (see fig. 10.9).

Figure 10.8

The graph with Tension at 50.

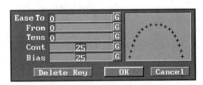

Figure 10.9

The graph with Tension at 0.

The Continuity button controls the angle at which the graph enters and leaves the keyframe. Higher values force the frames near the keyframe into their own curves above the keyframe (see fig. 10.10). Lower values produce results similar to a tension setting of 50 (see fig. 10.11).

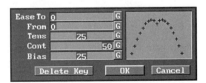

Figure 10.10

The graph with Continuity at 50.

Figure 10.11

*The graph with
Continuity at 0.*

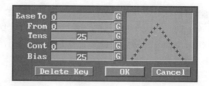

The last button, the Bias button, controls the overshoot and undershoot of the motion through the keyframe. Higher values cause the motion of the object to overshoot the position of the key (see fig. 10.12). Lower values cause the object to undershoot the position of the key (see fig. 10.13).

Figure 10.12

*The graph with
Bias at 50.*

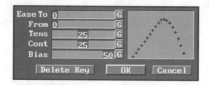

Figure 10.13

*The graph with
Bias at 0.*

To the right of each slider, the Global (G) button applies the values of each slider to all the keys in the track. (See the TrackInfo section for more information about tracks.)

Below the motion graphs and sliders is the Delete Key button. This is a handy tool when you assign a key you do not want. Should that happen, simply choose KeyInfo, click on the object with the key assigned to it, and click on Delete Key to delete the key from the animation.

When you choose one of the other KeyInfo types, such as Rotate (see fig. 10.14) or Scale (see fig. 10.15), only the Position slider section of the dialog box changes. The position section changes to rotation and scale values for each of the other key types.

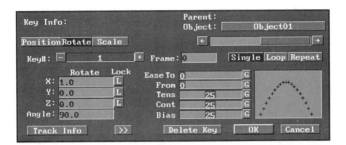

Figure 10.14

The KeyInfo dialog box for Rotation.

10

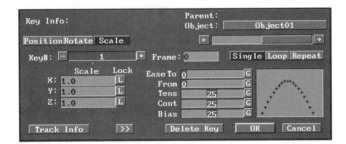

Figure 10.15

The KeyInfo dialog box for Scale.

Now that you have been introduced to the KeyInfo dialog box, it is time to look at a practical application of some of the tools in this box, using the bouncing ball example from the beginning of this chapter. The following exercise makes use of the CH10TUT1.3DS file found on the accompanying CD. Load this file and switch to the Keyframer before starting the exercise.

The CH10TUT1.3DS file has an animation of a bouncing ball. Here, the ball is assumed to bounce consistently in the same place. Clearly, this never happens in real life—but it does make a good exercise. All keyframes necessary for the animation have been assigned. The exercise focuses on how to adjust the keys. The total animation length is 60 frames, or two seconds. Before you begin the exercise, use the double-arrow button to play the animation so that you can see the motion before you make the changes. A light and camera are in the scene, but only default materials are assigned.

Adjusting a Keyframe

The most important keyframe in this exercise is the key located at frame 30, where the ball is at the top of its motion.

Using the slider at the bottom of the Keyframer screen, move to frame 30	Displays the ball at its top position (it should be white, to indicate that a keyframe is here)
Choose KeyInfo	Enables you to start the KeyInfo dialog box
Click on Ball	Enables you to look at the KeyInfo for the ball at this key (see fig. 10.16)

As the motion of the ball approaches its *apex* (the top of the motion), gravity causes it to slow down. To accomplish this effect, you must adjust the Ease To slider.

Adjust Ease To to 50	Moves frames before key closer to the key
Choose the double-arrow button	Plays back animation

At this point, the motion before the ball starts to fall back to the ground looks pretty good. But not quite right. The From values need to be adjusted to give the ball a sense of speeding up as it heads back toward the ground. Repeat the previous two steps, but change the From slider to 50 instead of the Ease To slider. Now render the animation to a Flic file to see if it plays back correctly. If the values of 50 for Ease To and From are too much, the ball seems to hang in the air a little too long. A readjustment may be necessary. Simply repeat the previous steps and choose different values for Ease To and From. It is suggested, at this point, that you play with the other sliders for the key as well, to see how they affect the motion. You may just find another combination that works better than adjusting Ease To and From to correct the motion of the ball.

Figure 10.16

The KeyInfo dialog box for the ball at top Position.

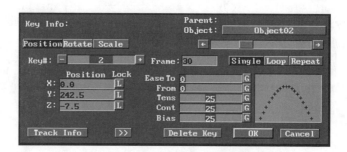

As you can guess, it might take some time for you to get used to adjusting keyframes to get the exact motion you are looking for.

Adjusting Keyframes with TrackInfo

The TrackInfo dialog box allows you to view keyframes in relation to each other and the rest of the animation. The KeyInfo dialog box only allows you to adjust individual key frames. TrackInfo lays out all keys in the animation on a time line. TrackInfo also allows you to add Hide keys that you cannot add anywhere else.

TrackInfo for Objects

The KeyInfo dialog box is used for adjusting individual keyframes. You can use the TrackInfo dialog box to adjust all the keyframes assigned to an object.

To access the TrackInfo dialog box (see fig. 10.17), choose the TrackInfo key in the Keyframer and select any object. You do not have to be at a keyframe to use the TrackInfo dialog box.

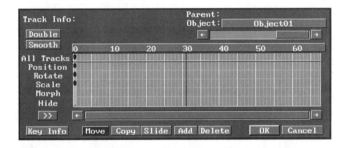

Figure 10.17

The TrackInfo dialog box.

To access this dialog box from the KeyInfo dialog box, click on the TrackInfo button in that box.

The first thing you will notice in the TrackInfo box is the large graph. This graph is broken down vertically into frames, and horizontally into six tracks: All Tracks, Position, Rotate, Scale, Morph, and Hide. If a keyframe of any of these types is assigned, a black dot appears in the frame column to which the keyframe was assigned, and on the track row of its type. All objects have a key at frame zero in all tracks. The current frame in the Keyframer is shown as a light-colored column. A black vertical bar represents the last frame of the animation. This setting is based on the total number of frames set in the Keyframer.

The All Tracks track shows you all the keys in the animation, in each keyframe they are assigned. This makes it very easy to track where you have keys and where you do not have keys.

The Position track enables you to see where you have keys that are moving the position of lights, cameras, and mesh objects.

The Rotate, Scale, Morph, and Hide tracks also enable you to see where keys of these types are assigned. Fortunately, because 3D Studio is smart enough to know when a key is a rotation key or a morph key, you do not have to provide this information.

Outside of the tracks graph are several useful buttons. In the upper left corner are the Double and Smooth buttons. The Double button doubles the length of the animation and makes an exact copy of the existing animation in the second half of the longer animation. The Smooth button smooths out the spacing of the key frames, to smooth the motion. If you are having a problem controlling the consistency of the speed of your animations, you can try to smooth the animation by using this button. These two global buttons affect all frames in the animation for the current object.

To select individual objects, use the box or slider in the upper right corner of the dialog box. In the lower left corner of the dialog box is a button that enables you to access the KeyInfo dialog box. To display information about a particular key, simply click on the KeyInfo button and then on the black dot that represents the key you want to look at. This switches you to the KeyInfo dialog box. Above the KeyInfo button is a double-arrow button with which you can play back the animation after you make changes.

To the right of the KeyInfo button is a series of useful buttons for manipulating keys: Move, Copy, Slide, Add, and Delete. As you can guess, each button performs its respective operations on a key in the graph. The only one whose effect might not be apparent is the Slide button, which slides keys up and down the time line. The only difference between it and Move is that Slide slides all the keys on that particular track, keeping them spaced a constant distance from one another. This can be a handy feature when you want to move a segment of animation to another time frame.

Finally, you can adjust the track information on a world scale instead of an object scale. When you right-click on the TrackInfo button, you get the world version of it (see fig. 10.18). Here, you can adjust all the keyframes in the animation.

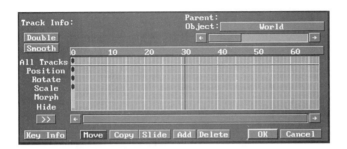

Figure 10.18

The world TrackInfo dialog box.

Now it is time to take a closer look at the TrackInfo dialog box. Load the CH10TUT2.3DS file from the companion CD, and switch to the Keyframer. This is the same animation created in the last exercise, but with a few twists added to it. In this animation, the ball rotates as it moves up to frame 20. The ball also gets smaller from frame 0 to frame 40, at which point it stays consistent. Use the double-arrow key to play back this animation so that you can see what it looks like at this point. You are going to use the TrackInfo dialog box to make some minor changes to the animation.

Before you begin the exercise, take a look at the TrackInfo for the ball. This is the only object you need to be concerned with. Simply click on the TrackInfo button, and then on the ball, to display the TrackInfo dialog box with Track information for the ball (see fig. 10.19).

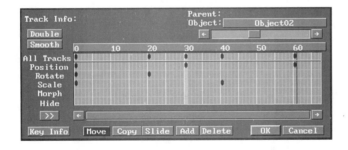

Figure 10.19

The TrackInfo dialog box for the ball.

Play the animation inCH10TUT02.3DS before beginning this exercise. The file is found on the companion CD.

Working with TrackInfo

When you play back the animation, you probably will notice that the ball continues to shrink in size after it reaches the of the motion. Some people might find this strange. By making a small change made with TrackInfo, you can move the scale key from frame 40 to frame 30 to correct this problem.

continues

continued

Choose Move from the bottom of the TrackInfo dialog box.	Enables you to move a key
Click on the dot in frame 40 of the Scale track	Enables you to move the Scale key
Move the dot to frame 30, and click again on frame 30	Moves the key to frame 30
Click on the double-arrow button	Plays back the animation

Now the animation is starting to look a little better. Notice that the rotation of the ball stops before the ball reaches the top of the animation. This can be corrected to produce a smoother animation.

Choose Move from the bottom of the TrackInfo dialog box	Enables you to move a key
Click on the dot in frame 20 of the Rotation track	Enables you to move the rotation key
Move the dot to frame 30, and click again on frame 30	Moves the key to frame 30
Click on the double-arrow button	Plays back the animation

Now the ball finishes its rotation at the top of the movement. These two adjustments could also have been made in the KeyInfo dialog box, using the Frame field. For fun, double the length of the animation to see how that works.

Choose Double from the top of the Track Info dialog box	Enables you to double the length of the animation
In the Warning box, choose Yes	Tells system that you want to double the length of the animation
Click on double-arrow button	Plays back the animation

Notice that the animation is now 120 frames, and you have two copies of the same animation. Now, just for fun, you are going to add a keyframe that hides the ball from frame 20 to frame 40.

Choose Add from the bottom of the TrackInfo dialog box	Enables you to add a keyframe
Click in frame 20's Hide track	Adds a Hide key at frame 20

Notice the white and gray line now in the track (see fig. 10.20). Where the line is white, the object is visible; where it is gray, the object is hidden.

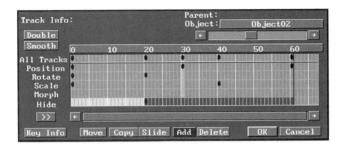

Figure 10.20

*The Hide track,
with a key.*

Click in frame 40's Hide track	Adds a Hide key at frame 40
Click on double-arrow button	Plays back the animation

Now the ball is hidden in the first repetition of the animation. You can continue to add hide keys in the Hide track as many times as you like. Notice that the gray area stays between the Hide keys (see fig. 10.21).

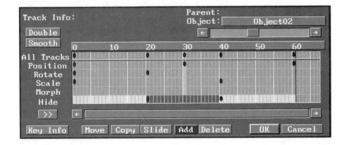

Figure 10.21

*The Hide track,
with two keys.*

As you can see, the TrackInfo dialog box gives you another measure of control. By combining TrackInfo with KeyInfo, you gain a high level of control over the use of keyframes in an animation.

TrackInfo for Lights

The TrackInfo dialog box provides different tracks for lights than it does for objects. The tracks work in the same way they do for objects, but affect the specific parts of the lights (see figs. 10.22, 10.23, and 10.24).

Figure 10.22

TrackInfo for a spotlight.

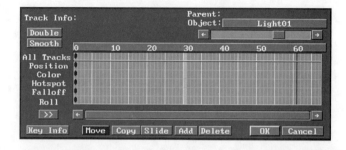

Figure 10.23

TrackInfo for a spotlight target.

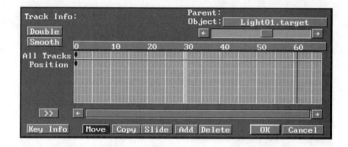

Figure 10.24

TrackInfo for an omni light.

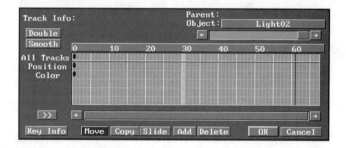

As you can see, you can adjust each part of the light over time.

TrackInfo for Cameras

As with the TrackInfo dialog box for lights, the one for cameras contains camera-specific tracks that can be manipulated over time (see fig. 10.25). The TrackInfo for a camera target is the same as for a spotlight target (refer to fig. 10.23).

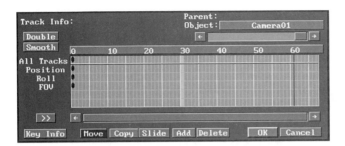

Figure 10.25

TrackInfo for a camera.

Combining TrackInfo with KeyInfo

The TrackInfo and KeyInfo dialog boxes were made to work hand in hand with each other. As you have seen, the KeyInfo dialog box allows you to adjust the individual keyframes, where the TrackInfo dialog box allows you to adjust the keyframes on a time line where you can see the relationships between keyframes.

Both TrackInfo and KeyInfo dialog boxes have a button allowing you access to the other dialog box. If, for example, you are looking at a keyframe for an object in KeyInfo, you can see the keyframe position relative to others simply by clicking on the TrackInfo button. When TrackInfo comes up, the keyframe you were viewing in KeyInfo will be highlighted.

TrackInfo also allows you to adjust two key types that KeyInfo does not, by default. These key types are Morph and Hide. You have seen how to use the Hide key in the previous exercise. The morph key will be discussed in the next section. When you add Morph or Hide keys, they appear on the time line as normal. When you choose KeyInfo and click on a Morph or Hide key, you will get a slightly different KeyInfo dialog box (see figure 10.26).

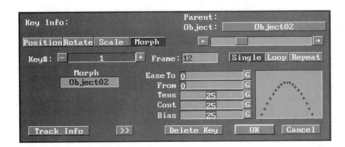

Figure 10.26

The KeyInfo dialog box with a Morph key.

As you can see, the only difference is the addition of a few key types at the top of the dialog box.

This interrelationship between the KeyInfo and TrackInfo dialog boxes is very important because it enables you to have a high degree of control over both the position and effect of each and every key. This control is simply not possible without the KeyInfo and TrackInfo dialog boxes. When you have gained enough experience with them, you will find that you will make heavy use of both dialog boxes.

Controlling Anticipating Motions

Frequently, you want an object to move to a certain point, remain there stationary for a time, and then begin moving again. Because 3D Studio will try to curve-fit the path through the same point in space over two different times, the object will not remain stationary during the intended pause. Instead, it will anticipate the upcoming movement by backing up before the keyframe that starts the second half of the motion. The next exercise shows how to control this effect.

In this exercise, you will to work with a cube animation (in which the cube travels through an L-shaped path). The goal of the exercise is to have the cube sit at the corner of the L shape during frames 12 through 18, before it proceeds through the rest of the motion. Using what you know of the TrackInfo dialog box, this goal would seem fairly easy to accomplish.

Pauses in Motion

Load CH10TUT5.3DS	Loads file
Click on the TrackInfo button in the Keyframer menu, then click on the cube	Displays the TrackInfo dialog box, with position keys indicated at frames 0, 15, and 30 (see fig. 10.27)
In the dialog box, click the Move button	Activates the button, which turns red
In the Position row, click on the keyframe indicated at frame 15, and slide it to frame 12. Click again to place the key	Now the spots occur at 0, 12, and 30 (see fig. 10.28)
Click on the Copy button	Activates the Copy button, which turns red

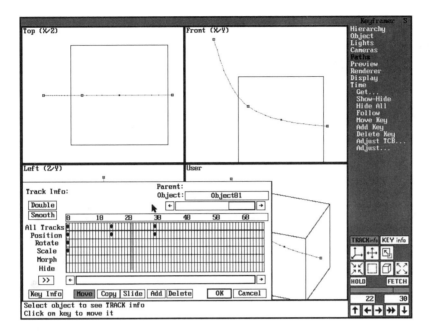

Figure 10.27

The cube's current TrackInfo, with position keys at 0, 15, and 30.

10

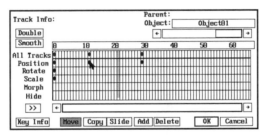

Figure 10.28

The key at frame 15 now occurs at frame 12. The object will move faster now, to get the same distance in fewer frames.

Click on the spot at frame 12, and move the copied key to frame 18 (see fig. 10.29)

Now spots occur on the position track at frames 0, 12, 18, and 30

You know that the exact same position data is in the keyframes at 12 and 18.

Click on OK to approve the changes and exit the dialog box

The dialog box disappears; the path now has a little loop in the corner, and the legs of the L shape are straight, rather than curved (see fig. 10.30)

Click on the play animation icon (the double-right-arrow icon at the bottom of the Keyframer menu)

The cube faithfully follows the path, including the little loop where the cube was supposed to be stationary

continues

continued

Figure 10.29

Copying the key at frame 12 to frame 18. Because the information is the same, the object will have keys that force it to be in the same position at frame 12.

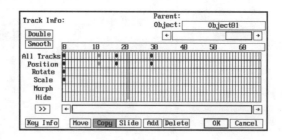

Figure 10.30

With keys overlapping in space, but separated by a few frames, the spline motion forces a loop in the path.

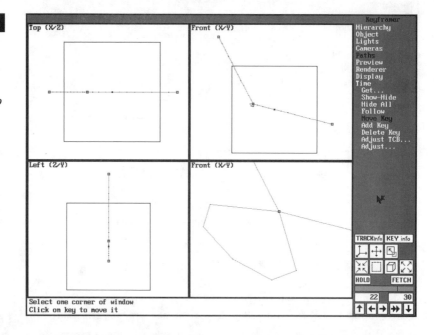

To fix the anticipatory motion of the cube during the time in which it is supposed to sit motionless, you must change the TCB values for the keyframes at frames 12 and 18.

Click on the KeyInfo button in the Keyframer menu, and choose the cube	Displays the KeyInfo dialog box
Choose the Position button at the upper left of the dialog box	Four keys are apparent in the Key# slider
Click in the Key# slider to select key 2	The dialog box reflects key 2's settings

Click and drag the indicator in the Continuity slider all the way to the left	The slider indicates 0
Click in the Key# slider to select key 3	The settings in the dialog box reflect key 3's parameters
Click and drag the Continuity slider as before, to set a continuity of 0	The slider indicates 0 (see fig. 10.31)
Click on OK	The dialog box disappears, and the path has no loop in its corner (see fig. 10.32)
Click on the double-right-arrow icon to play the animation	The cube now pauses at the corner

10

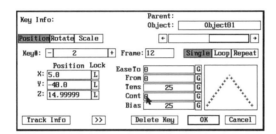

Keying with Continuity displayed.

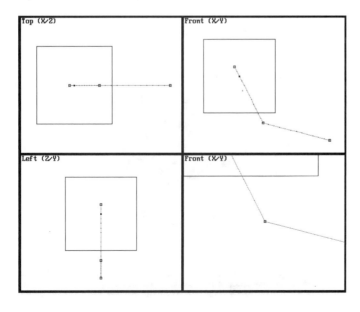

Figure 10.32

With the two middle keys' continuity set to zero, the loop disappears and the object moves through the path and pauses correctly.

Morphing with Keyframes

Because one of the key types discussed here is a morph type, this is a good place to explain how to use 3D Studio to create morphs.

Morphing is the process of transforming one object into another. In 3D Studio, you can morph from one object to another and from one material to another.

Morphing Objects

Morphing from one object to another is a little more difficult than morphing from one material to another. The process of morphing from one object to another includes several restrictions. The most important restriction is that both objects must have the same number of vertices. If the two objects you want to morph between do not have the same number of vertices, 3D Studio cannot morph the objects. Clearly, if the 2D Shaper and 3D Lofter were used to create the objects, simple control of the detail and path steps can provide different objects with the same number of vertices.

Assigning a morph key is a very simple process. Move the time line at the bottom of the Keyframer screen to the frame where you want the end of the morph to be. Choose Object/Morph/Assign in the Keyframer menu, then click on the first object. A morph dialog box is displayed that shows you all the objects currently in the scene into which you can morph this object (see fig. 10.33).

Then, simply choose the other object to morph to. At this point, you can use the Keyframer's Display/Hide option to remove the other object from the scene, because it is not needed. Do not delete the object, however.

If you choose an object that does not have another object it can morph to, you see the message No Morphable Objects. This means that one of the two objects you want to morph between does not have the same number of vertices as the other.

The following exercise shows you how to morph from a straight cylinder to a bent cylinder. Both cylinders were created by using the 2D Shaper and 3D Lofter, to ensure the same number of vertices in the object.

Before you begin this exercise, load the CH10TUT3.3DS file from the companion CD, and switch to the Keyframer. In this exercise, you create a one-second morph, based on 30 frames.

10

Morphing an Object

Move to frame 30	Moves to the selected frame to set key
Choose Objects/Morph/Assign	Enables you to assign a morph key
Choose the Cylinder	Chooses the cylinder as the first morph object, and displays the Morph dialog box (see fig. 10.34)
Choose Object1	Selects bent cylinder to Morph to
Choose OK	Displays Keyframer, with Bent cylinder displayed in place of cylinder (see fig. 10.35)
Choose Display/Hide/By Name	Enables you to hide an object
Choose Object1	Hides object1
Choose OK	
Click on double-arrow button	Plays back animation (see fig. 10.36)

As you can see, the cylinder morphs into the bent cylinder. This is just a simple example of morphing. Imagine what you can do with more complex objects, if you take the time.

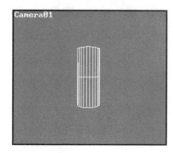

Figure 10.34

The cylinder at frame 0.

Figure 10.35

The cylinder at frame 15.

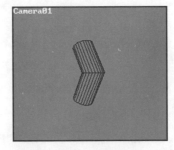

Figure 10.36

The cylinder at frame 30.

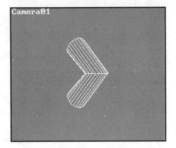

As you can see, morphing is fairly simple, provided that both objects have the same number of vertices. After you have assigned the morph key, you can use TrackInfo and KeyInfo to adjust the motion of the morph as another standard key.

Morphing Materials

Morphing materials is easier than morphing objects. Again, both morph objects must have the same number of vertices.

The following exercise takes you through the process of creating a morph of materials. This exercise shows you how to morph a solid box into a transparent box. Load the CH10TUT4.3DS file from the accompanying CD, and switch to the Keyframer. Two boxes of exactly the same size are in the scene. One has the default material, the other a material named *transparent*. The transparent material has the transparency slider to 100; nothing else is set.

Morphing Materials

Set Current frame to 30	Sets the frame for morph key to 30
Choose Object/Morph/Assign	Enables you to assign a morph key
Choose Object01 (the blue box)	Selects object for morph key
Choose Object02 to morph to	Chooses the morph-to object
Choose OK	Displays the Keyframer
Choose Object/Morph/Options	Enables you to set the Morph options
Choose Object01 gain	Selects object to change morph options
Choose Morph Materials	Tells object to morph materials (see fig. 10.37)

Choose OK.

Render Animation as normal.

You cannot use any of the preview methods to see a morph of materials. Morphed materials show up only in the final rendering. Because of the number of colors used in a morph of materials, FLIC files do not make a good output method for morphed materials. Because a FLIC file will show you the end result, however, render the animation to a FLIC, and play it back as you normally would. As with other morph objects, after you have assigned the morph key, you can hide Object02.

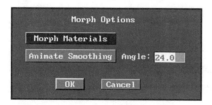

Figure 10.37

The Morph Options dialog box.

As you can see, morphing materials is fairly easy and can be a very powerful tool. Use your imagination, and have fun morphing.

Keyframing in IPAS Routines

Just a brief note about keyframing and its use in IPAS routines: Many routines, especially the IK routine that comes with Release 4, use keyframes to set up their animations. If you use an IPAS routine to create part or all of your animation, be careful when you go about adjusting keyframes with KeyInfo and TrackInfo. You don't want to mess up what the IPAS routine generated for you.

Tips and Techniques in Keyframing

The following are some tips and techniques for effective use of keyframing to create good, clean animations:

- Keep the number of keyframes to a minimum. Use TrackInfo and KeyInfo to adjust variances between keyframes, when possible.

- Always keep in mind how fast your animation will be played back when setting keys.

- Be careful when you use the Smooth and Double routines in TrackInfo. They might not always produce the results you expect.

- When you morph objects, make sure that both objects have the same number of vertices and the same materials applied, unless you want to morph materials at the same time.

- To accelerate redraw times in the Keyframer, always hide the morph-to object after you have set up the animation. Do not delete the morph-to object.

- When you morph materials, use the highest possible color depth for your output. This makes the morph of the materials look better.

- Make use of all of your animation preview capabilities before you generate the final animation. Catching mistakes beforehand is much easier than trying to catch them afterward.

Tips for Optimal Keyframing

The following tips will help you as you become more familiar with the Keyframer. These tips will help you optimize your keyframing skills, making your animations better.

1. **Always Check Frame before You Do Anything.** The current frame is always indicated at the bottom of the Keyframer menu. Because every change you make is almost always time-dependent, you must always confirm that what you are changing should be

changing at the current frame. If you hastily change object positions, you can easily (and accidentally) add undesired motion, or motions, at the wrong time. For changes on items that are not animating, make sure you are at frame 0 before you make any changes.

2. **Add Keys Sparingly.** By using the TCB controls, you should be able to accomplish most motion with relatively few keyframes. Smooth positional and rotational changes of an object are always best handled with dummy objects used as parents. This technique is described below.

10

> If you are creating dozens of position keys to accomplish a certain complex motion, unless the motion is extremely erratic there probably is a simpler way.

USAGE TIP

3. **Use Camera-Man Mentality.** Think of the camera as the viewer's head, and the camera target as the focus point of the viewer. A walk-through animation then makes much more sense when it's animated with the camera moving through a path, and the target rotating left and right, as a viewer's head might.

4. **Always Ease Movements, Except for Struck Objects and Robots.** When an object starts or stops moving in the real, physical world, its mass and inertia cause it to begin slowly and accelerate or slow before it stops. This applies to rotational movements as well as positional movements. Because 3D Studio, by default, keeps the Ease To and From settings at 0, you must go back and raise these values anywhere that an object is going to be stationary for a time.

5. **Use Paths/Show to See Actual Spline Motion.** As the TCB exercise illustrated, selectively displaying the paths of moving objects provides a direct and visual way to control where an object is going.

6. **Use Dummy Objects for Smooth Rotation.** Dummy parent objects move only to cause a smooth transitional move; as parents, they do not affect the child object when it moves at other times.

7. **KeyInfo Settings Apply to Color and Morphing.** Remember that the TCB and Ease settings apply to other animation also, such as morphing and light color changes. Although it's more difficult to visualize, the same sort of anticipatory spline problems can occur

with nonspatial types of animation, such as light color. A light that changes from red to green, stays green for a while, and then changes back to red, animates with the color equivalent of the loop seen in one of the exercises. In this case, the light would loop somewhat past the green hue, into a blue shade, during the time it was supposed to be a nonvarying green color.

8. **Think Physically when You Animate Collisions.** When objects are supposed to strike each other, add the reactional motion for realism. For example, when an object hits a floor plane, bounce the object briefly before the object settles on the ground. If the object is supposed to be very heavy, you can also animate the position of the camera and camera target to simulate the shock of the floor being hit.

9. **Hide Objects when Out of Scene.** There are many uses for the Hide track illustrated in the TrackInfo exercise. To improve rendering times in complex scenes, you can add hide keys to objects for the periods during which they are out of the camera view. If the object is casting a shadow, make sure that the shadow is also out of the scene before you Hide the object. When a complex object is hidden behind other geometry, it may also be appropriate to use hide keys to improve rendering speed during the hidden frames.

Summary

As you can see, keyframed animation is fairly easy. You might need a little time to get used to interpreting time when you assign keyframes, but 3D Studio provides many tools to help you find mistakes before you render the final animation. 3D Studio provides a high degree of control over keyframes. Use these tools—they will make your life easier.

The next chapter explores the Video Post, a powerful tool for creating special effects and compositing animations. Prepare yourself for some fun.

Chapter Snapshot

This chapter introduces different aspects
and capabilities of Video Post, and explains
their use. Video Post is 3D Studio's answer
to graphics needing special effects that
cannot be created in any of the modules
found in the 3D Studio program. The following sections are covered in this chapter:

- Splicing animations

- Transitions and fades

- Alpha channel compositing

- Image processing using IPAS routines

- Compiling still frames into an
  animation

Video Post

When you create animations in 3D Studio, you eventually
might need to create special effects that you cannot create
using any of the modules in 3D Studio. 3D Studio provides a
special tool, called *Video Post*, for these special effects.

Uses for Video Post

Video post is a powerful tool that can help make your animations flow more smoothly and look more professional. Some of
the uses for Video Post include the following:

- **Splicing Animations.** When you create many FLI or FLC
  animations in a project, you might eventually want to
  combine one or more of these animations into a single file.
  To do this in 3D Studio, you use Video Post. Otherwise,
  you would have to resort to an external program, such as
  Adobe Premiere or Razor Pro, to combine the animations.
  Certain shareware programs, such as Dave's Targa animator, also can be used to combine Flic files.

- **Transitions and Fades.** When you combine animations,
  you might want to create special effects (such as transitions and fades) between the animations, to make a
  smoother transition from one animation to the next.

- **Alpha Channel Compositing.** In alpha channel compositing, you composite one image over the top of another. As an example, you might create a rendering of a building and composite that rendering over a digitized photograph of the site. 3D Studio uses files with a color depth of 32 bits to accomplish this. The extra 8 bits of color are used as the *alpha channel*, or transparency channel, to composite the two images together.

  This can be also done in 3D Studio Release 4 by using the perspective match feature, with a digitized photo as a background.

- **Image Processing.** Video Post also has the capability to process each rendered image after it has been rendered, but before it is saved to disk. This procedure is called *image processing*. An example of image processing over time might be to create a rippled water effect in which your animation looks as though it is under a surface of rippling water. Video post uses powerful IPAS routines to accomplish this effect. Some of the more powerful IPAS routines are Pennello, from Xaos Tools, and Kai's Power Tools, from HSC.

The Video Post Layout

Now that you have an idea of what the Video Post is used for, it is time to take a look at the Video Post interface, which you must access through the Keyframer. If you choose Render/Video Post from the menu, you access the Video Post dialog box (see fig. 11.1).

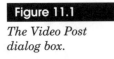

Figure 11.1

The Video Post dialog box.

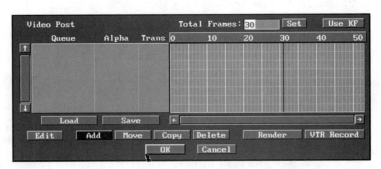

Notice that the Video Post dialog box is divided into four basic sections: the Queue column, the Alpha column, the Trans column, and the time line.

Video Post works as a linear time line, from top to bottom and left to right. As 3D Studio processes information, it works with the first item listed in the Video Post dialog box, then moves to the second, then the third, and so on. These items can be queues, alphas, or transitions.

You can add items to the Video Post by clicking on the Add button in the dialog box, and then clicking on a blank space in the Queue, Alpha, or Trans column. You will immediately see an entry displayed in the column, with a red line to its right, in the time line (see fig. 11.2).

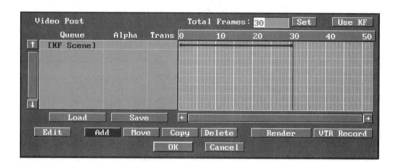

Figure 11.2

The Video Post dialog box with an entry.

By clicking on the Queue column, you add items to the queue for processing. The Alpha and Trans columns are used to determine whether the item in the queue is to be used for an alpha channel blend or a transition. The time line is where you define the length of the item in the queue, in frames.

The dialog box has several buttons. At the top of the dialog box, a Set button is next to the Total Frames field. This is where you set the overall number of frames for the animation (including queues, transitions, and alphas). Simply type a number and click on the Set button to set the overall length. If you want to use the number of frames defined in the Keyframer, simply click on the Use KF button to set the total number of frames to that of the Keyframer.

The most important buttons are the Add, Edit, Delete, and Copy buttons, which enable you to add, edit, delete, or copy Video Post entries. Add and Edit are the two buttons you will use most frequently.

The Render and VTR Record buttons, located in the lower right of the dialog box, work exactly like the Render and VTR Record buttons in the Keyframer—they bring up the exact same dialog boxes. The only difference is that they use the Video Post settings instead of the Keyframer settings.

As their names imply, the Load and Save buttons, on the left half of the dialog box, enable you to load and save Video Post settings. The files are saved with a VP extension. The capability to save settings can be very helpful because it enables you to save common and repetitive settings.

Of course, you also have the standard OK and Cancel buttons.

Adding and Editing Items in Video Post

Take a closer look at adding and editing items in the Video Post queue. Adding an item to the Video Post queue is very easy; just click on the Add button, and then click in an open space in the Queue column.

USAGE TIP

Make sure you click in the Queue column, and not in the Alpha or Trans column, unless the entry in the queue is to be an alpha or a transition item, too.

When you have added an entry to the queue, it shows up as a [KF Scene]. Notice that a red line with two dots is in the time line on the right. The first dot is the starting frame for this item in the queue, and the second dot is the ending frame of the animation. You can change the starting and ending points simply by clicking on either dot, and moving that dot to the frame you want.

The order in which you enter the queue entries is very important also. Say, for example, that you want to composite an animation of an aircraft over a sky background. You would have two entries in the queue—one for the aircraft, and one for the sky. The aircraft must come before the sky, so that it will be on top of the sky.

After you have added the entry, you must set the entry to do what you want. You can set up the entry by clicking on the Edit button, and then clicking on the entry itself. This will display the Queue Entry dialog box (see fig. 11.3).

You will notice in this box that you have many buttons to choose from. First, you must decide what kind of entry you are making. The six basic kinds of queue entries are Solid Color, Gradient, Bitmap, KF Scene, Process, and Inactive. A button for each is located on the left side of the dialog box. Simply click on the appropriate button to activate it.

The Solid Color button enables you to set the current entry to be a solid color. You can adjust the color here as you would adjust the color of a background when rendering, simply by clicking on the color swatch to the right of the Solid Color button. You would use a Solid Color if you wanted to overlay a rendered image on a different background.

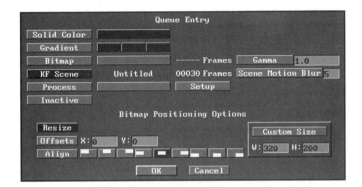

Figure 11.3

The Queue Entry dialog box.

The Gradient button is similar to the Solid Color button, but enables you to specify a color gradient, just like a background.

The Bitmap button enables you to choose any bitmap, or series of bitmaps, as the current entry in the queue. You add bitmaps to the queue by clicking on the blank button to the right of the Bitmap button. Clicking it displays the Select image to use: dialog box shown in figure 11.4.

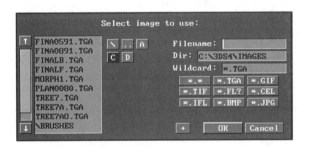

Figure 11.4

The Select image to use: dialog box.

You use this option to compile a series of still images into an animation. In the aircraft example mentioned earlier, you can set up the background as a series of bitmap images, or the frames from a piece of digitized video, to make the aircraft fly on top of a moving sky instead of a static background.

The KF Scene button tells the Video Post to use the default Keyframer scene for the current entry in the queue.

The Process button probably gives you most of the power in the Video Post. This is the button to use when you want to specify which image-processing IPAS routines to use. Simply click on the blank button next to the Process button to display the IXP Selector dialog box (see fig. 11.5).

The IXP Selector dialog box enables you to select any IXP IPAS routine located in your process subdirectory. After you have chosen the IPAS routine, you can choose the Setup button to set up the parameters for the IPAS routine. (You learn more about IPAS routines later in this chapter.)

Finally, you can specify the entry to be inactive. Specifying this disables the entry. You might want to make the entry inactive when you are testing the animation. By turning off entries you know are correct, you can reduce rendering time.

The following exercise shows you how to add two entries to the Video Post: a bitmap entry and an IPAS entry to produce a subtle blur in a still image.

Video Post Entries

Switch to the Keyframer (F4)

Choose Render/Video Post	Selects the Video Post option
Click in any viewport	Displays the Video Post dialog box
Enter **1** in Total Frames field	Sets the total number of frames to 1
Choose Set	Sets the sequence to 1
Choose Yes	
Choose Add	Enables you to add an entry

Click in Queue column	Adds entry to queue
Choose Edit	Enables you to edit entry
Click on [KF Scene]	Chooses entry to edit, and displays Queue entry dialog box
Choose Bitmap	Selects Bitmap option
Click on blank button next to Bitmap	Enables you to choose a file
Select Valley_l.tga from the Maps Dir.	Selects an image
Click on OK	Returns you to Video Post
Choose Add	Enables you to add an entry
Click below first entry	Adds new entry below the first one
Choose Edit	Enables you to edit an entry
Click on second entry	Selects second entry to edit
Choose Process	Selects process
Click on blank box next to Process	Enables you to choose an IPAS routine
Choose VBLUR	Selects the vblur.ixp routine
Choose OK	Returns you to Video Post
Choose Render	Selects the Render option
Save or delete file when finished	

Render as you would any other file. This exercise loads the Valley_l.tga file and applies a vertical blur to this image. You can adjust the resolution of the rendering in the Rendering dialog box.

The exercise you just completed is just a simple one-frame example of how you can use the Video Post. You can set up Video Post to work over time, as well.

Managing Time in the Video Post

The Video Post time line, located to the right of the transition column, is where you specify the length or duration of each entry in the queue. When each entry is entered into the queue, two lines appear in the time line. The first is a red line, with a start dot and an end dot. The second, a black line, usually is located under the red line (where you cannot see it). Some entries, called *single-range entries*, have only a red line. Entries with both lines are *double-range entries*.

In a single-range entry, you can change only the length of the entry. To move the entry without changing its length, hold down Ctrl and click on the red line.

A double-range entry has both black and red lines. The black line represents the total length of an animation that is to be composited. The red line is the range of frames (in that animation) to be used. The red line usually covers the black line so that you cannot see it, but the black line can extend beyond the total number of frames in the segment. If you extend the red line beyond the black line, the animation will start over again and play until it reaches the end of the red line.

When you are adjusting the end points of either type of entry, watch the status line. It will tell you where the frames start and end and whether the segment you set up is a looping animation.

Controlling time in the animation is as simple as placing Video Post entries at the appropriate frame numbers. Just remember that the priority in processing is from top to bottom (of the queue) and from left to right (in the time line).

Creating Transitions and Fades in Video Post

Creating fades in Video Post is a very simple process. Transitions, on the other hand, are a little more difficult and require a little more work. Both effects make use of the Trans column in the queue of the Video Post. You cannot use a transition with two types of queue entries: a KF Scene entry or a Process entry. Most of the time, because you are going to use a transition with existing bitmaps, you would be using a Bitmap entry. You can also use Solid Color and Gradient entries.

To add a transition or fade, simply choose the Add button, and click on the Trans column in which you want the fade or transition to occur. Then choose the Edit button, and again click in the Trans column in the same box you chose the transition or fade to occur in. This brings up the Transition dialog box (see fig. 11.6).

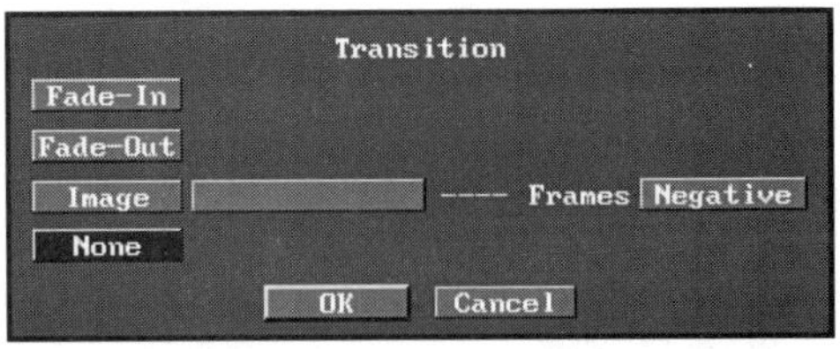

Figure 11.6

*The Transition
dialog box.*

Notice that this dialog box has four options: Fade-In, Fade-Out, Image, and None. A fade-in transition takes the bitmap and enables it to fade from black to the image over a specified time interval. You specify the time interval by choosing a start point and end point on the time line in the Video Post dialog box. When you choose a fade-in, the entry FadeI shows up in the Trans column.

The opposite happens when you use a fade-out. The image starts full and fades to black over a specified time frame. In this case, an entry of FadeO appears in the Trans column when you choose this option.

The most interesting option is the Image option. The Image option works best with black-and-white images, to create all sorts of unique fades and transitions. You could, for example, create a black-and-white animation of a 45-degree wipe, in which a line moves across the screen at a 45-degree angle, leaving everything white after it passes. 3D Studio will interpret the white as full opacity and the black as full transparency. Thus, when you create the transition, a line will cross the screen, leaving your image behind it.

The only problem with using an image transition is, where do you get the image or animation? The answer is, you probably will have to make it yourself. For the transition mentioned in the preceding paragraph, programs such as Animator Pro, or the new Animation Studio, from Autodesk, are great for creating such effects.

The following two sections provide you with a set of exercises to create some basic transitions and fades. Although these exercises use the Valley_l.tga file in your maps subdirectory, you can substitute any bitmap image or animation you like.

Transitions

The following exercise uses a Flic file, created in Animator Pro, to create a transition animation of a still image. The transition animation has been created for you. The file is located under 113DSBT1.FLC. Before you start the exercise, take a look at the transition animation with Aaplay or choose View, Flic in 3D Studio.

Because 3D Studio treats what is white as totally transparent, wherever you see a white dot, you will be able to see through to the underlying image. If you create a transition with grays, you will be able to have variations in the translucency of the item.

A Custom Transition

Start 3D Studio, and go to the Keyframer	Loads 3D Studio, and displays the appropriate module
Choose Render/Video Post	Selects Video Post option
Click in active viewport	Displays Video Post dialog box
Choose Add	Enables you to add an entry
Click in Queue column	Adds entry to queue column
Choose Edit	Enables you to edit the entry
Choose last entry	Displays Queue entry dialog box
Choose Bitmap	Selects Bitmap option
Choose the blank button next to Bitmap	Enables you to select a bitmap or Flic to use
Choose Valley_l.tga in your Maps directory	Chooses the file to use
Choose OK	Closes the Queue entry dialog box
Click in Trans column of same entry	Enables you to edit the transition of the entry
Choose Image	Enables you to choose an image to use as the transition
Choose blank button next to Image	
Choose 113DSBT1.FLC	Chooses the transition image
Choose OK	Displays Video Post
Check total frames = 30	Verifies the length of the transition

Figure 11.7 shows the Video Post dialog box settings before rendering.

Choose Render	Enables you to render the scene

Render the file as you normally would, but set the resolution to 320×200, and check the Disk button to save the file to disk.

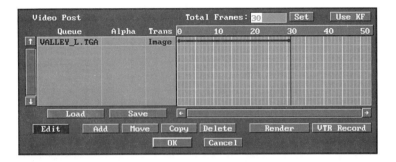

Figure 11.7

The final Video Post settings.

After about four or five minutes of processing, you should have an interesting transition for the Valley_l.tga file. You can play back the animation by using either View/Flic in Studio, or Aaplay in DOS. Aaplay is recommended, because you can slow down the play-back speed so that you can see the transition. Because this transition was created in 30 frames, it is approximately 1 second long and moves pretty quickly when played back.

The file 113DSBTF1.FLI, which is provided on the CD, is the completed animation. The animation is approximately 1.1 MB in size. The Transition animation is approximately 750 KB in size. You can substitute any still image or animation for the Valley_l.tga file.

USAGE TIP

Please note that the transition Flic is a 320×200 Flic and is 30 frames long. You should be careful to match your transition elements to the final length and resolution, so that you do not have any problems.

Fades and Wipes

The following exercise creates a fade-in for the same Valley_l.tga file. You can do a fade-out in the same way—just use Fade-Out instead.

Creating a Fade in Video Post

Start 3D Studio, and switch to Keyframer	Selects appropriate module to use
Choose Render/Video Post	Starts Video Post

continues

continued

Click in any active viewport	Displays the Video Post dialog box
Choose Add	Enables you to add an entry
Click in Queue column	Adds item to the queue
Choose Edit	Enables you to edit the item
Click on last entry	Displays Queue Entry dialog box
Choose Bitmap	Selects bitmap as the entry type
Click on the blank button next to Bitmap	Enables you to select the file
Choose Valley_l.tga from the Maps directory	Selects the file to use
Choose OK	Displays Video Post
Click on Trans column of last entry	Enables you to set up a transition
Choose Fade-In	Selects fade-in as transition type
Choose OK	Displays Video Post
Check Total Frames is set to 30	Verifies the length of the animation

Figure 11.8 shows the final Video Post dialog box setting before rendering.

Render as before

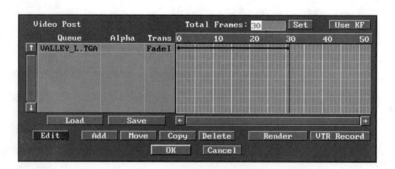

Figure 11.8

The final Video Post settings.

Again, use Aaplay or View/Flic to replay the final rendered animation.

The following exercise combines the two preceding exercises to create an animation that does a transition into a still frame, holds on the still frame for one second, and then fades out to black. Again, you use the Valley_l.tga file.

Multiple Fades and Transitions

Beginning with the custom transition exercise, do the following steps:

Enter **90** in Total Frames field of Video Post dialog box	Sets animation to 90 frames
Choose Set	Sets the overall length

Repeat the preceding Transition exercise.

Move start point of first red line to 0	Starts this segment at frame 0
Move end point to frame 30	Sets end of this segment at 30

Figure 11.9 shows the Video Post dialog box after setting the first transition.

Choose the Add button	Enables you to add an item to queue
Click in Queue column, below the transition entry	Adds entry below the first one
Choose Edit	Enables you to edit the entry
Select second entry in queue	Selects the second entry
Choose Bitmap	Selects Bitmap as entry type
Click on the blank button	Enables you to select a file
Choose Valley_l.tga	Selects the file
Choose OK	Displays Video Post
Move end point of second red line to frame 60	Defines end of this segment
Move start point of second red line to frame 30 (see fig. 11.10)	Defines start of segment at frame 30

Repeat Fade-In exercise, but use a fade-out, and add it as third entry in queue

When finished, Video Post will have three entries. Entry one runs from frame 0 to 30, entry two from 30 to 60, and entry three from 60 to 90.

Move end point of third red line to frame 90	Sets end of segment at frame 90
Move start point of third red line to frame 60 (see fig. 11.11)	Sets start of segment at frame 60

Render as before

Again, use Aaplay or View/Flic to view the final rendered animation.

Figure 11.9

*The Video Post
dialog box,
after setting
the transition.*

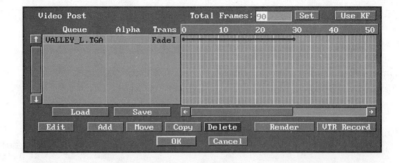

Figure 11.10

*The Video Post after
setting the transi-
tion to still image.*

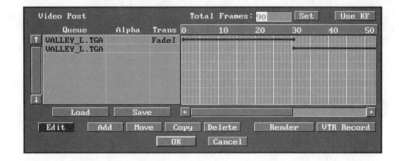

Figure 11.11

*The Video Post,
before rendering.*

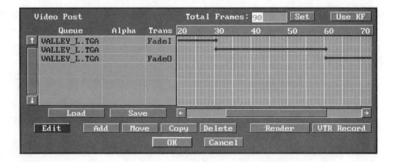

Now that you have seen some of the power of transitions, you can explore them on your own. Remember, the more imaginative you are with transitions, the more interesting your animations can be. It is highly recommended that you pick up either Animator Pro or Animation Studio to create transitions. Both programs provide a variety of tools for creating 2D animations that are well suited for use as transitions in 3D Studio.

Alpha Channel Compositing in Video Post

3D Studio enables you to use a special attribute of 32-bit color files, called the *alpha channel*. You can use this feature to composite one rendering on top of another, or on top of an animation or any still image. Although much of this work can be done by using Perspective Match and backgrounds, Video Post enables you to composite two still images without having to rerender the images.

The only limitation for compositing two images is that you must have 32-bit color files to do the job effectively. Otherwise, you have to resort to the intensity of the colors in the image. The best way to get a 32-bit file is to turn that option on during the rendering process. If you choose Options in the Render dialog box, you can use the Render Options dialog box (see fig. 11.12) to tell 3D Studio to generate 32-bit files.

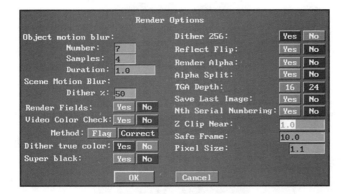

Figure 11.12

The Render Options dialog box.

Simply set the Render Alpha option to Yes, and you will be generating 32-bit files with an alpha channel. The button below the Render Alpha button, the Split Alpha button, enables you to create a separate file that contains the alpha information.

USAGE TIP

Make sure that the Targa depth is set to 24 and Dither 256 is turned off before you generate these files. The Dither 256 option reduces the file to the best 256 colors in the image, and produces a lower quality output.

The Alpha Channel: What Is It and How Do You Use It?

Image files with an alpha channel have a color depth of 32 bits. These files are really 24-bit files with an 8-bit alpha channel. The extra 8 bits are used to assign up to 256 levels of transparency to each pixel. This enables you to overlay one image on top of another effectively.

If you do not have an image with an alpha channel, the RGB color values can be used. In this case, the intensity of the colors specifies the degree of transparency. Unfortunately, the results produced by RGB color values are not as good as those produced by an alpha channel.

To access the alpha channel controls in the Video Post dialog box, simply add an entry to the queue. This entry cannot be a KF Scene entry or a Process entry. Then choose Edit, and click on the Alpha column of the entry. This displays the Alpha dialog box (see fig. 11.13).

Figure 11.13

The Alpha dialog box.

The two basic sets of buttons are those that apply to alpha channel compositing and those that apply to RGB compositing.

The Queue Alpha Channel button tells Video Post to use the Alpha channel of the image in the queue. The Queue RGB button tells Video Post to use the RGB values of the image in the queue.

With the next two buttons, you can choose whether to use an RGB mask or an alpha mask. (A *mask* is a method of hiding parts of an image.) Both buttons will mask off part of the image before compositing it over another image. A large blank button, located to the right of the mask buttons, enables you to choose the file to use as the alpha or RGB mask.

The next button, None, is the default. When this button is active, no alpha channel or RGB blending will occur.

The next section of the dialog box—the RGB transparency section— enables you to control how 3D Studio interprets the colors of a file that does not have an alpha channel. The first button is the Key Color button, with which you can choose the color that will remain completely opaque or solid. The default is black. In this instance, white is considered completely transparent, and all other colors fall somewhere in between.

The Blur Edges button tells 3D Studio to add a slight blur to all the edges in the image, producing a much softer image. The Intensity button tells 3D Studio to base the transparency values on the intensity of the colors.

The last section of the dialog box is the modifiers section. The first modifier is the Negative button, which essentially reverses all the other settings—where white was transparent, now black is. The last setting is the Opacity Threshold—the point at which a color is completely opaque and nontransparent.

Depending upon the options you choose, you will get a different notification in the Alpha column of the Video Post dialog box. For example, if you choose an Alpha mask, the marker says Amask, whereas RGB Mask says Rmask.

The following section leads you through an exercise in which you composite one image on top of another. Animations can be handled similarly, except that you will not have an alpha channel to work with, and must use RGB blending. The only way to do this with an animation is to save the animation as a sequence of Targa files, run them through Video Post to composite them, then compile them into an animation.

Compositing Still Images

The following exercise composites an image of the marble vase sample file over the Valley_l.tga file, using an RGB mask to mask off part of the image.

Before starting this exercise, you need to render the marble vase sample file (included with 3D Studio) at 320×200, with Render Alpha on and Dither 256 off. Save the rendering as a Targa file, under the filename VASE1.tga.

Compositing with Video Post

Load 3D Studio and switch to Keyframer	Loads appropriate module
Choose Render/Video Post	Starts the Video Post
Click in any active viewport	Loads Video Post dialog box
Choose Add	Enables you to add items to the queue
Click twice in Queue column	Adds two items to the queue
Choose Edit	Enables you to edit the entries
Click on first entry	Enables you to edit the first entry
Choose Bitmap	Sets entry type to Bitmap
Click on blank button	Enables you to select a file
Choose Vase1.tga	Selects file you previously rendered
Choose OK	Returns you to Video Post
Click on Alpha column of same entry controls	Enables you to edit the alpha channel
Choose Queue Alpha Channel	Tells 3D Studio to use the alpha channel of the image in the queue, in this case Vase1.tga
Choose OK	Returns you to Video Post
Click on second entry in Queue column	Enables you to edit the second entry
Choose Bitmap	Sets the second entry as a bitmap
Click on blank button	Lets you choose a file
Choose Valley_l.tga, from maps subdirectory	Chooses the file
Choose OK	Returns you to Video Post
Click on Alpha column of second entry	Lets you edit the alpha channel controls of the second entry
Choose Queue RGB entrys RGB intensities	Sets the transparency to use the queue
Choose OK	Returns you to Video Post

Figure 11.14 shows you the Video Post dialog box settings before rendering.

Choose Render	Enables you to render the file

Render as normal, but render only a single frame, not an animation. When the rendering is complete, notice how the colors of the marble vase file were interpreted when overlaid over the Valley_l.tga file.

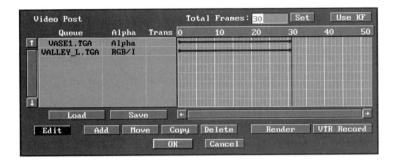

Figure 11.14

The final settings in Video Post.

Using Video Post to Compile Animations

One of Video Post's handy features is the capability to compile a series of still images into an animation. Why don't you have the animation compiled at render time by choosing the Flic file format? There is a good reason not to do this. When you are rendering directly to a Flic file, the animation must finish rendering for the Flic file to look correct. If the power goes out while you're rendering to individual files, you simply start with the next frame, and continue rendering. Then compile the still images into a Flic at the end.

The following exercise shows you how to compile a series of still images into a Flic file, using Video Post. To do this exercise, you should have a series of still images ready to composite. You can choose any sample file in the Meshes subdirectory that has animation in it. Then render out 30 or so frames to individual files. You will end up with a group of files with names like this: REN0000.tga to REN0030.tga. (3D Studio will take the first three or four letters of the filename and use those letters in place of the REN mentioned here.)

Compiling an Animation

Load 3D Studio and switch to Keyframer   Loads appropriate module

Choose Render/Video Post   Loads the Video Post

continues

continued

Click in any active viewport	Starts the Video Post dialog box
Set total frames to number of images you are going to compile	Sets overall length of compiled animation
Choose Add	Enables you to add an entry to the queue
Click in Queue column	Adds entry to queue
Choose Edit	Enables you to edit the entry
Click on last entry	Starts Queue entry dialog box
Choose Bitmap	Sets the entry type to Bitmap
Click on blank box	Enables you to choose a file
Choose directory in which files are located	Sets the correct path
Choose filename with wildcard, such as REN*.tga	Selects all files with these parameters
Choose OK	Returns you to the Video Post dialog box
Set red line to match black line on time line	Sets the range to be rendered to match number of files found
Choose Render	Enables you to render the file

CAUTION

Be aware that any location you use for images in the Video Post must also be in your map paths.

Render as usual, and choose Flic as your file output type. A few things you should note here: When you create the entry in the time line, you will see a double range bar. The black line represents the number of files 3D Studio found of the type you specified. The red line represents how many 3D Studio will render. Generally, you should set the red line to match the black line.

Using IPAS Routines in Video Post

The Video Post's capabilities to use image-processing IPAS routines probably are among 3D Studio's more powerful capabilities. You might wonder, however, what image processing is.

Image processing takes an image, whether a rendering or a digitized photo, and changes the look of that image, according to some algorithm. Some effects that you can produce with image processing are blurring, creating a rendering that looks like an oil painting, creating a water ripple in the image, and so on. All of these processes occur after the rendering process.

Video Post is used for image processing because you can add the IPAS routine to the queue after the rendering. In that way, all render images are processed in order. Finally, you can set up some of these IPAS routines to perform over time, thus creating unique effects.

Setting Up IPAS Routines for Use in Video Post

The process of setting up an IPAS routine is highly dependent on that particular IPAS routine and what it is capable of doing. Simply add an entry to the queue in Video Post. Edit that entry and assign it a process type. Then click on the blank button next to the Process button to assign a specific IPAS routine. All the IPAS routines will be located in your process subdirectory. After you have selected an IPAS routine, click on the Setup button. This enables you to set the parameters for specific IPAS routines.

Some Popular Image Processing IPAS Routines and Their Uses

Many popular image-processing IPAS routines are available today, with more coming every week. Two of the more powerful IPAS routines are Pennello and Kai's Power Tools. Penello is a subset of Xaos Tools' Pandemonium software, which runs on Silicon Graphics workstations.

Kai's power tools are the same type of plug-ins that run under Adobe Photoshop. If you use Photoshop a lot, then you are probably familar with what Kai's Power Tools are and what they are capable of doing.

Both of these packages are now available as IPAS routines, and perform the same functions in Studio that they do in their native environments. Both provide a suite of tools for creating just about any type of image process you want.

In addition, several IPAS routines are provided with 3D Studio, and you can use several shareware IPAS routines. (Most of these are light versions of the full packages.)

11

If you have access to CompuServe or other online services, you generally can find full working demos of most of these IPAS routines—in particular, Penello and Kai's Power Tools—which makes it very easy to decide whether you want to purchase these routines for use in your office.

Saving Video Post Setups

Loading and saving Video Post setups is a fairly simple procedure. Simply click on the Load or Save button in the Video Post dialog box. Then choose the file to load, or give the file a name to save in. All Video Post setup files have a VP extension.

If you set up many complex Video Post routines, saving the settings to a file for future use is a good idea.

Tips and Techniques for Using Video Post

The following tips and tricks should be helpful when you work with the Video Post:

- Be careful of the order in which you place your queue entries. 3D Studio processes the queue in order.

- Make use of other programs, such as Animator Studio, to create unique transitions.

- Save your Video Post setups for future use.

- Obtain demo copies of IPAS routines, and see which of them you might want use in your work. IPAS routines provide a high degree of power and flexibility, and can be used over time.

- Be careful when using the time line. Remember that the red line indicates where the queue entry is active in the overall animation.

- Remember that you cannot use KF Scene or process entries with alpha channel or RGB compositing.

- If you want to use alpha channel compositing, make sure that your image files contain an alpha channel. You can generate this channel by turning on Render Alpha in the rendering options.

- When you create Flic files, render to individual files, and then use Video Post to compile.

- Use Video Post to splice animations together. Use a fade or transition between the two to create a smooth animation.

Summary

In conclusion, the Video Post is a powerful compositing and image-processing tool. Explore it and use it. Although the alpha channel compositing might seem a little confusing at first, you will get used to it after a couple of tries. Above all, explore the creative options provided by the Video Post's transitions and IPAS-routine capabilities—they can add a lot of class to your animations.

The next chapter introduces you to the methods available for printing or viewing stills and animations.

11

Chapter Snapshot

Presentation, where you create the final output from the rendered image, is one of the most rewarding, yet frustrating, parts of the rendering process. Depending upon the output method chosen, you can use a variety of software to create the output in a variety of formats. The following issues are covered in this chapter:

- Output options

- Printing rendered images

- Printable media

- Playing animations

- Recording animations

Output Issues

Presentation can be rather frustrating when the output doesn't look like you want it to. Any of a number of things can go wrong when you print or produce the output of an image. The color balance can be wrong, the image may look fuzzy or blurry, it might be too large or too small, or it might not be the quality you are looking for.

In today's world, many methods are possible for producing the output of a rendered image. These methods can be divided into two categories: online and printed. Online presentation methods involve displaying the rendered image, or a series of rendered images, on the computer screen, using a variety of software. Printed methods include printing to any of a wide variety of printers, plotters, film recorders, VCRs, and so on.

When you have the output image in a format you want, you have something you can be proud of.

Output Options

3D Studio enables you to choose from a variety of output file formats and options. The choice of the correct file output options is critical to the overall quality of the rendered image or animation.

In 3D Studio you choose the file output format by using the Options button in the Render dialog box in either the Keyframer or the 3D Editor. By choosing the Options button, you display the Device Configuration dialog box (see fig. 12.1), in which you choose the appropriate file format, any options associated with that format, and the resolution of the output.

The only difference between the 3D Editor options box and the Keyframer options box is that the Keyframer has the capability to choose an animation format. 3D Studio supports the following file formats to save rendered images and animations: TIFF, Targa, JPEG, GIF, BMP, and Flic.

File Output Options

When you decide to create a rendering in 3D Studio, the most important question is which file format to render to. Before you look at the specifics of each file format, you need to understand two basic concepts about these formats: resolution and color depth.

A rendering is recorded as nothing more than a series of color or grayscale dots. These dots, called *pixels*, are placed close together, forming a picture. As you can imagine, the more dots you have in a given space, the crisper the appearance of the image. A typical rendering might have a resolution of 640 pixels by 480 pixels. This resolution is fairly close to TV quality, and is generally considered standard VGA resolution. The different file formats that 3D Studio supports just encode the pixels in different ways, for different reasons.

An animation is a series of still images played back quickly enough to give the illusion of motion. An animation file format is similar to a series of still images. The animation file is encoded in a way that enables a computer or piece of software to play back the animation smoothly enough to look like motion.

Depending upon the output you are looking for, you will render to various resolutions. For still images, these resolutions can get extremely large— as much as 8,000 pixels by 8,000 pixels. Resolutions in animations rarely exceed 750×480, because that is close to the resolution of a TV (depending upon your recording hardware, if you have any).

The *color depth* of an image is the number of colors you can have in the image. Each pixel in the image can be assigned a single color. This color is chosen from a palette of colors, depending upon the file format. As you can guess, the larger the color palette you can choose from, the more colors you can have, and the better the image will look. The color depth is usually referred to in terms of bits. This is a general computer term, but very easy to understand. Say, for example, that you have an 8-bit graphic file. How many colors are in the palette? The answer is 256 colors, or 2 raised to the eighth power. You can calculate all color depths with this method. The other common color depths you see frequently are 16-bit (32,000 colors), 24-bit (16.7 million colors), and 32-bit (4 billion colors).

You, as a human, can distinguish roughly 4 million colors simultaneously. Thus, a color depth of more than 24 bits is rarely used. Many programs use a 32-bit color depth, where the extra 8 bits of color are called an *alpha channel*. This alpha channel is used for blending two images or creating fades or transitions in an animation. (For more information about alpha channels, see Chapter 11, "Video Post.")

Now that you have an idea of the basic components of the file formats 3D Studio uses, it is time to take a closer look at each file format.

Targa

A Targa file is one of the older formats you can save a rendering to. It was the first 24-bit color format, and was invented to work with Targa video boards. This file format supports 8-bit, 24-bit, and 32-bit color output, as well as compression to reduce the file size. Targa files generally are fairly large. A Targa file that is 752×480 at 24-bit color is generally about 1.1 MB, uncompressed, and around 300 KB, compressed. Targa files are fairly portable to other systems, and widely used for output to video tape.

TIFF

TIFF files are similar to Targa files in that they are 8-bit, 24-bit, or 32-bit files and can be compressed. TIFF files generally are used when you want to import the rendering into some other program, such as PageMaker or Microsoft Word. TIFF is the most widely used graphics format on both the Macintosh and IBM-PC platforms.

GIF

The GIF file format was created by CompuServe and Unisys to be highly compact, with fairly good image quality. It was invented to enable people to transfer graphic images rapidly across telephone lines, using modems. The GIF file format is compressed, and is restricted to an 8-bit color depth. Hence, it might not look as good as a 24-bit Targa or TIFF, but the file size is much smaller. GIF is a good file type for archiving or transferring files over phone lines.

BMP

The BMP file format, because it was developed by Microsoft for use with Microsoft Windows, is not used as frequently as the other formats. 3D Studio supports writing 24-bit and 8-bit BMP files.

Flic

The final format in the group is the Flic format. There are two types of this format: FLI and FLC. A FLI file is simply an animation rendered at 320×200 or less resolution, whereas a FLC file is rendered at resolutions higher than that. A Flic file has a palette of 256 colors. Because this is an animation format, it contains many frames, each encoded to produce the best results when played back. Because the entire Flic file has the same 256 color palette, the Flic format is not the best for playing back animations. Also, high-resolution renderings, such as 640×480 or higher, can tax a machine's capability to play back the animation.

You can choose any of these file formats when you render your still images and animations. The following sections describe what you can do with the different formats and how to output them, using a variety of printers, plotters, and other equipment.

Online Methods of Presentation

Online presentation methods offer the advantage of not having to print the image on a printer or a plotter. The disadvantage is that the person or people to whom you want to show the images must either view them on your computer or have a computer capable of displaying the files.

To be able to view rendered images online, you need several things: a computer capable of displaying the images, software to display the images with, and an order of presentation.

Hardware Requirements

The hardware requirements for viewing renderings online vary greatly, according to the type of presentation. You don't need a fast machine to display still images, for example, but you need a very fast machine to display animations.

For the display of still images, the following system specifications should be considered a minimum:

- 80386/16 or higher
- 640×480×256 color graphics
- 40 MB hard drive
- 14-inch color, noninterlaced monitor

Given this very simple system, the most important requirement is the graphics card. The higher the resolution and color depth, the better the image will look. This is reflected also in the need for a decent monitor through which to view the images. A larger monitor is always beneficial to both the viewer and the worker. A 17-inch monitor is generally considered a good-sized monitor for online displays. A 21-inch (or larger) monitor would be optimum.

To play back animations at a decent speed, or for high-resolution color images, your system should include the following:

- 80486 or Pentium
- 16 MB of RAM
- 1024×768×256 color graphics, or higher
- 17-inch color, noninterlaced monitor
- 500 MB SCSI-2 or Enhanced IDE drive

This system is capable of replaying all rendered images and most animations. The faster your machine, the better it will play animations. In this

12

system, 24-bit color on the graphics card is very important for playing back still images. Animations, on the other hand, are generally encoded in 256-color file formats when they are played online; a 256-color display is enough in this circumstance.

A large hard drive is necessary to hold the still images, animations, and any programs necessary for playing back these images and animations. The faster the drive, the better the animations will play back.

Operating Systems

After checking your hardware requirements, you need to decide which operating system you are going to use to play back the images and animations. The two basic choices are DOS and Windows. Each has advantages and disadvantages.

The advantage of DOS is that it requires less memory than Windows and can run a large assortment of programs. The disadvantages are a lack of high-color and high-resolution video drivers for many applications, and sometimes difficult-to-use programs.

Windows, on the other hand, generally has all the necessary video drivers in the operating system itself, not the individual programs. So, it is easier to find high-color and high-resolution video drivers for Windows. With Windows, on the other hand, all the necessary video drivers generally are included in the operating system itself, and do not depend on an individual program. For this reason, finding high-color and high-resolution video drivers for Windows is easier than for DOS.

As you can see, both operating systems have advantages and disadvantages. You can choose one or the other, or both. After you have chosen an operating system, you have yet another choice—the program or programs you want to use to display the images and animations.

Shareware Online Image Viewers

Several good shareware programs for viewing online images are available. These programs can be used to view individual images and slide shows. (To learn more about shareware, see the "Various Shareware Programs" section, later in this chapter.)

Printing Rendered Images

Printed presentation is a very interesting (and confusing) aspect of presentation. The two basic types of printed presentations are still images and animations. Still images can be printed to paper transparency, film, or special papers. Animations, on the other hand, generally are printed only to film or video tape.

Before you begin printing still images, an understanding of the basic types of printers available to you—depending upon how much money you are willing to spend—is helpful. These are the five basic types of printers: laser printers, inkjet printers, thermal wax printers, dye sublimation printers, and laser film recorders.

You need to consider certain printer aspects: the printer's resolution speed, and the type and size of paper the printer accepts.

When you consider printing rendered images, the most important aspect of a printer is its resolution. A printer's resolution is expressed in dpi, or *dots per inch*. The more dots per inch, the higher the resolution of the printer. Most of today's printers are 300 dpi printers. If you match the dots on a printer to the pixels in an image, at 300 dpi, you would have to render an image at 3072×2048 to fill an 8 1/2-by-11-inch sheet of paper. Most of the time, rendered images are printed well below the stated resolution of the printer. A standard printing resolution for images is 72 dpi. At this resolution, a 750×480 image will cover the whole sheet of paper when printed. Some of the newer laser printers are capable of 600, 1,200 dpi—or even higher.

Your next consideration is the size of the paper the printer will accept. Most printers accept only 8 1/2-by-11-inch paper, or at most, 8 1/2-by-14 inches. Some of the newer laser printers can support up to 11-by-17-inch paper. Of course, the larger the paper, the better. Unfortunately, the larger the paper and the higher the resolution at which you print the image, the more memory you need in the printer. At 300 dpi, for example, a rendered image may need only 2 MB of printer memory to print. But at 600 dpi, you probably will need 6 MB or more. With color printers, this number can be much higher.

Black-and-White Laser Printers

Black-and-white laser printers are, by far, the most common type of printer found in the standard office. Most black-and-white laser printers are capable of printing at 300 dpi on 8 1/2-by-11-inch white paper. Print speeds vary, according to the printer and its resolution.

Some of the newer laser printers can print at 600, or even 1,200 dpi, on up to 11-by-17-inch paper. Hewlett Packard's Laserjet IVMV is a good example. This 600 dpi, 11-by-17-inch, 16 page per minute (PPM) printer is an excellent black-and-white printer for rendered images, if you can afford it.

Color Laser Printers

Color laser printers are a rather new technology. They are based on a technology similar to that of regular laser printers, but print in color. Most color laser printers are capable of 300 dpi, but can take several minutes per page to print.

Generally, color laser printers are used for business graphics, such as graphs, where bright, solid colors are needed. You can use a color laser printer for printing rendered images, but better printing solutions are available, for less cost.

Color InkJet Printers

Color inkjet printers are probably the most popular color printers, because they are cheap and produce fairly good results. Inkjet technology uses small spray nozzles to spray ink onto the sheet of paper as the print head passes over the paper. These printers can usually print between 300 and 720 dpi, depending upon the model you get.

Hewlett Packard, Canon, and Epson make the three most popular inkjet printers. At the time of this writing, these printers are in the $500 price range. Each printer prints with one black cartridge, and either a three-color cartridge or three individual color cartridges.

Another advantage of inkjet printers is the variety of media to which you can print with them. An inkjet can use bond paper, transparency, and special glossy paper. The downside is that you have to use paper made for inkjet printing; otherwise, the ink soaks through the paper and produces a very dark, muted print.

Finally, inkjets are scaleable. Hewlett Packard and others now make inkjet plotters capable of printing 300 dpi full-color images at scales up to 30 by 42 inches. With certain types of paper, these large printing images can approach the quality of a poster. Unfortunately, these plotters are usually rather expensive to buy and use. A full-bleed color print, at 30×42, can cost about $30 per print on an inkjet plotter—compared to a couple of pennies for an 8 1/2-by-11-inch print on the same printer.

Another method of producing larger-scale printouts is called *tiling*. Depending upon the software (see the "RenderPrint" section, later in this chapter), you can tile the image across several smaller pages, then piece these pages together to produce a larger print. This can be a cost-conscious alternative to a plotter. The downside is that there will be seams between each page of the tiled image, and aligning all the edges of each sheet can be difficult.

Thermal Wax Printers

Thermal wax printers are very different from both laser printers and inkjet printers. Thermal wax printers use ribbons of colored wax and special paper. The ribbons of wax are composed of cyan, magenta, and yellow color patches. Each color patch is the size of a sheet of paper. The paper is specially made to accept both the heat and the wax from the printer. Generally, you have to use paper that is approved by the printer manufacturer. In some cases, this paper is proprietary—and available only from the printer manufacturer.

As the paper passes under the print head, the wax is melted onto the paper. Because there are three colors, the paper must pass under the print head three times, making for slower prints.

Fortunately, the trade-off is worth it. Thermal wax printers produce nice final prints. They are considered *continuous-tone* printers, meaning that you cannot see any dots in the final image. With both inkjet and laser printers, you can generally see a pattern of dots (called *dithering*) in the final print.

Thermal wax can be rather expensive, however. On average, it costs about $.60 per page. You can print only a set number of pages per color ribbon (whereas both inkjets and laser jets use ink only as necessary). Thermal wax printers make good prepress color proof printers.

Dye Sublimation Printers

Dye sublimation printers are similar to thermal wax printers, except that they use melted dyes instead of wax. Generally, dye sublimation printers are the closest to photo-realistic you will find at this time.

12

Printing with a dye sublimation printer is rather expensive—on average, about $3 to $5 per page. When using a dye sublimation printer, you must use paper approved for use with that printer. You cannot use bond, transparency, and so on, unless the printer manufacturer approves it. Dye sublimation printers are excellent final-print quality printers.

The Fargo Primera Pro is worth mentioning here. This printer is unique, because it supports both thermal wax and dye sublimation printing. This printer is also relatively inexpensive: about $1,200 to $1,500 for the printer, $.60 per page for thermal wax, and $3.00 per page for dye sublimation. The Primera Pro can print up to 300×600 dpi. A newer version of the printer now supports paper up to 11×17, but is more expensive. If you are going to do a great many dye sublimation prints on a tight budget, get this printer. It produces excellent results for the money.

Laser Film Recorders

Laser film recorders are not commonly used, but are worth mentioning. With a laser film recorder, you can digitally record your images directly onto standard 35mm film. Then, just have this film developed. You can use slide, print, or instant film with these printers.

Why would you want to use a film recorder? Well, you can record a rendered image to slide and project the image on a wall. If you project the image large enough, it can give the illusion that you are standing in the rendered image. Laser film recording is also a good way to archive your renderings.

Unfortunately, laser film recorders are rather expensive. They start at about $3,000. After that, your only other costs are film and film developing.

Comparison of Output Methods

Figures 12.2 through 12.5 (in the four-color insert) illustrate the differences between these print methods (except laser film recording and color laser printing). Each image is printed at the same resolution, using the same settings from the printing program.

Printable Media

The print media can make the most difference in the quality of your final printed image. This is especially true of inkjet printers. For some printers, you should use thicker, heavier paper; for others, you have to use special paper. The four general types of paper are bond, transparency, glossy, and special paper.

Bond Paper

Bond is the most common type of paper. This is the type of paper you might see in a Xerox machine. The two important types of bond paper are standard grain and long grain. Long-grain paper is generally considered laser printer bond. This type of paper works well in laser printers and inkjet printers.

The weight of the paper is also important. The heavier the paper, the more ink it can absorb. Most inkjet printers like paper weights between 16 and 24 lbs. Long-grain laser paper is generally between 20 and 24 lbs.

If you are using an inkjet printer, look for paper specific for inkjet printers. Also, consult the documentation that came with the printer, which should recommend some paper manufacturers whose paper has been tested and found to work well with the printer.

When you use bond paper with inkjet printers, you probably will find the colors a little darker than you might expect. This is a result of the way the paper absorbs the ink. With laser printers, absorbency is not a factor.

Transparency

Transparency paper is nothing more than clear film. For inkjets, this clear film has a rough side, designed to take inkjet ink. Transparency papers are available for inkjet, laser, and thermal wax printers.

When you print to this paper, the colors may seem a little on the light side. When you place the transparency against a white background, you get a better idea of the color depth.

Make sure that you set the printer driver to use transparency paper before printing to the paper, or too much ink will be laid down on the transparency and it will smear. (Your printer driver documentation tells you how to do this.) Also, do not let the final print get wet at any time. The ink comes off fairly easily, because this is a piece of thin plastic film.

12

Glossy Paper

Usually, glossy paper is used with inkjet printers only. This is a very special paper, with a high gloss, or sheen. This type of paper costs about $1 per sheet, and generally produces the best results on an inkjet printer. You can approach thermal-wax quality prints with this paper using an inkjet printer.

When printing to this type of paper, make sure that your printer driver is configured for it, or it will not print correctly. As with transparency, do not let the final print get wet.

Special Paper

For dye sublimation or thermal wax printers, you must use a special paper, specific to each type of printer. Therefore, you have very little choice in the type, color, or shininess of the paper. About the only choice you do have is the size of the paper, which can be as large as 12×18, depending upon the printer you are using.

Film

There is not much to say about film. Film recorders use standard 35mm film, or 4×5 negative film (if you have one of the larger film recorders). Develop and handle the film as you would any other type of regular photographs or slides.

Programs for Printing Rendered Images

The program you use to print your rendered image can make a great difference in the quality of the final print. Unfortunately, you can use hundreds of programs (including 3D Studio) to print your images. Generally, each of these programs handles colors and resolutions a little differently. The mind boggles! Among the more notable programs are Adobe Photoshop and RenderPrint.

Photoshop and Other Image-Editing Programs

Adobe Photoshop is a full-blown image-editing program. Other programs, such as Aldus PhotoStyler, Corel PhotoPaint, and Micrografx Picture Publisher, do similar functions, but Photoshop is generally considered the best.

Here is a list of a few things you can do to an image in Photoshop:

- Rescale the size and resolution of the image
- Change the color balance of the image
- Add text to the image
- Create special effects, such as blurred images
- Change the brightness and/or contrast
- Convert the file to other formats
- Print the image

This is just a short list. If you are going to do much serious rendering, you will inevitably need Photoshop or some similar program. For example, if you render a still frame that takes three hours to render and comes out too dark, you can use Photoshop to lighten the image in a matter of minutes (no three-hour wait).

Photoshop also gives you a high degree of control over the printing process. Because of this high degree of control, you can adjust many parameters that directly affect the output quality. Figuring out the combination that best works for you can be frustrating and time-consuming, but well worth it in the end.

12

RenderPrint

The RenderPrint program was developed specifically for the purpose of printing rendered images at the highest resolution your printer can handle. This program is almost a must-have, especially if you cannot afford Photoshop or other such programs.

RenderPrint runs in both DOS and Windows, and has drivers to run in AutoCAD 12 and 3D Studio. RenderPrint uses a process called dithering to create images that print at 300 dpi.

To print an image at the full resolution of the printer, you must render the image at a very high resolution, such as 2,048 pixels by 1,536 pixels. RenderPrint prints lower-resolution images at the resolution of the printer, by interpreting the missing information through the dithering process. RenderPrint supports some 1,200 or more printers and a variety of dithering methods. RenderPrint also supports scaling and tiling of images across several sheets of paper, if necessary.

RenderPrint is actually a RIP (*raster-image processor*). A RIP converts the RGB colors of a rendered image to the CMYK colors necessary for printing. This can be a slow process. RenderPrint can RIP most images in less than 10 minutes. How long it takes to completely print the image depends upon your printer.

You definitely should consider RenderPrint for printing your images if you cannot afford more advanced programs. The output from RenderPrint is excellent, especially with laser or inkjet printers (see figs. 12.6 and 12.7).

Figure 12.6

A laser print with RenderPrint.

Figure 12.7

An inkjet print with RenderPrint.

Table of Resolutions and Output Types

Table 12.1 contains a set of standard resolutions and the resulting file sizes (in uncompressed 24-bit file format) for a variety of output methods.

Table 12.1
Table of Resolutions and File Sizes

Resolution (Approx)	Usage	File Size
320×200	CGA, Low Res Anim	100 KB
640×480	VGA, Mid Res Anim	500 KB
752×480	For Recording to a PAR	1.1 MB
756×486	For Recording to Vista Board	1.1 MB

continues

Table 12.1, Continued
Table of Resolutions and File Sizes

Resolution (Approx)	Usage	File Size
800×600	SVGA, Mid Res Print	1.4 MB
1024×768	SVGA, Mid Res Print	1.8 MB
2048×1536	High Res Print Low Res Slide	9 MB
3072×2048	High Res Print MidRes Slide	15 MB
4096×3072	High Res Print High Res Slide Large Print >18×24	24 MB
8096×8096	High Res 4×5 Negative High Res Large Print Typesetting Resolution	100 MB

As you can see, files can become very large in size and very high in resolution.

Various Shareware Programs

Many shareware programs are available for viewing, editing, and storing rendered images (or any graphic image, for that matter). A few worth looking at are Lview31, Thumbs Plus, Compushow, MMGif, Graphics Workshop, Image Alchemy, and others (all are included on the accompanying CD-ROM).

Lview31

Lview31, a Windows-based, image-editing shareware program, contains a basic set of tools for manipulating bitmap images. Lview can read Targa, JPEG, GIF, and BMP files. Lview is particularly useful with JPEG format files, and provides a good set of tools for image manipulation and printing.

Thumbs Plus

Thumbs Plus is a great program for cataloging your rendered images, maps, or any bitmap images you have. It creates a catalog of small thumbnails of each image. You can then browse the catalog, or even print the catalog so that you can quickly access your graphics images. Thumbs Plus also has a good set of image-manipulating and printing utilities. The main function here is cataloging, though. This is a Windows-based utility.

Compushow

Compushow is a DOS-based file viewer and slide show manager. It can be used to view any images you like. A slide show script can be written to play back images at given intervals—a handy feature for trade shows or office displays.

MMGif

MMGif is a neat little multimedia program. It enables you to embed WAV or MIDI sound files in a GIF image, so that the sounds are played when the GIF image is displayed. You need a sound card by MMGif. Again, you can use this program to create a simple slide show—but with sounds!

12

Graphics Workshop

Another shareware program to look at is Graphics Workshop. This Windows-based image-manipulation program is one of the more popular programs because it is simple and easy to use and supports a variety of manipulation and printing features.

Image Alchemy

Finally, a great utility to have is Image Alchemy. Image Alchemy is nothing more than a file-format conversion utility, but it can convert almost any format to any other format. Image Alchemy can also do batch-file conversions. Alchemy is a simple command-line DOS program. The shareware version included on disk can handle only limited-size files, but if you register the program, you can convert any size files you want.

Many more programs are out there, more each day. These are just a few that are pretty good. Shareware does provide a lot of software for a little money. Remember to register your software if you decide to keep using it!

Playing Animations

After you have generated your animation, you have to decide how to best play back the animation. The two possible approaches are playing the animation online, or recording the animation to tape and then playing it back. The second option clearly is more time consuming and expensive, but has a much higher quality.

The problem with online playback systems is the frame rate of the playback. Most animations are tuned to 30 frames per second. Unfortunately, most computers cannot play back at that speed. Many computers are lucky to be able to play back an animation at 15 fps!

Shareware Players

A variety of shareware players can play back animations. Autodesk makes several of these players, including Aaplay, aaplayhi, and Aawin. Autodesk is shipping Aniplay and Aawin with AutoVision 2.0. Aniplay is Animator Pro's animation player, and the equivalent of Aaplayhi.

Aaplay is a simple DOS animation player that plays back FLI files of up to 320×200 resolution. A FLI file is Autodesk's animation format. This version can play back animations at up to about 20 frames per second.

Aaplayhi, a more powerful version of Aaplay, can load both FLI and FLC animations. (A FLC animation is the same as a FLI, but at a higher resolution.) Aaplayhi also loads the animation into memory, if it will fit, which increases considerably the playback performance of the player. Aaplayhi generally plays back animations a little more smoothly than Aaplay.

Aawin is the Windows equivalent to Aaplayhi, with a couple of exceptions. Aawin has the capability to run scripts that play one or more animations and sound files with transitions between them. This is much more flexible than Aaplayhi, thanks mostly to the Windows interface. Aawin can be configured to run full screen or in a window, and to load the animation into memory, if possible.

Other shareware animation players exist, but these are the most widely available players. Also available is a nice little utility, called Video For DOS (VFD), that converts FLC files to Video for Windows or Mpeg file formats, and vice versa. If you need to use multiple file formats, VFD is the way to go.

Recording Animations

To record animations, you simply put the animations onto video tape. There are three ways to do this: capture the video output of one of the players mentioned earlier, record frame by frame, or real-time recording.

Frame by Frame

Frame-by-frame recording is the most popular and widely used technique for recording animations to video tape. Unfortunately, it requires a great deal of special hardware to accomplish, and is rather expensive and time consuming. For the occasional animator, it makes very little sense to invest in the appropriate hardware and software to do frame-by-frame animation.

To do frame-by-frame animation, you need the following:

- Frame-accurate VTR (not VCR)
- VTR controller card
- Controller software

This is just a short list. If you want to do any kind of editing, you need a second deck, as well. Each deck costs at least $5,000.

The process is fairly simple. First you stripe the tape with a time code. Then, you start recording. When the tape reaches the appropriate time code, a frame is laid down. The tape is then rewound, and the process is repeated for the next frame. Newer software enables you to record every tenth frame or so in one pass. As you can guess, the VTRs take quite a bit of punishment, and any misalignment can create a small glitch in the animation.

Real Time

Thanks to some newer technology, real-time playback is possible, using some specialized equipment. This equipment is usually a motion JPEG board, with a dedicated hard drive attached, and video output on the card, as well. Two popular systems use this technology: DPS's PAR and Matrox Studio.

12

Digital Processing System's PAR

The Digital Processing System's *Personal Animation Recorder* (PAR) is the most popular method of recording animation. The PAR uses a motion JPEG algorithm on a card with a dedicated hard drive. The PAR has three video outputs on the back: composite (VHS), S-VHS, and BETA-SP. Each is of progressively higher quality than the previous output.

For every 100 megabytes of hard drive space on the PAR hard drive, you get about 1 minute of video. The PAR accepts Targa files only. You can render directly to the PAR from 3D Studio and other such programs. Otherwise, you just use the PAR software to copy the files to the PAR drive. Then hook up something as simple as a VCR to the PAR, and play back the animation in real time.

When using certain software, you can edit the animation, create effects such as transitions and fades, and synchronize sound through nonlinear time editing. This makes the PAR very flexible and easy to use. A complete PAR setup can cost as little as $2,300, with about 12 minutes of video storage.

Matrox Studio

Matrox Studio is similar to the PAR, but a little more expensive. Matrox Studio also requires an EISA expansion slot. The PAR needs only a standard ISA slot. Thanks to the EISA slot, Matrox Studio has a higher throughput than the PAR, but the quality is fairly close.

When you want to output your rendered images or animations, you have many choices ahead of you. Along with these choices comes frustration whenever you get a bad output, and reward each time you get a good output.

Summary

There are many choices for software to use outside 3D Studio. It might take you some time to figure out which software to use. Some packages, most notably Photoshop and RenderPrint, were outlined in this chapter. You will have to explore the choices and decide for yourself which software packages work best for you.

Menu Bar Commands

Command	Description
	Info Commands
About 3D Studio (!)	Displays version number and serial number of your currently running version of 3D Studio.
Current Status (?)	Displays statistics about the number of objects present in the various modules. Also displays RAM usage and swap file size, useful for gauging 3D Studio's current need for RAM. The swap file is created when not enough RAM is available for the calculations 3D Studio must perform. Free space on the hard drive is used as a substitute for RAM when this occurs, and is called a swap file. Because the hard drive is much slower at moving data to and from the computer's processor, swap files cause slow performance.
Configure (*)	Used to set the various paths used by 3D Studio. 3D Studio assumes that the files it will need are stored in the hard disk directories listed in the Program Configuration dialog box. Also, mouse speed is set

Command	Description
	here. Mouse speed relates the amount of movement in the screen cursor with the amount of movement of the actual mouse. If the mouse must be moved an extreme amount to cause the cursor to cross the screen, increase this slider's value.
System Options	Brings up a dialog box for some of 3D Studio's more frequently adjusted switches. Less frequently adjusted switches are set by editing the 3DS.SET file and restarting 3D Studio.
Scene Info	Creates a detailed text report of all the objects, lights, cameras, materials, and other specifics about the current scene in the 3D Editor.
Key Assignments	3D Studio enables you to assign twelve of your own custom "hot keys." This command lists the settings for the twelve available keys (Ctrl+F1 through Ctrl+F12). These hot keys are set by holding Ctrl while selecting the menu option that is to be assigned.
Gamma Control	Adjusts the gamma values of the screen, files, and the frame buffer. Gamma alters the midtones of an image to compensate for non-linear brightness in a display. For example, a monitor might recieve an image whose data would create a mid-level gray, but still displays a gray that is much brighter than a gray that is perfectly halfway between the monitor's displayed black and displayed white.

File Commands

Command	Description
New	Clears all data from the current module.
Reset	Sets 3D Studio to the same state as if it were just started (this command has no effect on the swap file status of 3D Studio). All the modules are cleared and all the default settings are restored.
Load	Loads a 3DS file. Also can be used to import an ASC, FLM, or DXF format file. These types of files contain information for the 3D Editor and Keyframer only.
Merge	Enables you to import selected lights, cameras, or objects from a 3DS, DXF, or FLM file. These objects can retain the animation data from their source file if desired.

Command	Description
Replace Mesh	Used to delete an existing object by replacing it with the same-named object from a saved 3DS, DXF, or FLM file.
Save	Saves the existing 3D Editor and Keyframer data in a 3DS file. Optionally can be used to export to DXF or ASC format data files. Note that DXF format files do not include animation, materials, cameras, or lights.
Save Selected	Saves only the currently selected objects, instead of the entire scene.
Load Project	Project files contain much more than 3DS files; they include all the settings and scene data of all the 3D Studio modules. This command loads a saved project file (PRJ).
Save Project	Saves all settings and scene data of all of 3D Studio's modules to a PRJ file.
Merge Project	Enables you to import selected lights, cameras, or objects from a PRJ file. These objects can retain the animation data from their source file if desired.
Archive	Creates a single file that is a packed archive of all of the separate files required to render the current scene. Because many scenes use external image files that 3D Studio does not include in any of its saved file formats, this command is useful when transferring scene data to another computer. The Archive command commonly is used with the shareware utility PKZIP to create a compacted archive of a group of files.
File Info	Displays statistics about several types of image files.
Rename	Enables you to rename any file on your hard disk without leaving 3D Studio.
Delete	Enables you to delete any file on your hard disk without leaving 3D Studio.
Quit	Exits 3D Studio. Clears all RAM and hard disk swap space that 3D Studio is using.

A

Command	Description
	Views Commands
Redraw	Causes the active viewport to redraw. Often, some operations leave viewports in a messy state. Two objects that overlap, for example, will leave a near-blank screen when one of the two objects is deleted. The Redraw option fixes this.
Redraw All	Causes all displayed viewports to redraw.
Viewports	Brings up a dialog box that enables the selection of different viewport arrangements. Also enables you to set each viewport to any available viewpoints.
Drawing Aids	The snap and grid spacing are set numerically in the dialog box brought up by this option. Also, the Angle snap is set here. Grid, when active, displays regularly spaced dots in the viewport for reference while creating and editing. Snap, when active, constrains mouse movement to regularly spaced intervals. Angle snap forces rotation-related editing to be constrained to regularly spaced angle intervals.
Grid Extents	Enables you to describe an area with the mouse over which the grid dots will display.
Unit Setup	Enables you to define what the units in 3D Studio relate to in real world measurement units, such as feet, inches, or meters.
Use Snap	Activates Snap mode for the selected viewport. The mouse will be constrained in the viewport to the intervals set in the Drawing Aids dialog box.
Use Grid	Activates Grid mode for the selected viewport. Displays regularly spaced dots.
Fastview	Activates a mode where the scene redraws much more quickly by drawing only part of the lines that describe a scene. Useful when scenes are so complex that viewports redraw very slowly after each change.
Disable	Disables the current viewport. Temporarily turns off a viewport's display.
Scroll Lock	While creating or editing, if the mouse reaches the edge of a viewport, the viewport's boundaries will automatically move—a feature called scrolling. If scrolling is not desired, Scroll Lock disables it.

Command	Description
Safe Frame	Displays a boundary around the active viewport, to indicate the area that might be obscured during output to video. Because the front bezel of a television covers up to ten percent of the outer border of the screen, it is important to keep your animation's action out of the undisplayed area.
See Background	A static or moving background image can be applied to an animation. Normally, this background image is not seen until the scene is rendered. Using See Background, a simple gray approximation of the background image will appear in the selected viewport for use as a reference.
Adjust Background	See Background displays images using four gray levels. The middle two gray levels can be adjusted for the brightness level of the source image that they correspond to by using the Adjust Background command.
Vertex Snap	In the 3D Editor, when Vertex Snap is active a moved vertex will automatically be placed on a nearby existing vertex.
Save Current	This command will store the configuration of the active viewport in a temporary buffer. Occasionally a viewport will be perfectly positioned for editing one feature of a 3D object. The viewport's precise point of view is temporarily held by the Save Current command.
Restore Saved	This command will restore the configuration of the active viewport from the data stored with the last Save Current command.
Angle Snap	Activates Angle Snap mode. This affects most rotation commands. Rotation actions will be constrained to exact intervals of rotation. The Angle snap is set in the Drawing Aids dialog box.

Program Commands

Command	Description
2D Shaper (F1)	Switches to the 2D Shaper module.
3D Lofter (F2)	Switches to the 3D Lofter module.
3D Editor (F3)	Switches to the 3D Editor module.
Keyframer (F4)	Switches to the Keyframer module.
Materials Editor (F5)	Switches to the Materials Editor module.
Browser	Activates the Image Browser plug-in.

A

Command	*Description*
Camera/Preview	In the 3D Editor, this activates the Camera Control and Match Perspective plug-in. In the Keyframer, this activates the Quick Preview plug-in.
IK	In the Keyframer, this activates the Inverse Kinematics plug-in.
Keyscript	This activates the Keyscript Editing dialog box.
DOS Window	This option temporarily exits to DOS from 3D Studio. 3D Studio is still loaded in memory during the DOS window operation. The DOS window is exited by typing **EXIT** at the prompt.
Text Editor	Activates 3D Studio's built-in text editor.
PXP/KXP Loader	Loads a dialog box that lists all the available plug-in modules. In the 3D Editor, the plug-ins are PXPs, and in the Keyframer the plug-ins are KXPs.

Network Commands

Slave	Puts the machine into Slave mode. Any projects in the network queue will begin processing. Network rendering is where multiple machines render the frames of an animation cooperatively. Also, a single machine can operate in Slave mode to render a collection of projects unattended.
Configure	Brings up a dialog box that lists the paths used by the machine during network rendering. Also sets the machine ID and display used by the machine when it is network rendering (in Slave mode).
Edit Queue	Enables you to choose the order of projects that are to be rendered by the network. Also allows individual projects to be deleted.

Index

Symbols

N-O

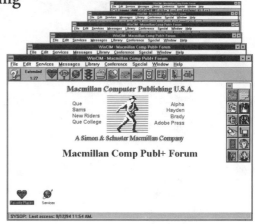

WANT MORE INFORMATION?

CHECK OUT THESE RELATED TOPICS OR SEE YOUR LOCAL BOOKSTORE

CAD and 3D Studio

As the number one CAD publisher in the world, and as a Registered Publisher of Autodesk, New Riders Publishing provides unequaled content on this complex topic. Industry-leading products include AutoCAD and 3D Studio.

Networking

As the leading Novell NetWare publisher, New Riders Publishing delivers cutting-edge products for network professionals. We publish books for all levels of users, from those wanting to gain NetWare Certification, to those administering or installing a network. Leading books in this category include *Inside NetWare 3.12*, *CNE Training Guide: Managing NetWare Systems*, *Inside TCP/IP*, and *NetWare: The Professional Reference*.

Graphics

New Riders provides readers with the most comprehensive product tutorials and references available for the graphics market. Best-sellers include *Inside CorelDRAW! 5*, *Inside Photoshop 3*, and *Adobe Photoshop NOW!*

Internet and Communications

As one of the fastest growing publishers in the communications market, New Riders provides unparalleled information and detail on this ever-changing topic area. We publish international best-sellers such as *New Riders' Official Internet Yellow Pages, 2nd Edition*, a directory of over 10,000 listings of Internet sites and resources from around the world, and *Riding the Internet Highway, Deluxe Edition*.

Operating Systems

Expanding off our expertise in technical markets, and driven by the needs of the computing and business professional, New Riders offers comprehensive references for experienced and advanced users of today's most popular operating systems, including *Understanding Windows 95*, *Inside Unix*, *Inside Windows 3.11 Platinum Edition*, *Inside OS/2 Warp Version 3*, and *Inside MS-DOS 6.22*.

Other Markets

Professionals looking to increase productivity and maximize the potential of their software and hardware should spend time discovering our line of products for Word, Excel, and Lotus 1-2-3. These titles include *Inside Word 6 for Windows*, *Inside Excel 5 for Windows*, *Inside 1-2-3 Release 5*, and *Inside WordPerfect for Windows*.

Orders/Customer Service **1-800-653-6156**   Source Code **NRP95**

New Riders Publishing   201 West 103rd Street ◆ Indianapolis, Indiana 46290 USA

REGISTRATION CARD

3D Studio for Beginners

Name _____ Title _____

Company _____ Type of business _____

Address _____

City/State/ZIP _____

Have you used these types of books before? ☐ yes ☐ no

If yes, which ones? _____

_____

How many computer books do you purchase each year? ☐ 1–5 ☐ 6 or more

How did you learn about this book? _____

Where did you purchase this book? _____

Which applications do you currently use? _____

_____

Which computer magazines do you subscribe to? _____

_____

What trade shows do you attend? _____

_____

Comments: _____

_____

_____

Would you like to be placed on our preferred mailing list? ☐ yes ☐ no

☐ **I would like to see my name in print!** You may use my name and quote me in future New Riders products and promotions. My daytime phone number is: _____

New Riders Publishing 201 West 103rd Street ◆ Indianapolis, Indiana 46290 USA

Fax to **317-581-4670** Orders/Customer Service **1-800-653-6156** Source Code **NRP95**

Fold Here

- -

BUSINESS REPLY MAIL
FIRST-CLASS MAIL PERMIT NO. 9918 INDIANAPOLIS IN

POSTAGE WILL BE PAID BY THE ADDRESSEE

**NEW RIDERS PUBLISHING
201 W 103RD ST
INDIANAPOLIS IN 46290-9058**